MARGINALIA

Marginalia

READERS WRITING IN BOOKS

H. J. Jackson

Yale University Press   New Haven and London

Designed by Rebecca Gibb.
Set in Fournier type by The Composing Room of Michigan, Inc.
Printed in the United States of America by Lightning Source.

Library of Congress Cataloging-in-Publication Data
Jackson, H. J.
Marginalia : readers writing in books / H. J. Jackson.
        p.   cm.
Includes bibliographical references (p.   ) and index.
ISBN: 978-0-300-09720-7
1. Books and reading—History. 2. Marginalia—History. I. Title.
Z1003 .J12 2001
028'.9'09—dc21
00-043721

A catalogue record for this book is available from the British Library.

10 9 8 7 6 5 4 3 2 1

For Robin Jackson

CONTENTS

INTRODUCTION

We all know the reader-annotated book of the present day, and we prefer not to think about it. It's a scruffy thing. Somebody has used yellow highlighter to mark significant passages—most of the text, it seems. Perhaps it was the same person who scribbled some page numbers in ballpoint pen inside the back cover, with the odd word to show what subject the page numbers refer to, and who wrote a disparaging comment on the title page, just under the author's name. If it is a library book, there will be no way of telling who marked it up, but if it is private property, the owner's name will almost certainly be on the first blank page inside the cover, at the top right-hand corner. If it is left behind on a bus, nobody will carry it off: it is unlovable and unsalable.

On the other hand, the British Library in 1998 proudly announced the acquisition of its second copy of Galileo's work on sunspots, *Istoria e dimostrazioni intorno alle macchie solari* (Rome, 1613). A publicity flyer describes it as follows:

> The special interest of this copy lies in the copious annotations in Italian which have been written in the margins throughout the book. While it is not known who wrote the annotations, there appear to be three different hands, all dating from the early seventeenth century.

The annotations have not been transcribed or studied in any detail, but it is clear that they were written by contemporary readers who were interested in recent developments in astronomy and were competent enough to comment in detail on Galileo's observations and findings. These annotations are important evidence for the impact of Galileo's ideas on his contemporaries and give a glimpse of the excited interest and polemical discussion which Galileo's work often provoked.

In this case, apparently, readers' notes greatly increase the market value of the book. I do not question the purchase or the purchase price, but I am interested in the justification offered. The Library did not need another copy of that edition, rare and valuable though it might be. The book is not an association copy: the notes are not Galileo's, nor does it contain even his autograph. The notes were written, so far as we know, not by some other famous person but by unidentified contemporaries of no guaranteed authority. In fact the notes have not been "transcribed or studied in any detail," so we don't actually know yet what they contain, and it is possible that they are not original, perhaps not even directly relevant to the text at hand. Nevertheless they are valued *as a contemporary response,* and may be valued all the more, nowadays, for being the work of nameless readers. The same criteria could be applied to the book on the bus, but its annotations have negative value. How do we explain the discrepancy between worthless notes and priceless ones?

There are obvious and less obvious answers. It is easy to dismiss the products of our own age: they are all around us and easy of access. Early-seventeenth-century Italy is another matter, for the historical record is scant and any new piece of evidence is welcome, particularly in underdocumented areas like the history of science. There is rarity value: a very old book abandoned on a bus—even a book of the 1930s or '40s, or any hardcover book—might attract attention, whereas a recent paperback would not. Then too, Western consumer societies are inclined to despise used goods. People fear contagion, literally and metaphorically. It should be pointed out, moreover, that my hypothetical bit of garbage is featureless. I made it up, generalizing on the basis of common experience. We haven't really looked at it and in a sense there is nothing to see. Suppose I had given it an author and a title, put a name to the annotator, and been able to quote some of the notes. Suppose it turned out that the annotator was known to us. What effect would it have on our estimate of the notes if we knew the annotator personally, or if the annotator were a celebrity—say, Madonna? Little by little the book becomes more interesting. It is still, however, merely a mental exercise, less vivid to us than the Galileo. Let me make it more concrete.

About the time that the British Library displayed its Galileo, I had an opportunity to pick through a batch of books rejected from a college book sale. There I found an object answering pretty well the description I gave earlier. For this first modern example—and only for this one—I shall begin at the beginning and work step by step through to the end. It is a paperback copy of a book by Joseph Fletcher called *Situation Ethics: The New Morality* (Philadelphia, 1966). All markings are in ballpoint ink. Inside the front cover are an address and two owners' names; the notes were written by the second of them. On the first page, which is the half-title, she has written, "criticism in book store by Ramsey"—a bibliographical reference for further reading. The Foreword is unmarked. Given the fact that throughout the text passages are set off with underlining and with lines down the margin, the absence of markings in the Foreword suggests that it was skipped over. The first note in the text occurs on page 19, where the word "casuistry" is underlined and a definition is given in the margin: "study of right and wrong." The reader, certainly a student, appears to be conscientious enough to look up unfamiliar terms. At page 41, she begins cautiously to express her own opinions in reaction to the developing argument: "good," she says. At page 55, she first registers disagreement, underlining the sentence, "For the situationist there are no rules—none at all," and commenting, "DON'T AGREE should have some rules or could screw it all up." So the response continues, the comments being generally brief and, to be honest, banal: "don't know whether agree or not" (p. 63); "good idea" (p. 99); "can't see how it is possible to love an enemy" (p. 103); "example is right but it would be a very hard thing to do" (p. 115)—that is, to rescue the medical genius and not your own father from a fire; and so on. At the end of the index, which is the last printed page, the annotator sums up the volume in her own words:

nothing is no-no—everything is relative in face of love—must love neighbour—only 1 absolute—L O V E—idea of "summum bonum"—higher good—says must do things for the good—end could turn out bad but as long as the goal is good then it's o.k.—the means to the end—feels there should be no laws—how can you bring children up that way?—remember 6 propositions

Finally, on the back cover, she has bracketed a part of the publisher's copy that states the thesis of the book, and marked it "N.B."

We have no way of knowing whether the notes in the Galileo are any more sophisticated than these. It is quite likely that they, too, are students' notes, and if we were in a position to compare them, we might be able to say something about changes in educational methods and results over time, though we would need to know a good deal about the subject already in order to interpret the evidence that particular examples provide. This copy of *Situation Ethics* might be described as a middling case. It's not as uninformative as the book that contains nothing but underlining, nor as thrilling as a copy that provides privileged information or bold and significant criticism. But it repays attention, and as time goes by its kind of record is very likely to increase in value, if not in commercial terms then at least in terms of potential use by the sociologist and cultural historian. Something could be made of this modest volume, as I hope to demonstrate in the course of this book. For the moment, however, I wish to use it to make a few general points.

Readers' notes in books are a familiar but unexamined phenomenon. We do not understand it well. We have mixed feelings about it, sometimes quite strong ones, such as shame and disapproval. Why do we? Why should we? What advantage did the student reader find in marking up her own copy of a book she was reading, rather than taking notes on separate pages, or writing her notes in pencil so that they could be erased when the book was resold or passed on? What difference does the presence of notes make for the reader who follows? Under what circumstances could such notes be considered value added to the book, and for what audience—for the author or his agent, for the teacher, for the psychologist of reading?

Though the annotator herself can hardly have been aware of the fact, her practice in annotation is consistent with centuries of tradition reaching back far beyond the birth of print, through the ages of manuscript culture. If you ask annotators today what systems they use for marking their books and where they learned them, they generally tell you that their methods are private and idiosyncratic. As to having learned them, they have no more recollection of having been taught the arts of annotation than of having been taught how to fasten on a wristwatch. If you listen to their accounts of what they do, or if you are allowed to examine their books, however, you find (with very, very few exceptions) that they reproduce the common practices of readers since the Middle Ages. These are traditional practices culturally transmitted by the usual tacit and mysterious means—example, prohibition, word of mouth. They are taken for granted as part of the common reading experience, and it looks as though they will continue so. Computer books and databases already come equipped with provision for annotation, as in the DynaText program that accompanies Cambridge CD-ROMs and the prototype E-book, SoftBook.

Finally, the student copy of *Situation Ethics* illustrates a fact that many serious readers deplore: even when less invasive alternatives are available, people go on guiltily disfiguring books. Those same serious readers might be prepared to make an exception, though, for marginalia associated with public figures. They would be stirred by the sight of the copy of Shakespeare that circulated secretly among the prisoners at Robben Island in South Africa when Nelson Mandela was there. (The prisoners' custom was to sign their names at their favorite passages, and in 1977 Mandela chose *Julius Caesar* II ii 32–37, "Cowards die many times before their deaths," et cetera.) They would understand the buzz over Marilyn Monroe's books in September 1999, when some of her personal effects came up for sale. (The "most telling" of them was said to be a copy of *The Little Engine That Could* containing "childish pencil scrawls at the end," possibly hers. The auctioneers alleged that she carried this book to the Kennedy birthday ball where she sang "Happy Birthday, Mr. President"—though some readers of the *New York Times* probably shook their heads, as I did, and suspected myth-making.)[1]

If they thought about it a bit, they would see that these exceptional books also reflect commonplace experience. Other children besides Marilyn Monroe scribble in their picture books; other adults cling to souvenirs of their childhood. Other groups besides Mandela's affirm their cohesion with the documentary evidence of albums and autographs. Special cases can lead us to seek a better understanding of ordinary practice, and later sections of this book will be concerned with children's marginalia and with the social functions of the annotated book. In these pages I hope that specialist and non-specialist readers alike may discover common ground and develop a measure of fellow-feeling toward annotators of the near and distant past, for readers' notes are and always have been part of the landscape, and we might as well get to know them.

Given the recent shift of attention from the writer to the reader and to the production, dissemination, and reception of texts, marginalia of all periods would appear to be potentially a goldmine for scholars. And so they are, but they are a contested goldmine. Some excellent basic bibliographic and historical work has been done, and there are a few fine case studies, most of them dealing with Medieval and Renaissance texts. The subject has stimulated intelligent theorizing. For a few famous writers, the corpus of marginalia has been the focus of a critical edition. Critics disagree, however, about the reliability of readers' notes, and consequently about the ways in which they might legitimately be used to reconstruct either a reading environment or the mental experience of a particular reader.[2]

This book aims to describe and illustrate the behavior of annotators in the English-speaking world during the past three centuries, and to test current assumptions about the potential value of readers' notes for historical studies of reception and reader response. Not primarily a history but a genre study, it is based on archival work, the examination of more than two thousand annotated books in great public or academic libraries. For reasons that will be elaborated later, the sample set of works has no claim to being exhaustive or representative or even statistically significant. It is large and diverse enough, nevertheless, to expose basic patterns in readers' practice; and the quest turned up some outstanding individual examples of the annotator's art that would otherwise have gone unrecognized. To my surprise I found that many of these remarkable books, though faithfully preserved and catalogued, and available for decades and sometimes for centuries to public view, were wrongly described because, as it appeared, no one had actually read them. Like the British Library Galileo, they were still awaiting detailed study.

It was as an appreciative reader and then as the editor of marginalia by S. T. Coleridge that I began to notice other readers' comments in books, and to collect and keep track of them. Coleridge occupies a pivotal position in the history of marginalia in English, for his is the name associated with the publication and popularization of the genre. Before his time, annotation was widely practiced and marginalia of special interest or quality circulated privately. His friends knew about and encouraged his habit of writing comments in the margins of books. They lent him books of their own to comment on. (Coleridge well understood the sentimental value of his notes in other people's books. In Charles Lamb's copy of the plays of Beaumont and Fletcher he wrote, "I will not be long here, Charles!—& gone, you will not mind my having spoiled a book in order to leave a Relic.") From roughly 1807, when he was thirty-five, the number of books that he freely annotated grew steadily until he began to see this library as a marketable resource, and to capitalize upon it. One of Charles Lamb's best-known essays celebrated his skills as an annotator. Thomas De Quincey published some of the notes that Coleridge had written in books of his. In November 1819, Coleridge himself, under cover of an editorial fiction, published his "marginalia" on Sir Thomas Browne in *Blackwood's Magazine,* bringing the word *marginalia* from Latin into English and permanently changing the conditions under which readers wrote their notes.[3]

Once a reader's notes are published on their own account, as Coleridge's were, it becomes possible that any of them might be publishable, and all annotators become more self-conscious in their work. The profile of Coleridge as an annotator here in Chapter Five attempts to account for the force of his example. The word itself, which Coleridge may well have used ironically to make light of his own pretensions, has stuck: readers seem to find that its Latinity confers a degree of seriousness and erudition that "notes," "remarks," "comments," and even "annotations" lack.

After Coleridge's death, his executors made an effort to assemble all the annotated books so that his notes could be published. Following a small selection in *Literary Remains* (1836–39), specialized collections based on topics—politics, literature, religion—appeared, in several volumes each, catering to the Victorians' curiosity about Coleridge himself as well as to their interest in his opinions about books and authors. Some of Coleridge's eldest son's marginalia were included among his own posthumously collected papers, as were, eventually, his daughter's.[4] In 1880, the British Library purchased a large number of Coleridge's annotated books; a second collection was acquired in 1953; and odd volumes have been added steadily over the years. Other libraries and private collectors compete with one another for the occasional stray. The canonization and institutional recognition afforded to Coleridge's marginalia were the result partly, no doubt, of intrinsic merit, but also of strenuous publicity and editorial labors that both reflected and influenced public opinion. It is largely because of the Coleridge family that marginalia are taken seriously outside narrow academic areas of specialization. At the narrow academic level, however, it is also worth noting that the latest round of publication for Coleridge's marginalia—the appearance of what aimed to be a definitive scholarly edition in the Bollingen Edition of his *Collected Works*—coincided with growing interest in reader response as a subject of study and a multifaceted approach to the interpretation of texts, which was itself followed by historicized studies, with the result that now, as Anthony Grafton puts it, "The history of reading is hot."[5] Perhaps it is mere coincidence; or perhaps the climate was finally right for the full-scale acceptance of what used to be considered a negligible form of writing.

Another recent development that made the present study feasible was the evolution of searchable electronic library catalogues. Without them, it would have been extremely difficult to identify a large body of annotated books. Public libraries understandably prohibit the writing of notes in books. It would seem counterproductive to make a rule and then to celebrate the breaking of it, so, by and large, libraries do not encourage annotators by drawing attention to the manuscript annotations in their collections. In any case, having a category for manuscript (ms.) notes adds to the complications and expense of cataloguing. Catalogues therefore normally record the presence of marginalia only when they are authorial or associated with a famous name. Several writers are known partly for their marginalia—Coleridge, Horace Walpole, William Beckford, William Blake, Charles Darwin, Thomas Babington Macaulay—but you cannot write a general account on the basis of a few great anomalies. And even notes associated with names like these may be hard to trace. Sometimes they are recorded as manuscripts and are not included among the library's books at all; sometimes they are merely of autograph or association interest. I was looking for what I thought of, tendentiously, as "real" marginalia, discursive notes, preferably by minor or unknown readers. For a while, when I began this study, I tried to work with provenance files, the boxes of index cards that give the books' pedigrees, with evidence of ownership; but where these files recorded "notes," they were usually presentation inscriptions or simply owners' marks. I made some progress by throwing myself on the mercy of librarians and asking whether they knew of any way of using the catalogue to locate annotated works, or whether they could direct me to particular examples in their collections. (A librarian at the New York Public rolled her eyes and said, "You should see our Occult section." I hope someone may try that, someday.)

But the breakthrough came, for me, with the publication of Robin Alston's *Books with Manuscript: A Short Title Catalogue of Books with Manuscript Notes in the British Library* (1994). Alston, who had served an apprenticeship with Coleridge too, used the newly on-line version of the British Library catalogue to locate everything recorded as containing manuscript features. Although some entries are not relevant to my purpose—books with letters tipped in, for example—and although Alston does not pretend to do more than list items already identified as containing manuscript materials, knowing quite well that there must be many, perhaps hundreds of thousands of books in the collection containing notes but not so described, still *Books with Manuscript* gave me easy access to a huge miscellaneous assortment of just the kind of annotations I had been seeking. With this precedent, I turned to other large collections. The Bodleian Library maintains a "field" for ms. notes that turned up twelve hundred entries in their catalogue; at the Beinecke Library at Yale the librarians and I netted nearly six thousand. From these and similarly generous offerings elsewhere I made my selection. My choices reflect a desire for breadth in chronology and number of annotators, and a prejudice in favor of notes that were written as an end in themselves rather than as a stage in the production of something else, such as a new edition or a lecture or a review—though these categories are not impermeable and I have not attempted to be absolutely rigorous about exclusions. Few notes, if any, can be called perfectly disinterested: Chapter Three explores some of the hidden agendas underlying the most spontaneous-looking marginalia.

Old-fashioned methods can still be productive too. A Renaissance term for scholars' notebooks is *adversaria,* and the libraries of Cambridge University have a long-established interest in adversaria—loosely defined to include printed books with readers' notes in them—that resulted in the introduction of an actual cataloguing category, "Adv.," in the 1930s.[6] Cambridge had by then already published a slim bibliography, Henry Richards Luard's *Catalogue of Adversaria and Printed Books Containing MS. Notes, Preserved in the Library of the University of Cambridge* (1864); better still, they continue to keep handwritten lists of significant annotated works, and there is a card index of annotators. Because the university has a history of attending to marginalia, collections including annotated books come their way, and catalogues are duly prepared and sometimes published, as in the case of the magnificent Rothschild collection at Trinity, the Hayward collection of T. S. Eliot manuscripts at King's, and the Pepys collection at Magdalene. Every table in the university library has on it the same notice: "Marking of Books is FORBIDDEN."

Some of the limitations of my survey may be apparent even as I list the major archives. Ordinary libraries seldom have the will or the resources to catalogue marginalia; special collections contain special books. The great institutional libraries of England and the United States that I have relied on will by the nature of things present a skewed sample. If books are listed as containing ms. notes it is likely to be because the books were purchased for the sake of the notes, in which case they are almost by definition not typical or representative. But what, in this context, can "typical" or "representative" mean? (I shall return to this question in Chapter Eight.) Then there are geographical, temporal, and social imbalances. The great majority of the books that I examined because they happen to have been recorded as containing readers' notes were published in London and read and annotated in England, by well-to-do men in the book business as writers, editors, scholars, publishers, or reviewers. A disproportionate number of the ones I describe here were annotated in the late eighteenth century or in the early nineteenth. Are these limitations defensible? I think they are; in fact I think they are unavoidable. First of all, I acknowledge them, and urge the reader to keep them in mind as I proceed. Second, I have found that many books with ms. notes found their way into these collections and were catalogued as containing notes because the cataloguing system was set up to do that, although the notes themselves were *not* the reason for the purchase; the collections are less carefully controlled than they might at first sight appear to be. Books are bequeathed and donated, and may have had a full life before they enter the library; rare books may have to be accepted with ms. notes because no clean copy can be found. A copy of Samuel Johnson's *Plan of a Dictionary* now at the University of Toronto is a case in point: its eighteenth-century owner, Samuel Maude, used it for his diary (fig. 1).

Writers' archives come into libraries as they are, often with boxes of books that nobody has looked at for many years, until the cataloguer has to deal with them. I have paid particular attention to titles and annotators outside the mainstream, and made an effort to consult small collections and local or subscription libraries as well as mammoth public ones. Books printed in cheap formats for the poor, such as the chapbooks sold by itinerant peddlers and manuals of practical arts like farriery, give occasional glimpses of the practice of working-class readers. That most familiar and homely of cases, the annotated cookbook, turns up more frequently than you might expect. The National Library of Scotland's *Aberdeen Cookery Book* (1931), for instance, contains manuscript recipes

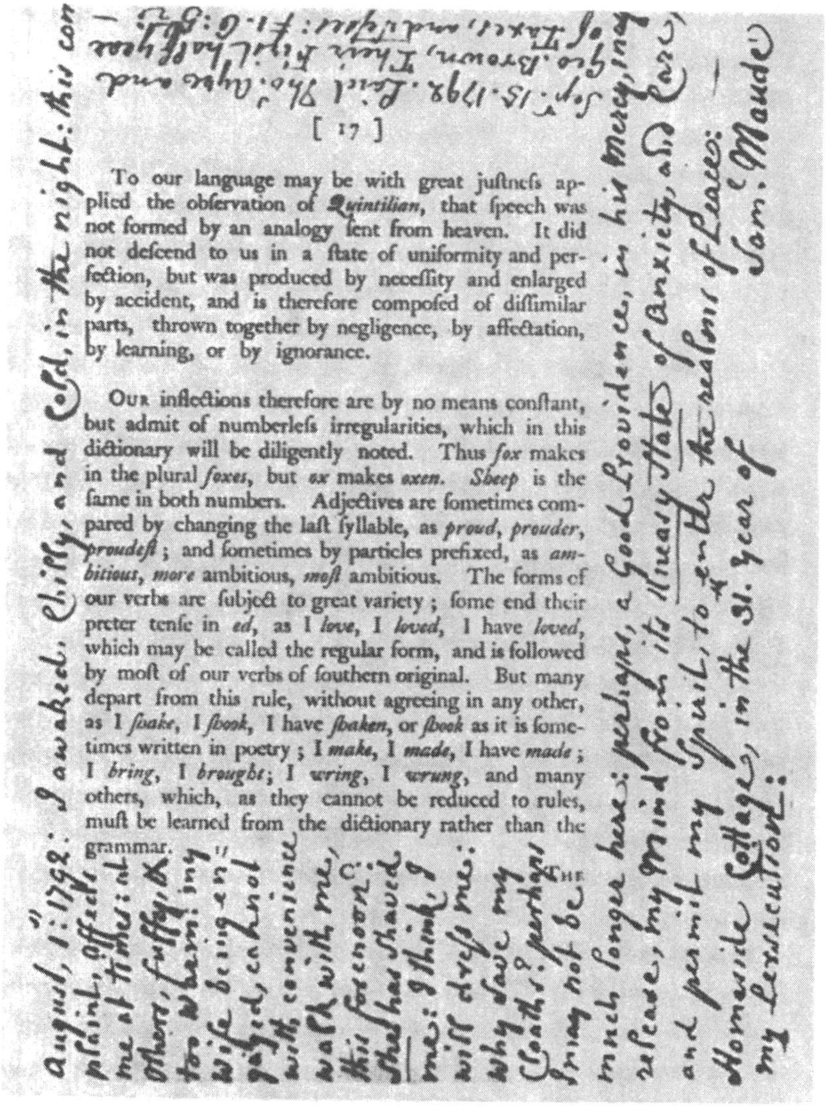

[17]

To our language may be with great justness applied the observation of *Quintilian*, that speech was not formed by an analogy sent from heaven. It did not descend to us in a state of uniformity and perfection, but was produced by necessity and enlarged by accident, and is therefore composed of dissimilar parts, thrown together by negligence, by affectation, by learning, or by ignorance.

Our inflections therefore are by no means constant, but admit of numberless irregularities, which in this dictionary will be diligently noted. Thus *fox* makes in the plural *foxes*, but *ox* makes *oxen*. *Sheep* is the same in both numbers. Adjectives are sometimes compared by changing the last syllable, as *proud*, *prouder*, *proudest*; and sometimes by particles prefixed, as *ambitious*, *more* ambitious, *most* ambitious. The forms of our verbs are subject to great variety; some end their preter tense in *ed*, as I *love*, I *loved*, I have *loved*, which may be called the regular form, and is followed by most of our verbs of southern original. But many depart from this rule, without agreeing in any other, as I *shake*, I *shook*, I have *shaken*, or *shook* as it is sometimes written in poetry; I *make*, I *made*, I have *made*; I *bring*, I *brought*; I *wring*, I *wrung*, and many others, which, as they cannot be reduced to rules, must be learned from the dictionary rather than the grammar.

THE

FIG. I Samuel Johnson, *The Plan of a Dictionary of the English Language* (1747). (Used by permission of the Thomas Fisher Rare Book Library, University of Toronto)

("Milk and Macaroni Soup") just about as distasteful to later imaginations as the printed "Sheep's Head Broth" (p. 13)—and a bonus slip recording bridge scores ("We" and "They") besides. I have introduced a few examples from novels and poems for the insight they offer into people's attitudes toward marginalia, and for their influence on readers' behavior. I have also tried to vary my approach in order to counteract the bias inherent in the selection process. The portion of Chapter Five dealing with the reception of James Boswell's *Life of Johnson*, for instance, draws on many annotated copies not so described in the catalogues. Finally, I would point out that this survey is the first and (I hope) not the last word on the subject. It is a starting point. It does not aim to be comprehensive, only to set out the history and conventions of a widespread custom by reference to a substantial body of specific cases.

Besides these built-in restrictions, some boundaries had to be drawn to keep the topic under control. They are indicated in the key terms of an early version of the title—"Marginalia: Readers' Notes in Books, 1700–2000." "Marginalia," the plural of the Latin neuter singular *marginale*, from the adjective *marginalis* meaning "in the margin," was imported into the language by Coleridge when he first published some "things in the margin" of his own, as I have said, in 1819. (Books in Latin with scholarly apparatus had of course been using the term for centuries.) Coleridge is an acknowledged master of the form and played a crucial part in its history, and it therefore seems fitting that his word should be used. I use it with some latitude, however, as Coleridge himself did, taking it to refer to notes written anywhere in a book, and not merely in the margins.

"Readers" in these pages usually, though not invariably, means readers other than the author of the book being annotated. While it is true that an author becomes a reader once the book is in print, authorial reflections and revisions are marginalia of a special kind, refinements to the text, and of limited interest, as a rule, to anyone but the producer. This is true even of such famous cases as Sir James Frazer's copiously annotated copies of the several parts of *The Golden Bough,* now in the Wren Library at Trinity College, Cambridge. As each edition appeared, he added notes and new references in manuscript, to be incorporated at the next opportunity. Toward the end of his life, he had a set interleaved—that is, specially bound with a blank page facing each page, to take notes—and had someone copy into it all the notes not yet published, from all the other copies. He continued to add the occasional new bit of information himself. The biographer of Frazer or the editor of *The Golden Bough* might be grateful for this evidence of his methodical habits and of the process of composition of an extraordinarily influential work in anthropology, but from the point of view of reading practice it is all too predictable. For the same reason I seldom cite books marked up by an editor for a new edition. (This policy had the accidental benefit of sparing me Edmond Malone's horrible hand as revising editor in multiple copies of Boswell and Shakespeare.)

"Notes" are to be distinguished from asterisks, fists ☞, exclamation marks, word by word translation, and similar signs of readers' attentions. As Roger Stoddard's pioneering exhibition catalogue, *Marks in Books* (1985), shows, readers write in their books for many reasons, using expressive non-verbal codes. Most of the conventional marks will be touched on in this study, but on the whole I have chosen to concentrate on original discursive notes that express a reaction to the text or an opinion about it, as opposed to the minimal and equivocal witness of the question mark or cross, the use of blank spaces as scrap paper (as in the Johnson example cited above), or the copying-out of somebody else's remarks. I could afford to: the quantity of material is next to unmanageable. That is not to say that the lesser marks are not also susceptible of interpretation. A scholar tracing Wordsworth's reputation among the Victorians can interpret Darwin's quick mark against "Surprised by Joy" as "poignant"; with suitable caution, students of Emily Dickinson read the evidence of dog-eared pages in books from the family library.[7]

They have to be notes "in books." There are significant differences between notes made on separate sheets of paper or in a notebook and notes made in the book that become part of the book and accompany it ever after. Only notes actually written into the books are admitted here. "Books" also implies exclusions. People do not annotate newspapers. They do sometimes annotate other ephemera, such as playbills, advertisements, and menus, but those kinds of printing are beyond the scope of my study.

The dates 1700–2000 are not arbitrary. The terminal date needs no justification, except perhaps to point out that examples from the late twentieth century are scarce in these pages—partly because rare-book libraries tend not to have them, and partly because as far as I can see, readers even of the late twentieth century follow models established long before. The starting point is more questionable. For reasons that I shall go into in Chapter Two, discursive and original readers' notes of the kind I am concerned with are rare before 1700 and increasingly common (in relation to other forms of annotation) thereafter. During the period from about 1750 to 1820, this kind of writing developed rapidly and became highly sophisticated. Good specimens were copied out and imitated, so that by 1820 they were ready to be launched as publishable. Hence examples from this time have been prized and preserved; hence the special emphasis on cases from that time of transition.

This is not exclusively or primarily, however, a historical study. As a literary scholar, I am interested in interpretation and in the *progress* of interpretation, both in the individual reader and in the great society of readers over time. Every record of a particular reader's engagement with a book will have both historical and ahistorical or transhistorical elements. As physical objects, books have changed in shape and texture over the years, but some features remain constant. As intellectual objects, they act upon—or rather interact with—the reader's mind in different ways upon different occasions, but again there are constant features: the words on the page do not change, and the range of meaning is not wide open. As I present the evidence of readers' responses to books, expressed in their marginalia, I try to bear these complementary claims in mind; therefore the several chapters of this book adopt diverse approaches to the subject, and in most of them, illustrations are selected for the topic and not by period. Since this book is the product of a personal quest—what the scientists call "curiosity-driven research"—I have also felt free to introduce obscure and atypical examples because they delighted me and it would have seemed a pity to let them go unnoticed.

Nor am I referring only to readers' notes. Marginalia are responsive; they need to be read as they are written, in conjunction with a prior text. Much of the pleasure of my work lay in the discovery not only of good annotations but also of out-of-the-way, thought-provoking, neglected, sometimes simply weird books. The pages that follow should convey something of the variety and charm of hitherto unvisited readers and writers. Negligible in isolation, they are collectively exciting.

Editors and presses have struggled with the special problems of the presentation of marginalia since the early nineteenth century without achieving any kind of consensus. I shall address this question more at length in the Afterword. For the purposes of this study, I have adopted a few routine procedures and technical conventions. Since the materials come mostly from unpublished sources and either the annotator or the work itself is liable to be unfamiliar to many readers, I generally introduce them with as unobtrusive a summary of relevant facts as I can manage, but then quote extensively. Endnotes supply page references, identify relevant scholarly publications, and occasionally provide additional examples. The Bibliography of Annotated Books Cited lists these books alphabetically by author; the Bibliography of Secondary Works Cited includes published editions of marginalia such as Darwin's, Macaulay's, and Coleridge's. Annotators may be traced through the Index. In all quotations from marginalia, I preserve the spelling and punctuation of the manuscripts but ignore cancellations and incorporate insertions into the text without special notice. Words underlined in manuscript are recorded as underlined, not as italicized, unless they are quoted from printed sources in which they have been italicized. Notes on flyleaves are cited by assigning numbers to the blank pages front and back, counting backward from the first printed page and forward from the last: -4 means the fourth page back from the first printed page, and $+2$ the second page following the last printed one. In quotations from annotated books, underlining represents not italic print but the annotator's added underlining.

I begin, in Chapter One, with the physical features of the annotated book, observing the way in which particular spaces have come to be identified with particular kinds of annotation. Chapter Two surveys the history of annotation, demonstrating the high degree of continuity of practice as well as variations and evolution over time. In Chapter Three I address what I take to be a fundamental theoretical issue, namely the occasion of the written note, or possible motives for writing; a key question here is that of the addressee. Another matter of debate is the usefulness of marginalia. What are they good for? What are we to make of them? Chapters Four and Five offer examples of two of the more obvious sorts of responsible use, namely author studies and case studies—the first showing what might be done with particular exceptional copies and the second profiling a major annotator and a major book. Some extreme cases are considered in Chapter Six, which shows what can be and has been done to books by the set of readers that I have come to think of as obsessive, those who fasten on one book and make it the repository of their intellectual and emotional lives in a way that may appear, in retrospect, to be either therapeutic or dangerous. Chapter Seven proposes an aesthetics or poetics of marginalia, outlining criteria for best and worst practice. Chapter Eight considers the dark side of the annotating habit, asking why it continues to provoke resistance and distaste, and showing how well founded these objections often are. The Afterword turns to advocacy and suggests means by which marginalia might be given more credit and more visibility.

chapter one

PHYSICAL FEATURES

The physical features of books have changed really very little since 1700, at least from the annotator's point of view. It is true that formats changed, from the handsome folios of the seventeenth century to the neat octavos of the eighteenth, and from the luxury quartos of the Romantic period to the triple-deckers of the Victorian era and the closely printed paperbacks of the mid–twentieth century. Printing technology passed from monotype to stereotype and linotype and so to computer composition. Paper shortages led to experiments with wood pulp and other substitutes for rag content, with serious and irreversible consequences. In terms of layout, the phasing out of printed marginal glosses in favor of the footnote—a development of the early eighteenth century—and the still unresolved rivalry between the footnote and the endnote have no doubt influenced the annotator's practice, as has the generally diminishing provision of empty space between lines, in margins, and in flyleaves.[1] Books nevertheless continue to present themselves in a familiar shape. They have covers, half-titles and title pages, front and back endpapers, and chapter divisions that leave convenient blanks at the bottoms and tops of certain pages. Annotators throughout the period can be seen to make distinctly different, though standard, use of these various spaces—that is to say, custom and perhaps physical necessity dictate appropriate kinds of use for separate areas in the book. In this chapter I shall describe the typical physical features of manuscript annotation, subordinating content as far as possible. Content, however, is a force of nature: you can drive it out with a pitchfork, but it will soon find a way back. I have not even attempted to suppress it altogether.

All the front area of a book, from the inside of the front cover to the beginning of the text proper, presents an opportunity to provide introductory material, and the first impulse of any owner appears to be the impulse to stake a claim. Ownership marks are far and away the commonest form of annotation. The inside front cover, whether it is the paste-down of the endpaper or the actual verso of the cover itself as in a modern paperback, is the traditional place for a bookplate. Presentation inscriptions there or on the title page are likewise statements about ownership not written by the owner. More usual, however, is the owner's signature or initials, generally to be found on the top right-hand corner of the first free page, whether it is a flyleaf or the title page. An owner's initials constitute the minimum of annotation.

The marginalia of children are instructive, and a case can be made for their revealing fundamental readers' attitudes in a particularly raw state. Before they can read, children may scribble—pretending to write—or draw pictures in books that come their way, but as soon as they can read and write, they write their names, often over and over again in the one book. A work in which the annotations are conveniently dated 1700, exactly the starting point for this study, a copy of Claude Mauger's *French Grammar,* contains no notes whatever in the text, and no notes having any connection with French grammar, but voluminous writings on the endpapers: the owner, Grizel Baillie, writes her own name several times with various spellings ("Grisall," "Grisell," "Grissell"), and her address, and an upper-case and lower-case alphabet, and a lot of fists, and four copies of a short letter to her cousin—all with the same wording, so the practice must have been for penmanship. Such behavior was and continues to be perfectly normal.[2]

One of the rare cases I have been fortunate enough to find of a barely literate but, on the evidence, adult reader shows similar features. Listed in the Bibliography under "Wesley," it is actually a heavily used collection of English and American sermons of the later eighteenth century. All the notes are in pencil and by the same unformed hand. One or two notes in the body of the text ("Salvation" as the subject of one of the sermons, for instance) indicate that the owner understood its contents, but practically all the writing is on the front and back flyleaves and endpapers and has nothing to do with the sermons. There is the standard ownership claim, in this case a list of names, apparently because the book was a family treasure: "Mary an Banks | Martha Banks | Eliza Banks | William Banks | Sarah Banks | William Henry Banks." And then there are miscellaneous memoranda: a list of prices of household goods, such as matches at two cents, lard at eight cents, cotton at five cents; some scribbles; some figures; a bit of verse mildly risqué for early America; and a declaration of love—"my Dear Mister Brown i love you With all my heart and i Hope you do the same"—that seemingly could not be suppressed. These are readers with little experience of books who have not yet learned the customary use of different areas for annotation, and whose very irregularity proves the rule. For the library reader such volumes are a lucky dip—you never know what may turn up.

A marvelous fictional example of the lucky dip into the mind, via the marginalia, of an immature reader is the experience of the narrator, Lockwood, in Emily Brontë's *Wuthering Heights*. In his bedchamber, unable to sleep, Lockwood examines a few musty old books with Catherine Earnshaw's name in them:

> Catherine's library was select, and its state of dilapidation proved it to have been well used, though not altogether for a legitimate purpose; scarcely one chapter had escaped a pen-and-ink commentary—at least, the appearance of one—covering every morsel of blank that the printer had left. Some were detached sentences; other parts took the form of a regular diary, scrawled in an unformed, childish hand. At the top of an extra page (quite a treasure, probably, when first lighted on) I was greatly amused to behold an excellent caricature of my friend Joseph,—rudely yet powerfully sketched. An immediate interest kindled within me for the unknown Catherine, and I began forthwith to decipher her faded hieroglyphics.[3]

Besides the supporting evidence that this passage provides of the use of books for scrap paper, continuing into the nineteenth century, Catherine's marginalia illustrate the value of marginalia as a literary device. In *Wuthering Heights*, they are a means for introducing a new voice in a particularly direct and personal way, a means for securing interest for Catherine through the reaction of the narrator, and a means for obliquely indicating the distance between them—as a respectable man, he is rather shocked by her flouting of "legitimate" usage. They also trigger Lockwood's dramatic dreams about her. But they are a credible reflection of reality as well as a useful narrative technique.

The Osborne Collection of children's books includes enough annotated books to show patterns that are constant over time, in the relatively stable experience of child readers, as well as some striking individual aberrations.[4] On the whole, preschool children are not real annotators. Coloring black-and-white illustrations does not count. Writing notes in response to a text appears to be a habit acquired at school. Very young children who can read and write use their books rather as spare paper for drawing or writing practice, and confine themselves to the blank leaves at the front and back. A charming case from the late eighteenth century is a copy of John Aikin and Anna Laetitia Barbauld's *Evenings at Home*. The first owner, Hannah Andrews, wrote her name in ink on the front flyleaves and opening pages of the text. A later owner used the back endpaper for her own writing practice, first copying the name "Hannah Andrews" several times and then finally in triumph writing her own name, Lucy Weldron or Meldron, and adding, "I am much improved in my writing since I wrote that ugly Hannah Andrews." Elvie Favet's copy of *The Babes in the Basket*, a gift from her aunt, is decorated front and back with delicate watercolor paintings of birds, mostly owls in pink and blue.

Under instruction, children learn to mark the text conservatively, and to use the endpapers for institutionally approved, standard kinds of note-taking. Florence Nightingale's copy of Mrs. Trimmer's *New and Comprehensive Lessons, Containing a General Outline of the Roman History* (1818) has Nightingale's autograph in pencil on a flyleaf (p. -1) and penciled marks—an "x" or an "A"—at the ends of chapters to show

how far she had got with her reading. A copy of A. E. Marty's *Ontario High School Reader* (1919) that was passed down in the Clements family displays, immediately upon opening, the signatures of successive child owners; a drawing that is surely a portrait of the class teacher; and a list of reading assignments, with page references—all in ink—besides a library bookplate giving the name of the donor, herself presumably the last of the original signatories (fig. 2). More advanced versions of these school readers and similar textbooks do contain manuscript notes within the text, especially definitions of terms, solutions for mathematical problems, and some notes from class, such as the birth and death dates of an author, or comment on a specific passage. Carrie Rae's copy of *Five Longer Poems* (1927), a fifth-form textbook, includes interlinear and marginal notes that gloss words like "wassail-bowl" ("beverage") and paraphrase lines of the text. She also attempted some of the questions proposed at the back of the book, explaining the appeal of Wordsworth's poem "Michael," for example, thus: "It tells us of their simple life & sets an example for us by showing us that even although Luke was well brought up there were things in the city which tended to contribute to his disgrace. It is so original, different, love for his son." Historians of education and of criticism could work with material like this to ascertain, not merely by retrospective reminiscence and anecdote, what went on in the classrooms of a given place at a given time.

Besides these representative examples of normal use one sometimes encounters oddities like the Osborne Collection copy of *Tommy Trip's Valentine Gift* (1785), which contains an account of the origin of St. Valentine's Day, together with improving moral tales and illustrations that are now colored in. The neat inscription in ink on the front pastedown reads, "Edwin Griffith | the gift of his wife | Eliza Noble | 1790"; to it an untidy child's hand has added "and three"—meaning, not 1790 but 1793. On the same page in the same hand are two further notes, "March 4th 1793 | a nice book" and "Fred brought me this for Easter." There are no reader's marks in the text, but the back flyleaves (pp. +1–+5) are filled with notes that reaffirm ownership and provide a vivid impression of the owner's circumstances and feelings. Eliza Noble was a playmate, the play "wife" of young Edwin. These are the notes in full: "Edwin

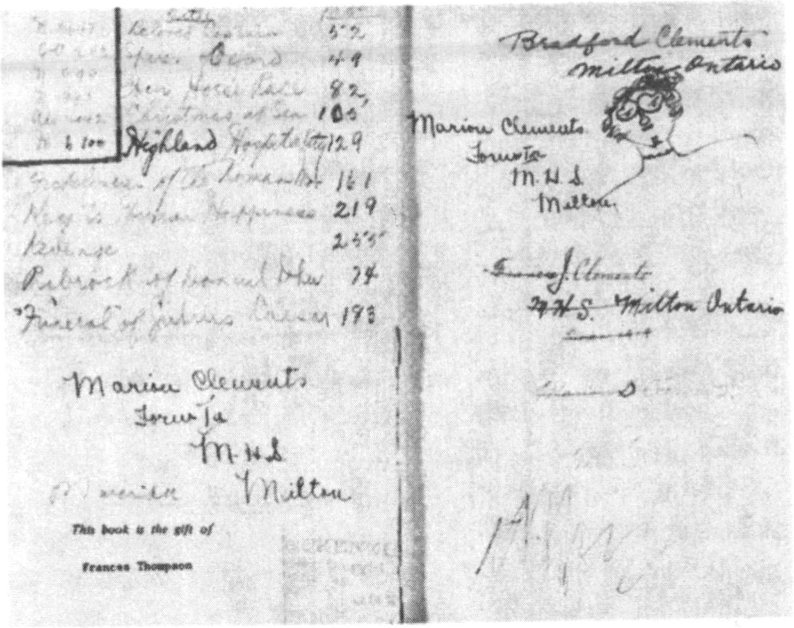

FIG. 2 A. E. Marty, ed., *Ontario High School Reader* (1919). Front endpaper and flyleaf. (Used by permission of the Osborne Collection of Early Children's Books, Toronto Public Library)

Griffith the Gift of his wife—March 4 1793 Edwin G[.] I shall keep this book as Long as it is in being. I shall show it to my wife every time she comes here—. My Grandmother and my Aunt is here playing at cards just by me—. Mrs Noble is at home with Eliza Noble for she has got the whooping cough and cannot come here which I am very sorry about, for she is a charming girl[.] I hope none read this for it is sad[.] Nonscence I am going to bed it is nine a Clock—Farewell[.] This now given to me at 10 a Clock[.]"

Edwin Griffith is like other young annotators in using the blank leaves in his book for writing paper without reference to the text.[5] He is remarkable, in a way that makes one aware of the internal or external restrictions that usually apply, in declaring an opinion about the "nice" book, and even more so in using the book to display the emotions of the moment. I wish I knew what became of Edwin Griffith. I suspect he may have been set already on the road leading to the fanaticisms of Chapter Six. Nevertheless, the point should be made that although the content of his notes is unusual, the way he uses the blank spaces of his book is not: the introductory inscription and assertion of ownership are where convention dictates that they should be, and the personal notes at the back are in a way an extension of the initial assertion. Like Samuel Maude, he affirms his property rights as he turns the book into a diary.

When they go beyond the basic declaration of ownership, child and adult readers alike tend next to fill in details of acquisition. Tradition gives children more scope than adults, who are expected to be drily factual, and brief. An adult owner often supplies an address, a date, and the name of the source—bookseller, for instance, or book sale. Ann Owen Hay's copy of Lambert's *Little Henry* (1823) also gives an address on the front flyleaf. It was written at first in pencil, and later overtraced in ink as a permanent record: "Ann Owen Hay | Hadley | Barnet | Middlesex | England | Great Britain | Europe | P. Ocean [*sic*] | World | Air | Nothing." The first note on the front flyleaf of an eighteenth-century school edition of Cato reads, "William Curzon Is My Name And England Is My Nation Breedon Is My Dwelling Place And Heaven Is My Habitation. July. ye. 19th. 1737[.]" (When I was at school we completed the rhyme with "destination," but "habitation" could be a legitimate variant.) Dates, like addresses, are open to adaptation under circumscribed conditions. Hence William Makepeace Thackeray dated his battered "Collection of English Poems," when he was at school in the 1820s, with a typically ritualistic list, counting down the days "to the holidays" from "Only 2 weeks" to "Only 13 days" and so on down to one.

William Curzon goes on to provide the next indispensable thing— still reinforcement of the ownership claim—as the second note in his Cato, further down the page: "Steal Not This Book For Fear Of Shame For Here You See The Oners Name William Curzon His Book July ye. 19 1737[.]" Iona and Peter Opie divide such anathemas into two categories, "book protection" and "book desecration."[6] A longer version of this one is the first in their collection. They do not have the one Robert Odell of Petrolia, Ontario, used in his *Third Reader* in 1897, and perhaps it is a colonial creation: "Steal not this book for fear of life for the owner has a big jackknife." Adult readers like Joshua Earnshaw, who acquired a second-hand copy of Joseph Townsend's *Physician's Vade Mecum* in 1824, may prefer more sophisticated wording (Earnshaw adopts the Latin "Hic Nomen pono | Quia Librum perdere nolo"—"I put this name down because I do not wish to lose the book"), but the impulse is the same. Holbrook Jackson documents traditional anathemas already in use as early as the twelfth century.[7]

Possession established, owners often begin the process of customizing their books by introducing in the preliminary blank spaces the sort of material that they might have encountered in the apparatus of textbooks. At the most mundane level, the owner of a composite volume containing several short items—plays, poems, sermons, or tracts—may provide a manuscript Table of Contents. (The list of readings shown in figure 2 provides that sort of guide.) The British Library contains many books annotated by John Mitford, who was a clergyman, a classical scholar, editor of the *Gentleman's Magazine* from 1834 to 1850, and a lover of English literature. Mitford was systematic. He marked text in his books sparingly, but at the front he always carefully wrote in his name and the date of acquisition, and then filled the opening pages with pasted-in clippings from booksellers' catalogues or extracts from periodicals; bibliographical notes in his own neat, small hand, in ink; and passages about the book or the author, copied out from other books. In his Rabelais, for example, he noted in 1812, "'Garagantuas is decisively Francis I and Henry II is Pantagruel, and Charles V, Picrocole. Rabelais imitated in many passages, the Literae Virorum Obscurorum.' Warton's Pope V. iv. p. 273. and see the Preface p. xxxvi."

Not scholars or ex-scholars only, but readers of all sorts similarly collected, in the front of their books, materials from other books that could be used as aids and reinforcements for the reading of the book at hand. Notes of this kind are not original, but they indicate by the principles of selection and by the trouble taken to preserve them the frame of mind that the reader considered appropriate in the approach to the work. John Keats's friend Richard Woodhouse used some of the front pages of a copy of Keats's *Poems* (1817) that is now at the Huntington Library for a collection of quotations, some from Keats and some from other authors,

of a kind that might be appropriate as epigraphs—"Verses from which
the soul would never wean," for instance. His *Endymion* (1818) also begins with short passages quoting Keats himself on the nature of poetry,
as well as other authors whose words can be construed as tributes to him,
all by way of psychological preparation for the reader—like the old editions of Shakespeare that begin with poetical testimonials; like modern
publishers' blurbs. With less piety, an irritated reader of Jonathan Edwards's *Dissertation Concerning Liberty and Necessity* (1797) provides an
epigraph from Milton on the title page, right after the author's name: "So
spoke the Fiend, and with NECESSITY, / —excused his dev'lish
deeds."

Generally more personal are the expressions of opinion that readers
put down on the opening pages of their books. These appear to be intended, normally, either to serve as an aid to memory for future reference, or—like their equivalents in print—to make introductions, to act
as a mediator between the text and later readers. Francis Hargrave, a
lawyer and legal scholar whose collection of annotated books was purchased for the British Museum in 1813, patiently explains the bibliographical status of his 1614 edition of John Selden's *Titles of Honour* on
a front flyleaf, and gives his reasons for keeping this copy:

> In 1631 Mr. Selden published a folio volume with the same title; &
> stiled it in the title page a second edition. It is divided into two parts, as
> this first edition is. But the first edition is scarce a third of the second in
> point of quantity; & the latter is in great measure a newly written
> work. Yet this edition has its use. It contains the author's first
> thoughts. Some matter here, though of importance, is omitted in the
> second edition; & an instance of this may be found in the author's ac-
> count of the beginning of feuds in chap. 8. of 2d. part in this edition.
> Besides this edition has the advantage of various indexes none of
> which are in the second. The dedication & preface to this edition are
> different from those in the other. F. H. 28. Aug. 1803.

Hargrave's note combines scholarship and personal judgment in a
way that is typical of conscientious readers before and since—though

the proportions vary. Sir Arthur Conan Doyle endorses many of the volumes in his collection of books about spiritualism and parapsychological experience with a signed note on the title page: of L. Margery Bazett's *After-Death Communications* (1918), for example, he says, "A very useful little book with many good cases entirely beyond Criticism." When you open the American poet Witter Bynner's copy of Dante's lyric sequence *The New Life* you find an original poem, "Perhaps they laughed at Dante in his youth," which he must have written after reading the book, but which he chose to put at the front. It is a sensitive, striking, and strikingly appropriate response to the text. If he gave even a moment's thought to the location of the note, he would have said to himself that the front of the book was where such a response belonged, that's where one would expect to find such a thing; but back of that thinking is a long tradition of prefatory apparatus. The front flyleaves of Coleridge's books also often contain a general assessment, sometimes in the form of a warning. This practice he adopted quite early, for example in a copy of Gerhard Voss's *Poeticarum institutionum, libri tres* (1647): "I have looked thro' this book with some attention, April 21, 1803—, and seldom indeed have I read a more thoroughly worthless one."

In the body of the text, different functions are assigned to different spaces. The top margin, naturally, is for "heads"—in a printed (or for that matter manuscript) book, the section or chapter title that tells you where you are, or, more narrowly, the subject heading that summarizes the content of the page. Readers as a rule put their own heads at the outer edges of the page, top right on the recto, top left on the verso. In books printed since 1700, the bottom margin, the foot of the page, is commonly reserved for footnotes. Readers occasionally mimic the conventions of print by putting footnote cues in the text that are keyed to their own notes below—Alexander Pope's copy of Boileau is a case in point. This practice, however, appears not to be common. Some readers put their subject heads at the foot of the page—as long as it's always in the same part of the page so that you don't have to scan the whole page at every turning, it does not make much difference whether it's top or bottom—but most of them use the bottom margin simply for overflow from the sides. When the side margins are narrow, readers have to use what space they can find elsewhere, not only the bottoms of pages but also the odd bits of lines left blank at the ends and beginnings of paragraphs. The one thing they hardly ever do is trespass into the text itself to write heads or commentary between the lines: that space is reserved for a special kind of reader's aid, the interlinear gloss or word by word translation of the kind I mentioned earlier in my account of schoolbooks. (If there is no room for words between the lines, however, readers' aids will spill out into the margin.)

The side margins, then, are universally, in English-language books, the favored place for the reader's running commentary on the text. Because most of the rest of this study will have to do with notes of this kind and from these spaces, I offer only brief samples here.

Readers' marginal comments range from hasty marks to extended essays. The most basic marks are signs of attention, a line across the margin or running vertically down it, or underlining of the text itself.[8] These are often coupled with a fist or an asterisk, or one of the conventional symbols indicating approval or disapproval: the check, exclamation mark, cross, or question mark. Multiples are used to heighten the effect, five exclamation marks expressing perhaps the maximum of astonishment. Like other systems of notation this one is tried and true, easy to use, readily understood, but crude and unrefined. Now and again, for private purposes or for greater discrimination in communication, readers experiment with systems of their own. When Coleridge was invited to comment on William Blake's *Songs of Innocence and of Experience* in 1818, he tried introducing a ranking system: "N.B. Ɨ signifies, It gave me pleasure. Ɨ, still greater— ɨɨ, and greater still. ⊙, in the highest degree, ○, in the lowest."[9] We do not know whether he used these marks on the work itself; we rather hope not.

The fate of that copy of *Innocence and Experience* is not recorded, but a large part of the manuscript of William Godwin's play *Abbas*, with Coleridge's commentary dating from 1801, has recently come to light, and there also he adopted a set of symbols for common problems, "false or intolerable English," "*flat* or mean," "common-place *book* Language," and "bad metre."[10] He did the same for a copy of *Joan of Arc* that he annotated in 1814. *Joan* is an epic poem, revolutionary in its politics, that had been jointly written by Coleridge and his brother-in-law Robert Southey and published in 1796. Nearly twenty years later, with a history of difficult family relations between them, Coleridge devised and used a shorthand system to criticize Southey's part of the poem:

S.E.   means *Southey's English,* i.e. no English at all.

N.   means Nonsense.

J.   means discordant *Jingle* of sound—one word rhyming or half-rhyming to another proving either utter want of ears, or else very long ones.

L.M. = ludicrous metaphor.

I.M. = incongruous metaphor.

S. =   pseudo-poetic Slang, generally, too, not English.[11]

In this case the very terms of the system, application aside, convey the settled hostility of the annotator: in contrast to the Blake one, there is no room here for commendation. But schemes like these are devised for particular occasions and seem not to last. Every time you invent a custom-made system, you have to explain it somewhere, so that it is liable to be more trouble than it's worth. There may be annotators with private codes that they used over and over again, but I have not come across them.

The next step up is the brief word or phrase. It offers more scope and more precision than the standard marks, though it takes a little longer to write. The "don't agree" and "good idea" of the student annotator of Fletcher described in the Introduction belong to this category, which is, however, capable of greater nuance. John Ruskin's copy of Philip Nichols's *Sir Francis Drake Revived* (1626) illustrates the potential range of such brief jottings: within a few pages, he writes, "very obscure" (p. 27), "Fleche?" (p. 28, against the line, "a Fletcher to keepe our Bowes and Arrowes in order"), "Where?" (p. 33, "*Diego* the Negroe aforesaid"), "don't understand at all" (p. 41), and "Panama—first mention?" (p. 52). These few notes fluctuate between resistance and engagement as they register Ruskin's reactions: some passages he finds difficult, and is inclined to blame the author; but others lead him to make connections and note small discoveries—the origin of the word "fletcher" in the French word for an arrow, and possibly the first reference to Panama in an English publication. Running notes like these are perhaps on balance more likely to be negative than positive. An author and an annotator himself, Thackeray was ruefully aware of the reader's capacity for negative criticism. He tries to anticipate and defuse it when he imagines the reaction to the scene in which Amelia leaves her boarding school, at the beginning of *Vanity Fair:* "All which details, I have no doubt, Jones, who reads this book at his Club, will pronounce to be excessively foolish, trivial, twaddling, and ultra-sentimental. Yes; I can see Jones at this minute (rather flushed with his joint of mutton and half-pint of wine), taking out his pencil and scoring under the words 'foolish, twaddling,' &c., and adding to them his own remark of *'quite true.'*"[12] For readers like Jones, marginalizing with single words or brief phrases is a careless habit; for readers like Ruskin, it appears to be an intellectual discipline that keeps them alert.

There is an obvious correlation between the level of interest and absorption in the reader and the length of the reader's notes. Some particularly intense readers respond sentence by sentence and even point by point, especially when they disagree with the author. In 1783, Richard Watson, the Bishop of Llandaff, published *A Letter to His Grace the Archbishop of Canterbury* as part of an unsuccessful campaign to have the revenues of the Church of England redistributed. At least one copy fell into the hands of a member of the clergy who was opposed to any such change, and who makes his views quite clear in his marginal notes. (Sometimes books are annotated this way as preparation for a published response, but that does not appear to have been the case here.) His use of the space in the volume is quite revealing. The first eleven pages of this nice quarto volume with generous margins are neatly filled with a torrent of invective; then it stops. The reader appears to have gone on reading, however, for there is one more isolated note, a note to a footnote on the very last page (p. 54). His opinion is summed up not at the back but, according to custom, at the front of the book, on the half-title, where he completes the publisher's line "A Letter to His Grace the Archbishop of Canterbury" with a subtitle that introduces his own contribution as though he had been the editor of the volume: "with critical Notes & Observations to elucidate, explain, & clear ye Obscurity false Reasoning not to say palpable gross Lies which this impudent Son of the Church has wrote & published to ye World supposing them to be blind & could not see, ignorant & knew not, & ye worst of Slaves to submit ye Understandings which ye Great GOD ye Fountain of all Knowledge has given them to use for his Glory (to submit I say their Understandings) to ye Devil, ye Pope, his Conclave or any of his *Apes,* existing in any Kingdom of Utopia."

Within the text, the reader's notes present themselves directly opposite the printed sentences and in a larger size, in a "struggle for control of position," as Evelyn B. Tribble would say.[13] In order to reproduce in print the in-every-sense adversarial effect of the marginalia in this volume I shall quote all the notes from one page (p. 11), splicing author and annotator, first giving Watson's text and then on a separate line the reader's response. The underlining is by the annotator.

I am far from saying or thinking, that the Bishops of the present age are more obsequious in their attention to Ministers than their Predecessors have been,

Sing tantararara Bow All!

or that the Spiritual Lords are the only Lords who are liable to this suspicion, or that Lords in general, are the only persons on whom expectation has an influence;

What Business have You with any Lords besides Lords Bishops?

but the suspicion, whether well or ill founded, is disreputable to our Order;

Dont your Practice countenance support & declare to all ye World yt [that] it is so?

and, what is of worse consequence, it hinders us from doing that good which we otherwise might do; for the Laity, whilst they entertain such a suspicion concerning us, will accuse us of Avarice and Ambition,

Fie! dont accuse ye Laity by laying ye Faût of Suspicion on them for you have confest it concerning yr Brethren!

of making a gain of Godliness, of bartering the dignity of our Office for the chance of a translation, in one word of—Secularity—; and against that accusation they are very backward in allowing the Bishops or the Clergy in general, such kind of defence as they would readily allow to any other class of Men, any other denomination of Christians,

ye other Classes of Men & any other Denominations of Xristians should have been out of ye Question as they are not our Lords Bishops

under the similar circumstances, of large families and small fortunes.

The annotator who can put this amount of energy into the disruption of a single sentence is a formidable opponent, at least on the page. Still it is worth emphasizing that he accepts the physical limitations of the margin and the page, and that he attempts to work within the existing conventions of book format, writing subtitles and side-notes—the equivalent of the printed marginal glosses that had been the norm a century before, and that continued to appear long after the introduction of the footnote—and not just blowing off steam in random abuse of the author.

The legend that everyone knows about writing in the margins of books is the story of the French mathematician Pierre de Fermat who declared, in a note written about 1637 and published posthumously in 1670, that he had a proof for an important problem, but that the margin was too small to contain it. This tantalizing statement occupied mathematicians for centuries after.[14] It is not clear that it was seriously and not just teasingly meant. Had Fermat been in earnest, however, and had he had his wits about him, the solution to the logistical problem should not have been hard to find; the mistake lay in tamely accepting, like Watson's otherwise rough reader, the constraints of the page. Had he been less inhibited, more imaginative, or more strongly impelled to persist, he would simply have turned the page and continued on the next page and the next until he had laid out his proof. There are also other ways of resolving the problem. Sometimes readers start a long note at the relevant point in the text and continue it at the foot of the page or, with a cue such as "turn to," on a later page with more blank space, or on a flyleaf. One of the Shipleys coped with the extremely narrow margins of a cheap trade paperback by turning the book ninety degrees and writing along the margin instead of across it, as we have seen Samuel Maude do.[15] This trick gives you a long run in the side margins where you might otherwise have to break words frequently; but your note no longer looks anything like a printed gloss.

Another option, one that was until recently quite readily available, is interleaving. For as long as binderies were plentiful, and especially during the period when books were issued in boards or paper covers so that you could have them bound to your own specifications—up till roughly the middle of the nineteenth century—it was relatively easy to order a book bound with a blank leaf (or, less commonly, two blank leaves) following every printed leaf, so that for every page of text there was a blank page facing to accommodate the reader's notes. In some cases publishers anticipated demand and offered books in an interleaved format, or with extra blank pages at the back of the book. In 1787, for example, the publishers of a guidebook entitled *A Supplement to the Tour of Great-Britain, Containing a Catalogue of the Antiquities, Plantations, Scenes, and Situations, in England and Wales . . . by the Late Mr. Gray* solicited readers' corrections and improvements by adding a set of pages with printed headings (for example, "Bedfordshire"; "Antiquities"; "Scenes and Situations") at the end. The work itself had been based, as the title indicates, on Gray's *Catalogue*, which in turn was based on Gray's interleaved annotated copy of Thomas Kitchin's *New Geographical Description of England and Wales*. So strategic interleaving contributed to the advancement of knowledge and the book trade.

33

There is something premeditated about this convenient arrangement, however, that is at odds with the spirit of impulsive marginalizing, and I have found few examples in which interleaved pages are not used for work-related purposes such as authorial revision, editing, or lecturing. Richard Woodhouse's two Keats books, mentioned earlier for their front matter, may be among the exceptions to this general rule. Both were interleaved to take Woodhouse's notes, and it is instructive to discover what that ideally sympathetic contemporary reader thought that he or others might want to know about Keats's verse. He supplies some variant readings based on the collation of manuscripts; offers relevant biographical details; provides definitions for unusual words like "ouzel," but also for colloquialisms like "peer about"; and quotes literary sources or parallels. It is not clear whether he was actually contemplating an edition or whether, as seems more likely, these volumes were simply part of the collection of papers and scrapbooks that he assembled as a custodian of Keats's reputation. In any case, Woodhouse contracted tuberculosis and died in 1834 without having published his commentary. Nor is it by any means systematic or complete. The interleaved pages are far from full. In fact it is my impression that interleaved volumes often go this way: annotators begin enthusiastically, but after a while the prospect becomes discouraging—all those blank leaves still to fill—and unless the book is very important to them, or the task quite imperative, they give up.

Interleaving seems to have been routine for students, especially in the professions. Interleaved textbooks and lecture outlines or syllabi are a potentially valuable resource for the history of science, medicine, or law, or for the history of education in those subjects, for they make it possible to compare a published statement with the actual content of the lecture series. William Wollaston's *Plan of a Course of Chemical Lectures* (1794), for example, announces the subject of "The bulk and specific gravity of a mixture of sulphuric acid with water" (p. 9), but the student's note on the facing interleaf reads, "a flask filld with water ½ pourd out the same quantity of Sul[phuri]c acid pourd into the flask does not fill it"; thus we find out by what demonstration Wollaston proved his point.

Outside the lecture halls, readers also made up study guides for themselves. The genteel vogue for botanizing that began in the eighteenth century must have generated many fascinating cases like the British Library's interleaved copy of Samuel Saunders's *Short and Easy Introduction to Scientific and Philosophic Botany* (1792)—one of many presentations of Linnaean botany in the period—interleaved to take the notes of a contemporary reader, almost certainly a woman. The text itself is only lightly marked, with a little underlining and a few notes. Most of the annotation is on the interleaved pages. Given the two folding plates bound in at the back, consisting of watercolor illustrations with manuscript text, the volume technically counts as extra-illustrated, but the notes are the reader's more important contribution. (The subject of extra-illustration will be discussed at length in Chapter Six.) The notes add information and explanations; they appear not to have been copied from other books, but to be the annotator's own words. They offer a mixture of contemporary science and popular plant lore. On the leaf facing page 73, where the class "Polyandria (*many males*)" is introduced, the annotator observes,

> The plants belonging to this class are usually of a poisonous nature. When the nectarium or honey cup is distinct from the petals or flower leaves the plant is always poisonous.

At the more basic level, when the author writes generally of leaves as "the most useful and ornamental parts of plants" (p. 17), the notes provide a glimpse of contemporary housekeeping as well as of the mindset of the amateur botanist:

> A branch of a tree may be kept alive for some time, provided two or three of its leaves are suffer'd to be under water. Hence if you wish to preserve flowers for ornament you should never strip the stem of its leaves.
>
> Plants should never be water'd but in the Evening. If the water be not of the cleanest, so much the better.
>
> The upper surface of a leaf is always darker than the under in consequence of the action of light upon it.

Interleaving is a practical solution to the physical constraint of margins. For a methodical owner like this one, it provides an opportunity to turn a single volume into a tailor-made compendium. Reference books are often interleaved.

For readers who do not have the means, or the forethought, to interleave their books especially to take their marginal notes, accidental spaces within the text are naturally a blessing. These too have their conventional uses. The space at the start of a new chapter or section invites the annotator to summarize the contents; the space at the end, to express a general view of the section, as opposed to responses to specific statements. In Chapter 5 of his *Biographical Sketch of the Life of William B. Ide* (1880), Simeon Ide tells the story of the capture of the garrison of Sonoma, and of the following month in 1846 when California became a republic under the Bear Flag. His narrative relies heavily on quotations from a letter by W. M. Boggs, who had known several of the participants. Boggs's own copy uses the margins to reinforce the witness of the letter with such assertions as, "I have heard more than a dozen of the Bear Party relate these facts" (p. 54). He uses the space at the end of the chapter for a solemn testimonial: "I wrote the foregoing pages for Mr. Simeon Ide Author of this Book and I vouch for the Truthfulness of his Narrative of his Brother W. B. Ides History in California in 1846–7. Wdl Boggs | Napa | March 11th 1883." Boggs's situation is unusual, no doubt, but his instinct about where properly to place his notes is in conformity with common usage.

If the last page of a chapter is the right location for general remarks about the chapter, the last page of a book, especially when it declares "Finis" or "The End," might seem to be the obvious spot for an assessment of the work as a whole. Readers do sometimes make use of the space for that purpose; and in that case, if there is no room on the page itself, they will turn to the verso or to the facing flyleaf—the nearest possible blank space—instead. A typical example is Johnson's friend Hester Lynch Piozzi (known to him as Mrs. Thrale), who loyally wrote, following "The End" of a copy of his philosophical tale *Rasselas*, "—of a Book unrivalled in Excellence of Intention, in Elegance of Diction; in minute Knowlege of human Life—& Sublime Expression of Oriental

Imagery" (p. 184). There's also Leigh Hunt's response to the coda of his copy of the *Meditations* of Marcus Aurelius Antoninus, "depart, therefore, contented, and in good humour; for, he is propitious and kind, who dismisses you." Hunt courteously adds, "Thanks, and love to you, excellent Antoninus. L. H. Feb. 7th. 1853. His second regular perusal."

The practice of writing at the end in this way had been recommended by Michel de Montaigne in an influential essay on books. He engagingly admits that he adopted it after finding that he often picked up a book as new to him, only to find the margins full of his own notes. By writing a summary note at the back of the book when the experience was still fresh in his mind, he could spare himself the trouble of rereading.[16] But it is much more common for the general assessment to appear where we have already seen it, with the front matter. That prominent position makes it more likely to be useful as a guide to future reading, whether by the original annotator or not. And besides, the back flyleaves and paste-down of a book are usually reserved for another purpose—the reader's index.

Like the published index, the reader's manuscript index by tradition appears at the back of the book. (I had a chemistry teacher once whose favorite dictum was, "All chemicals are white except the ones that aren't." What he meant was that this held for the overwhelming majority and that if we had to guess, say on the final examination, we should guess white. The same logic holds true for the manuscript index. I do know of one book, an early edition of Boswell's *Life of Johnson,* where the index appears at the front, but any reader would be surprised to find it there. Of course, it is quite a bit more likely that a reader's index will be at the front than that the published one will.)

"Index" is a rather grand term, usually, for what I am describing— the list of subject headings with corresponding page numbers that the reader scribbles on the back endpapers. In its humblest form, it consists of page numbers only. A list of page numbers is the quickest and simplest form of reference because it entails minimal interruption of the reading process, but it is the least efficient in the long run because when you consult it later you have to page through the book to find out which number, if any, will enable you to locate the passage you are seeking. The conventional practice is for readers to write down, as they come upon them (therefore normally in page order from beginning to end and not in the alphabetical order of the published index), the page reference and a word or two to indicate the subject of the passage noted. To an observant, informed, and dedicated later reader, these simple memoranda can be quite revealing. The total number of notes may be an indication of the degree of the earlier reader's interest. The order of page references may reflect the order of reading—was the book read through, or dipped into?—and the number of readings. The selection of topics gives an impression of the kind of thing the reader was looking for, or arrested by. If you know enough about the annotator, you may be able to tell whether the list was made for private or for professional purposes—for example, as a set of materials to be used in an anthology, a review, or a memoir. Some readers group topics in separate areas on the endpapers rather than making a single list; anything with more system to it than a list is evidence of habits of mind strong enough to override conventional usage. The subject headings are usually very basic and the path of least resistance is to use the words of the original author; annotators who put things in their own words are unusual and noteworthy.

The flamboyant and eccentric William Beckford (1759–1844) adapted the conventional reader's index in a quite distinctive way. I shall be returning to him again later, but a few examples from among his books at this point will serve to establish his customary practice and to illustrate the value of the reader's index and its customary placement.

Beckford was born to great wealth, and was educated privately. From 1777 until 1792 he spent a great deal of time abroad, mostly in Paris and Switzerland. As a very young man, he tossed off the decadently erotic "Oriental" tale *Vathek*, which he wrote and eventually published in French; an unauthorized English translation appeared in 1784. In 1796, he settled down on the family estate at Fonthill and embarked on a ruinous program of building and collecting. He was obliged to sell Fonthill in 1822, but he took many books and the best of his pictures with him into retirement. A major sale of books took place in 1882–83; there had been lesser sales earlier, in 1804, 1808, 1817, and 1823.[17]

Beckford was a well-known collector and a well-known annotator, so purchasers tended to record the provenance of books from his library, and there are hundreds and hundreds of them still extant. They are—uniformly, in my experience—remarkably beautiful: Beckford employed excellent binders. It may have been partly out of fastidiousness that he developed his personal method of annotation, which preserves the pages of the text unmarked and keeps the notes confined to the flyleaves. He seems generally to have annotated a book as soon as he got it, before it was bound; the binder took care to preserve the notes from cropping by folding in the relevant pages. (Other binders, less elegantly, would slit the page above and below a note and fold in just the flap containing it.) Beckford ordinarily used pencil. He started his note-taking at the front of the book but would continue to the back if he ran out of space. His handwriting is small, fine, and clear. The notes are presented in an orderly way, with a page number at the left followed by an indented block of words. To this extent, Beckford conforms to the standard method of "indexing," though his list comes at the beginning rather than at the end of the book. His innovation is in the length of the entries. Some are, in the ordinary way, brief subject headings. Most, however, are several lines long, for they typically consist of actual extracts from the text. These are by no means neutral or impersonal. The selection itself implies judgment—Beckford chooses passages that he likes or dislikes. Furthermore, he tends to edit and paraphrase as he goes, changing the original to emphasize the qualities that appealed to him in it. Now and again he expresses an opinion of his own.

Richard Garnett, in the entry on Beckford for the British *Dictionary of National Biography,* where he concludes that Beckford's was, "on the whole, a wasted life," describes the library as follows: "A large proportion of the volumes contained copious notes in his handwriting, more frequently evincing whimsical prejudice than discriminating criticism." Without knowing what volumes Garnett had access to, it is not easy to challenge this harsh judgment. Beckford's overtly critical notes are forcefully expressed; they do not affect the balanced air of "discriminating criticism." Of the poet laureate Robert Southey's little volume of ballads, *All for Love; and The Pilgrim to Compostella* (1829), for instance, he remarks, "All for pelf rather than all for Love in this breathing world—Nothing but the desire of adding to his stock of pence, and the laudable view of presenting his little friends, sweet listening dears,—with comfits & sugar-plumbs, could have induced the Laureate to put forth such a doodlesome publication." But hardly any of Beckford's notes *are* explicitly critical. For the most part, they consist of quotations or a blend of quotation and précis. (The intent must have been to enable Beckford, when he took the book off his shelf later on, to recapture the experience of the first reading. The index is a retrieval device.)

Garnett's irritated statement might perhaps be defended, however, by a careful study of the patterns of selection. Beckford was struck by salacious details and by ludicrous, especially pompous, phrasing; his selection and light editing of passages from the books he read testify to his love of the ridiculous and to his mocking, irreverent spirit. To take a very modest example, his copy of a collection of biographies of central figures in the French Revolution, Stewarton's *Revolutionary Plutarch* (1806), has notes in only the first of three volumes, and they refer to fewer than a hundred pages of text. Beckford's notes fill half a page, as follows:

179   Murdering en masse at Toulon by Brutus Buonaparte Citizen
       Sans-culotte
183   Barras & his entourage
260   Angereau for one night put 16 young Nuns into requisition for
       himself & his staff—
261   delightful Fète given by this gallant general in the principal
       Church of Bologna . . . described in a work printed at Verona
       1799 called les Crimes des Republicains en Italie—

The first and second entries are taken verbatim from the text, the first from a footnote—so Beckford was reading attentively. The third is presented by the author as a particularly abhorrent act, but Beckford appears to have enjoyed the incongruity of the military term "requisition" in this context, and perhaps the sadistic titillation of the report. In the fourth entry, Beckford draws on the wording of the text but ironizes it, "delightful Fète" and "gallant" being phrasing of his own for what Stewarton had described as "inhuman and sacrilegious abominations."

It is understandable that a reader like Garnett should have objected to the frivolity of the annotator's attitude. Though Beckford is not making a direct critical comment, criticism is implicit in his selection and modification of quotations.

An amusing and instructive copy of another book with Beckford's notes is Robert Southey's poem *A Vision of Judgement* (1821) now at the Pierpont Morgan Library in New York. In this work, Southey used his position as poet laureate to make a ferocious attack on Lord Byron and "the Satanic School" of poetry. Byron successfully counterattacked with a parody, *The Vision of Judgement,* in 1822, so that Southey's poem is now known only as the occasion of Byron's. The Morgan copy once belonged to Byron. It contains a transcription, in ink, not necessarily made in Byron's lifetime, of Beckford's satirical but defensive annotations to the work. This transcription is significant for two reasons. In the first place, it indicates that the notes had a wider circulation than Beckford's own copy—that is, that they were valued enough to be duplicated in manuscript. (George Whalley, the founding editor of the Coleridge marginalia, coined the phrase "ms facsimile" for this phenomenon, which is a boon to an editor if it preserves the annotations after the original has been lost, but a trial when it leads, as it sometimes does, to mistaken attributions.) But the second unusual feature of this copy is that the transcription is not in fact an exact facsimile, for the notes have been copied onto the relevant pages of the text rather than being kept to the flyleaves. In a few cases, when Beckford's note is a direct critical remark, this procedure may work; but when—as is more often the case—his note is simply an echo of the text, it doesn't. "Firm in his Father's steps hath the Regent trod, was the answer" does not provide much illumination for "Right in his Father's steps hath the Regent trod, was the answer: / Firm hath he prov'd and wise" in the text. These are properly "index" notes. They don't belong in the margins.

A tour of the annotated book from front to back, whether we consider conventional use or idiosyncratic variations, reveals that our customs and expectations, constant over time, are based on the conventional format of the book itself. In more ways than one, marginalia *mirror* the texts they supplement. Considered from another perspective, the distri-

[handwritten marginalia:] close and far

[handwritten marginalia:] distance from text / physical features

41

bution of marginalia also represents a progressive distancing from the text. Both processes are aspects of assimilation: by the first, readers accommodate themselves to the work and identify with it, adopting the author's train of thought and the structure by which it is mediated; by the second, they gradually separate themselves from it. The notes that are in the closest physical proximity to the text are the interlinear glosses that traditionally move word by word, as readers' aids, translating or defining or paraphrasing the original. These are, as we paradoxically say, the same but different: the words have changed, but the meaning is as nearly identical as we can make it. Marks and commentary in the margin of the same page, however, express a distinct position pro or con, or offer supplementary material from an external source, such as literary parallels or additional evidence. The index at the back extracts from the whole text just those passages that the reader might want to refer to again, and the summary judgment at the front or back formulates an opinion that is decidedly the reader's and not the author's. The psychological sequence works not so much from front to back, then, as from the inside out. The process of withdrawal can be traced farther as readers pass from writing in the pages of the book to writing in a notebook or commonplace book, and from articulating views in immediate response to a printed text, to reformulating and reorganizing those views in their own compositions. And "farther" in this case is not just a metaphor, for as long as the physical link is maintained—while the words of the annotator are on the same page or between the same covers as the words that prompted them—author and reader act visually as checks on one another, but once it is broken that is no longer so. For this reason, marginal notes are particularly well calculated for minute criticism and "close" reading.

Before leaving the subject of typical physical features of marginalia, I'd like very briefly to mention other physical issues that are worth bearing in mind when marginalia are examined. One of the great dividers of kinds is the medium used: are the notes in pencil, or in ink? In one color, or more than one? Are they by one hand only, or by more than one? If there are two annotators, what appears to be the relationship between them—does the later annotator ignore the first, or is she or he drawn to passages the other has marked? If they are by one hand, are they the product of one reading, or of more than one? Do repeat readers return to their own notes, and comment on them? Are all sections of the book evenly marked? Are the notes dated? Are they signed or initialed? Are they in the same language as the text? Is the annotation roughly contemporary with the text, or not? And in all these cases, *why so?*

The answers to this last question may be not at all obvious. For example, we might assume that a note in ink was intended to be public and permanent, whereas a note in pencil was intended to be private and temporary since it could be easily erased. But readers use pen or pencil for various reasons. Beckford was probably mindful of the beauty of his books, and perhaps of the indiscretion of his notes. Coleridge generally used ink, but he made a point of choosing pencil for a book "lent to me by a friend who had himself borrowed it," and he had to use pencil for some of his German books because the paper was so spongy that ink soaked through it and writing became illegible.[18] The student who marked up Fletcher's *Situation Ethics* probably used a pen because it was there, without thinking about whether she wanted her notes to be with the book forever or not. Sometimes, even into this century, notes that were written in pencil came to be overtraced in ink later. Was it by the same hand or by another? On what occasion? These questions have to be addressed case by case, with as much knowledge of the historical and personal context as we can muster.

Interesting idea...

chapter two

HISTORY

The marginalia that we see and write today are in a direct line of descent from those of two thousand years ago. Indeed the custom may be as old as script itself, for readers have to interpret writing, and note follows text as thunder follows lightning. Over the centuries, of course, technological and social developments led to modifications in the practice of annotation, so that the unified empire of marginalia could also be said to be divided into distinct kingdoms. In the English-speaking world in the modern period, since the advent of print, we could define three such kingdoms, with border-posts about 1700 and 1820—the first part, that is, ending around 1700 (where this study properly begins), the second running roughly from 1700 to 1820, and the third from 1820 to the present. While I cannot resist giving them names—the Kingdom of Competition, the Kingdom of Sociability, the Kingdom of Subjectivity—honesty obliges me to say at the outset that my labels bring out differences that are in fact relatively superficial. Although the main divisions of this chapter deal with each kingdom in turn, therefore, they all contain examples from other periods in order to reinforce the theme of continuity. The history of these several kingdoms or ages is a history not of revolution but of expansion, as the conventions of scholarly annotation spread to secular, vernacular texts and were exercised by a wider and wider range of readers. In the crucial period of the eighteenth century, marginalia became both increasingly personal and increasingly public; but at the same time, the practices of earlier periods quietly persisted. I begin, therefore, by giving the broad outlines of the history of marginalia before 1700.

Glosses, rubrics, and scholia are the basic particles of the matter generated by annotators. We find them attached, seemingly from the start, to the most revered of texts circulating in manuscript: the great works of classical literature, the Bible, and the legal code. "Gloss" and "scholium" are derived ultimately from Greek terms, *glossa* and *scholion*. "Rubric" is a latecomer from the Latin *rubrica*, referring to the scribal practice of writing or marking certain words in red. A "rubric" in the context of annotation is, as the *Oxford English Dictionary* defines it, "A heading of a chapter, section, or other division of a book, written or printed in red, or otherwise distinguished in lettering; a particular passage or sentence so marked." The rubric corresponds to the subject heading, or "head," that is so common a feature of the modern annotated book described in Chapter One. Glosses and scholia, likewise, are the exact equivalents of the familiar interlinear gloss and the marginal comment. The gloss, in its primary sense, translates or explains foreign or obscure words; its expanded forms are the translation and the paraphrase. It operates at the most literal of levels, and aims to be faithful to the text it mediates. The scholium, on the other hand, is a note that introduces information from outside the work that some scholar (usually) has judged relevant to it— a grammatical or textual point, an elucidation, a new illustration, a historical reference, a confirming or contradicting authority. All these forms of interpretative labor mount up, so that a sufficient mass of individual glosses can become a free-standing glossary, a mass of rubrics an index, and a mass of scholia an independent commentary. But in pre-print eras, the most important texts were copied with a ready-made apparatus. The Bible and the Justinian Code, specifically, acquired standard sets of notes, in each case called the *glossa ordinaria*.[1]

Early printed books, modeled on manuscripts, imitated the physical features of manuscripts. Editions of the classics continued the manuscript tradition of leaving room between the lines and in the margins for students' notes.[2] Glosses and scholia were printed in the margins, and when necessary, as with the Bible and its Glossa Ordinaria, completely surrounded the central text. In some cases, manuscript details were added to printed books before they left the shop. Paul Saenger and Michael Heinlen have discovered, for example, that what might appear to be readers' notes in very early printed books may actually be manuscript readers' aids supplied by the printer, reflecting "a division of labour in late medieval scriptoria which appears to have been simply transferred to the printshops or monastic scriptoria that specialized in the confecting of incunables."[3] Old and new techniques of publication thus evidently drew strength from one another and maintained a peaceful coexistence for many years after the introduction of the printing press.

Early modern marginalia also perpetuated the practices associated with manuscript books: readers continued to add to books just as their ancestors had done. The kinds of note they wrote were conditioned by example—now including the example of *printed* glosses and scholia (fig. 3)—as well as by education, for teachers advised pupils on methods of annotation and supervised and encouraged their efforts. The last is a point worth pausing over.

Education aims to transfer knowledge to students so that they may in their turn use and increase the stock of it. Children learning to read begin with the rudimentary interpretation of letters and words and progress through basic levels of comprehension to more sophisticated contextualization and appropriation. At every stage, students working with books have used the tool of annotation. The broad divide is between note-taking of the kind represented by heads and translations, and the bolder activity of book improvement. Bernard M. Rosenthal's descriptions of 242 early annotated books include many examples of students' notes, including not only interlinear and explanatory glosses and paraphrases but also complete commentaries *dictated* by their instructors.[4] Their schooling over, readers were presumably qualified to make their own additions to the books in their care. The norm in these cases is for relatively neutral, impersonal, and not necessarily original material.

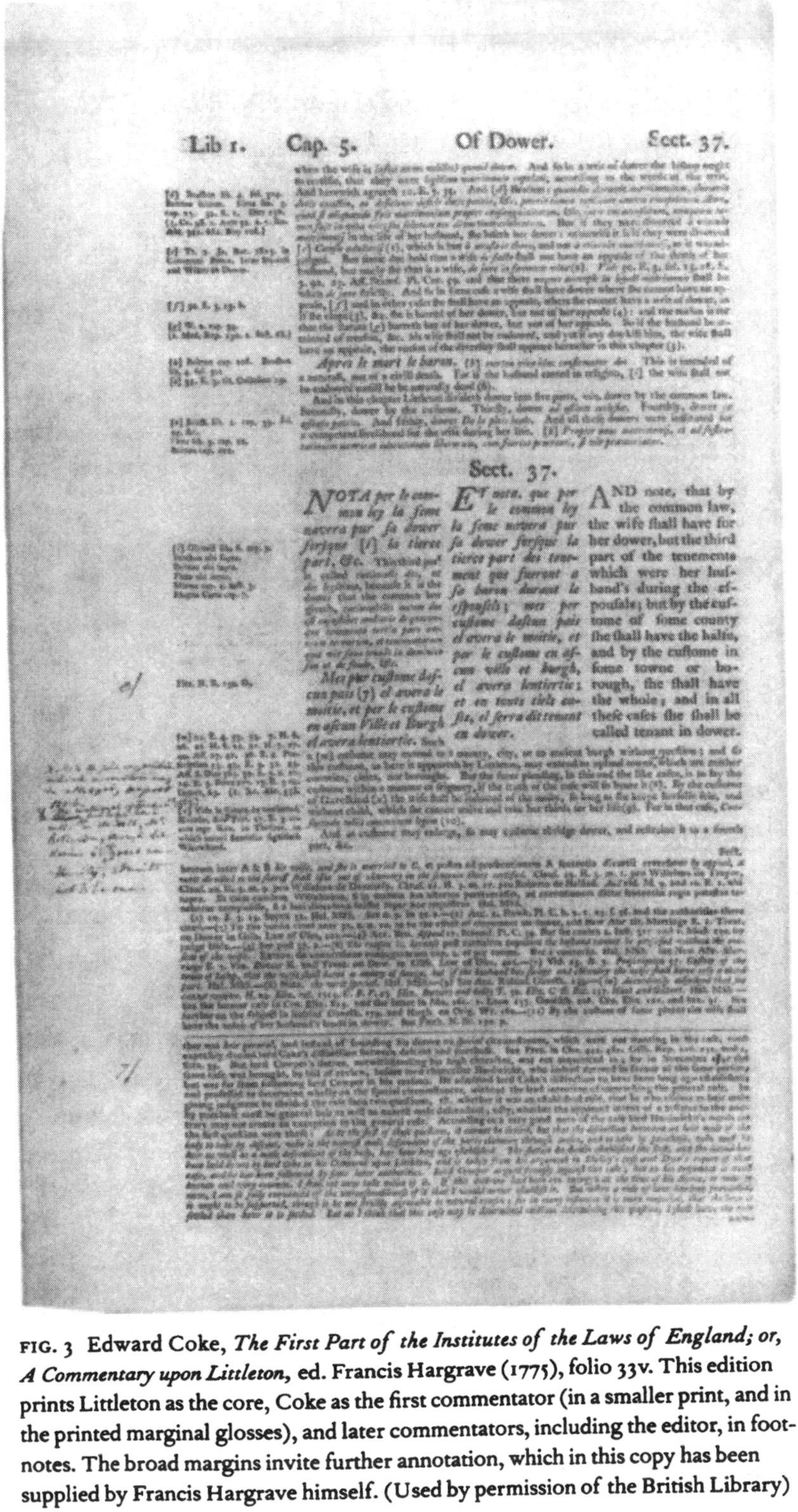

Sect. 37.

NOTA per common ley la some nectura par si aver serfyne (f) la tierce part, &c. ...

ET note, que per le common ley la some nectura par si dower serfyne le tierce part des tenements que furent a si baron durant le spousfals; mes per custome desfinz puis d'avera le moitie, et per le custome en ascun vills et burgh, d'avera lentiertie; et en touts thés ausfis, el serra dit tenant en dower. ...

AND note, that by the common law, the wife shall have for her dower, but the third part of the tenements which were her husband's during the espousals; but by the custome of some county she shall have the halfe, and by the custome in some towne or borough, she shall have the whole; and in all these cases she shall be called tenant in dower.

FIG. 3 Edward Coke, *The First Part of the Institutes of the Laws of England; or, A Commentary upon Littleton,* ed. Francis Hargrave (1775), folio 33v. This edition prints Littleton as the core, Coke as the first commentator (in a smaller print, and in the printed marginal glosses), and later commentators, including the editor, in footnotes. The broad margins invite further annotation, which in this copy has been supplied by Francis Hargrave himself. (Used by permission of the British Library)

In one sixteenth-century text Rosenthal finds, for example, both interlinear glosses and "marginal notes of several kinds" representing considerable scholarly labor—emendations, explanations of unfamiliar terms, paraphrases of the author's meaning, citations of literary sources, historical notes, and references to other commentaries (p. 206). Expressions of personal opinion or literary judgment are rare in Rosenthal's collection, though they do occur (p. 202), and there is some evidence that they too would have been encouraged as part of the learning process.

Over the centuries, recommendations about writing marginalia constitute a minor theme in educational theory. Erasmus's advice on how to study makes a useful starting point: "Informed then by all this you will carefully observe when reading writers whether any striking word occurs, if diction is archaic or novel, if some argument shows brilliant invention or has been skilfully adapted from elsewhere, if there is any brilliance in the style, if there is any adage, historical parallel, or maxim worth committing to memory. Such a passage should be indicated by some appropriate mark. For not only must a variety of marks be employed but appropriate ones at that, so that they will immediately indicate their purpose." Erasmus is addressing students at an advanced note-taking stage, when they have progressed far enough to begin culling from the authors they read materials that they may use in their own speech or writing. They are to exercise their own judgment in selecting these materials, and to devise a system of special marks to differentiate one category from another. They are not yet at the stage of being able to improve the books they study: Erasmus stops short of recommending discursive additions. He does tie the system of marks to other mnemonic devices, recommending the use of a commonplace book into which fine passages would be copied under subject headings, and suggesting some tricks to exercise the memory. Writing in books comes in here too: "In the same way you will write some brief but pithy sayings such as aphorisms, proverbs, and maxims at the beginning and at the end of your books; others you will inscribe on rings or drinking cups; others you will paint on doors and walls or even in the glass of a window so that what may aid learning is constantly before you."[5]

The great authority of Erasmus articulated and reinforced the common practice of many centuries. In the marginalia of assured readers like Gabriel Harvey, John Dee, and John Evelyn, in the sixteenth and seventeenth centuries, we see the full range of readers' manuscript additions to books: special private marks, impersonal additions to the text, and here and there "personal reflections, introspections, and precepts."[6] And the advice given by Erasmus is reiterated through the centuries. Ellen Terry annotated a copy of David Pryde's *Highways of Literature; or, What to Read and How to Read* (1882) knowing she had the author's full approval—at least for her method of reading. He might not have been altogether pleased to see her comment that "David Pryde had a bit of John Knox in him" (p. 207). Pryde promotes a system of note-taking followed by written digests in the reader's own words: "If the keeping of a note-book be a care too harassing for you, then, if the book be your own, write your notes on the margin with a pencil. . . . Note-taking may thus be done in various ways, but done in some way it must be. Without it you cannot be intelligent readers. For how can you be intelligent readers without being discriminating; and how can you be discriminating without distinguishing between the good and the bad, the remarkable and the commonplace; and how can you distinguish between these without affixing some distinctive marks? You will find, too, that all great scholars have been great note-takers" (p. 29).

Pryde follows Erasmus and convention in advocating the systematic marking of texts as a means of forming judgment, and in associating the writing of marginalia with scholarship. The American educator Mortimer J. Adler did the same in a well-known article, "How to Mark a Book," in 1940. (His editors rather wickedly chose to publish with the article, ostensibly as "an example of how *not* to mark a book," a photograph of a page from Adler's earlier *How to Read a Book* covered with mildly abusive and very slovenly annotations, whereas Adler had proposed marking as a matter of professional discipline.) Examples of this century reveal teachers both practicing and advocating the annotation of books. Vladimir Nabokov's teaching copy of Franz Kafka's *Metamorphosis* contains notes that he must have read aloud to his students, including the injunction, "Use space at bottom of pages for your notes"

(p. [11]); F. R. Leavis dedicated a collection of essays, *Nor Shall My Sword* (1972), "To the York students who gave me a new Blake with clean margins to write in." So annotation has its place in an honorable educational tradition.

In the long period that includes the circulation of manuscript books and the first century or so of what we now call print culture, readers wrote in books as part of the process of learning, whether as students under the authority of teachers or as scholars themselves contributing to the world of learning. Ordinary and acceptable additions to books consisted of notes modeled on those of the classical grammarians and editors, namely textual collations and corrections, explanations of hard words and obscure passages, references to sources, and illustrative examples. Expressions of opinion, as I have said, were rare: like editors, annotators seem to have been expected to suppress private views in the interests of cumulative scholarship.[7] The fact that personal opinions appear at all, however, suggests that it was not force of example merely that conditioned a reader's behavior in the early years of print. Private ownership and the expectation of continued possession also played a part, affecting readers' attitudes toward books and their ideas of the uses that might be made of them.

Saenger and Heinlen have argued that the evidence of manuscript features in incunables "implies a psychology of reading incunables distinctly different from that of modern books" given that "The modern reader, if he or she adds marginalia, records personal reactions to the reading of the text. In contrast, the late medieval reading notes found in incunables reflect a preoccupation with clarifying the text on behalf of the community of the lettered through the removal of all visual ambiguity" (p. 250). This remark seems to suggest that in the good old days of manuscript culture, readers were public-spirited and self-effacing, whereas later on they became emotional and self-centered. The authors probably did not intend moral judgment and were merely echoing a common generalization about an era in which books, being scarce, were revered, and one in which, being comparatively plentiful, they were abused; one in which reading was a social and responsible activity as opposed to one in which it became solitary and self-indulgent. But this easy assumption of radical discontinuity never did bear examination. Whether the "modern reader" inhabits the twentieth century or any period later than the early sixteenth century, it is not true that he or she invariably "records personal reactions to the reading of the text." Readers continue to this day to do what readers did in the Middle Ages, besides doing much more in the way of recording individual impressions. They mark up their books as a way of learning and remembering what they contain, and improve them by correcting errors and adding useful relevant information. Some early readers engaged themselves in argument with the books they read, or expressed distaste for or disapproval of them; they were admittedly in a minority, but the minority included Montaigne. I suggest that the gradual shift (not a complete about-face) from one kind of annotation to the other has little or nothing to do with psychology of reading, and much to do with available models and with the steady increase of private ownership of books.

In England in the sixteenth century, the Reformation and the print revolution coincided to bring more books—especially books in English—to more people and to present readers with new models of annotation. Writers, the book trade, and government itself were all aware of the risks involved in sending books into the world with no guidance for the reader. The widely adopted solution was to provide printed commentary in order to control the reader's efforts at interpretation. Familiar literary examples of this phenomenon are Edmund Spenser's *Shepheardes Calendar* (1579), with endnotes to each eclogue by the fictional or semi-fictional "E. K.," and John Bunyan's *Pilgrim's Progress* (1678), with printed marginal glosses that give cross-references to the Bible and offer explanations of the allegory. John Harington's 1591 translation of Ariosto's *Orlando Furioso* was printed with both marginal glosses and endnotes. In his pioneering study of printed marginalia in Renaissance books, William Slights lists alphabetically fifteen functions that could be served by such notes, from amplification through justification and parody to translation.[8]

Attempts to restrain interpretative activity have their own pitfalls, most noticeable where there is most at stake. Tribble's book on the early printed page describes the typical relationship between the text and the printed gloss in this period as "a battle" for authority (p. 10). Like Saenger and Heinlen, Tribble sees a fundamental change of attitude arising in the early years of print: "the premodern book," she says, displays "the social and collaborative nature of literary production" (p. 100), the writer's words being surrounded normally by friendly apparatus that clearly establishes the limits of interpretation, whereas the sixteenth and seventeenth centuries saw the limits extended, denied, or removed altogether, by hostile or discordant printed glosses. She does not speculate about the "psychology of reading," however, and her examples, from the notorious case of the English Bible through editions of the classics and so to contemporary literature, are compelling. Successive versions of the Bible, for instance, smothered the text with commentary but typically found it necessary to back up a doctrinally correct reading with a refutation of erroneous ones, thereby publicizing error in the name of orthodoxy. The printed gloss that was meant to indicate the bounds of conformity may even have fueled controversy.[9] Grafton describes a "raft of editions" of major and minor classical authors published between 1650 and 1730, "in all of which the voices of the arguing commentators threatened to drown the thin classic monotone of the original text."[10] Imitating such models in their own marginalia, readers of the sixteenth and seventeenth centuries were freed to quarrel with their books.

In manuscript marginalia of the seventeenth century, Steven Zwicker has also found changes that he attributes to the combination of political turmoil and an active press. He maintains that the English Civil War and the pamphlet warfare of the 1640s turned annotators from docile supporters into "contesting readers"; furthermore, that by the end of the century, a proliferation of ready-made indexes and commonplace books had made the traditional function of the annotating reader redundant, thus sending "the world of humanist annotation" into eclipse, "crowded out by other kinds of marking and other technologies of reading."[11] On this latter point the eighteenth-century poet George Crabbe would have agreed with him. Crabbe blamed Grub Street and the temptations of cribs, publication in parts, and light reading for a general loss of concentration and readerly stamina:

Our patient Fathers trifling themes laid by,
And roll'd o'er labour'd works th'attentive eye;
Page after page, the much-enduring men
Explor'd the deeps and shallows of the pen;
Till, every note and every comment known,
They mark'd the spacious margin with their own;
Minute corrections prov'd their studious care,
The little Index pointing told us where;
And many an emendation prov'd the age
Look'd far beyond the rubric title-page.

    Our nicer palates lighter labours seek,
Cloy'd with a Folio-number once a week;
Bibles with cuts and comments thus go down,
E'en light Voltaire is number'd through the town;
Thus Physic flies abroad, and thus the law
From men of study, and from men of straw;
Abstracts, Abridgements, please the fickle times,
Pamphlets and Plays, and Politics and Rhymes.[12]

But Crabbe seems to imply that nobody was annotating anything any more. Far from it. Traditional humanist annotation may have been in eclipse, but it was not extinguished: the schools continued to teach it, and editors and commentators to practice it. The British Museum and university and college libraries were deliberately collecting books annotated by scholars like Richard Bentley and Isaac Casaubon; book auction catalogues invariably referred to annotations as an added attraction.[13] It was simply no longer the only way that readers could, or did, use their books.

In the first phase of the history of marginalia in English, a habit associated with scholars and textbooks filtered through to other kinds of books, readers, and reading modes. This process continued and was accelerated in the publishing boom of the eighteenth century. But the dominant form of annotation in the eighteenth century had a different character again from that of the seventeenth, as even a brief illustration may demonstrate.

Let me propose one that is ready to hand to me at the University of Toronto. It is a mid-century copy of the ninth edition (1754) of Thomas Gray's well-known *Elegy Written in a Country Churchyard*, a runaway best-seller originally published in 1751. A modest quarto pamphlet of only eleven pages, it was probably still in the paper covers that it came in from the shop when it was annotated. The notes consist of a donor's inscription ("From K. L. | Neptune at Sea"), on the title page, and a few notes by the owner in the body of the text. He underlined two words, and two whole lines word by word—"The paths of glory lead but to the grave" and "On some fond breast the parting soul relies." There are reflective remarks at four points: for example at "They kept the noiseless tenor of their way," he says, "Many indeed are not fitted for any Active Part in Life," and at "A Youth to Fortune and to Fame unknown," his comment is, "Yet were he on this score less happy?" These annotations might easily be dismissed as slight and banal. They have been preserved and prized because they were written by General James Wolfe, who had the poem with him on his last campaign, and who according to legend declared, the night before the capture of Quebec, "I would rather have been the author of that piece than beat the French tomorrow."[14] The book is valued for its historical connections, and the notes acquire considerable pathos from the myths surrounding them.

But if we pretend that the annotator is an unidentified reader of no special significance, we can still tell that these are notes that could not have been written a century—nor even perhaps a half-century—earlier. They are neither impersonal contributions to scholarship nor aggressive displays of disagreement. Unassuming as they are, they implicitly judge the text by concurring with or questioning the ideas it expresses. They do so in an independent way that evokes the personal interests and views of the reader. They are nevertheless not as private as they may seem, for the book was a gift from Wolfe's fiancée Katharine Lowther and he probably expected that she would see it again sooner or later; at any rate, he associated the book with her and those associations must have colored his reading and consequently his annotating. This little book represents the distinctive features of marginalia of the second period, which are typically critical (in the sense of evaluative), personal, and designed to be shared. How did they get to be that way? Answers have to be sought in particular circumstances of the book trade, as well as in general social trends.

Publishing was in a flourishing state in England at the beginning of the eighteenth century and continued so, although for new books at reasonable prices and for mass-market production one has to wait another hundred years. Recently available figures give a rough indication of the rate of growth: "by comparison with the 400 or so surviving books known to have been published in England in the first decade of the sixteenth century, about 6,000 were published during the 1630s, almost 21,000 during the 1710s, and more than 56,000 in the 1790s . . . [and] around 325,000 separate items [were] published during the 1870s."[15] These numbers represent only *titles* published; they do not include imports, and as yet little is known about sizes of print runs. But they do dramatize the state of the market.

While it is always risky to generalize about the "audience" for books—at any time, there are multiple audiences—it is clear that the main area of development at the end of the seventeenth century and beginning of the eighteenth was in an urban middle class influenced by the tastes of the court. This was the audience defined (we might say "targeted," but "defined" carries with it an appropriate sense of actual bringing into being) with stunning success by the periodical press, especially by Joseph Addison and Richard Steele in the *Spectator* of 1711–12. These readers had money and time to devote to reading. They were not generally as frivolous as they were made out to be by Crabbe and the satirical tradition. They may have had little or no classical learning, but they were prepared to put themselves to school to English critics like Dryden, Addison, and Johnson, who could make learning agreeable. The demands of this new audience involved the producers of books in new devices and approaches, which in turn affected the way books were received and used by readers. As models of printed annotation changed, so did marginalia.

From a technical point of view, the great innovation of about 1700 was the choice of the footnote to the virtual exclusion of other forms of printed annotation.[16] This move appears to have been part of the printers' efforts to modernize layout as they increasingly distanced themselves from the original manuscript models, but it had further subtle consequences.[17] The footnote made a visual statement about the relative importance of the author and the editor or interpreter by firmly demoting commentary to the bottom of the page and a smaller typeface (though printed glosses had also normally been smaller than the "central" text).[18] It played a part in the evolution of the author as an independent agent, along with developments in copyright—debated and disputed throughout the century—and in the various contractual arrangements that gradually replaced the patronage system. It looks to me as though it also contributed to the evolution of the *reader* as an independent agent, by separating the author from the editor, and by leaving the margins alongside both authorial and editorial text clear for readerly intervention.

More important for the history of marginalia than any of these other considerations is a change in the content and spirit of printed annotation that seems to have accompanied the change in format. Alexander Pope, a writer of marginalia himself, was a leading practitioner of the reformed style. Pope is the classic example of a spectacularly successful, ruthlessly self-promoting author. By cultivating his contacts, publicly mocking his rivals, manipulating the book trade, and turning subscription publication into a best-selling business, he kept himself before the public eye and proved that it was possible to earn a living as a writer without depending either on patrons or on Grub Street publishers. Though he never went to school and his formal education was uneven, he was bookish and ambitious. Of his library of perhaps six or seven hundred volumes, about 170 survive; some of those volumes contain his annotations.[19] These books are interesting in a number of ways. They allow us to be confident about his having read certain works, such as the essays of Montaigne. The marginalia, though relatively sparse, provide an example of what one reader of the early eighteenth century thought noteworthy. And later owners' notes about provenance demonstrate that Pope's books were prized and preserved for their association value even in his lifetime. A copy of his *Works* (1717–35) "Given me by the Author," according to a note on the title page by Jonathan Richardson, passed from

Richardson to Edmond Malone, John Wilson Croker, Reginald Heber, and Jerome Kern, all of whom have left their marks in it; in this case, however, the alleged marginalia by Pope may be no more than Richardson's collations from Pope's manuscripts.[20] The proud owner of Pope's copy of John Oldham's *Satyrs upon the Jesuits* published Pope's brief "index" list (p. +1) of works he approved—the only note he wrote in this volume—as part of his own edition of Oldham, in 1770, with the comment, "We are apt to catch at the most trivial Observations of Men of illustrious Genius; and though the above Remarks are small, yet they prove the good Opinion that Mr. *Pope* entertained of Mr. *Oldham,* and his ingenious Compositions."[21]

The books in which Pope's annotations, though scanty, are undoubtedly authentic include a copy of the racy poems of the Earl of Rochester in which Pope filled in some of the concealed or deliberately omitted names. (This was common practice, a kind of parlor-game, throughout the long eighteenth century. When satires were published with fictional names or blanks to disguise living subjects, readers rushed to fill them in. Very often they did so not on the basis of personal knowledge but on the authority of published "Keys" or of other annotated copies, which might themselves have relied on Keys. That said, some identifications *were* based on personal knowledge, and so contemporary or near-contemporary annotated copies are often worth consulting.)[22] It also contains just three substantive notes, one in which he criticizes a passage for "false thought" (p. 13), one in which he says that an observation about the distribution of wit is taken from Descartes (p. 83), and one in which he regrets the absence from the edition of Rochester's letters to Henry Saville (p. +1). His copy of Boileau contains subject headings written in as footnotes. Pope collected copies of attacks on his own work, and the notes in these tend understandably to the defensive, as in the occasional sarcastic comment in pamphlets by John Dennis: when Dennis complains, for instance, of a dream temple suspended in air, that it "is contrary to Nature, and to the Eternal Laws of Gravitation," Pope grumbles, "wch no dream ought to be."[23] Alluding to this tract in a note to Dennis's earlier *True Character of Mr. Pope,* when Dennis promises "plainly" to prove Pope's incompetence as a critic, Pope sneers, "as he did ye next yr in his *Remarks on Homer*" (p. 16). In books that he admired, on the other hand, he was given from an early age to marking especially good passages with inverted double commas.[24]

In Pope's own books, though the number of his notes is small, we can see something of the general character of his annotation. Extending the concerns of literary scholars to English authors, he notes editorial lapses and unacknowledged indebtedness. Like a promising student, he takes note of memorable pieces of writing. But he does not fill the margins with cross-references and citations of authorities. And like the controversialists of the seventeenth century, he feels free to contradict his authors in their margins.

Pope was conspicuously active, in both negative and positive ways, in the movement for user-friendly annotation. He and his friends of the Scriblerus Club made fun of humorless pedants who stuff themselves "with all such reading as was never read," who contrive to "make Horace flat, and humble Maro's strains," and who "crucify poor Shakespear once a week"—as Pope wrote in the withering lines of the *Dunciad*. The *Dunciad* itself, originally published in 1728 with minimal annotation and with most of the names left blank, was reissued in 1729 as the *Dunciad Variorum* (the *Dunciad* with "notes by various hands"), its massive mock scholarly apparatus attributed to Martin Scriblerus. Parodic in form as fitting to the satire, the notes nevertheless do supply authorial identifications and evidence. By these means Pope contrived to have his cake and eat it too: he was able to preempt other commentaries and tell his readers what to think, while at the same time enlisting those readers as allies in a joke about the absurdity of overzealous commentators. The *Variorum* notes are topical, extravagant, and witty. The line about crucifying Shakespeare, for example, leads to a long note which asserts (inaccurately) that Lewis Theobald, the main object of Pope's attack, had for a time published regularly in a weekly journal "a single remark or poor conjecture on some *word* or *pointing* of *Shakespear,* either in his own name, or in letters to himself as from others without name"—and reprints some verses by other writers on the occasion.[25]

Like the first version of the *Dunciad,* Pope's poems had regularly come accompanied by authorial commentary, usually very brief, that provides vital information in an accessible form. *The Rape of the Lock*, for example, in both the short version of 1712 and the familiar five cantos of 1714, was published with footnotes in a few places so that readers should not miss significant classical allusions and imitations. When he came to prepare his own edition of Shakespeare and his translations of Homer, Pope again tried to share his learning without adopting cumbersome scholarly apparatus, and to convey the message that taste was in any case more important than learning. Both works were initially published by subscription, in very handsome, expensive quarto editions with virtually clear text. Both contained critical introductions that established the standards by which the works were to be judged. Neither employed printed marginal glosses. In the Homer, Pope's commentary appeared as endnotes or "Observations" following each Book of the poem, and in the Shakespeare, though there were footnotes on the page, they were very few, and typographical symbols took the place of detailed critical commentary. Pope eliminated from the text of Shakespeare some passages that he thought "excessively bad," printing them in the footnotes and leaving only an asterisk in the text. Fine passages he highlighted with inverted commas in the margin—as in his own annotated books—and fine scenes he starred.[26] His rare footnotes made some effort to suggest that textual scholarship must be justified by literary judgment: of *Lear* IV iii, for instance, he says, *"This scene, left out in all the common bookes, is restor'd from the old edition; it being manifestly of Shakespear's writing, and necessary to continue the story of Cordelia, whose behaviour is here most beautifully painted"* (3:78).

Pope was not alone in the desire to make commentary serve artistic values, though he was spectacularly successful. (Tribble exaggerates when she declares, "It was Alexander Pope who attempted to find a new critical use for the note, one that would eschew both the prolixity of an Ogilby and the pedanticism of a Bentley.")[27] There were precedents in the French critics whose works gained prominence in England after the court returned from France in 1660. There was a precedent in Pope's own publisher's list. Bernard Lintot, who published Pope's translation of the *Iliad* volume by precious volume from 1715 to 1720, had already brought out, in 1712, a modest English prose translation by John Ozell, based on the 1711 French version by Anne Dacier and including critical notes printed in double columns at the foot of the page (unlike hers, which were printed as endnotes). Pope's notes were—as he freely and publicly acknowledged—very much indebted to Dacier's. When his translation had to be reprinted in a cheaper format in 1732, in response to piracies, his critical notes were changed from endnotes to footnotes and in appearance and apparatus his *Iliad* no longer differed greatly from Ozell's. But Pope's was far more widely distributed. Toward the end of the century, Johnson summed up the opinion of the age in his praise for both the translation and the footnotes. The translation he called "the noblest version of poetry which the world has ever seen." He liked the notes "subjoined to the text in the same page" (the word "footnote" had not yet been introduced) because they were "more easily consulted" than endnotes. In response to complaints that Pope's notes, especially those addressed to female readers, were full of "unseasonable levity," he observed stoutly that "the notes of others are read to clear difficulties, those of Pope to vary entertainment."[28]

By the example of commentators like Pope—and it bears repeating that he was only part of a general movement in English criticism and book production—readers of the eighteenth century were encouraged to make independent critical observations about their reading on the margins and flyleaves of their books. Unlike the anonymous contributions of generations of annotators before them, these notes would be identified with named individuals (normally the owners of the books) and understood to reflect their personal views. Of course "personal" carries a range of meanings, and Pope's notes do not strike us as personal in the same way as Wolfe's remarks on Gray's *Elegy* do. But the published notes to Homer, Shakespeare, and Pope's own *Rape of the Lock* and *Essay on Man* display the judgment and artistry of a named, living critic, and thereby implicitly convey an impression of his individual character. The notes to the *Dunciad Variorum* attack certain named contemporary figures and seek to justify the author's claim to higher moral ground: they can be called "personal" too. Pope's manuscript annotations in his own books, being private, might be supposed to be even more reliable indications of his true responses than published notes, and they certainly express thoughts that occurred to him as he read. Nevertheless they remain matters of judgment, and Pope's marginalia lack the emotional warmth that we find in Wolfe's brief jottings—a consequence probably of their connection with Wolfe's love life. The most intensely personal marginalia of this period owe that quality to their having been produced in a social context, written like a personal letter to foster intimacy. (The eighteenth century was the golden age of the letter too.) At every level the personal element in eighteenth-century marginalia can be linked to their social function.

It may be objected that in the pre-print era and in the early years of print, annotations were also written in the expectation that they would be seen, registered, and perhaps copied by other readers. That is true, and in learned circles the custom continued. The difference is that the notes were no longer anonymously transmitted. A work of contemporary literary scholarship that is often found in an annotated or extra-illustrated form, for example, is Gerard Langbaine's *Account of the English Dramatic Poets*, an alphabetically arranged biographical dictionary. One of the interleaved British Library copies of the 1691 edition graphically represents the circulation of annotated books in the eighteenth century and the early nineteenth, for it contains not only the notes of the current owner in 1813, John Haslemere, and those of his predecessor Richard Wright, but also notes transcribed from another copy that had been annotated by George Steevens who had himself collected notes from yet another annotated by Thomas Percy and William Oldys. Each layer of annotation is carefully distinguished from the others and attributed to the appropriate writer.

According to the *Dictionary of National Biography*, Oldys, the earliest of these annotators—who was known in his lifetime for his systematic method of collecting and filing information by writing in the margins and between the lines of books in his collection—had filled one Langbaine before 1727 and went on to do at least one more afterward. His notes in this and other works combined traditional bibliographical, biographical, and historical materials with original critical observations. In a copy of Samuel Butler's satirical Restoration poem *Hudibras*, for example, he names Samuel Luke as the original of Hudibras (p. 17), identifies some literary allusions such as the reference to "Dol Common" ("a Character in Ben Jonsons Alchimist," p. 331), complains of a line justified only by the rhyme (p. 15), and explains the author's purpose where it might appear obscure: "This whole Page points out ye strange foolish affected Tone ye Fanatical Ministers used to draw ye poor ignorant People into Rebellion and Confusion" (p. 20). To the customary subjects of academic criticism, now extended to modern literature, Oldys and his contemporaries added personal judgment.

Oldys's marginalia and their like not only circulated under their writers' names early in the eighteenth century; they also circulated within a defined group. When Oldys published his substantial life of Walter Raleigh in the 1736 edition of Raleigh's *History of the World,* he made up some copies with seven extra folio pages in manuscript for the sake of "a few worthy and honourable Friends," containing "some Additions and Amendments . . . wch were Communicated too late to be interwoven in their proper Places." This supplement he provided by way of thanks for contributions that he had received and by way of encouragement to more, "hoping they will continue their Communications where they shall find any thing, as well to be amended as enlargd, in the foregoing Sheets; none being more willing to reform an Error, or desirous of being led by the Light of Truth."[29] Oldys was an active participant in a network of like-minded scholars; his marginalia were written to be shared with his friends.

Similar cases of marginalia circulating among scholars are legion in the eighteenth and nineteenth centuries but it is difficult even for another academic to whip up much enthusiasm for the details, and I shall not multiply examples of marginalia for specialists. An exception must be made, however, for Francis Douce, a learned and well-known annotator of a later generation. Douce also operated in a select scholarly network. When John Brand had a copy of his *Observations on Popular Antiquities* (1777) interleaved to take materials for a revised edition, he drafted a paragraph of acknowledgments with specific reference to Douce, "who had enriched an interleaved Copy of my former Book with many very pertinent notes & illustrations furnished from his very extensive reading on the subject and from Books in his invaluable Library."[30] Douce died in 1834, bequeathing his magnificent collection of more than nineteen thousand volumes to the Bodleian Library, where it is still preserved as a collection under his name. Many volumes contain his erudite and expert notes, carefully written (he drew lines in pencil to guide his pen) and valuable to this day. Like Oldys, Douce improved his books for the use of his colleagues and successors; like him, he combined scholarly precision with personal reflection. On the subject of Elizabethan portraiture, for example, in response to James Granger's enthusiasm for Isaac Oliver, he remarks, "Beautiful as are the miniatures of Oliver, they have been perhaps exceeded by some of those in the best illuminated Manuscripts of the 15th and 16th centuries. See particularly a most elegant Psalter in the Royal Library 2A.XVI, done for Henry the 8th with his portrait and that of Will Summers. And what can be more exquisitely painted than the books adorned by Julio Clovio & Julio Romano, or some of the devotional volumes with illuminations by the Flemish & Italian Artists?"[31] Of a song—"As blithe as the linnet sings in the green woods"—in *Robin Hood's Garland,* he says, "Many a time and oft have I heard honest Philip Constable sing this Song at the meetings of the Toxophilite Society at Leicester House. He was the last surviving member of the Finsbury Archers."[32]

But Douce made two explicit exceptions from his Oxford bequest, and they are the reason for my mentioning him at this point. He must have been in some ways a prickly and difficult man. He was Keeper of Manuscripts at the British Museum for a short time; he resigned that position after a falling-out with the trustees. Nevertheless he bequeathed two showy books to the Museum. On front flyleaf (p. -1) of John Whitaker's *The Ancient Cathedral of Cornwall Historically Surveyed* (1804), he wrote, "It is my desire that after my decease this volume, as well as my quarto edition of Whitaker's History of Manchester in two volumes, be presented to the British Museum." So they were, and every successive reader of those copies has had the benefit of Douce's clear and extensive notes, which must have occupied him for many bitter hours. Whitaker's attitude toward his predecessors is not generous. Douce had been one of them. In *The Ancient Cathedral of Cornwall,* Whitaker quotes him on the origin of the term "rook" in chess, declares him wrong, and proposes that he must have been confused at the time and have meant to write something other than what he did write. Douce's long note at this point is understandably choleric:

> We have here and in what follows a notable specimen of the most consummate arrogance with the profoundest ignorance & stupidity that can be imagined. I meant to write what I <u>have</u> written, & not the nonsense that Whitaker has published. . . . This comes of garbled quotation, & of that precipitate manner of reading that W. must have been accustomed to from his innumerable blunders & misconceptions, & which mislead him to criticize with unparalleled insolence & stupidity on other men's opinions. (2:391)

What is remarkable is not so much the note itself as its destination. Having unburdened himself of his feelings at a personal attack, Douce took measures to make sure that not only on this point but on hundreds of others where he disagreed with the author, posterity should know about it. Then he acquired a copy of *The History of Manchester* and gave it the same treatment—backing up a sarcastic note (1:vii) about the defects of the author's style and his overreliance on sentences beginning with the conjunctions "and" or "but," for example, by underlining every single instance of a sentence beginning with "and" in the two volumes. Douce's notes on Whitaker, the first but not the last example that we shall see of marginalia used for revenge, supplement and correct the original text as scholarly annotations had always done, but they are also characteristic of their period in being critical, personal, and designed to be shared.

Nor was it only in scholarly and professional circles that annotated books were shared about. All presentation inscriptions by definition testify to the popularity of books as gifts, but I refer specifically to the exchange of books with marginal comments. Mary Astell returned a borrowed copy of Pierre Bayle's *Pensées diverses* (4th ed., 1704) to the owner, Lady Mary Wortley Montagu, with the first volume profusely annotated. On the flyleaf she wrote a general impression, beginning with a cursory apology: "I ask pardon for scribling in Y[ou]r

La[dyshi]ps Book. The Author is so disingenuous & inconsistent yt no lover of Truth can read it without a just Indignation."[33] When Samuel Richardson asked his friend Lady Bradshaigh for her opinion of his novels *Pamela* and *Clarissa*, she sent him her annotated copies—and he "devoted some of his last days to reading her comments and to making his own comments on them."[34] Samuel Johnson, who marked up books professionally for use in his *Dictionary*, also annotated a copy of a religious work in 1755 so that he could exchange views with a woman he loved, Hill Boothby. In the accompanying letter he wrote, "I beg you to return the book when you have looked into it. I should not have written what is in the margin, had I not had it from you, or had I not intended to show it you."[35] Hester Piozzi, who with her first husband sheltered Johnson for many years, annotated dozens of books to give away to friends. (Her marginalia will be discussed at some length in Chapter Four.) Coleridge at the owners' urging wrote some of his best notes in books belonging to his friends Thomas Poole, Charles Lamb, Henry Crabb Robinson, and Joseph Henry Green. Felicia Hemans was in the habit of enriching books lent to her "with the thoughts excited by their perusal, and with such parallel passages from other writers as bore upon their subject."[36] The exchange of annotated books among friends continued through the Victorian period and into the twentieth century, but the practice was established in the eighteenth century, when—as they well knew but we are just beginning to realize—reading was more often than not a *social* activity.

The history of reading is a relatively new area of investigation, but the formulations of the first generation of scholars are already being challenged and dismantled—in some cases, by the formulators themselves. The familiar assumption invoked by Saenger and Heinlen, among others, that the coming of the printed book in short order put an end to public, communal, highly directed reading and led to silent, solitary, anarchic reading, no longer seems to have many adherents, though for a time it borrowed strength from a new but related idea. In 1974, Rolf Engelsing published a detailed account of what he saw as a dramatic alteration in reading practices in Germany in the second half of the eighteenth century, when both the quantity and the mode of reading appeared to change so that instead of reading a very small number of works in a lifetime, but reading them "intensively," people were found to be reading many more books, but more casually a. d "extensively." Though his hypothesis had commonsense appeal, it di‹ not travel well: case studies concerned with French and English markets and readers failed to confirm it, and it now appears to be an overstatement at best. In its place we have the equally commonsensical view that every really literate person is and always has been capable of a repertoire of reading modes suited to different occasions and different materials.[37] This new orthodoxy will no doubt also be contested, but in the meantime the process of investigation has turned up fascinating information about the actual habits of readers in the past, and forced us to revise our ideas about them.

As far as the eighteenth century is concerned, several case studies (with their accompanying documentation) in the collection of essays edited by James Raven, Helen Small, and Naomi Tadmor cast doubt on the supposedly solitary experience of reading in the period. Not only did public reading out loud persist as an important part of the culture (notably, in churches), but there was a great expansion in domestic reading, that is, reading aloud in small circles of family or friends. Anna Larpent's diary reveals the apparently unremarkable practice of one household:

> On 1 July 1780, for instance, after hearing her sister Clara read Rollin's *Histoire ancienne* (a history much recommended to young women), Anna "spent two hours in the family circle reading and working". While her friends were engaged in different sorts of women's work— embroidering and making cushion covers—she read them a great favourite, the sentimental novel *Marianne*, by Pierre Marivaux. After dinner Anna worked while another guest read Henry Kelly's comedy, *School for Wives;* and, after supper and in mixed company, she returned to Marivaux, reading further passages from his novel.[38]

Such performances of reading quickly spread from the domestic to the public sphere, and to reading tours of the kind we still see today. Even so-called private reading—silent reading to oneself—was seldom really solitary, being carried on in shared household space or outside the house in coffee shops, bookshops, and circulating libraries.[39] To the evidence of novels, diaries, letters, and contemporary prints we may now add that of eighteenth-century marginalia, which would not have the personal and critical qualities that distinguish this period from earlier ones but for the generally social character of reading itself. Writers of marginalia at this time usually worked with an audience in mind, not a nebulous scholarly community merely, but known individuals in their own social circles.

As a by-product of the exchange of books between friends and associates in this period, we may briefly consider the evolution of a minor poetic genre, the verse inscription. The Chadwyck-Healey database English Poetry gives access to hundreds of poems composed between 1500 and 1900 that represent themselves as "lines written in" this or that book, usually "on a blank leaf" of it. In fact the earliest in this particular collection are by the Marquis of Montrose, a seventeenth-century Scottish poet. In his case, the titles were supplied posthumously, probably in the nineteenth century. The Montrose poems are all epigrammatic tributes to a Latin author or hero; they express the reader's admiration for the book, just as Witter Bynner's sonnet for Dante does. In both these cases the poems actually were written into copies of the books they celebrate. The convention eventually took on a life of its own, however, and poets learned to take advantage of a convenient fiction. I do not doubt that, more often than not, the poem "written in a blank leaf" was not literally so. For my purposes it does not really matter. What I do find intriguing is the fact that after the meager representation of seventeenth-century examples, the database gives dozens of instances for the eighteenth century, and hundreds for the nineteenth; and that most, though not all, of these are not simply a reader's tribute to a book but presentation inscriptions in which a third party is involved, or else (this becomes more complicated) records of the presentation by the new owner, that is, something corresponding to those authentic ownership inscriptions that take note of the circumstances in which the book was acquired.[40]

An early example, Lady Mary Wortley Montagu's "Lines Written in a Blank Page of Milton's *Paradise Lost*"—another case of a real book but of a title supplied by an editor—contains reflections on relations between the sexes prompted, perhaps, by Milton's description of Adam and Eve, but also directly relevant to Lady Mary's conversations with the donor, the Duke of Wharton.[41] Aaron Hill, a fringe member of Pope's circle, wrote several inscriptions that were published with his collected works in 1753: "Sent to Lord Chesterfield; writ on a blank Leaf, of a Poem, called, The Religion of Reason"; "To Lord Bolingbroke, writ on a blank Leaf of a Poem, which was sent him, by the Author"; "Writ on a blank Leaf of *Merope;* sent to Mr. *Garrick,* by the Author"; "In a blank Leaf of a Book, sent to *Miranda*"; and so on. Whether the author or an editor was responsible for the title, the genre was soon well established and proved susceptible of adaptation for many purposes— criticism, condolence, satire, seduction. Eighteenth-century examples include Barton Booth's "Written *Extempore* on a Blank Leaf in Rymer's Remarks upon Shakespeare," Thomas Warton's "Written in a Blank Leaf of Dugdale's Monasticon," James Thomson's "Stanzas . . . on the Blank Leaf of a Copy of his 'Seasons' Sent by him to Mr. Lyttelton, Soon After the Death of His Wife," Samuel Bowden's "Written on the First Leaf of a Lawyer's *Coke* upon *Littleton,*" William Cowper's "The Critics Chastised. Written on a Page of *The Monthly Review,*" and—the most long-winded of all titles—Robert Burns's "Written on the Blank Leaf of a Copy of the Last Edition of My Poems, Presented to the Lady Whom, in so Many Fictitious Reveries of Passion, but with the Most Ardent Sentiments of Real Friendship, I Have so often Sung under the Name of Chloris."

The vogue for this type of society verse I take to be at once a reflection of actual annotating practice and an incentive to it. An example in the *carpe diem* tradition is Lord Chesterfield's "Verses Written in a Lady's Sherlock upon Death," which I came upon in a copy of Robert Dodsley's popular miscellany annotated by Thomas Percy—himself a contributor to the collection—who like the good scholar he was supplied attributions for poems published anonymously.

Mistaken fair, lay Sherlock by,
  His doctrine is deceiving;
For whilst he teaches us to die,
  He cheats us of our living.

To die's a lesson we shall know
  Too soon without a master;
Then let us only study now
  How we may live the faster.

To live's to love, to bless, be blest
  With mutual inclination;
Share then my ardour in your breast,
  And kindly meet my passion.

But if thus bless'd I may not live,
  And pity you deny,
To me at least your Sherlock give,
  'Tis I must learn to die.[42]

Chesterfield's poem plays cleverly upon literary and social conventions. We imagine lovers exchanging books, and not letters only; a respectable religious tract is made to serve personal desires. I know of no instance before the eighteenth century of marginalia furthering the cause of love; in that period it became possible. Another fictional example is Mary Wollstonecraft's unfinished novel *The Wrongs of Woman*, in which the heroine is attracted to another inmate of the madhouse in which she is unjustly confined, when she is brought a bundle of his books and notices his comments, "written with force and taste," in a copy of Dryden's *Fables*. She adds a few sympathetic comments of her own, sends the books back to the owner, and a correspondence begins.[43]

A real-life example from the end of the second phase in the history that I am surveying is a copy of William Mudford's *Nubilia in Search of a Husband* (1809), with notes by an unidentified reader—presumably the "A. Urquhart" who signed the title page in 1812, since the hand appears to match that of the annotations. Some of the notes are in pencil, some in pencil recopied in ink, and some in ink from the start; all are neat and legible. Many passages are marked with a line or a cross. A few of the notes merely supply subject headings ("Collins. His 2nd Eclogue praised," p. 236; "The power of Imagination," p. 333) or provide definitions (Nubilia is named "From the adjective Nubilis, marriageable, ready for a husband," p. 1). But most of them respond to the text and express opinions about it. It is clear on internal evidence that they were written at a single, first reading.

Under the guise of fiction, *Nubilia* is a vehicle for Evangelical doctrines—a worthy counterpart to its model, Hannah More's *Coelebs in Search of a Wife*. The events of the flimsy plot are introduced chiefly to justify essays and pseudo-dialogues about literature and social issues; the author himself disarmingly acknowledges that this is so, in the preface. But the overall effect is preachy, and Urquhart chafes at it. At the end of Chapter 4 we encounter the following note:

> The preceding observations on tuition are, I make no doubt, very just;
> some of them, I am persuaded are particularly so. The title of this
> book, would very naturally, lead one to expect much adventure; and
> this expectation, as naturally, generates a hope of being much enter-
> tained. The author however very kindly at the beginning (see the pref-
> ace) tells his reader that they are to expect no such thing as adventure;
> which of course implies that it is improvement alone, and not enter-
> tainment, that he has in view. Improvement of course, is of more con-
> sequence, than mere entertainment; but I think that a sufficiency of the
> latter, might have been brought into play, without excluding any of
> the former which it was essential to retain. And that this was not the
> consequence, the evident effect is, that the book becomes less agree-
> able. Nevertheless it is well worthy a careful reading.

"Careful reading" is what these notes are all about. Fiction is less commonly annotated than other genres are. This book is an exception to the rule. *Nubilia* is not a particularly successful example of its kind, though, so perhaps it hardly counts. But why did Urquhart persist? The notes become increasingly rebellious. Nubilia, at first regarded as a mildly objectionable idealization, becomes positively irritating toward the end. "There is no pleasing some people, and Nubilia is one of these fastidious creatures," says Urquhart on page 326. A passage in which she gushes about an Aeolian Harp but excuses herself by saying that anyone who had heard one would understand, and that her "rapture will appear extravagant, if not ridiculous" only to someone who had not, elicits a response that incidentally reveals that Urquhart was a man: "Why, Nubilia, you are right—one of your readers does really think your 'rapture' extravagant; and to confess a truth, somewhat ridiculous, also!—But it is possible that you are right—which of course, by a parity of reasoning, puts him in the wrong.—" (p. 341). When she expresses her longing to go home "to rural quiet and rural innocence," he encourages her: "Return, for you can be spared" (p. 365). When she sadly remarks that there is no true friend to be found "in the ranks of social life," he objects that "This belief, I hope, is as untrue, as it is illiberal" (p. 438).

This book is an excellent example of spirited reader response from the end of a period that cultivated the art of reading and valued personal, critical marginalia. What distinguishes it from both predecessors and successors is its having been produced to fulfill a social function. Urquhart did not write notes as a private record but as a stimulus to friendship and perhaps as part of a courtship. He would not have needed to be reminded, since he knew it, of the origin of the name Nubilia; he would not have advised *himself* to "see the preface." He was writing to somebody else. The last note quoted—about friends in the ranks of social life—contains a covert reference to his own situation and that of his presumed future listener, whom he tenderly addresses on other occasions. Noting a rather absurd phrase early on, he half apologizes for his own interventions. "I have dipped my pencil in the living tints of nature" (p. 134) leads him to ask, "Have I not 'dipped my <u>pencil</u>' enough, gentle reader! since I began the reading of Nubilia?" An earnest exhortation by *Nubilia*'s author calls out the reinforcement of underlining—"Were I asked, what <u>possible</u> condition could produce the <u>greatest earthly happiness</u> to man, I should reply—MARRIAGE. There is not, there <u>cannot</u> be, a state superior to it in this world. But for me, it must be differently constituted to what it now is"—followed by a request from the annotator, "Let a certain fair reader attend to this passage" (p. 194).

Lovers will seize on whatever means of communication are available to them, and books with marginalia often turn out to be a record of affection.[44] So Johnson's notes in the book belonging to Hill Boothby would be, if they survived, whatever their attitude toward the text itself. So are the notes in books exchanged by Thomas Hardy and Mrs. Henniker at the end of the nineteenth century, and those of Helen Spencer and Rolfe Humphries in the early twentieth. Samuel Clemens (Mark Twain) seems to have started off as a writer of marginalia by writing in books to amuse his fiancée. In the 1960s Philip Larkin, a librarian as well as a poet, enjoyed bawdily altering books with his companion Monica Jones, and Joe Orton and Kenneth Halliwell were convicted of defacing library books.[45] Joanna Coles's column in *The Times* of London on 25 June 1999 describes the way a friend's disappointing date attempted to make amends: "He was toweringly repentant though. He sent me flowers and then a week later, Philip Larkin's *Collected Poems* which he'd annotated" (p. 5). I do not claim that the sharing of marked or annotated books came to an end after 1820, only that it ceased to be the norm.

I propose 1820 as a watershed date for several reasons. It is a round number. It roughly coincides with the set of social and technological changes, charted forty years ago by Richard Altick in *The English Common Reader,* that led to mass production in the 1820s and consequently to lower prices and almost universal private ownership of books. It marks a pair of events—Coleridge's publishing his own "marginalia" under that name in 1819, and Lamb's quirky tribute to his artistry in 1820— that brought the notes of the lay reader into the public domain and set a standard. Once marginalia had gone public in this way, they became part of the literary culture. In the 1840s Edgar Allan Poe adopted the collective title "Marginalia" for a set of brief disconnected observations—not actually based on his notes in books—about books and authors, published in popular magazines.[46] Substantial bodies of notes found their way into print, slowly but surely—in chronological order Coleridge's,

Hartley Coleridge's, Thackeray's (marginal *sketches*, a special case), Keats's, Macaulay's, Piozzi's, Blake's, Twain's, Herman Melville's, Darwin's. Slighter instances appeared in specialist articles or as parts of single-author studies.[47]

These developments seem a natural enough culmination of the rage for reading and the increasing activity of annotators in the late eighteenth century and the early nineteenth, but they also prompted a reaction. The book-collecting, book-enhancing habits of well-to-do readers like William Beckford and Horace Walpole, celebrated under the name "bibliomania" by John Ferriar and Thomas Frognall Dibdin in 1809, were about to be imitated by lesser mortals, and there seem to have been fears that it had all got out of hand.[48] Along with the encouragement offered to annotators, therefore, came a strengthening of prohibitions against the marking of books, intensified with the growth of the public library system after 1850, that aimed to repress the annotating habit. Readers were torn two ways, spurred on by opportunity and by the example of celebrities, but held back by fear of exposure and disapproval.

I should call the period from 1820 to the present a period of ambivalence, but that surviving annotated volumes actually show little evidence of ambivalence. They are as confident as ever. What seems to have happened is that by and large readers retreated into themselves, and annotation became predominantly a private affair, a matter of self-expression. Annotating readers went underground. Personal systems of marks become more common—like Coleridge's scheme for annotating Blake, but without the explanatory key that enabled another reader to follow it. Darwin's and Melville's books make good examples. In them, manuscript indexes with the briefest of subject headings take the place of discursive notes: they would be sufficient for the owner, and no other reader was thought of. William Ewart Gladstone, prime minister in England on and off between 1868 and 1894, left a most remarkable record of his reading in his huge library, including uncounted numbers of annotated books, preserved intact at St. Deiniol's at Hawarden in Wales, together with diaries that methodically recorded his daily reading for the whole of his long life, but he does not seem to have been a very forthcoming annotator. His editor and biographer describes him as "a careful, if rapid, reader. He annotated his books with lines, ticks, and crosses, and wrote the odd comment in the margin, writing 'ma' (the Italian for 'but') when he disagreed with the author. He often compiled a short index on the back inside cover, books in those days rarely having a printed index."[49]

Gladstone's example is not exceptional. As reading became less sociable and marginalia were vulnerable to publication, readers' notes themselves became less accessible and less engaging than they had been in the heyday of the long eighteenth century. But there are compensations for this loss. In the first place, there are many wonderful exceptions to the general rule; in the second place, though they may be less charming, when readers do confide in their books, the results are often more revealing than before. If books are to be shared even with intimate friends, readers will be on their mettle and on their guard, putting on—however unconsciously—a kind of performance.

The taboo against writing marginalia—sometimes called "the Crime against the Book"—is the subject of Chapter Eight, and I shall not spend much time on it now except to acknowledge its inhibiting presence. It was not a creation of the Victorians. Earlier readers also experienced some guilt associated with their practice of annotation. Mary Astell, as we have seen, apologized for scribbling in a borrowed book. Hester Piozzi confessed to her diary in 1790, "I have a Trick of writing in the Margins of my Books, it is not a good Trick, but one longs to say something. . . ."[50] Coleridge on occasion made awkward excuses. But until 1820 or so, bookish people were on the whole receptive to marginalia, accepted them as natural accretions, and valued particularly useful or entertaining specimens. Astell, Piozzi, and Coleridge may have hesitated but they were not deterred. Later on, the balance shifted so that the prevailing and respectable attitude was much more negative. Writing notes even in one's own books, let alone in someone else's, let alone in ink, came to be thought of as irresponsible, weak, or transgressive. Lockwood in *Wuthering Heights* might have been prepared to accept learned commentary, and he is amused by Cathy's entries, but the way the heroine is introduced signals that she is a rebel. Another Brontë heroine, carelessly making ornamental drawings—"little leaves, fragments of pillars, broken crosses, on the margin of the book"—is rebuked by her tutor, who observes that none of his books would be safe with her.[51] These examples are fictional but they would not be convincing if they did not draw on familiar views and situations.

In the face of general condemnation, some readers restrain themselves, some become defiant, but many more just quietly get on with it. In the nineteenth and twentieth centuries, if they tended to keep their notes to themselves, readers still wrote in books by way of note-taking, in the interest of learning; to correct and supplement them, either for personal use or as part of a process of book-making; and to record their private opinions on the spot, so that the books would always be accompanied by their comments. With the exception of a craze for extra-illustration that will be described in Chapter Six (and even that had its origins in the eighteenth century), I do not find formal innovation after 1820. Annotators are not anarchic—bad press to the contrary. They are as subject to convention and tradition as any other writers. And the chief determinant of convention in this case seems to be the genre of the host book itself. At the risk of belaboring what ought to be self-evident, I wish to say something about such customary usage as it persisted after 1820, before ending this chapter with a volume that bridges the eighteenth and twentieth centuries.

The constraints of genre are more obvious in some cases than in others. In all manner of textbooks, for instance, we can expect to find students trying out the tools of the trade—in languages, supplying translations; in mathematics, solving problems; in history, adding references; in editions, questioning the editor's critical judgment. Fermat's proof would make no sense in a copy of *The Bacchae*. Likewise practical manuals. Cookbooks generate recipes, not literary criticism. The broader principle underlying the conventional association of certain kinds of notes with certain kinds of books is the principle that marginalia must be responsive. They do not stand on their own, but are permanently attached to the text that stimulated them; they are consequently restricted in their range of reference. (In fact there is an element of mimicry about marginalia that I shall be considering in Chapter Three.) The annotations in tourist guides and travel books invariably add details to the guide's descriptions. Field guides to birds and wildflowers get neat records of local sightings, sometimes with the addition of drawings or pressed flowers. As Sir Walter Elliott, in Jane Austen's *Persuasion*, kept his copy of the *Baronetage* up to date on developments in his own family, so the real owners of reference books freely supplement them with information from other sources. Collectors improve their favorite catalogues with entries the compilers had missed. All narratives in which names have had to be concealed—satires, secret histories, romans à clef, allegories—invite knowing readers to reveal them. An Oxford in-joke by C. L. Dodgson (Lewis Carroll), *Notes by an Oxford Chiel 1865–1874* or *The New Method of Evaluation as Applied to* π would be completely impenetrable now without his key to the code.

In areas that are not strictly matters of fact, wherever judgment and interpretation come into play, the role of the annotator is less clearly defined though still likely to be governed by the original text. In the law, which evolves under the influence of cases and statutes, and which has a very long history of margination and commentary, annotations may be restricted to references to relevant new laws and precedents but there is also scope for reasoned debate about past decisions. All the more so in reflective nonfiction writing such as political, polemical, and biographical or autobiographical prose, when either facts or opinions may be disputed. Walter Savage Landor's copy of *Conversations of Lord Byron with the Countess of Blessington* takes issue with Byron's declaration that if they were married, he and the Countess Guiccioli would "be cited as an example of conjugal happiness," by giving the counterevidence of a contemporary: "yet Trelawny told me he was wearied to death by her fondness—."[52] An Irish nationalist annotating the autobiographical *Life of Theobald Wolfe Tone, the Founder of the "United Irishmen"* (1845) identifies the pseudonymous author of the "Dedication," thereby adding useful information to his copy, but is also moved to register his views about the history of his country. When Tone, for example, says that General Clarke "still seemed, however, to have a leaning towards the co-operation of our aristocracy, which is flat nonsense," he agrees:

"The Irish Aristocracy always opposed to the independence of Ireland—being Anglo-Irish in political feelings & interests—& the tools of England—no patriots—but forming the English garrison in this country—."[53] (In fact the spirit of these annotations is so strongly engaged that a later owner found it necessary to censor them: on several pages words are scribbled through and rewritten to soften the meaning.) Exactly a hundred years later, W. R. Titterton's *So This Is Shaw* (1945) fell into the hands of John Kirkby, who had known Shaw and was able to leave in the book a detailed statement about a disputed incident in Shaw's career—an eye-witness correction of the record.[54] In this case also, a few other notes are rubbed out or covered over, possibly reflecting second thoughts of the annotator himself.

At the opposite end of the spectrum from textbooks and field guides, works of fiction and imaginative literature—plays, poems, novels, and romances—seem, perhaps surprisingly, to have been the least attractive to annotators. Mudford's *Nubilia*, described earlier, is an exception, but *Nubilia* is a vehicle for the author's opinions and more like a collection of essays than a novel; and in any case, the annotator was writing notes for a friend. Of course it is possible that works of fiction simply do not find their way into the sort of special collections libraries that I have been depending on; but even Macaulay, otherwise a prodigious reader and compulsive annotator, did not annotate his copies of Jane Austen except to record the dates of reading and to correct a very small number of typographical errors. The absorbed state of mind normal for reading fiction seems to be incompatible with the practice of annotation, unless the reader is a teacher or fellow writer.[55] (In the last thirty years of his life, Graham Greene used to take a book to a restaurant to read over dinner, and he annotated a good deal of contemporary fiction that way.)[56] For all these general truths, however, there are endless individual variations and fascinating exceptions; every annotated book is singular and potentially instructive.

A case in point is a copy of Jean-Jacques Rousseau's most famous political essay, *A Treatise on the Social Compact,* in a translation of the late eighteenth century, now in the British Library. It is annotated in two hands. The first annotator wrote only one note, in ink, on the front flyleaf. It is a version of the provenance inscription that claims possession and tells where the book came from.

> This book fell by lot to me from the Shrewsbury Library; in consequence of a resolution of a majority of the Subscribers, at a general meeting May 4th. 1798—that the following books, should be expelled from the Society.
>
> New monthly Magazine
> Analytical Review
> Sir William Jones's Principles of Government
> Rousseau's Social Compact
> Knight's progress of civil Society
> Wakefield's answer to Paine—
> D[itt]o.————Do. to Wilberforce—
> Do.————————Do. to Watson—
> Wolstonecrafts Rights of Woman.
> Do.————remarks on ye French Revolution.
> Mackintosh's Vindiciae Gallicae.
> Godwin's Political Justice.—
> Do.————Enquirer.
> Royal Recollections
> Rousseaus Confessions
> Caleb Williams
> Hugh Trevor

The inscription itself is a useful bit of historical evidence about the political climate of 1798 and about the history of libraries, for with the exception of the first two items, which may simply have been out of date, everything on this list, whether novel, journalism, or pamphlet, was politically sensitive, and the expulsion of Rousseau, Godwin, Wollstonecraft, and the rest from the library shelves was an act of calculated caution, if not of conservative reactionism. The writer is at pains to indicate that he acquired this dangerous volume "by lot" and not by choice; it may be significant that he does not give his name. This is a statement designed to explain, to anyone else who might come upon it among his books, that it got there more or less by accident.

The second annotator appears to have been at a school, either as senior pupil or as a junior master: his ownership inscription reads, "H. B. L. Webb | Brent House | Master Brace | 30th Dec. 1909. | (Bought at old Bennett's in Castle St.)."[57] All the notes in the margins are in his hand, and in pencil. They seem to have been made at a single reading shortly after the book was acquired; one note (p. 163) refers to the 1910 elections as though they were current or very recent. There is some underlining, and many passages are marked with a single or double line in the margin. About half of these marked passages also provoked comments, some of them brief ("very flimsy here," p. 19; "Pah!" p. 64), but several of a sentence or two in length. Nearly all of them register resistance or objections to Rousseau's argument, and do so in a distinctive voice. When Webb spots a contradiction, he says, "Hullo! Cf. page 228" (p. 231). He is keen to bring his learning from other sources to bear: when Rousseau defines a tyrant as "any individual who assumes the royal authority, without having a right to it," he invokes the Greek origin of the word to challenge the definition (p. 150). When Rousseau recommends farming over commerce, Webb quotes George Meredith against him: "G. Meredith says 'the young who avoid the region of romance escape the title of fool at the cost of a celestial Crown.' The nation which avoids commerce and the arts is not likely to produce a Shakespeare or a Rousseau" (pp. 85–86). To Rousseau's assertion that "In this age, however, we think that a most absurd part of erudition, which relates to the identity of the deities of different nations, and according to which it is supposed that Moloch, Saturn and Chronos were one and the same god . . . as if any thing could be found in common between chimerical beings bearing different names!" he replies, "And yet, Jean Jacques, comparative mythology has told us a different tale about this 'absurd part of erudition'!" (pp. 228–29).

The two sets of notes in the one little volume dramatize both the distance and the resemblances between the Kingdom of Sociability and the Kingdom of Subjectivity. Many readers more nearly contemporary with Rousseau must have reacted to his words as Webb did—and may have done so in the margins of their books—but they are unlikely to have done so in such a casual, colloquial way, as though in private conversation with the dead, and without regard to other readers of their own time or yet to come. Or is the apparent difference a difference of emphasis only, and do annotators read always with a divided mind, part attending to the text at hand and part to their own image? We assume that Webb was writing for his own amusement, but we cannot be sure: the book had had other owners before him and would most likely have others after. The next chapter considers not the history but the psychology of the annotating impulse.

chapter three

MOTIVES FOR MARGINALIA

In 1892, Kenneth Grahame (of *The Wind in the Willows*) published a playful little essay entitled "Marginalia" in the *National Observer,* reminiscing about his own childhood love of margins as places for drawings and jokes; he whimsically spoke up for "the absolute value of the margin itself" and wondered when the world might hope for "a book of verse consisting entirely of margin." This essay, reprinted in Grahame's *Pagan Papers,* prompted an admirer to make him a present of a blank book entitled *Margin,* which he accepted with graceful, ironical thanks for "a copy which I understand exhausts the Edition & baffles the clamorous Public."[1] Not wishing to break a butterfly on a wheel or take a chainsaw to a birthday cake, I have to protest, all the same, that a book without text is a book without marginalia. The essential and defining character of the marginal note throughout its history is that it is a responsive kind of writing permanently anchored to preexisting written words. Chapters One and Two considered the spatial distribution of readers' notes and their evolution over time, their geography as it were, and their history; they addressed the questions of where and when. This one turns to transhistorical (long-standing but not transcendent) features of marginalia, and asks the question, *why?*

Annotators are self-conscious readers, so we can begin with their own justifications. They often plead irresistible impulse. Hester Piozzi's words, already quoted, speak for many: "one longs to say something." But that is hardly a searching explanation. Blake takes it a little further, writing in the margin of his copy of Johann Lavater's *Aphorisms*, "I hope no one will call what I have written cavilling because he may think my remarks of small consequence For I write from the warmth of my heart, & cannot resist the impulse I feel to rectify what I think false in a book I love so much, & approve so generally." Coleridge, annotating Schelling, likewise declares, "A book, I value, I reason & quarrel with as with my-self when I am reasoning." In a letter to Coleridge, writing about his cheerless social life, Charles Lamb confesses, "I can only converse with you by letter and with the dead in their books."[2] The vocabulary of con-versation, friendly talk between equals, continues to be used of and by annotators, and although it is misleading in some ways, it reminds us that there are always at least two parties involved, the book and the reader, with some sort of give-and-take between them. The perception, wide-spread if not universal among annotators, that reading is interactive is consistent with recent theory and its emphasis on the reader's role. Reading is "an intertextual process governed by an active reader." Read-ing "allows the minds of two people to be more intimately joined than any other form of social contact."[3] The current orthodoxy puts to rest the old model of the passively receptive reader—supposing any reader ever actually believed in that model. But even the new view is too simple and self-congratulatory to deal with the complex reality of marginalia, which are not always friendly and not usually the product of a meeting of equals.

The writer of marginalia acts on the impulse to stop reading for long enough to record a comment. Why? Because it may be done and has been done; it is customary. Under certain conditions (subject to change) it is socially acceptable behavior. But it is seldom *required* behavior; not all readers write notes in their books. Those who choose to make the effort to register their responses must foresee some advantage for some-one; so the question of motive resolves itself into another question, *cui bono?* For whose benefit is it done? And that in turn leads to the question of the addressee.

As far as conscious motive is concerned, most annotators appear to assume that there are just two parties, two "voices" involved, and that they (the annotators) are talking either to themselves or to the author. If Blake says, "Mark this," or "Note this," he is most likely talking to himself, making a minimal remark just one step up from a line or a cross, to assist his memory or to jog his attention upon rereading. If he says "Excellent!" or "True!" or "Well said!"—as he does sometimes even in the case of his enemy Sir Joshua Reynolds—there is an added element of congratulation to the writer, dead at least ten years by the time Blake annotated his work. But if he says, as he does in a copy of Francis Bacon's *Essays*, "Villain! did Christ seek the Praise of the Rulers?" he seems to be forgetting himself and expressing his outrage directly to the author as though he were present. (John Hollander, writing about marginalia, uses the apt phrase, "the dead whom we are shouting at.")[4]

Annotators often address the author directly. John Horne, later John Horne Tooke, gave his copy of Joseph Priestley's *Disquisitions Relating to Matter and Spirit* (1777), a gift from the author, an attentive critical reading. It may be a sign of the intensity of his engagement with the book that from time to time, instead of referring to Priestley in the third person, he addresses him as "you." This sentence from the Preface he first underlined and then commented on: "I have at this time by me several tracts, particularly *Letters* addressed to me, on those subjects, and which have been much applauded, which I have not looked into, and which I profess I never intend to look into" (p. xx). "Then why keep them by you," Horne asks familiarly. In a more mocking spirit, whoever annotated the British Library copy of an eyewitness account of incidents during the French invasion of Ireland in 1798 regularly addresses the self-important author—not named on the title page but easily identifiable, on internal evidence, as Joseph Stock, the Bishop of Killalla—with questions and sarcastic suggestions: "What is ye mean[in]g of this my good Bishop!" (p. 2); "What a surprizing fellow you are Bishop" (p. 54); "This[,] Bishop[,] is really extremely interesting,"— the Bishop has told how he and his wife and four children had to crowd into one room along with four neighboring children and their mother— "but you sho[ul]d have added to the interest by giving us the names &

ages of the Children" (p. 133). When Macaulay took up his copy of Joseph Milner's *History of the Church of Christ* in 1836, he reacted in the same way, chiding the author. "Your style and your chronology are on a par" (1:62), "I believe so on your system" (1:95), "You bolt every lie that the Fathers tell as glibly as your Creed" (1:410)—and so on until, halfway through the third of five volumes, most remarkably for the dogged Macaulay, he stopped, fed up with Milner's company: "Here I give in. I have done my best—But the monotonous absurdity dishonesty & malevolence of this man are beyond me. Nov 13" (3:217).

For a modern example take a polemical political book that had to be withdrawn from the library system for mutilation—in this case, heavy annotation by several hands. René Levesque's *An Option for Quebec* (1968) says, in passing, that "maximum size is in no way synonymous with maximum progress among human societies" (p. 17), and the annotator agrees: "no, that is very true, but you just finished saying that Quebec's lack of progress in educ, sci, & technology was holding it back. The justification, here, is a compromising one, and not very rational." The frame of mind in which a reader can address a book as though it were another human subject, and present, is one we must all recognize. It can be compared to the more often discussed dramatic illusion, our voluntary and habitual submission to the conventions of the stage. It is not that we are actually hallucinating, believing the actors to be the persons they represent, and us invisibly in their company. Nor does any reader believe the writer of the book to be speaking the words in it, and available for conversation. That fact does not prevent us from cherishing the illusion of intimacy, much as we do in the theater.

When annotators address books as personifications of their authors and call them "you," does it mean that they expect their objections and improvements to reach the actual authors somehow? Do they write for their benefit? Only in those rare cases when the authors have specifically solicited commentary, and under those conditions annotators are likely to be circumspect.[5] No; when Webb invokes "Jean Jacques" chummily in his copy of Rousseau, he is engaging in what Lamb called conversation "with the dead in their books"—that form of harmless fantasy, a common feature of the reading process, that sustains and rewards readers. They "speak" to us, and we reciprocate. Only of course there can be no real conversation or dialogue, since the author has no opportunity to answer back. Nor can a reader's contributions properly be likened to collaboration, unless it is as a collaboration foisted on the original writer. Writing marginalia has much in common with letter-writing, and a great annotator often proves to be also a gifted correspondent (Piozzi, Walpole, and Coleridge are cases in point), but books do not answer readers in that sense either. Writing marginalia is not so much akin to conversation or collaboration or correspondence as it is to talking back to the TV set—and readers like it that way.

In an essay about the psychology of reading that has implications for marginalia, Marcel Proust disposes with characteristic subtlety of the cliché that reading is conversation with the best and wisest. "[T]he essential difference between a book and a friend," he says, "is not their degree of greatness or wisdom, but the manner in which we communicate with them, reading, contrary to conversation, consisting for each of us in receiving the communication of another thought, but while we remain all alone, that is to say, while continuing to enjoy the intellectual power we have in solitude, and which conversation dissipates immediately, while continuing to be inspired, to maintain the mind's full, fruitful work on itself."[6] Proust's revision of the "conversation" model as a "communication" model was and is refreshingly corrective; it will confirm readers' intuitive sense of the difference between live social engagement and the enchanted mental space of reading. Proust describes communication of a strictly limited kind: the text expresses itself to the reader, who responds as culture, education, reading experience, and so forth permit. He gives the reader far and away the more active role in the relationship, the book being the stimulus to a process of reflection that soon leaves it behind. He puts the reader securely in command of the situation. This attractive scenario, however, fails to take into account either the different kinds of experience that most readers are aware of or, more critically, the ambivalences of reading. The relationship between book and reader may be as fraught as any close human relationship, with the special frustration of one partner's being insensate and unchangeable. Theorists, in fact, maintain that the experience of reading always involves an element of contest or struggle, and an oscillation between surrender and resistance, identification and detachment.[7] Marginalia lend support to this view. Blake's copy of Lavater's *Aphorisms*, for instance—"a book I love so much, & approve so generally," but in which he felt compelled to record points of disagreement—concisely illustrates the conflict associated with the normal business of reading, let alone with such overt hostilities as mark Macaulay's reading of Milner.

If it is not for the benefit of the author personally, would it be fair to say that marginalia are written for the good of the work itself, impersonally? Yes, sometimes. All cases of authorial or editorial revision by means of annotation fall into this category, as do all corrections of press errors, statements of fact, supplementary information, and improvements of the line of argument that might find their way into a revised edition. Readers do not normally expect their comments to be turned to such practical use. They do, however, expect to keep the book on their shelves in its "corrected" condition, so their own copy would be, to their eyes at least, the better for their work with it. It has been customized for them—a dictionary with more words, a catalogue with extra entries, a polemical tract with a sounder position. But this reasoning leads us back to the reader again.

If there are two parties to the transaction but marginalia are not written for the benefit of the author to whom they are ostensibly addressed, nor for the work itself in any serious sense, then we need to consider advantages to the reader. These are many, and important, though readers themselves may be only dimly aware of them. I do not refer to the most obvious worldly advantages, to the ways in which books may be marked up for professional use by editors, reviewers, lawyers, teachers, auctioneers, et cetera. Those we may take for granted. I mean personal benefits to lay readers, and to the professionals when they are not in their professional mode.

The first experience most readers have of writing in books after they have learned to "listen" to the author, that is, to read, and so passed beyond the stage of seeing only blanks in books, comes with note-taking. (By "author" here and hereafter I normally mean not the actual writer but Wayne Booth's "implied author"—the person inferred from the text on the page, the one we have seen annotators address as "you.")[8] Annotation used to be taught as part of the routine of learning. Marking, copying out, inserting glosses, selecting heads, adding bits from other books, and writing one's own observations are all traditional devices, on a rising scale of readerly activity, for remembering and assimilating text. Psychologically, these techniques seem to function by forcing the reader to slow down (or stop) and go back over the material, and by driving a wedge between the author and the reader. Critical marginalia, especially, typically arise over points of difference, oblige the reader to find words to articulate that difference, and thereby foster independence. But self-awareness is the key thing: conscious agreement and dissent alike contribute to the construction of identity. ("Construction" is the modish term, but "discovery" might be better: it generally *feels* more like discovery.) A marked or annotated book traces the development of the reader's self-definition in and by relation to the text. Perhaps all readers experience this process; annotators keep a log.

The reverse of the process happens when outsiders study marginalia for clues to the identity of the writer—"access to the inner life," as John Powell says, speaking of Gladstone (p. 13).[9] Because we assume that marginalia express a reader's impulsive and unguarded reactions to a book, we consider them to be an exceptionally reliable guide to personality. Novelists have for many years exploited and thereby reinforced this somewhat shaky assumption. Maria Edgeworth's Belinda, for example, comes upon a copy of John Wesley's *Admonitions* in the worldly Lady Delacour's dressing room, "marked in pencil, with reiterated lines, which she knew to be her ladyship's customary mode of distinguishing passages that she particularly liked." When Lady Delacour realizes that Belinda has looked into her books, she pretends to have been reading the Methodists only to laugh at them; Belinda "concluded that the marks of approbation in these books were ironical, and thought no more of the matter." But the reader knows better: faced with a discrepancy between what one character says to another and what she says to her books, we trust the evidence of the books. In *The Strange Case of Dr. Jekyll and Mr. Hyde,* again, marginalia tell the truth though they contradict the public persona: "There were several books on a shelf; one lay beside the tea things open, and Utterson was amazed to find it a copy of a pious work, for which Jekyll had several times expressed a great esteem, annotated, in his own hand, with startling blasphemies." The postmodern twist comes when a character plants an annotated book "in the shelves with its spine to the wall," to suggest that she had been contemplating suicide (as in fact she had been).[10]

But I digress from the subject of what it is that induces readers to expose themselves by writing marginalia in the first place. Using a notebook or keeping a reading diary might be neater, but it is a quite different procedure that increases the distance between reader and text and emphasizes the autonomy of the reader. Writing notes on the page takes less time than turning aside to a notebook and poses less of a threat to the reader's concentration. In the long term, it has potential benefits for both parties. As long as the notes are permanently attached to the text, the text stands as a reminder of the source and a corrective check on the interpretation. Annotated books also constitute a ready-made filing and retrieval system. Readers know where to find their notes on physiognomy, church history, and Quebec separatism—in their Lavaters, their Milners, their Levesques. But they are reminded every time they go to them where their ideas came from: they arose out of intense mental involvement, amounting at times to complete identification with someone else. Coleridge's introspective observation is shrewd: "A book, I value, I reason & quarrel with as with myself when I am reasoning." The simplicity of the phrasing here should not conceal the sophistication of the insight, which manages to avoid either of the easy and insufficient answers to the question of the addressee. Coleridge does not claim to be talking to the author or to himself, but to the book *as though* to himself.

The sort of fluid merging and separating that Coleridge identifies as typical of his own reading might account for an element of mimicry common among writers of marginalia. Though in one way they affirm their separateness when they write notes, in other ways they contradict themselves and seem to adopt the identity of the author. Difference and sameness are blended in their interventions: even Beckford's extracts, described in Chapter One, that use the very words of the text, display by the nature of the selection and by verbal variation the distinct sensibility of the annotator. To some extent the imitative quality can be accounted for by the decorums of genre, as I have said before: cookbooks attract recipes, editions acquire manuscript notes similar to the printed ones. The aphorisms published in the Berg Collection's copy of Coventry Patmore's collection *The Rod, the Root, and the Flower* (1911) are interspersed with aphorisms in manuscript by his son Tennyson. But the resemblance goes beyond the requirements of genre. Annotators often write their notes in the language of the text rather than in their mother tongue, this habit suggesting that they were thinking in the other language. Jonathan Swift, who annotated his Latin books in Latin and his French books in French, belongs to this camp. Montaigne, on the other hand, made a point of sticking to French, saying that whatever language his books spoke to him, he spoke to them in his own. Others, interestingly, vacillate. T. S. Eliot sometimes slipped into French in a French book, but on at least one occasion he used French in a Latin book, and no Latin.[11] Mary Astell's notes in Lady Mary Wortley Montagu's Bayle are all in English, but Lady Mary herself used French for some of the (relatively few) notes in her Montaigne.

Roland Barthes says of all reading that it is subject to the structure imposed by the text, it needs and respects it—but it also perverts it.[12] This hypothesis is confirmed again and again by marginalia from readers of all sorts. Annotators like to declare themselves independent of the text, but they never really are so. It is curious, for instance, to find annotators responding to verse with verse. The penciled notes to *The New School of Love*, a tiny Scottish chapbook of the kind sold by itinerant peddlers to the poorest readers, were certainly made before the collection was assembled in 1828. This closely printed little book of just twenty-four pages is a guide to the arts of courtship, including the significance of marks on different parts of the body and the meaning of dreams. It includes model love letters, love songs, "Toasts, Sentiments, etc." A cynical reader made use of such space as he (presumably, he) could find among the poems, in one case adding to the end of a plaintive poetical epistle from "a Love-sick Youth to a scornful Maid" and incorporating the heading of the next poem, her "ANSWER," in verses of his own. The Youth's poem ends, "I live to wear the chain, and live in pain /

And, 'till I know my doom, I must remain / Yours, &c. &c." The marginalia follow on from "remain": "As large a fool as ever lacked a brain. / Now hear the ANSWER of the bitch again." It is not an uncommon reaction, parody: it is a way of criticizing from within. Its mimicry voices the usually unspoken uneasiness of the reader's relation to the text.

All annotators are readers, but not all readers are annotators. Annotators are readers who write. Annotation combines—synthesizes, I should say—the functions of reading and writing. This fact in itself heightens the natural tension between author and reader by making the reader a rival of the author, under conditions that give the reader considerable power. The author has the first word, but the annotator has the last. Even in those cases in which the annotator appears most subservient to the text and probably felt quite innocently helpful, for example in filling up the names left blank or adding new references to bring the book up to date, the annotator is implicitly critical, presuming to know better and taking over authorial functions. As Thomas McFarland says, apropos of Blake, marginalia are always invasive.[13] If political and military metaphors seem heavy-handed for so minor and so private a phenomenon, let me put it another way and propose that all marginalia are extensions of the ownership inscription, which itself expresses the primary impulse of claiming the book as one's own. Every note entails a degree of self-assertion, if not of aggression. The reader leaves a mark and thereby alters the object.[14] Usually the implicit rival is the author, but not always. Ezra Pound, having acquired a copy of Algernon Swinburne's *Laus Veneris* already annotated by somebody else, took pains to dissociate himself from the other's views: "Some damn fool had this book before I bought it. I am not responsible for the notes in his handwriting" (p. −2). This note is superfluous—whoever *would* imagine Pound responsible for notes in another hand?—but emotionally it makes sense. Pound claims possession and dismisses the usurper.[15]

Pound's note also implicitly endorses the view that marginalia express personality. (Though the previous owner reveals himself a fool, Pound wants to make it plain that *he* is no fool and has no patience with fools.) If the early practice of annotation supports the development of a distinct personality, the full-blown habit serves to maintain and strengthen it. A case in point is Samuel Clemens's Tacitus, full of notes disparaging the ineptitude of the translator: "Execrable English" (1:122); "Doubtless this translator can read Latin, but he can't write English" (1:202); "To quote a man puts the man's remark in the first person, but this fossil doesn't know that" (1:215); "This book's English is the rottenest that was ever puked upon paper" (2:101). The level of complaint implies that the annotator could do better; the flamboyant style proves it. Clemens's self-consciousness as a reader is comically paraded later on, when he reads about the appointment of Arretinus Clemens as commander of the praetorian guard, a post his father had held with honor before him. "The same name," Tacitus explains, "would be welcome to the soldiers; and Clemens himself, though a member of the senate, would be able to discharge the duties of both stations." Clemens the reader underlines the name and comments wryly, "An error of judgment. There was never yet a Clemens who could creditably fill two stations at the same time" (2:247).[16]

Marginalia can be used to construct and to *monitor* identity. Victor Plarr was so troubled by misogynistic remarks in his friend Ernest Dowson's marginalia that he had to suppose that those remarks, and those only, had been written to fulfill the requirements of a pseudonym (p. 46). Closer to home, the experience of coming on one's own notes written years before may be chastening or it may—as it did for Blake—confirm integrity of character (fig. 4):

Burkes Treatise on the Sublime & Beautiful is founded on the Opinions of Newton & Locke on this Treatise Reynolds has grounded many of his assertions in all his Discourses I read Burkes Treatise when very Young at the same time I read Locke on Human Understanding & Bacons Advancemt of Learning on Every one of these Books I wrote my Opinions & on looking them over find that my Notes on Reynolds in this Book are exactly Similar. I felt the Same Contempt & Abhorrence then; that I do now. They mock Inspiration & Vision Inspiration & Vision was then & now is & I hope will always Remain my Element my Eternal Dwelling place. how can I then hear it Contemned without returning Scorn for Scorn—[17]

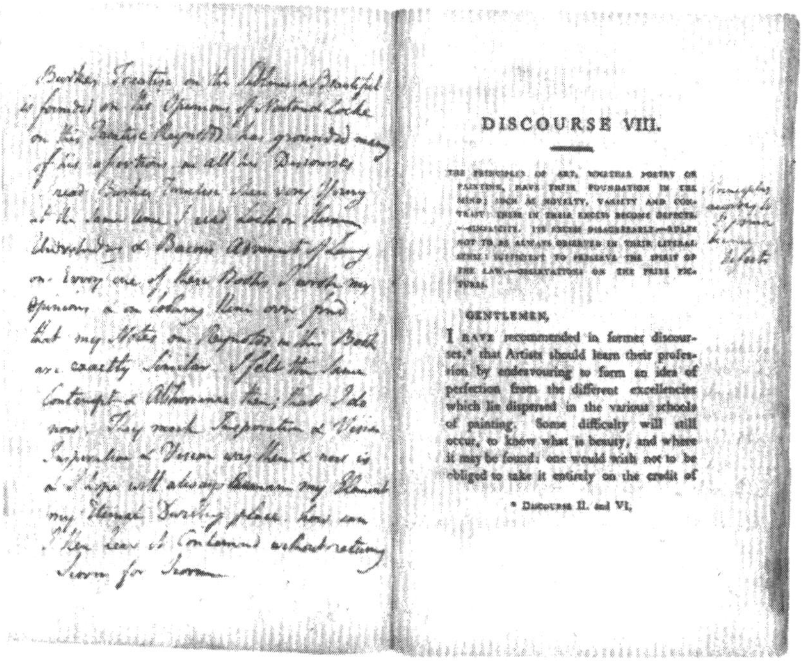

FIG. 4 Sir Joshua Reynolds, *Works* (1798), 1:[244–45]. Annotations by William Blake. (Used by permission of the British Library)

This comment of Blake's applies two criteria for constancy of character. Besides strongly asserting personal identity by opposition to what one is not (in this case, not Reynolds or Edmund Burke or John Locke), it requires emotional consistency—"I felt the Same Contempt & Abhorrence then that I do now." This remark highlights another of the blessings of annotation to annotators, namely the outlet that it gives them for expressing their feelings—their joy when the author says exactly what they think, their dismay when the bond with the author is broken, and their fluctuating reactions to the course of an argument or narrative. It is a cheap and convenient form of therapy.

Annotators who "long to say something" can have the satisfaction of saying it. The records are, in consequence, especially rich in abuse that was perhaps expected to be kept quietly shut up inside the covers of the book. Now and then, inevitably, it gets out.[18] Evelyn Waugh's books, many of them annotated as reviewers' books tend to be, were acquired by the Humanities Research Center of the University of Texas at Austin. Alan Bell reports that after Cyril Connolly, passing through Austin, saw the notes Waugh had written in a copy of Connolly's book *The Unquiet Grave,* "He was deeply upset, and soon after sold many of his inscribed Waugh first editions at Christie's."[19] There was also some consternation (and some glee) in the publishing world when Graham Greene's books went to Boston College, for he was a habitual annotator and his books were known to contain sharp remarks about contemporary authors.[20] By way of example, the summary note at the end of the first volume of his copy of Malcolm Muggeridge's *Chronicles of Wasted Time*—a presentation copy inscribed "affectionately" from the author— says, "And yet after reading this absurd, not very honest, badly written volume, I still find an affection for the clown, Malcolm—his absurdity produces a sort of affection as one might have for an *only* dog. I have, like him, used too many adjectives—his last paragraph of 28 lines contains 37 adjectives."

Greene's comment on Muggeridge would appear to be a clear-cut case of the note written purely for the annotator. It articulates the feelings of the moment and finds an original image for them; it makes a critical observation of a technical kind that at one blow disparages Muggeridge and acknowledges a weakness that Greene himself knows he ought to be vigilant about. So it vents feelings, demonstrates and improves self-awareness, and constitutes a permanent record of the reading experience. It was certainly not intended for the eye of the author of the book. (It may seem surprising that presentation copies like this one often contain distinctly ungrateful notes by the recipients, but after all they—the recipients—did not ask for the books and yet feel obliged to read them—a situation that is not conducive to charitable reading.) But private documents do run the risk of becoming public, especially when the writers are celebrities. Greene knew that, and so did Waugh. Marginalia had been published before. Does the impulse to "say something" overwhelm all caution?

It is a complicated issue, the privacy of marginalia, and it will come up again later. In this case, I think the answer must be that Greene was *not* writing just to please himself, and that he probably knew it. He wanted to make a statement to clarify his attitude toward Muggeridge. As long as *Chronicles of Wasted Time* remained in his keeping, the notes would exist for him only, the use of them being under his control, but if he ever disposed of the book, at least his reservations would go with it. A colleague of mine once told me that he annotated his books so that no one should think he accepted what they said when he didn't. It seemed to me just so much unnecessary labor at the time, but there's something to it and for him it filled a need. I believe that like him, Greene also understood that as physical objects, books are likely to outlive their owners and therefore provide an opportunity, perhaps even a responsibility, for communication beyond the immediate conjunction of author and reader. Surely this is why memoirs and biographies seem especially to attract expansive, direct, indiscreet, often artful marginalia, designed to set the record straight.

A telling example is Harriet Martineau's copy of Elizabeth Gaskell's *Life of Charlotte Brontë* (1857), now in the Houghton Library at Harvard. Martineau's notes are all in pencil. Comparing this copy with a later edition, she notes some of the significant cuts that Gaskell had been induced to make (1:55–57). She confirms with her initials her authorship of a statement about *Jane Eyre* in the obituary of "Currer Bell" (2:11) and expresses her judgment of George Henry Lewes ("a Humbug," 2:44). When Brontë is quoted as promising to try "diligently" to read Jane Austen, she comments, "She tried here, & cd not get on. Said nothing of any former controversy. H. M." (2:56). But the notes are relatively scanty before Chapters 9 and 12, which include accounts of "Her Visit to Miss Martineau" and "Misunderstanding with Miss Martineau." Here the text induces a rash of corrections and contradictions, especially of statements in Brontë's letters. Martineau irritably underlines and interrupts the text: "I believe she is not at all conscious of her own absolutism. <u>When I tell her of it</u> (HM: 'never did'), she denies the charge warmly; <u>then I laugh at her</u> (HM: 'imaginary altogether')" (2:199). "Stuff!" says Martineau, in the margin. When Gaskell maintains that Brontë was "disturbed and distressed" by the publication of Martineau's letters, she denies it: "Her letters to H. M. say the contrary. Being besought to let them alone she <u>claimed</u> a copy, & praised them for 'reverence & earnestness' &c, & asked, 'Who cd be angry?'" (2:203). Gaskell's assertion that "hundreds have forsaken her" she dismisses briskly as "Hallucination" (2:282). These notes may reflect the indignant impulse of the moment, but like others of their kind they were allowed to stand unrevised. Martineau did not need to defend herself *to herself* through the medium of marginalia, but she left the book as a record of her version of events. She can hardly have realized that the tone of the notes would only corroborate Brontë's opinion of her "absolutism."

The illusion of being alone with the author is so strong in many kinds of reading that when readers write in books they tend automatically to address their remarks to the author or to themselves. The theorists of reading likewise assume that they have only two parties to deal with. This easy assumption needs to be reconsidered, however—at least for the reader of an annotating habit. The ostensible addressee is not the only addressee. It is not only the sociable readers of Chapter Two, marking books deliberately to send to a particular friend or a circle of colleagues, who share their experiences with a third party. The physical nature of the book and the history of the circulation of books ensure that there always is a third party tacitly present at the writing of marginalia. When the reader takes on the role of a writer and leaves traces in the book, the communication between reader and text necessarily involves not only their two speaking parts but also the silent audience that will sooner or later witness the performance. It becomes a semipublic occasion on which annotators have an opportunity to show what they can do. One of De Quincey's reminiscing essays complains about William Wordsworth's cavalier handling of books and compares him unfavorably with Coleridge. Not only was Wordsworth seen to cut open a book with a buttery knife, but he "rarely, indeed, wrote on the margin of books; and, when he did, nothing could less illustrate his intellectual superiority. The comments were such as might have been made by anybody."[21] De Quincey appears to believe that marginalia are written competitively and that an annotator *ought* to demonstrate "intellectual superiority." Over whom, and for whose benefit? The implication is, over the ordinary run of readers; and for the sake of one's reputation (which is to say, for one's own sake, but by way of the opinion of others). De Quincey's ideal writer in the margins foresees the possibility of publication.

Annotators themselves display varying degrees of self-consciousness about the unknown prospective reader. Francis Douce, as we have seen, annotated books on purpose for future readers in the British Museum; Walpole, according to his biographer, wrote for posterity.[22] But when Blake set about correcting Lavater, he too anticipated the reaction of the unnamed future reader who might "call what I have written cavilling": he felt compelled to justify himself to that third party. Clemens knew that his family enjoyed his marginalia, and he played up to them as he wrote. Why should Pound have made such a point of differentiating himself from the previous owner, unless he foresaw the day when the book would change hands again? Coleridge annotated many books at the request of friends, knowing well that there was no controlling the use of the books once they went back to their owners. Even his own books were liable to be lent out, or lost, or pawned or sold to meet pressing needs. His copy of *Quentin Durward* includes a note that reveals his sense of public responsibility as an annotator. Sir Walter Scott's narrator has proposed that one of the advantages of foreign travel is that your purchasing power is missed at home—"my absence is both missed and moaned"—when otherwise the local shopkeepers might not care whether you were alive or dead. Coleridge comments, "For the sake of young Readers of this, my ever circulating Copy of Scott's Novels I feel it a duty to say, that this is written in a *bad* spirit. Why *should* the Butcher, the Barber &c feel any deeper regard for a Customer, than as a Customer? Esteem and Love are due only for Esteem and Love. If my Butcher behaves civilly and serves me honestly, he has fully balanced my doings toward him, chusing him for my Butcher, in the belief that I should be better served by him than by an other."[23] In this case, as in many others, the impulse to write evidently involved three factors: the idea expressed by the text, the reader's resistance to it, and the ghostly audience. Coleridge makes it clear that the audience tipped the scale; without it, the moment would have gone unrecorded.

Further complicating this three- or four-way transaction (text, reader, target audience, unknown future reader) is the variability of the reader's mood and approach. It takes time to read a book. Circumstances change. Levels of engagement and concentration change. The reading may be a rereading, and marginalia may be written on different occasions for different purposes. Coleridge's many notes to Jeremy Taylor's *Polemicall Discourses* include some addressed to the author directly ("A sophism, dearest Jeremy!"); some to the owner of the volume, Charles Lamb; and some to a hypothetical other reader who might "need other illustrations" enforcing Coleridge's argument.[24] The same could be said of Blake's Reynolds—he appears to address different people at different times—and of Urquhart's copy of Mudford's *Nubilia,* which shows the reader at some points quarreling with the narrator and at others thinking of his own "gentle" friend.

This sort of mixed use is more common than not. A Victorian edition of a legal classic, the *Institutes* of Justinian, shows signs of careful and laborious study, with an elaborate system of marking (underlining, bracketing, lines in the margin, multiple pointed brackets, etc.); heads for important terms and definitions; corrections to the translation; cross-references to other law books; and occasional comments on matters of history or interpretation. But a little more than halfway through this volume of 599 pages, all of them marked one way or another, comes a personal note: "Left off work at this pt to row head of the river 12th May 1864!" (p. 338). The British Library attributes the annotations to Charles Wentworth Dilke, and I'd like to think they are right: he was seventy-four at the time and died later that year.

The Irish poet and playwright Denis Johnston left among his books (many of which are annotated) a copy of A. S. Eddington's *The Nature of the Physical World* with notes that show how carefully he followed the argument step by step, sometimes addressing the author directly (where the text says, "Nor shall I discuss here how complete is the proof afforded by these experiments," Johnston added, "Better not," p. 5), sometimes letting off steam ("To hell with Fitzgerald," p. 60), and sometimes stepping back to say something to himself ("A very disarming person after all," p. 353, the last page). But he must have read the book more than once, and at some stage he wrote a set of notes that appears to have been designed to guide another reader. These are generally less terse than his notes to himself. Eddington's example of a pack of cards, for instance, gets first of all a simple contradiction, and then a fuller comment. On the subject of "The Running-Down of the Universe," Eddington writes, "If you take a pack of cards as it comes from the maker and shuffle it for a few minutes, all trace of the original systematic order disappears. <u>The order will never come back no matter how long you shuffle</u>" (p. 63). "Yes it may," says Johnston on his first pass. Then later: "A pack of cards is a very bad example & put me off the track of what he means for years. What the 'order' of the cards is is completely conventional, and shuffling has no significant effect whatever." Johnston's observation of particular cases of weakness in Eddington's reasoning leads him to a generalization that might have been formulated either as a memorandum to himself or as assistance to the other reader: "Eddington is however basically right though a desperately bad explainer, making it worse by his illustrations" (p. 39). Here as elsewhere it is probably impossible to extricate from one another different layers of annotation and different levels of motivation in the annotator.

Even when the primary purpose of annotation is strictly professional, readers often prove unable or unwilling to pass over passages that interest them though they may be irrelevant to the task at hand. When Edward Gibbon set out to revise his *History of the Decline and Fall of the Roman Empire,* he went about it in the traditional way by marking up an existing copy with new wording and additional information. The process of revision seems to have got him thinking, and he started to write down his reflections at the same time.[25] On the first page, as he corrects the account of his "design" for Chapters 1 and 2 for the printer, he asks himself:

> Should I not have given the <u>history</u> of that fortunate period which was interposed between two Iron ages? Should I not have deduced the decline of the Empire from the civil Wars, that ensued after the fall of Nero or even from the tyranny which succeeded the reign of Augustus? Alas! I should: but of what avail is this tardy knowledge? Where error is irretrievable, repentance is useless!

On the next page, he provides a glimpse of a meeting one would like to know more about. Gibbon had asserted that the whole world was concerned in the consequences of the fall of Rome, but he has been brought to reconsider that assertion: "NB. Mr Hume told me that in correcting his history, he always laboured to reduce superlatives, and soften positives. Have Asia and Africa, from Japan to Morocco, any feeling or memory of the Roman Empire?" And so it goes. In this case, routine revisions intended for the press are accompanied by the author's private reflections. The marginalia of reviewers like Macaulay, Waugh, and Edmund White, though written to supply raw materials for the eventual review article, always include comments that are not used—because they don't fit in with the position adopted in the end, or because they're too risky or too personal one way or another. Teaching notes prepared by eminent figures like Northrop Frye and Vladimir Nabokov often share the page with personal reflections and memoranda.[26] Ramsay Macdonald, prime minister in Britain's first Labour government in 1924, wrote reviews throughout his career. Unpublished remarks in his extant review copies and other books now in the Library of Scotland could supplement and perhaps clarify the record of his opinions, especially on political matters. His review of Olive Schreiner's *Woman and Labour* (1911) for the *Daily Chronicle*, for example, is generally supportive, quotes generously, and only hints disapproval of the prose style, but his annotated copy reveals some areas of significant disagreement. Here it is probably safe to assume that the less diplomatic marginalia are closer to Macdonald's actual thinking at the time, but it is also important to remember that the reading must have been influenced by the task at hand.

What I hope to demonstrate by these examples is that common assumptions about marginalia—that they are spontaneous, impulsive, uninhibited; that they offer direct access to the reader's mind; that they are private and therefore trustworthy—fail to take into account inherent complexities of motivation and historical circumstance. I by no means propose the opposite—that they are calculating, corrupt, and dishonest—but wish simply to emphasize the fact that readers who write in their books *are* writers, subject to the conventions and expectations that govern this responsive kind of writing, and influenced by many of the motives that drive other writers. Love, anger, pity, ambition, spite, emulation, partisanship—any and all of these may show up. On a scale of transparency from one to a hundred where a hundred constitutes maximum transparency, marginalia rank high but not all marginalia equally, for they are subject to the conventions not only of writing but of all human communication, which, as Stephen Pinker says, "is not just a transfer of information like two fax machines connected with a wire; it is a series of alternating displays of behavior by sensitive, scheming, second-guessing, social animals" (pp. 229–30).

For the collector who acquires an annotated book and for the scholar who wants to use the evidence of marginalia, it seems to me that there is a net gain in abandoning the notion that marginalia are innocent and transparent: if we have to let go a pleasing illusion, we end up with more human drama and come closer to the truth besides. Marginalia are the product of an interaction between text and reader carried on—since books are durable objects—in the presence of silent witnesses. They always have been both personal and potentially public, though the proportions of personal to public have changed from one period to another. And still every annotated book is unique. In this and the preceding chapters, I have attempted to establish the general framework in which marginalia were written between about 1700 and the present. In those that follow, I shall be exploring some remarkable particular cases.

chapter four

OBJECT LESSONS

You acquire a book with marginalia—a message to an unknown fellow reader, like a letter in a bottle. What next? "Rub them out and say no more about it," as I was once advised to do with new Coleridge material? Fair enough—it's your book now—if the sight of notes offends you, or if upon examination you find them to be really of no possible interest. Perhaps the rule should be, not if *or* if, but if *and* if. Both conditions need to be met. If you are so fastidious that you could not bring yourself to give shelf room to an annotated book, then you ought to pass it on as soon as you can to someone who will give the notes a bit of attention— at the very least, read them through—before taking a life-or-death decision. For myself (of course I am partial), annotation is part of the history of a book and I would choose to leave notes alone: evidence of use is less depressing than the signs of a book's having never been read. (Some extreme kinds of abuse, however, will be considered in Chapter Eight.)

At this point, in a more positive spirit, I introduce four case studies to show where the study of marginalia might lead. Although one of them turned out to be unexpectedly rich, these are not spectacular cases of the order of Gibbon on Herodotus, Coleridge on Luther, or Pound on Eliot; they were chosen to show what quite unassuming and even repulsive objects might have to offer by way of access to the past and understanding of the present. Because readers are the focus, I refer to these particular copies by the name of the reader instead of the author: they are Hester Piozzi's *Rasselas*, Rupert Brooke's *Introduction to Poetry*, Scriblerus's *Life of Johnson*, and T. H. White's *Two Essays on Analytical Psychology*.

For twenty years now, the Houghton Library at Harvard has housed an 1818 copy of Samuel Johnson's "Oriental" philosophical tale *Rasselas* annotated by a woman who had been his friend and confidante, Hester Lynch Piozzi. Piozzi came to be a celebrity in her own right after Johnson's death, and books with her marginalia have been preserved and written about before now, but the *Rasselas* has not had much attention, nor have the circumstances of the annotation been properly understood. Nevertheless, it is a fascinating copy and one for which it is possible to reconstruct a quite rich historical context.[1]

Hester Lynch Salusbury, a Welshwoman of good family, was a petted and precocious child. Besides the modern languages, French, Spanish, and Italian, she studied Latin with an excellent tutor. She wrote and published poems as a teenager. At twenty-two, in 1763, she made a marriage of convenience with Henry Thrale, a wealthy brewer, and she and her widowed mother went to live with him in the outskirts of London, first at Thrale's country house, Streatham Park, and then at the house at Southwark near his business. Their first child—the first of twelve, of whom four daughters survived to adulthood—was born in September 1764. In January 1765 they entertained Samuel Johnson at Southwark and he became a regular dinner guest; in the summer of 1766, in the aftermath of a period of severe depression, he accepted their invitation to join them at Streatham Park, and for the next sixteen years he was virtually a member of the household. Although he kept his own house, he was in and out of theirs: Johnson and the Thrales lived, worked, read, wrote, and traveled together. Both Henry Thrale and Johnson, in their different ways, encouraged Hester Thrale's literary talent. Her husband gave her handsome blank books ("Thraliana") to write in, and Johnson read and approved her anecdotes, domestic journal entries, and verses. Johnson helped his hosts to assemble a library.

After her husband's death in 1781, however, Hester Thrale alienated Johnson, her daughters, and most of her social circle by marrying her daughters' music master, the Italian singer Gabriel Piozzi. Johnson died in December 1784, five months after her second marriage. The scandalous marriage was unquestionably a personal success. For Hester Piozzi, it was also the beginning of a new career as a writer in which she turned to account her learning, her wit, and her languages. She and her husband traveled for two years and then returned to London. From the Continent, she published some poems in the *Florence Miscellany* (1785) and then the controversial *Anecdotes of the Late Samuel Johnson, LL.D.* (1786). There followed an edition of *Letters to and from Samuel Johnson* (1788), *Observations and Reflections Made in the Course of a Journey through France, Italy, and Germany* (1788), *British Synonymy: or an Attempt at Regulating the Choice of Words in Familiar Conversation* (1794), *Three Warnings to John Bull* (1798), and a world history entitled *Retrospection* (1801). The reviewers were not kind.

The Piozzis built a country house that they named Brynbella, in Wales, and adopted a five-year-old boy, Gabriel Piozzi's nephew, who came to them from Italy in 1798. This adoption was intended to make up for the coldness and occasional hostility of the Thrale daughters—"the Ladies," as their mother mockingly called them. After the death of her second husband in 1809, Piozzi depended more than ever on the society of family and friends. When her prospective heir, renamed John Salusbury, married in 1814, she gave him Brynbella and, in reduced circumstances herself, retired to Bath. Here her reputation and her unquenchable liveliness won her new friends and admirers, notably Sir James Fellowes, who encouraged her to talk about the past and saw or corresponded with her frequently until his marriage in 1816; Rev. Edward Mangin, eventually her first biographer, who also married in 1816; and the handsome young leading man of the Bath theater, William Augustus Conway, with whom she carried on an intense friendship from December 1818 until her death in May 1821. The annotated *Rasselas* was one of her gifts to Conway.

By character or by habit, Piozzi needed an appreciative man to attend to. Her heir had disappointed her; Fellowes and Mangin were at last disqualified by marriage; Conway was a godsend. He was almost fifty years younger than she, and like Johnson's old crony Richard Savage he had a cause. He believed himself to be the illegitimate son of a peer, Lord Conway. His mother, Susanna Rudd, let lodgings in Clifton, near Bristol; Piozzi died in one of her houses. In 1818, he was working as an actor, with mixed success. He was making fruitless attempts to have the relationship with Lord Conway acknowledged. He was courting a young woman whose family did not approve of him, but in this suit he also failed. After the Bath winter season of 1818–19, he went on to perform in Birmingham and London, returning to Bath for a few months at a time, and visiting his mother occasionally in Clifton. The record of his friendship with Piozzi, especially correspondence to and about him, dates from the spring of 1819, and the *Rasselas* was certainly given to him in that year. It would probably have amused but not surprised Piozzi to know that her name would be linked with Conway's in a posthumous scandal, with the publication in 1843 of *Love Letters of Mrs. Piozzi, Written When She Was 80, to W. A. Conway.*[2]

A serious and voracious reader, Piozzi was accustomed to make notes for herself as she read—sometimes in separate notebooks, sometimes in the books themselves. At a certain point, however, she realized that, far from spoiling them, her marginalia might increase the value of the books they were written in, and she began to capitalize upon her habit, making the gift of annotated books a means of intimate communication supplementary to and possibly more permanent than letters. She became one of those "sociable" readers described earlier. For Fellowes, a prospective biographer, she annotated books by and about herself: Nathaniel Wraxall's *Historical Memoirs of My Own Time* (1815), the Johnson *Anecdotes* and *Letters,* and her own *Observations* and *Retrospection.*[3] Four or five years later, when Conway left for Birmingham, she did her best to comfort him and to maintain her sense of connection with him by frequent letters and thoughtful little presents—"Lozenges for the cough—Books for the Shelf," as she wrote in June 1819. She must have put herself to a regular *course* of annotation. At one stage she points out that she is sending him new books that she herself has not finished reading: "these Books which I have just received from Upham, & not quite cut open; yet could not help my old Trick of making Mr. Deformed in the Margin." She sent him fresh copies of the books listed as given to Fellowes, and others besides. Some went to him by bequest after her death. When Conway himself committed suicide in America in 1828, his trunks contained her annotated copies of the *Letters* and *Anecdotes*, *Retrospection*, Wraxall, "a French translation of Johnson's *Rasselas*, and a Bible." She also voluminously annotated a Bible for Conway's mother.[4]

The 184 pages of the Houghton copy of *Rasselas* are quite heavily annotated in ink, with marks ranging from simple calls for attention—underlining, exclamation marks, and fists—to notes that fill all the margins of a page (fig. 5). Piozzi's hand is generally small but firm and clear.[5] There are altogether about 120 notes, some of them very brief ("charming! and how natural!" p. 12; "alas!" p. 49), others long and rambling. Evidence of the connection with Conway is entirely internal—there appears to be no other record of her having sent him this book—but nevertheless conclusive. Several of the notes and marks in the book are concerned with friendship, and others, such as waspish allusions to problem children on page 47 and to the loss of Brynbella on page 81, assume the sympathetic interest of a friendly reader. On page 9, Piozzi observes, "Enjoyment implies Friendship—one can enjoy nothing alone—at least I cannot. H. L. P." On page 128 she underlined two sentences: "She that has no one to love or trust has little to hope. She wants the radical principle of happiness." On page 163, in the chapter on old age, there is a long note. Johnson's speaker says, "to me, who am now declining to decrepitude, there is little to be feared from the malevolence of men, and yet less to be hoped for from their affection or esteem." Piozzi responds, "little indeed . . . except as they can wound me thro' a new-found Friend, whose Esteem even if I can flatter myself with deserving, I cannot keep long; & in whose Remembrance I can hardly hope to be retained, while every Blast of Fortune—good or bad,—will shake my feeble Tenure on his Affections; & every Current carry the poor Straw down the Stream, losing even the once-honour'd Name of H: L: P."[6] The object of all this sentiment is revealed in a note on page 113,

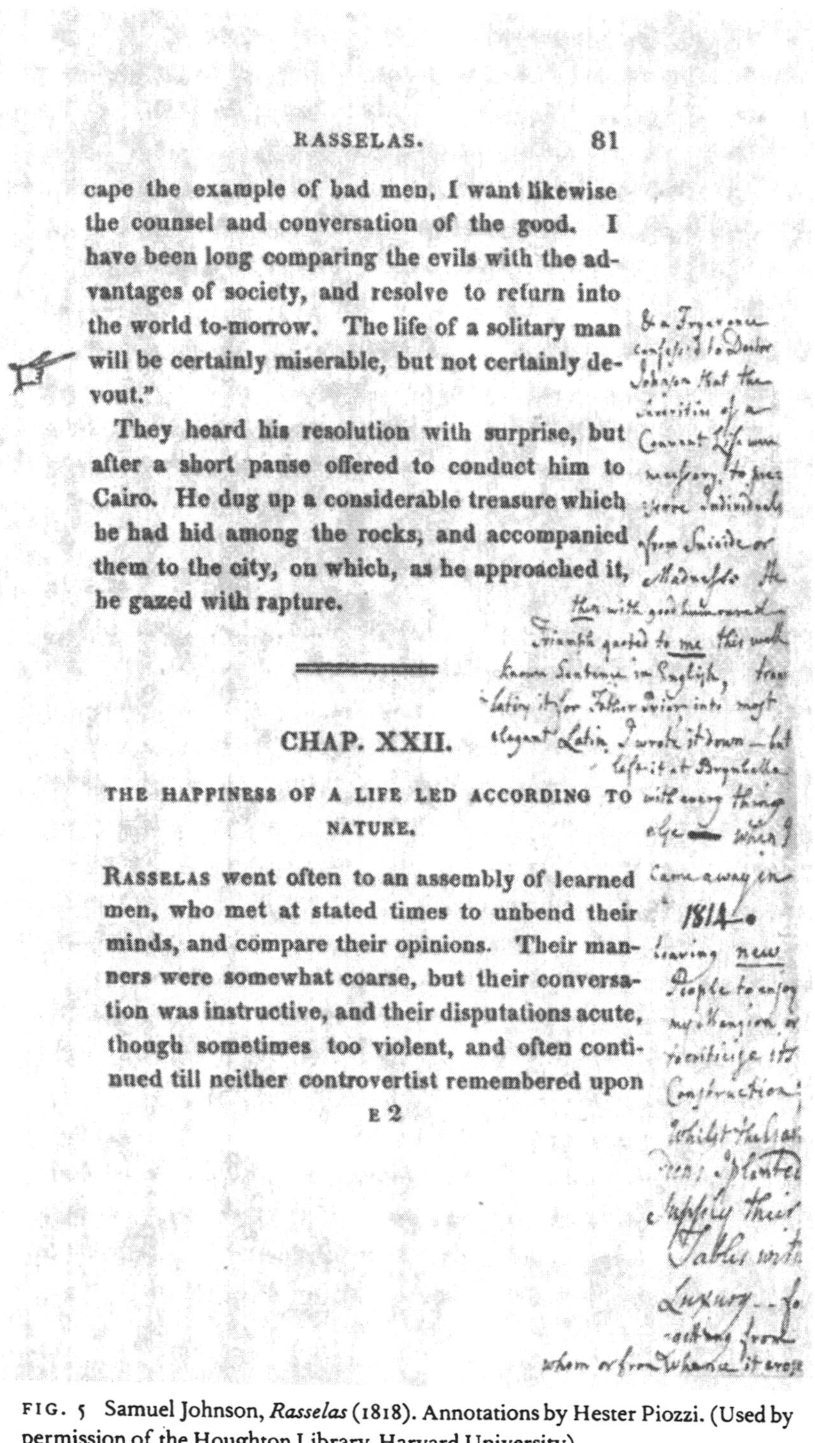

RASSELAS. 81

cape the example of bad men, I want likewise the counsel and conversation of the good. I have been long comparing the evils with the advantages of society, and resolve to return into the world to-morrow. The life of a solitary man will be certainly miserable, but not certainly devout."

They heard his resolution with surprise, but after a short pause offered to conduct him to Cairo. He dug up a considerable treasure which he had hid among the rocks, and accompanied them to the city, on which, as he approached it, he gazed with rapture.

CHAP. XXII.

THE HAPPINESS OF A LIFE LED ACCORDING TO NATURE.

RASSELAS went often to an assembly of learned men, who met at stated times to unbend their minds, and compare their opinions. Their manners were somewhat coarse, but their conversation was instructive, and their disputations acute, though sometimes too violent, and often continued till neither controvertist remembered upon

E 2

& a Ignorance confessed to Doctor Johnson that the Invention of a Convent Life was necessary to free some Individuals from Suicide or Madness He then with good humoured Triumph quoted to me this well known Sentence in English, translating it for Father Quin into most elegant Latin. I wrote it down — but left it at Brynbella with every thing else — when I came away in 1814. leaving new People to enjoy my Mansion, or criticize its Construction; Whilst the Trees I planted supply their Tables with Luxury — forgetting from whom or from Whence it arose

FIG. 5 Samuel Johnson, *Rasselas* (1818). Annotations by Hester Piozzi. (Used by permission of the Houghton Library, Harvard University)

when Rasselas and his party entertain a proposal to visit the Pyramids: "Coptic Mythology at last comes in as an Auxiliary you see—will it help me to endure the Absence of Mr. Conway?"

The poignancy that Piozzi felt in her relationship with Conway arose from her age and from the disparity between her age and his. Many of her notes dwell, naturally enough, on that theme. On the same page as the long note just quoted in which she writes of her "feeble Tenure on his Affections," she picks out the sentence, "'Praise,' said the sage, with a sigh, 'is to an old man an empty sound . . .'" and adds her own endorsement: "Oh! Truest Word of all this Pen has written,—of all these Eyes have read." And in the heavily marked chapters on the madness of the Astronomer, when the poet Imlac speaks of the "folly" of "visionary schemes" (p. 161), she remarks, "Imaginative People are doubtless all of them in some danger while Young of a Disease, over Which,—Wisdom has no Power, & Pity no Command. in old Age no Temptations to such Folly can arise. Our Fancy is blunted, & our Imagination Starved.— The mental like the natural Eye flattens by too long use; reverting foolishly to things past, not as in youth—stretching toward Things to come." In the first instance, then, the notes in the Harvard *Rasselas* have biographical value insofar as they add detail and emotional depth to our understanding of Piozzi and her warm friendship with Conway. Furthermore, as James Clifford observed in *Hester Lynch Piozzi* when he imagined the dispersed marginalia as a complete set, "they provide the most unquestionable proof not only of the variety of her reading but of her knowledge as well. They are the answer to those who have followed Boswell in sneering at both her intellect and her character" (p. 449). But even that "answer" represents only the narrowest and most obvious claim on present-day interest, for Piozzi was more than a maligned character: she was one of Johnson's inner circle.

Part of Piozzi's stock in trade was Johnsonian anecdote. This copy of *Rasselas* contains stories and sayings of Johnson, most of which are not published elsewhere. When Imlac tells Rasselas about the lady who "rejected my suit because my father was a merchant" (p. 49), her comment is, "Poor Imlac! but how Dr. Johnson knew the World: He meant Imlac as his own Representative to his own feelings; The Lady was Miss Molly

Aston who sate for the Portrait of Altilia in the Rambler; when she was Dame passée I believe. Johnson could not bear a Man who loved below himself—When Dr. Pepys—(—now old Sir Lucas—)—married Lady Rothes; some one said—He would have his Head Combed by a Countess; Well Sir! was the Reply; It would be worse to have one's Feet bastinadod by a Slave." Piozzi tells Conway that Chapter 10 ("A Dissertation on Poetry") was Johnson's favorite (p. 41), and that the philosopher in Chapter 22 was modeled on Gilbert Cooper (that is, John Gilbert Cooper), "a Man now I think wholly forgotten, tho' a very showy Talker in his Time" (p. 85). She confirms Johnson's lack of interest in scenery, saying that they found it impossible "to engage his Attention in France to the Beauties of the Country or the Climate,—he exclaimed—no Sir, a Blade of Grass is but a Blade of Grass, my Business is with Men & Women, let us see how these will be found to differ from those we have left behind" (p. 33). And when the Hermit describes the dangers of solitude—the way the "fancy riots in scenes of folly" (p. 80), she marks the passage with underlining and a line in the margin and writes, "a Danger Doctor Johnson deprecated beyond all other . . . . & seem'd to think more common than I can conceive. On this Subject however, Contradiction was insupportable to him, . . . & Discussion,—dreadful."

In addition to these reminiscences of Johnson, Piozzi offers the judgment of a practiced and privileged reader. Her response is admiring for the most part, though she ventures sometimes to question aspects of style or matters of opinion (notably in the debate about the immateriality of the soul). At the very beginning of the book she notes, "This is perhaps the only Work of which the End is the natural Result of the Beginning; and the concluding Sentence such as we might expect from the Introductory Paragraph" (p. 1); her parallel opinion at the end (quoted in full above in Chapter One) praises the book's "Excellence of Intention, . . . Elegance of Diction . . . & Sublime Expression." After the first paragraph, she makes the conventional comparison of Rasselas with Voltaire's Candide, which coincidentally appeared in the same year: "It was very observable at the Time—very observable indeed, that Rasselas & Candide should have come into the World together, inculcating precisely the Same particular Opinions of human Life—'Life with all its

Circles vain'—One, in the gross Terms of coarse Buffoonery & bitter ridicule,—one with Elaborate Elegance of Diction, & Sublimity Scarcely Surpass'd by Oriental Language[.] They are indeed acknowleged les Chefs D'Oeuvres of Johnson & Voltaire[.]" She also compares parts of *Rasselas* to other works by Johnson, as when she observes that the ideas in a page-long reflection upon pilgrimage were to be reiterated in a later book: "These Sentiments recur in Johnson's Journey to the Hebrides, as rising in his Mind at the Contemplation of the Island called Iona or Icolmkill; from thence they are recollected And quoted perpetually: I suppose because the Mode of Expression is compress'd; & fastens its Form more firmly on the Memory. Gold itself will not bear too great Expansion, . . . & with Regard to Style of Composition, he who wishes to please, must be diffuse; . . . but to be remember'd, he must be concentrated" (p. 44).

To a reader of the twentieth century, a great part of the value of Piozzi's notes is the insight they give into the topics of discussion and modes of thought of early-nineteenth-century Britain. This effect is perhaps most obvious in her critical discussion, as in the note just quoted, from which we learn that readers were still quoting Johnson then, fifty or sixty years after the works had appeared; that they were interested in certain rhetorical effects (the relative merits of brevity and amplification); and that they understood the caricatures or stereotypes of Johnson's fictions to have been also portraits of individuals. But there are other incidental revelations. Piozzi thought it very likely that the world would end "in 1950—or a little more, according to Mr. King's Calculations" (p. 83). The speculative "Dissertation on the Art of Flying" in *Rasselas* draws her out on the recent fad of ballooning: "& now they have learned the Art, & now that they do tower into the Air: . . . What's the Result? Nothing" (p. 24). And we hear old memories, for example when Johnson points out that "he who would fix his condition upon incontestable reasons of preference, must live and die inquiring and deliberating" (p. 65), and Piozzi adds: "So he must—and I remember a Wise Man James Bever by Name, when we were celebrating the Domestic Happiness of our King & Queen about the Year—1767— said he would engage to walk round Ranelagh blindfolded, & catching at the first Young Woman Chance threw into his Arms would pass the next 20 Years with Her as well, as the Man he spoke to would do with the Girl of his most deliberate Choice." The annotated *Rasselas* is valuable from a historical as well as from a biographical perspective, then, since it makes us aware of persons, events, and a *mentalité* or mind-set remote, in many ways, from our own, and adds to our understanding of a major cultural icon.

Finally, Piozzi's *Rasselas* enables us by inference to learn something about reading practices in the period. Although we have to exercise caution whenever we generalize on the basis of few (let alone single) or exceptional examples, all the same reading and writing are social arts—socially conditioned, socially transmitted—and are consequently dependent on sets of shared assumptions and conventions. If Piozzi expected Conway to be able to make sense of her guided tour of *Rasselas*, as of course she did, she had to be able to count on those conventions. Several of her notes expose them quite clearly. They indicate, for instance, that readers of fiction were to be alert critics, not passive receivers of dogma. They should be capable of distinguishing between authorial statements and ideas proper to the characters, as when Rasselas says to Imlac, "since thou art thyself weary of the valley, it is evident that thy former state was better than this," and Piozzi first underlines "evident" and then remarks, "not evident at all,—but the prince might think so" (p. 52); or when Nekayah declares that "Imlac favors not our search, lest we should in time find him mistaken," and she comments approvingly, "That's good; they had learned a little of the World I see" (p. 86). She also questions assertions made in the text, sometimes flatly disagreeing with Johnson's position.

When she does agree, still it is as no passive subject. She takes Johnson's propositions and tests them against her own experience, letting memory cast up appropriate associations. This process of filling in blanks is one that Johnson endeavored to induce in readers through his periodical essays as well as through fictions in prose and verse. In the first chapter, which tells of the delights of the Happy Valley and the custom by which "every year produced new schemes of delight, and new competitors for imprisonment," Piozzi notes, "Philosophers have told us that Extremes meet. & the solitary Grandeur of Alpine Scenery had the same Effect upon my Mind when new, as these fictitious Delights had on the Dancers here described, as Candidates for the Continuity of Pleasure: I thought the first Day too short for my Feelings, & the Second for my Expressions of admiring Praise; but on the Third my Faculties felt Weariness; & on the fourth, I was but too happy to descend from my painful Elevation—" (p. 4).

Perhaps the best—though less showy—displays of the active reader's mind occur in passages in which there is a sequence of short notes. In the following transcription I have recorded Piozzi's notes in square brackets as interruptions of the text; the underlining corresponds to hers. The Princess Nekayah is reflecting on the domestic life of families:

Poverty has, in large cities, very different appearances: it is often concealed in splendour, and often in extravagance. ["Oh, so it is.—"] It is the care of a very great part of mankind to conceal their indigence from the rest; they support themselves by temporary expedients, and every day is lost in contriving for the morrow. ["Oh admirably said, and wisely discover'd."]

This, however, was an evil, which though frequent, I saw with less pain, because I could relieve it. Yet some have refused my bounties; more offended with my quickness to detect their wants, than pleased with my readiness to succour them: and others, whose exigencies compelled them to admit my kindness, have never been able to forgive their benefactress. ["how often have we seen and felt this!!"] Many, however, have been sincerely grateful, without the ostentation of gratitude, or the hope of other favors. ["I know not how Many; but in fourscore years, I think I have found One."] (pp. 91–92)

An excellent annotator, Piozzi can here be seen to be following the words of the text closely and responding impulsively, as though listening to the author and urging him on. Literary appreciation happens concurrently with intellectual appreciation: hence "Oh admirably said," and the underlining of parallel words in the second paragraph. The number of notes, brief though they may be, is a sign of the intensity of her involvement. In fact, since shorter notes entail less distraction from the text, they may be a more certain proof of engagement than longer, more reflective and wandering ones. But over and above these typical features, we become aware of a personal subtext. Piozzi is writing for Conway, who knows her history and her circumstances. She knows about wealth and the show of wealth; her bounty, like Nekayah's, has been resented; and Conway is praised for being "sincerely grateful." The complexities of motivation outlined in Chapter Three are well represented by this annotated *Rasselas*.

On the face of it, Rupert Brooke's copy of Raymond Macdonald Alden's *Introduction to Poetry for Students of English Literature* (1909) is one of the least appealing items in the whole list of annotated books. Written as a handbook to follow the American professor's anthology *English Verse* (1903), it comes in institutional blue cloth boards and rather mean octavo pages. In six remorselessly thorough chapters, it covers the "Definitions and Origins" of poetry; "Classes or Kinds"; "Internal" and "External" bases; "English Metres"; and "Rime and Stanza Forms." The marginalia written by Brooke, who acquired the work in 1909 when he was twenty-one (he wrote his name and the year on a flyleaf), are a student's notes not unlike those in the copy of *Situation Ethics* described in the Introduction. Many passages are marked for special attention; some get a word or two expressing doubt or disagreement; a dozen or so elicit longer comments, none of them much out of the ordinary. The notes were clearly made on a single reading, and for the reader's own purposes—not, like the notes in Piozzi's *Rasselas*, upon an exceptionally informed rereading, nor with any effort to charm and entertain a friend. All the marks are casually formed, and in pencil. (They make it look as though Brooke might have been reading in bed, at any rate not at a desk or table where he would have been able to write firmly. That impression would be consistent with his habits: a friend remembered him a year or so later in a canoe, where "he would keep the paddle going with his left hand, and with the other make pencil notes on Webster, steadying the text against his knee.")[7] This woeful object would hardly seem to be worth a second look but for its association with the mythic Brooke, and even that distinction it shares with other annotated books that might seem naturally to have a stronger claim: his Shakespeare, for instance, and his Keats, both of them now in the same collection at King's College, Cambridge. But as it turns out, this unpromising volume has quite a lot to offer.

The first pleasant surprise is the ugly duckling itself. Marginalia are responsive, so it is helpful to understand what it is they are responding to. Alden frames his technical analysis of verse composition with a stirring philosophical defense of poetry as "the greatest of the arts" (p. 6). Conveniently organized and clearly written, his book constitutes an anthology of poetic theory and practice, for it includes extensive quotations from the writings of scholars and of poets from Chaucer right through to Yeats. It continued to be reprinted regularly well into the 1930s. (E. E. Cummings, later e. e. cummings, annotated a copy of the same edition that Brooke owned, probably just a few years later.)[8] The selection is up to date and remarkably eclectic; Alden draws on the work of Continental theorists like Friedrich von Schlegel and on American as well as British poets. In the quarrel between the quantity party and the accent party—those who argued that English verse should be analyzed on the basis of the number and length of syllables by analogy with Latin verse, and those who maintained that English was different and depended simply on the number of stresses in a line—he takes the commonsense and conciliatory position that both factors must be taken into account, for rhythm requires regular time intervals, marked by stresses (p. 156). On the vexed question of metrical innovation, however, his position is ultimately conservative: he maintains that English verse has always relied on a small set of tested and proven forms (p. 322), and in opposition to the free-verse movement he quotes a French critic who calls free verse "anti-social art" (p. 349).

Brooke came well prepared and well disposed to the reading of Alden's *Introduction*. Even as a schoolboy, he had followed the metrical experiments and aesthetic extremism of Swinburne and other "Decadent" poets. His papers at King's, where he read Classics, include many samples of metrical analysis. A letter written as early as 1905, when he was seventeen, argues "that a dodecasyllabic-lined sonnet can give sound effects that a decasyllabic ditto can't." And although he could make fun of his enthusiasm and even affect ennui ("The words *Anapaestic dimeter acatalectics* that fired me once, now leave me cold"), the passion certainly persisted, reinforced by his academic training, his ever deepening acquaintance with English literature, and his effort with his own poems. In January 1909 he explained to a friend the weakness of somebody else's verse: "I like her mind better than her metre. . . . Perhaps she wanted to write blank verse. If the latter is true she is very bold. There's the dear old rule that you begin de dúm de dúm or dum de de dum. A few (myself and Mr Phillipps), beginning rather hurriedly dúm de dúm, always put in a little 'de' later, somewhere, in the line. If we remember. But merely dúm de dúm de dúm de dúm de dúm (de). Oh! but its unusual! Chaucer a few times, Beaumont & Fletcher five times a play, Keats once. . . ."[9]

When he came upon Alden, soon after, his marks and notes show exactly what he was interested in. He used lines down or across the margin, check marks, and crosses—long or short—for passages he particularly approved; question marks to register doubt; and exclamation marks or verbal comments for disagreement. There are just over fifty marked passages without notes, and just under fifty with notes—about half of them very brief notes, and none of them very long. He calls Alden "fool" (p. 77) and "idiot" (p. 202), but such scornful remarks generally appear in sections on the drama, which was Brooke's forte and not Alden's. On balance Brooke seems to have liked the book, and his skeptical or contradictory notes are written in Blake's spirit (in Lavater) of friendly correction, not out of hostility. He catches Alden up, for instance, for referring to "the long syllable *ironed*" (Alden's italics, Brooke's underlining) when the word seems to him obviously to have more than one syllable ("oh! oh!" p. 182),[10] and out of hundreds of analyses of meter differs with him about three or four others also (pp. 169, 184, 255, 256). When Alden proposes that the "strange pleasure" that we take in tragedy arises from the stirring of deep emotions "provided one's own personality is not too intimately touched," and instances the pleasurable experience of "funeral pomp and the music of dirges," Brooke teasingly adds, "At the death of one's friend's friends, for instance" (p. 87). But what the marginalia unmistakably indicate is that he really *was* interested. He read the book through, and he read it attentively.

Although Brooke's notes are scattered throughout the volume, the most heavily annotated areas are those that deal with tragedy (pp. 85–90), the relation of poetry to beauty and truth (pp. 112–22), verse rhythm (pp. 164–90, in a chapter that Alden elsewhere identifies as "the most individual portion of this book"), and the pause and caesura (pp. 258–64). Since Brooke uses the marginal line, cross, and so on to mark attention, with further signals when he disapproves, it is possible to make out which of the ideas put forward by Alden he could endorse. His markings support, in the first place, idealistic statements about poetry as having special powers both for creating beauty ("a more perfect beauty than the world can show," marked p. 113) and for representing common or universal human feelings. Extracts from two long passages that he marked, quotations from Professors Walter Raleigh and F. B. Gummere, respectively, convey the general exaltation of the art that informs the book:

> It is they [poets] who preserve language from pollution and enrich it with new powers. They redeem words from degradation by a single noble employment. They establish a tradition that bridges over the treacherous currents and quicksands of time and fashion. . . . This, then, is why rhythm will not be banished from poetry so long as poetry shall remain emotional utterance; for rhythm is not only sign and warrant of a social contract stronger, deeper, vaster, than any fancied by Rousseau, but it is the expression of a human sense more keen even than the fear of devils and the love of gods—the sense and sympathy of kind. (pp. 138, 205)

And though Brooke might challenge Alden's pronouncements about the drama, he evidently accepted this statement about tragedy by H. B. Alexander, which he marked, singling out the word "promise" especially: "In beauty there is an eternity of promise which death cannot subdue, and the strange calm which succeeds the spectacle of tragic dissolution comes not from a sense of defeat but from awe of the fulfil-ment" (p. 91).

Other signs of approval by Brooke are associated with criticism of particular works or writers, and with specific issues, theoretical or tech-nical, such as the fancy-imagination distinction (p. 112), personification (p. 147), alliteration (p. 209), the regularity of trochaic verse (p. 281), or end-pauses (p. 262). Some of these are really practical tips, as with an observation and accompanying footnote that Brooke marked on page 139. The main text reads, "The chosen word of the poet is first of all the word which will recall the most vivid image to the imaginary impres-sions of the senses," and the footnote adds, "So Grant Allen points out, in his *Physiological Aesthetics,* that the poets show a preference for the more vivid color-words, such as *crimson, azure,* and the like." In the quite heavily marked section on rhythm, Brooke noted in particular a Wildean quotation from T. S. Omond: "The perfection of music lies in absolute accordance with time, that of verse in continual slight depar-tures from time. This is why no musical representations of verse ever seem satisfactory" (p. 193). A less epigrammatic statement by Alden himself on the subject elicits a question: "Two streams of sound pass constantly through the inner ear of one who understands or appreciates the rhythm of our verse: one, never actually found in the real sounds which are uttered, is the absolute rhythm, its equal time-intervals mov-ing on in infinitely perfect progression; the other, represented by the ac-tual movement of the verse, is constantly shifting by quickening, retard-ing, strengthening or weakening its sounds, yet always hovers along the line of the perfect rhythm, and bids the ear refer to that perfect rhythm the succession of its pulsations" (p. 188). "Yet does this absolute rhythm 'pass constantly through the inner ear?'" asks Brooke, either wondering about the purported experience of sensitive readers, or suspecting a con-tradiction in the statement—if the absolute rhythm is "never actually found" in real sounds, can it be said to pass even through the inner ear? Most of Brooke's notes exhibit this level of alertness. On several other occasions he justifiably complains of obscurity or careless reasoning (for example, pp. 7, 88, 117, 249).

The final category for Brooke's notes is the celebration of metrical language as opposed to prose and free verse. Here again the rhapsodies of the theorists are balanced by close analysis of actual examples in Brooke's selection from the text (such as pp. 15, 22–23, 194, 196, 204). On the rhapsodic side, Brooke marked a page in which Alden speculates that tragedy may be more bearable in verse than in prose: "This, we saw, might be regarded as partly due to the soothing and controlling effect of the regular stresses of the metre; it is still more clearly due to the fact that the metrical form lifts the material above the plane of crude reality. It not only softens and beautifies it, by imposing upon it the rhythmical form, but seems also in a sense to show its universal significance" (p. 200). He also took note of Alden's account of why and how changes of measure within a poem—a hotly argued topic at the time—sometimes worked and sometimes didn't (p. 251). He shows that he has grasped Alden's point, and contributes something of his own to it, when Alden explains that iambic verse is generally more successful than trochaic because the "line of division" falls "between rhythmical units" in iambic but "between words" in trochaic verse (p. 265). Brooke agrees and takes the argument a step further: "because it <u>emphasises</u> the metre less." This is a case in which theory and practice come together, but Brooke's comment on the next sentence is altogether practical. Alden expresses puzzlement about the overwhelming success of iambic verse—"Neither of these reasons would explain the preference for iambic to anapestic metres, and this does not seem to be a preference natural to the language"—and Brooke offers the simple explanation that "It's the difficulty of finding enough pairs of unstressed syllables." In summary, Brooke's marginalia to Alden exhibit open-minded and constructive reading. Brooke both takes and gives: he takes from the book some new ideas and some striking reformulations of old ones; he tests his knowledge against Alden's and sharpens up his own position; he offers some improvements. These are exemplary student marginalia.

Brooke's notes on Alden come to appear even more remarkable when we consider the circumstances under which they were written. Brooke probably read and marked this book early in April 1909, over the Easter break. It was a critical period for him: he was to take his examinations in May and he should have been cramming Classics. But he had willfully neglected his official subject and been busy with many other things. This is an old story, of course, but Brooke had his own version of it. He was a member of at least two select societies, the Cambridge "Apostles" and the "Carbonari" (which latter group he had formed, with a friend, at King's). He had joined the Fabian Society a year earlier and would be elected president of the Cambridge Fabians in the autumn. As a founding member of the Marlowe Dramatic Society, he had been heavily involved in their occasional productions. Since 1907 he had been writing poems and reviews for the *Cambridge Review;* he was about to be invited to take over as editor.[11]

Alden's *Introduction to Poetry* may have come his way, in fact, through the *Cambridge Review.* An embossed stamp on the title page reading "presentation copy" indicates that he got it free somehow, and the most likely source is the *Review* office. The author's preface is dated January 1909, so the book would have been hot off the press and only the reviews would have had access to advance copies. At the same time it is clear from the nature of the marginalia that he did not mark it up with a mind to reviewing. Neither the *Cambridge Review* nor the *Times Literary Supplement* ever did review Alden. As a textbook, and on a technical subject, and with an American author, it was not likely to have high priority. Brooke was as automatically and unselfconsciously anti-American as most of his contemporaries were. (The second sentence of his review of Ezra Pound's collection *Personae* reads, "He is—do not his name and his verse betray it?—a young American; and he writes *vers libre*.")[12] It is all the more creditable that he gave Alden's book such a serious reading. At some level, of course, it was grist to the mill: when Brooke did come to review a book on verse forms, Volume 3 of George Saintsbury's monumental *History of English Prosody* (1910) in 1911, he could do it with great assurance, judiciously observing, for example, "He is right in saying that a foot is not *necessarily* marked by accent; at least any actual foot is not. But he does not give sufficient importance to the 'norm' of the line and foot which has to exist in the reader's mind, and to which the actual verses have to conform within certain limits."[13]

But the annotation of Alden was not provoked by the immediate responsibility of reviewing. All the evidence indicates that Brooke read the book by choice and for pleasure—and that's what I find extraordinary about this case. A letter of April 1909 establishes the context—possibly the exact timing, certainly the emotional ambience—of his reading of Alden:

> I have done no "work" for ages: and my tripos is in a few weeks. All
> the old and dreary who control me are infinitely sick. And I am wholly
> radiant. This holidays I fled from my family for long. Part of the while
> I walked through Devon. Always it rained and always I sang. Then
> in a hut by a waterfall on Dartmoor, a strange fat Johnian and I
> "worked" for three weeks. He read—oh! Aristotle, I think! And I read
> the Minority Report of the Poor Law Commission; and books on Me-
> tre (I'm a poet, you know!); and Shakespere! It was a great time.[14]

This letter has to be read in the context of Brooke's relationship to the addressee, Jacques Raverat, and with some allowance for Brooke's attitudinizing. He had an image to protect.[15] But if the calculated frivolity of the letter is at odds with the seriousness of the marginalia, still it supports the impression derived from the notes themselves that for Brooke reading and marking such a book as Alden's was not a task but a labor of love. It suggests also that Brooke associated "books on Metre" with his vocation and hence with his identity. Only I wonder whether he may have slightly mistaken the vocation.

I am not about to argue that Raymond Alden's *Introduction to Poetry* made Brooke into a poet or that it profoundly affected his development as an artist. He does not appear ever to have named Alden in his letters or essays. I doubt that the *Introduction* had much effect on his writing; it was just one book among many. As a poet, Brooke may have picked up some practical tips from it. Very likely it reinforced his bias against radical innovation, but then that was, as it always is, just the current orthodoxy. Alden was not alone in telling him that new forms were not the way to go—though he does that repeatedly, notably in a passage Brooke marked, toward the end of the book:

> In general, recent English poetry is characterized by great freedom
> and ingenuity in the invention and variation of metrical forms, and

there is no reason to doubt that the present century may show as remarkable a development in this direction as the last. But whatever the
new forms of metre, and whether they be imitated from those of other
languages or devised *de novo* for our own, they must conform to the
metrical laws which we have been studying, speaking the rhythmical
language of the English race, or they will remain mere curiosities—
not real interpreters of our feelings and thoughts. (pp. 288–89)

This combination of nationalism and traditionalism suited Brooke well,
at that stage of his life. He might have met the same sort of argument in
the work of the standard English authority on meter before Saintsbury,
T. S. Omond, who addressed the threat of free verse in the person of
Walt Whitman by recalling the success of Brooke's idol Swinburne: "as
yet there is no sign of the old forms being effete. At the very moment
when Whitman was trying to cast them from him, the author of *Atalanta
in Calydon* was preluding a music soon to fill them with new life."[16]
Brooke himself invoked Whitman in his review of Pound a few months
later, praising his "metrical poems," deploring the fact that Pound had
"fallen . . . under the dangerous influence of Whitman," but offering
him "a little quiet reasoning" to correct Whitmanesque tendencies: "For
the truth of the matter is very clear. There are certain extremely valuable
'aesthetic' feelings to be got through literature. These can be got, it is
empirically certain, sometimes through prose, of the ordinary and of
the Whitmanic kind, often and more intensely through poetry, in which
the three elements of thought, words, and metre are employed. That
is the beginning and end of the whole affair."[17] The convictions that
Brooke expresses here go back to his school days and seem never to have
been shaken.

In the spring of 1909, nevertheless, Brooke's career was at a crossroads. He did not win the First that he had hoped for in the May examinations. He and his tutors agreed that he should at that point leave Classics behind and spend his final year concentrating on English literature;
eventually he wrote a dissertation on Elizabethan drama and won a College Fellowship. He moved out of his college rooms to less accessible
lodgings in Grantchester, partly in the hope of cutting back his social ac-

tivity. He declined the editorship of the *Review*, though he continued as an occasional contributor. He restricted his involvement in the theater to attending and reporting. After a year as president of the Fabians, he left that society, too, behind.[18] He saw a volume of his own, *Poems*, published in 1911 and became an advocate for other contemporary poets, notably through his work with Edward Marsh on the first volume of *Georgian Poetry* (1912), which is said to have sold out the first edition of five hundred copies on the day of publication.[19] The vocation he perhaps felt only dimly as he wrote his notes in Alden, but for which the devoted hard work of the next four years fully prepared him, was that of the poet-critic—like Dryden, Johnson, Coleridge, Matthew Arnold, Swinburne, and for that matter Alden and Omond (who also published as poets) before him. As Omond had said, in a declaration that nobody would deny, "English metre is made by poets, not by critics."[20] It falls to critics, however, to analyze and explain not only the workings of meter but also other aspects of the poet's art. A poet who is prepared to be a critic as well is ideally placed to do something for both poetry and criticism. Brooke's marginalia in Alden, slight as they may be, show him ready to take on that role, as do his later essays and reviews. It is a confident and creative critic who can write, as Brooke did of Saintsbury's contribution to the fifth volume of the *Cambridge History of English Literature,* "Professor Saintsbury's chapters among the rest stand out like a hippopotamus in an expanse of mud, clumsy and absurd, but alive." Brooke was pleased with that line.[21]

The moment at which Brooke annotated his copy of Alden was also a turning point for his chosen (double) profession. I have said that his intense interest in Alden's kind of work is unusual; although I have been teaching for a very long time, I have never met an undergraduate who would read a book on meter voluntarily. It seems likely, however, that Brooke's appetite was less unusual in his day than it has become since then. As we know from memoirs like Vera Brittain's wonderful *Testament of Youth* and cultural histories like Paul Fussell's *The Great War and Modern Memory,* the period leading up the First World War was one of widespread participation in poetry, when young people, in particular, regularly chose verse as a means of self-expression. They were excited by poetry and issues around it, even technical ones. Though different parties may have been divided by a preference for one sort over another, they do not seem to have been exclusive—rather the reverse. While he was still in school, Brooke gave a talk on modern (meaning contemporary) poetry partly based, as he acknowledged, on William Archer's catholic study of lesser poets of the 1890s, *Poets of the Younger Generation* (1902).[22] When he and Marsh organized the first volume of *Georgian Poetry*, they invited Pound to contribute; although he could not do so then, he was not unwilling on principle.[23]

The academic study of meter and versification was also booming. Whereas normally one might expect the market to bear a book like Alden's about once in a decade, the field at that time was crowded and controversial. Saintsbury's *Historical Manual of English Prosody*, which came out conveniently in 1910, lists in its short bibliography seventeen books about prosody published between 1900 and 1910, including his own massive three-volume *History;* and those are only the ones he thought "any student" should cover.[24] Obvious reasons for the boom include the popularity of poetry and of poetry writing, the challenge presented by the experimenters of Swinburne's generation, and the rise of the latest, Modernist rebellion. The ferment among poets was echoed in the academy in such a way that in 1907 Omond could declare "that we have as yet no established system of prosody" and that the whole area was at a crossroads: "We may reasonably look with expectation to what the next few years will bring. If the whole truth has not been reached, it is now recognized as attainable."[25] Scholarly critics were debating the merits of opposed systems of notation, speculating about the future of meter, and of course quarreling about method. In their theory wars, Saintsbury stood for English empiricism against various Continental philosophies. Omond and Alden tried to reconcile the two; Brooke, spokesman for a younger generation, seems to have found their approach more congenial than Saintsbury's.

In 1909, poetry's stock was high and experts were in demand. Brooke's *Introduction to Poetry*, capturing that moment, reveals features of the age as well as features of the reader.

One copy of the first edition of James Boswell's *Life of Samuel Johnson* in two quarto volumes (1791) is distinguished from others in the British Library by the catalogue description "COPIOUS MS. NOTES." Boswell's *Life*, in this edition particularly, contains features that have made it practically irresistible to readers of an annotating habit. It is concerned with characters who were at the date of publication living or only recently dead, celebrities known to many in person or through their works. It contains Boswell's own footnotes; printed annotations seem to justify handwritten ones, perhaps on the mimicry principle, perhaps because the single, steady narrative voice is already being interrupted. The account of Johnson is anecdotal (readers want to express opinions about anecdotes, and to add to them) and polemical (Johnson's conversation invites disagreement). The margins are unusually spacious. The work has never gone out of print and annotated copies are common, so it is not surprising that examples of the first edition, over two hundred years old now, should often appear in this state. Nevertheless, the British Library copy with contemporary marginalia has special claims on our attention, and only the fact that the identity of the author is unrecorded can explain our failure to have given it the recognition it deserves.

This copy was acquired by the British Museum from a bookseller, Thomas Rodd, in 1839, along with a few other miscellaneous works, for a total cost of ten pounds.[26] The price of the *Life* alone was fifteen shillings, roughly the going rate. It is interesting that Rodd's catalogue should have presented hostile notes as an attractive feature: "This copy has the margins filled throughout with Manuscript notes severely criticizing the work and the author."[27] In the 1830s, when Johnson's reputation was on the wane, such commentary might appear to be something to relish. The notes are not, in fact, uniformly hostile, but probably it was easier for Rodd to capitalize on their occasional severity than to explain their actual complexity.

The work has been very recently rebound, possibly at the cost of some identifying features, though if there had been bookplates, they would surely have been preserved. Although the binding unluckily makes it difficult to decipher some of the notes written in the inner margins, there are many perfectly accessible notes remaining—perhaps actually thousands of them, virtually all in ink. The annotator, who reveals his gender but not his name, refers to himself as "Scriblerus" and to his notes as scribbles.[28] (His hand is, notwithstanding, reasonably clear, so that the notes are legible, apart from those affected by some light cropping when the work was first bound.) Scriblerus has something to say on almost every page, frequently at more than one point on the page, though he never lets a note run over to the page following. He evidently read the *Life*, or at least dipped into it, more than once: a summary note from the end of his first reading is dated November 1791, but other notes include dates in 1792 and 1797.[29] One set of particularly faded notes appears to belong to the first reading, but they are certainly not the only ones from that period. It would be impossible completely to extricate one layer of annotation from the rest.

It is hard to generalize about the content of these marginalia beyond saying that the notes are extraordinarily diverse and uninhibited. Scriblerus's comments are critical and opinionated, but then the *Life* itself is provocative, and there is every sign that Scriblerus was also appreciative and attempting to be fair. "I am willing to suppose I may mistake," he says, "yet opinion is free, & no man can follow other than his own" (1:91). He likes to cite the authority of Sir Roger de Coverley—with whom, in some ways, he must have identified himself—to endorse the maxim that "Much may be said on both sides!" (e.g., 2:262). He expresses admiration for Johnson ("this good man," 1:69; "this great genius," 2:15), but also, repeatedly, irritation both at the apparent inconsistencies of Johnson's personality and at Boswell's attitude of veneration, which he calls "adoration" or "mania" (1:488, 489). Like other readers, he struggles with the contradictions of the text, breaking out in exasperation, "there is no End of <u>Shewing him</u> ridiculous & <u>Calling him</u> respectable, in the same breath—" (2:305), and commenting generally (on the occasion of Johnson's hilarity over the idea of Bennet Langton's making his will) that he was "a gentleman with beautiful Elements very awkwardly mixd indeed" (1:424).

Scriblerus gives the *Life* an alert and minute examination. At a technical level, he has the confidence to challenge Boswell about certain spellings (such as "shew" and "show," 1:178), and take Johnson to task for failures in the rhymes and measures of his verse (e.g., *The Vanity of Human Wishes*, 1:105). At the famous line in the Letter to Lord Chesterfield, "The shepherd in Virgil grew at last acquainted with Love, and found him a native of the rocks," he responds with vexation, "What does this mean? that Ld. Ch's heart was a Rock?—if so, to me it is very far fetched indeed! What also means the term, <u>love</u>?" (1:142). He objects particularly to Johnson's notorious use of hard words, citing his reputation as Lexiphanes (1:123), playing down the importance of the *Dictionary* (1:98), carping at what appear to be instances of pretentiousness, and praising Johnson when he adopts a plainer style. When Johnson refers to "a stage vehicle," for example, Scriblerus says, "Vulgarly Calld <u>Coach</u>"; when he describes "a gloomy, frigid, ungenial summer," Scriblerus scolds, "why cant you say <u>Cold</u> like the rest of ye world" (2:545, 541). On the other hand, class considerations (to which we shall return) may override principles of style: when Johnson reports that "Mrs. Thrale is big, and fancies that she carries a boy," the comment is, "Would not a Common man, or at least Common gentleman, rather have said here—Mrs. Thrale <u>is breeding</u>, 'and flatters herself with a boy.'—This I submit at least to better Judges" (2:100).

It is not unusual for annotators to spend most of their time raising objections even where, as in this case, the overall estimate is positive. Scriblerus regularly disagrees with Boswell in his estimate of works and characters—Johnson's and others'. Like many of their contemporaries, he thought that where Johnson was concerned, Boswell was simply infatuated. When at one point he finds him registering an opinion contrary to Johnson's, saying, "But I have ever thought somewhat differently" (1:488–89), Scriblerus tartly observes, "and so you have with all your Enthusiasm for this man often before, and yet you deduce nothing from it—still you go on—<u>he</u> is the <u>only</u> man of Sense or the first in the world. for gods sake Mr. B. cease this <u>mania</u> & be your Self." It is clear to him that even from a purely rhetorical point of view, overstatement can be counterproductive: "oh Mr. B. be something <u>nearer</u> to <u>fairness</u> or it will recoil on you, not honour your <u>favoured friend</u>" (1:123); "I maintain, it would <u>equally</u> bear to say, he was an Eminent <u>fool</u>, as <u>Wise Man</u>"

(1:488). He is sharply aware of the biographer's power over reputation, protesting, when Boswell shows Johnson preening himself as "a good humoured fellow" (1:486), "Lord Help us all! What a Solomon have you got!—I beg pardon,—have you MADE!"

In such observations, he speaks for the frustrated and vacillating readers of every generation. He enjoys and admires Boswell's wealth of particulars, but protests at the length and unevenness of the work and is made uneasy by Boswell's indiscretion: "Bozzy, Thou art an absolute Idiot to print this" (2:98); "Oh Bozzy Bozzy! Oh gibble gabble! I say not Ever so—but of these 2 immense Vols. how much is no more than what you might Collect from almost Every Company you fell into?" (2:146); "oh what would this book be without this great anecdote?—whether a hare or a rabit! how greatly said!—" (2:176). In summary, "Mr. Boswell is a frank or a freespoken man and often where I Confess I should not have been equally so. He more than Once through these Sheets Seems what they call to let the Cat out of the bag, when some might have kept Puss tyed up. Ex. gr. here is Dr. Hd. [Huddesford] brought forward as with Principles congenial to his own; (viz: Dr. J.'s;) and we must suppose his historian's. Those Principles it was notorious were fiery Jacobitism. Which in general I think Jacobites have kept to themselves" (1:155).

Over and above these common objections, Scriblerus expresses some views that are—collectively at any rate—distinctively his own. He has quite a lot to say about money, questioning Johnson's handling of subscribers to his edition of Shakespeare and his ability to bargain effectively with the booksellers (1:188, 2:112, 428). He appears puzzled by Boswell's account of Johnson's marriage, wondering why so little is said of it and whether Johnson and his wife were as ill-assorted as Boswell makes out (1:46, 88). He is so repelled by Johnson's harping on the fact that Mrs. Boswell does not like him that he objects to it almost every time it occurs and goes out of his way to counteract it with praise: "this Woman somehow pleases me Wonderfully, all she says and does not Say, do and not do Seems right" (2:428).[30] He defends some of Johnson's intellectual rivals, notably Gibbon, whom he greatly admires (1:478, 2:516); and he speaks up for country life even against Johnson's powerful advocacy of London (2:83).

Scriblerus presents himself as an arbiter of taste and tends to disparage Johnson's judgment in aesthetic matters, for example pouring scorn on the attribution to him of essays on agriculture and architecture: "I should have thought he did not know a field of barley from a field of wheat, any more than he knew one tune from another or a Raphael from his daubing Copyer. Is there any harm in Saying all this when it is to be decided how far & in what degree he was on the whole a man Superior to other men, which we are so much told he was?" (1:168). He is occasionally driven to deplore Johnson's failures in politeness ("Unwarrantable Insolencys," 1:306). In a similar way, he regrets what he sees as lapses of tact on Boswell's part. When Boswell records Johnson as having said, "When Shakespeare has got———— for his rival, and Mrs. Montague for his defender, he is in a poor state indeed," Scriblerus says, "according to my Sense of delicacy the printing all this of a living lady and so deservedly Eminent a one too, is very Extraordinary & Uncommon" (1:319). On the Wilkes dinner, he remarks, "Wilkes now alive certainly— and to read all this—Strange & most Strange to my poor taste & Comprehension Sure Enough" (2:83). And of Wilkes's quip that the oratory of a certain unnamed but celebrated speaker lacks taste as though it had been nourished with potatoes and whiskey, Scriblerus first asks, "is not this Burke," and then later adds, "yes I am clear it is Burke, aye and no bad remark on him—but! how strange in B———ll to insert it here to be read, by Burke!—" (2:391).[31]

The most forceful of such statements appears in his defense of Hester Thrale, a series of notes in which a certain protectiveness toward women, noted earlier, is combined with a confident sense of social decorum. A good example, longer than the notes I have been quoting hitherto but by no means untypical in its length (or in its show of humility), is the response to a discussion that Boswell and Johnson have about Mrs. Thrale's alleged "insolence of wealth" and "conceit of parts" (2:242):

I have read this 3 times, nay have rubd my Eyes—& yet They See
right and I am thunderstruck—why & how, I really cannot exactly
Say. the lady alive and merry to see it as well as me, too!—but this also

comes in with me and my poor small Philosophy compard with all those so much deeper holyer & admirabler, that, what is the footing Johnson stood upon in regard to that woman, be She what She will; why on that of being taken into her house & Protection from even "a Variety of Woe" A house of affluence credit honour Every thing that could be given from Liberality & generosity to real distress of body & soul. What then should HE say to & of this Person, even if she had spit in his face?—God preserve me from Such whether heros or Saints!

It must be apparent from even this small sampling of notes that Scriblerus is hardly a typical reader. Who is he, thus passing judgment on Johnson? Where does he get his assurance? The notes are plentiful and personal enough to suggest some answers. In the first place, Scriblerus is not entirely disinterested. He reveals casually that he has met several members of Johnson's circle—Burke, Langton, Reynolds, Charles Burney, David Garrick, Oliver Goldsmith, Giuseppe Baretti, Joseph Warton—as well as Johnson himself. It distresses him to learn about Goldsmith's self-aggrandizing lies: "new to me & not less Sorrowful!—the man I have seen often & the folly as well as (Oh what are They!) Parts.—but to hear at last of a Confirmed L I A R, and to know how little it told against him with these great & good, it really now in the moment painfully strikes my Mind" (1:225). On the other hand, he is pleased by the account of Reynolds as so absorbed in reading the *Life of Savage* that he found his arm had gone to sleep: "this is a trait of animation I should not have Suspected in that Cool Cautious and Phlegmatic Character. it raises it in my Mind" (1:89). He mentions having asked Johnson, at Dodsley's, how he liked Gray's odes, and on getting a dismissive reply, pressing him: "on which I said surely Sr. they are fine in their way, to which he replyd—then it is in a very bad way" (1:231). Having witnessed what he considered Johnson's rudeness and having had his opinion confirmed by Boswell's narrative, when he comes to read Johnson's letter of 2 September 1784 to Reynolds, which refers to the length of their friendship and the relatively little "cause of complaint on either side," he underlines "cause of" and comments:

If a Votary to the goddess with the bandage on her Eyes (which witness Heaven, I am) I must here Say the 2 monysyllables here Italicd are not unjustly So. Every Reader has seen his Spleen to Reynolds when terribly defending the Use of wine against his Strange Notions about it, to name nothing Else; & I my Self happend to witness his still greater rudeness to Reynolds on another question not a Soul joind him in at Dr. Burneys in a pretty large Company; which nothing but Reynolds' mild forbearance kept from a very disagreeable Altercation. (2:549)

He appears to have been a close contemporary of Johnson's: he caps Boswell's story about visiting the son of Edward Young (the author of *Night Thoughts*) with his own account of having called on the poet himself (2:400), and he is able to confirm testimonies about Pope's sociability from personal experience, saying, "he <u>was</u> a very lively nay talkative man as I know having Seen when a younker at dinner with him, at my Mothers" (2:354).

In one important respect he must have been quite unlike Johnson. The distance between them is evident even in a note that strongly endorses Johnson's observation that "People in general do not willingly read, if they can have any thing else to amuse them": "here I agree with Johnson. Reading seems a force upon Nature, all the days of my youth I almost hated the Sight of a book, nay years of youth. all through School I read none and how I was sufferd to Conduct School Exercises, so as to come away with hardly any latin at all I know not. at Oxford this was openly allowd, & I do not remember looking into a book there from 16 to 18 nor when Sent abroad from 18 to 20—2 or more in Italy rather" (2:453). The difference between them is not what it might seem to be, a matter of learning. If Scriblerus did not read as a young man, he made up for it later. His notes display enough acquaintance with Latin and even with Greek, as well as with English literature, to give his opinions reasonable credibility when he weighs in against Johnson. The difference is class. Scriblerus has been a carefree undergraduate (he mentions the drinking song of another college, in a note to 2:38) and has been to Italy on the Grand Tour. He is well connected. Just as he repeats remarks made by Reynolds or Burke, he may in passing quote Lord Holland or refer to the Countess of Harrington, who was instrumental in securing Johnson's support for Dr. William Dodd, as "my good Cousin the Countess" (2:135). Although he approves of Burke, whom "I have seen pretty often in my life," as "a very good humourd Civil & obliging man," he has to admit that he "had not to me the Carriage manners or perhaps Some of the tastes of what we Call <u>the gentleman</u>" (2:491).

It is perhaps to be expected that a man of the world would wish to minimize the amount of reading he had done, as Scriblerus did in the note above; appeal to the moral standards of the Continent in protest against the infamy attached to adultery (2:264); and defend the country-man's point of view, as he does when Johnson opposes raising the wages of day laborers, saying, "Dr. J——n was not a Country gentleman to see his labourers live with perhaps 6 or 8 mouths beside, on a shilling a day the same as 40 or 50 years ago, prices now doubled and trebled" (2:439).[32] He does not appear, however, to have been an insensitive snob. On reading about Johnson's reaction to the death of the Thrales' only son, for instance, when Johnson and Boswell discuss questions of male succession and the importance of preserving a name, he only hints at the risk of arousing a wrong reaction: "Suppose some one else had said this and some one else had heard it? is it quite sure he might not have laughd instead of Cry:—<u>the Name</u> of Thrale the <u>Brewer</u>" (2:39). For this reason, his views about Johnson's social standing should be of special interest. When Boswell compliments Lord and Lady Lucan for their hospitality but wonders why Johnson was not invited out more often than he was, Scriblerus offers another perspective:

> this Lord's sort of <u>respect</u> was perhaps more <u>truly</u> markd by Mr. B.'s own anecdote of his account of Johnsons both importance and speech in the Character of Executor to Mr. Thrales Will. nay people invited him to dinner to do themselves honour, or perhaps from Curiosity, or from fashion. how many laughd at him even this book tells.—how far All this does honour to his Character, nay how far he merited honour let even this book with all its amazing particlitys, not a little tell also!—Rational manly Men are I believe pretty well agreed as to his

amazing talents and even from thence his still more amazing and Contemptible proud Prejudices. (2:520)

The value of an extensive commentary on the *Life* by an acquaintance of Johnson's who shared his literary interests but had a different social position does not depend on our knowing the precise identity of the writer. As part of the historical record, it adds detail to our understanding of the period and of several significant figures in it.[33] It merits serious study also as a rare example of richly documented reader response, capable of telling us a good deal about how this reader approached a book, as well as about the immediate reception of this particular book. But as it happens, it is possible to ascertain the real name of Scriblerus (and thereby appraise his testimony more effectively) by putting together scattered clues and looking carefully at a group of notes that disclose the circumstances of his writing. Scriblerus's *Life of Johnson* was annotated over a period of several years. Most of the clues that reveal the identity of the annotator do not belong to 1791, because at that time Scriblerus expected that Boswell himself would read his notes before revising the work, and he wanted to preserve his anonymity. (The second edition of the *Life* shows that Boswell did make use of such contributions: in the Advertisement, he effusively expresses gratitude to his club-mate Lord Macartney for his annotations, and he acknowledges the assistance of "an anonymous annotator on my work" in the notes.)[34] So it was not an unreasonable or eccentric undertaking on the part of Scriblerus, though it may have been futile in the end.

As it happens, Scriblerus received the second volume of the *Life* first, and set to work without waiting for the first. The first note in Volume 1, commenting on Boswell's assiduity in recording Johnson's conversation, reads, "those were early days for you Mr. B. for you who are beginning that litterary Career I mean to follow you in.—in truth I have been anticipated by your 2d. Vol. which I first got" (1:2); and there is a later reference to the annotator's having "made most free with" Volume 2 already (1:116). To consider Scriblerus as on terms of friendly rivalry with Boswell—perhaps contemplating some memoirs of his own—and of Boswell as not a merely hypothetical reader considerably alters one's attitude toward the first-generation notes. Knowing that they were purpose-made under the peculiar circumstances of revision makes them appear rhetorically more suspect, more artful, less spontaneous. Scriblerus appeals to Boswell with tempting bits of information: "I happen to be able to tell Mr. B. an anecdote (if supposable he read this,) viz. that the great Burke holds Night Thoughts sovereignly cheap. This happens to be <u>known</u> to this writer" (1:117). He registers protests, as we have seen, for various sorts of indiscretion. He recommends pruning and reorganizing: "really and truly Mr. B. do you not think on more reflection that my idea of putting these passages into Sermons might do no hurt to your next Edition, and in many less foolish Eyes than mine?" (1:363). In the final note to Volume 1, he pleads for a fair hearing, assuring Boswell of his own "very real respect for his talents and his Character" (1:516).

The *Life,* with its first layer of marginalia, does seem to have been delivered as planned. A later note commenting on Johnson's remark about the value of keeping a diary up to date—"it will not be the same a week afterwards"—observes, "tho I say it now after the book is returnd me, let me not omit—<u>admirably said</u>" (1:395). The work must have left its owner's hands after 15 November 1791, and been back in them by July 1792 (1:516, 2:116), judging by dated notes. But given that few of the notes propose specific improvements, and that most of them are critical—an unlovable quality when the proposer is not known—it is not altogether surprising that Boswell appears to have ignored their suggestions. Although he altered the text at a few points criticized by Scriblerus, no revision undoubtedly reflects his influence. When he got the book back, Scriblerus continued to write notes in it, but from then on, as far as I can tell, he did it for his own delight and perhaps because he was in the habit of it.

At least two of the notes written during that first sitting contain coy clues to the identity of Scriblerus. The one that gave me my first positive lead is the one that describes the writer's call on Edward Young: he says he introduced himself "as friend to Hawk[th] I had just had not a little connection with about a certain *Reflections*" (2:400). Young died in 1765, which gives a latest-possible date for the visit. On the assumption that "Hawk[th]" was an abbreviation for "Hawkesworth" meaning John

Hawkesworth, of the *Adventurer* and other literary enterprises, I began to pursue his connection with "a certain *Reflections*." To make a long story short, the pursuit ended in conviction. Other manuscripts in the same hand, in British Library collections, reinforce a conclusion founded on internal evidence.[35] Scriblerus was Fulke Greville (1717–1806), grandson of the fifth Baron Brooke, husband of the author of "A Prayer for Indifference," early patron of Charles Burney, Envoy Extraordinary to Bavaria, and author of *Maxims, Characters, and Reflections*—a work that Hawkesworth sent to Johnson for an opinion in March 1756 without revealing the name of the author.[36] By 1791, however, its authorship was an open secret. Boswell quotes from it under Greville's name as a book "which is entitled to much more praise than it has received"; and Greville anonymously rises to the bait. (The note has suffered from cropping; speculative reconstitution is indicated by square brackets.)

It was & is <u>Caviar to the Multitude</u>[.] from common readers the book could not have any th[ing] they all laughd at it from the seeming discordance of bo[ok] & author, but to Superior readers it has had praise enough & gone through I th[ink] 5 Editions.—the train of thinking however of that book is in many respects not a little different from that of this o[ne] if Mr. B. carefully looks into [it] for <u>That</u> Book loves Truth dearly dearly and most dearly, and It loves (what let B. and Co: Say how far the Same, as this Object & Work) "the Man who is not Passion's Slave" and whom, <u>then</u>, (that is, <u>if</u> I could find him) I would "take to my heart, yea my heart of hearts my hearts Core—Even as I do (<u>not</u>) take Thee my good (not) Horatio[."] (2:507)

Out of context, this note may need some glossing. Greville's notes are laced with references to dramatic literature, English and French, so the allusions to *Hamlet* are not out of place. (Fulke and his wife, Frances, were known for amateur theatricals, especially at their Wiltshire home, Wilbury House.)[37] What is out of place—and with Greville's emphasis on tact, remarkably so—is the ungracious innuendo that Boswell, who is not Horatio, is not a great lover of truth. Although in Greville's notes direct insult is rare, diplomatic compliment common, and real enthusiasm apparent ("Well said Bozzy, take care I dont like your Jokes best," 2:30), this patronizing attitude might understandably have deterred Boswell from taking seriously any of the notes anonymously offered to him in this copy.

The existence of Fulke Greville's annotated copy of the *Life* makes it possible to flesh out what we know of the career of a minor but not negligible figure in literary circles of the second half of the eighteenth century, and especially to clarify his relationship with Boswell and Johnson—a relationship of which they must have been largely unaware.

Most of what was known of Greville until now depended on his connection with the Burneys, and on the image recorded in Fanny Burney's *Memoirs of Doctor Burney* (1832).[38] When they were both young men, Greville's influence was paramount: he took Burney into his fashionable household on the footing of a companion; he bought him out of his indentures with Thomas Arne and then freely released him even from obligations to himself; and he introduced him to new Continental models in music, as well as to English writers and artists (James Harris of Salisbury and John Hawkesworth, notably). For his part, Burney gave away the bride at Greville's clandestine wedding and acted as godfather to the first child, Frances Anne (later Lady Crewe), who became a lifelong friend of the family. Fanny Burney's *Memoirs* portrays Greville as "the finest gentleman about town" when her father first knew him, a member of White's and Brooks's clubs living in a "vortex of high dissipation" that left him at last with a greatly reduced fortune.

The Grevilles spent much time on the Continent, particularly between 1764 and 1770, when he held various diplomatic appointments. After they returned, Greville attempted to recover the three hundred pounds that he had paid for Burney's indentures, Burney refused to pay it back, and they quarreled; but the quarrel was made up about the end of 1773 and the friendship was renewed, though undoubtedly with less warmth than in the early days. In her *Memoirs* (2:101–14), Fanny Burney—Frances Greville's god-daughter—gives an amusing and poignant account of Burney's attempt formally to introduce the Grevilles to Johnson. The meeting did not go well, perhaps because Greville was reluctant to present himself as an author and therefore adopted "his most supercilious air of distant superiority" (2:106–7). No one was prepared to break the ice until, as Gabriel Piozzi sang, Hester Thrale crept up behind him and mockingly imitated his mannerisms. Johnson challenged Greville over his monopoly of the hearth. The party broke up. With this inauspicious beginning, both men striving to shine one way or another, it is no wonder that they did not become friends; but they continued to meet socially.[39]

Greville did not advertise his literary career; in fact, as the Burney *Memoirs* indicates, he was inclined to conceal the fact that he wrote. As a rule he published anonymously, though it is plain that some of his contemporaries knew or suspected his authorship, and a significant exception will be noted shortly. He must have had mixed feelings about writing for publication. As an amateur, he would have hesitated to rank himself with Boswell, let alone with Johnson; and the reviewers were not friendly. Furthermore, his career suffered a long hiatus, and may have appeared to have come to an end, after the publication of the *Maxims* in 1756. The Grevilles were raising five children, representing Britain at foreign courts, supervising their estates, and worrying about money. Although her "Prayer for Indifference" had been greatly praised—Roger Lonsdale calls it "the most famous poem by a woman in the period"—his *Maxims* had been criticized as having foreign airs, so Greville may well have concluded that authorship was not worth the trouble. (Hawkesworth having solicited Johnson's opinion of the *Maxims*—which was lukewarm—forwarded his response to the author; Greville's critique of Boswell might be taken as a sort of repayment in kind.) In 1774 Dr. Burney reports that Greville is "not about to publish anything he now writes."[40]

Frances Greville died in 1789. Even before her death, her husband, by then in his sixties, had ventured into print again with *A Soliloquy in a Thatched Building in a Retired Part of W—— Gardens* (1787) and (an expanded version) *Reflection, a Poem, in Four Cantos* (1790). The reaction to these efforts was not favorable; Greville fought back with *A Letter to the Reviewers of the Monthly Review; from Fulke Greville, Esq. Author of Reflection, a poem in four cantos* (1790).[41] We know from his remark about

Boswell's "litterary Career" that he was hoping for further opportunities at the time that Boswell's *Life* appeared. One of his notes alerts us to another recent composition. Commenting on Boswell's description of the *Dictionary* as the unaided work of one man, et cetera, Greville writes,

> all this about the Dictionary has been said over and over, but not quite so I think latterly, not to say very much the Contrary.—let any one open the book at hazard any where, and if he finds not Something to object to I shd. be not a little surprised. I have done this often to my Self Sometimes to others who have, yes, who have—Stared it is impossible here to particularize any thing but am I quite Singular in this? no, I have up & down heard the Same from many impartial & competent Judges. a new Dictionary is on the anvil, & Mr. Bosll. might even have seen in his Gentlemans Magazine many Critical letters to the proposed Editor Mr. Croft concerning the Work, one this Writer confesses anonymously from himself.
>
> P.S. (92) Mr. Crofts Proposals are now publishd and his account of the present Dictionary may be Seen. (1:98)

Herbert Croft had used the *Gentleman's Magazine* in 1787 to publicize his plan for a new dictionary and invite comments and contributions from readers; his letter elicited a flurry of response in 1787–88. A long letter in two parts, signed "A.B.C.," applauding the proposal, complaining about Johnson, and recommending specific improvements, must be the one Greville acknowledges as his own. Its style and its opinion upon particulars tally with his in the notes to Boswell. It observes that "no man of common intelligence" could open Johnson's *Dictionary* at random "without finding more than one instance of defect of some kind or other"; it takes as a sample to demonstrate Johnson's inadequacies in the realm of common usage terms "related to hunting, shooting, and coursing, and . . . the games of cricket, billiards, and tennis"; it urges the restoration of "-our" spellings in words such as "honour" and "favour," just as Greville does in the annotations.[42]

The last act in the relations between Greville and the Johnson circle is perhaps a typical but a sad one. He sent the annotated volumes to

Boswell. Boswell ignored them. Seeking another outlet, he brought out an anonymous pamphlet of eighty-seven pages, *A Letter to James Boswell, Esq. With Some Remarks on Johnson's Dictionary, and on Language* (1792). The *Monthly Review*, in its notice, is scathing about the failings of the prose: "let not this tiny scribbler again have the presumption to say of Dr. Johnson, 'This is a poor creature,' lest echo from every corner of the temple of criticism should reply—POOR CREATURE!" On the office copy of the *Review*, someone in the know at the time wrote, "By Fulke Greville, Esq.—as appears, without any doubt, from internal evidence."[43] The only recorded copy of the pamphlet itself, now at the Huntington Library, contains copious ms. notes by the author.

T. H. White died of a heart attack in 1964, aged fifty-seven, on board a cruise ship in the Athens harbor of Piraeus. He had just finished a lecture tour in the United States and was giving himself a holiday. A few years before, the musical *Camelot* (1960), based on his Arthurian novels, had brought him secure wealth and fame at once. Up to that point, his life as a professional writer had had the usual contours of chronic poverty offset by occasional windfalls, and chronic isolation relieved by pets and a few loyal old friends. Like others of his kind, White had struggled with alcoholism and despair. *Camelot* did not bring him happiness—he would have been the last to expect that it should. The now-standard biography by Sylvia Townsend Warner appeared in 1967. She had never met him, but she knew his work and had access to private correspondence and diaries from which she was able to quote extensively. Her biography, compassionate without being cloying, must have been quite a relief to his friends. Although Warner appears to have accepted White's own conclusion that the root of his lifelong loneliness was his troubled sexuality, which he blamed on a frigid mother and a severe school system, she chose not to write a sensational psychobiography of the kind that was being produced by the truckload in the late sixties, simply a comprehensive and well-balanced account of the vicissitudes of White's career and personal life.

After White's death, the books from his house in Alderney, in the Channel Islands, went en masse to the Humanities Research Center at the University of Texas in Austin. There are more than four hundred, many of them annotated.[44] Warner makes no reference to these books although she had seen them; there was no need, since she had plenty of material without them. They are a casually assembled set. Some had been with White a long time, others were acquired new as review copies or to meet the needs of a particular literary project. The annotations typically combine personal and professional concerns, so that a book sent for review may contain private observations and memoranda as well as ideas that could be developed in the review. There is an Everyman's Library edition of Sir Thomas Malory's *Morte d'Arthur* in two volumes that fed into *The Once and Future King,* and a battered Victorian copy of Boswell's *Life of Johnson* that became an important source for *The Age of Scandal,* but neither of them looks as though it was marked up purposefully with the later book in mind.

White was a good annotator, receptive and appreciative but also independent in his attitude toward his books. He generally followed conventional usage by marking particular words or passages, jotting down headings, and creating an index, but he was sufficiently sure of himself to choose his own wording, which is often wry or sardonic. On the evidence of selective annotation, he did not always bother to read books through: his copy of Grace and Philip Wharton's *Wits and Beaux of Society,* for example, has notes only in the chapter on Beau Brummell. Like Beckford, he tended to want to keep track especially of things that struck him as funny. Among these books, C. G. Jung's *Two Essays on Analytical Psychology* (1928) stands out as an unlikely candidate for amusement and indeed, although White's notes in this book do include jokes, they are far from being exercises in humorous detachment.

White's copy of *Two Essays* was published in 1928. He also owned Sigmund Freud's *Introductory Lectures on Psycho-Analysis* (1923) and Alfred Adler's *Practice and Theory of Individual Psychology* (1924), which are now in the Austin collection, both of them lightly annotated. He was a rapid reader—a friend describes him as having consumed "about ten books a day, or through the night" in Italy in 1962[45]—and his own small library represents only a fraction of what he covered in the course of a lifetime, but the survival of these three books is already proof of the importance of this kind of literature to him at a certain period in his life.

There is good reason to believe that he read them, and more like them, in his early twenties, certainly before 1932 when he was twenty-six. His sexual life was confused and tormented; he thought he was dangerously abnormal and probably mentally ill. Although some of his friends knew a little about his situation, for one reason or another he does not seem to have been able to talk seriously to them about it, nor did he seek professional help from an analyst until 1935. In the meantime he did what any educated, desperate person would do—he tried to figure it out for himself by reading the latest psychiatric textbooks.

White was born in India and was cared for first by native servants and then by his maternal grandparents in England. At fourteen he was sent in the usual way to boarding school—to Cheltenham, where the tradition of caning made him, as he put it later, "a flagellant," "a paederast," and a sadist. When he was sixteen the papers carried the news of his parents' final battle: his father had sued for restitution of conjugal rights; his mother had successfully countersued for a judicial separation. Today we might be interested in the role of the hard-drinking, violent father in the formation of the son's personality, but that's our bias. In keeping with the attitudes and theories of his own time White believed that it was his mother who had "managed to bitch up my loving women." White went from Cheltenham to Cambridge, where homosexuality (for men) was accepted, if not actually mandatory. During a year's break in Italy, where he went to recover from tuberculosis in 1927–28, he had an unhappy affair, which he at first tried to write about honestly: recast as a novel about heterosexual love, it was published under the pseudonym of James Aston as *First Lesson* in 1932.[46] After graduating from Cambridge, while trying to establish himself as a writer, he had to earn a living somehow, and the route he chose was that of the schoolmaster. For two years, 1930–32, he taught in a prep school at Reigate; in 1932 he was appointed as an English master at Stowe. He was popular with his pupils at Stowe—his feelings and frustrations, whatever they were, firmly kept in check—and although there was a bit of a flurry among the parents when *First Lesson* appeared and the cover of the pseudonym was broken, the headmaster supported him and he stayed until 1936, by which time he was earning enough freelancing to be able to cut loose and live independently.

I believe that White's reading of Jung's *Two Essays* belongs to the Reigate period, or possibly to the year before, when he was finishing at Cambridge and working on a biographical project, "Three Lives," still unpublished. Reigate is the more likely.

White's pencil notes and markings extend only to page 48 of the 280 pages of the book, but there is also a long note on an endpaper (p. +1), referring to text on page 7. Internal evidence indicates that White also glanced at a later page, 202; and after writing his notes he may have settled down and finished the volume. It is clear, however, that such notes as there are were written on a first reading, and that White's attention waned after fifty pages or so.

Jung presents his book as an advance in psychoanalytic theory and practice. He claims to build on the current orthodoxy, the validity of which is taken for granted, that mental illnesses (including homosexuality) are products of conflict between the conscious and the unconscious mind. Jung extends the concept of the unconscious to include a collective unconscious as well as a personal unconscious. He also represents his method of treatment as an improvement upon the opposite but, he says, equally one-sided Freudian and Adlerian systems, which he characterizes as respectively introverted and extraverted. All this has been covered by the point at which White may have stopped reading. Jung goes on to recommend his particular brand of analysis of dreams and fantasies as a means of engaging in dialogue with the unconscious, bringing its contents to light so that they may be "subject to insight and correction" (p. 92). He warns that the unconscious has great power and therefore ought not to "be made a source of social entertainment, or employed in light-hearted therapeutic experiments" (p. 116). His second essay focuses on the relation between the individual and the collective unconscious, and introduces the concepts of anima and animus.

White's notes typically start with the underlining of a word or marking of a passage. He argues with the text. He may well have stopped reading, eventually, because he could see that he and Jung were on a collision course with each other. At the very beginning, he defends medical intervention, as opposed to that of the specialist in psychiatry, from Jung's charge that cold-water cures, electricity, and so on are often a matter "of <u>disreputable</u> artifice, calculated to work upon suggestibility" (p. 2). "Such an artifice," White says, "can only be disreputable if the cure it effects is not permanent. If the cure is permanent, the logic of the means is of no importance." On page 7, Jung dismisses "the so-called trauma-theory, which affirms that the hysterical symptom, and, in so far as symptoms compose maladies, hysteria in general, results from <u>psychic injuries (traumata)</u> of which the impression persists unconsciously for many years." At this stage in his thinking, White must have been an adherent of the despised trauma theory. He underlined the one phrase, wrote a very long note about his own psychic injuries on the back endpaper, and referred to it in the margin with a brief memorandum, "cf my appendix" (his addition to the book, on p. +1). I shall return to the long note in a moment.

On page 12, White was entertained by the account of a young woman, courted by a suitable young man but actually attracted to one of his married friends. By chance, she and the husband were thrown together. "On one occasion they went boating. In a burst of exuberant merriment she suddenly fell overboard. She was not a swimmer and Mr. A. rescued her with great difficulty, pulling her into the boat in a semi-conscious state." White comments, "The young lady seems to have behaved in a very womanly way throughout"; and he makes a note of the page number for his index at the back of the book—"p. 12. The burst of exuberant merriment." On page 19, Jung turns to the debate about methods of treatment: "how can I most quickly and satisfactorily arrive at an understanding of what is happening in the unconscious of the patient?" In order to clear the way for his preference for dream analysis, he discredits the earlier techniques of hypnosis and free association. From the long note (p. +1) it appears that White was accustomed to practice free association. He also speaks up for hypnosis, however, which Jung describes as "primitive and unsatisfactory." "I wish you would explain why" is White's reasonable protest.

But on pages 20–21, he marks a long paragraph outlining Freud's theory of dream analysis, and urges himself, "Read this repeatedly." He was obviously excited by Jung's concise and cogent summary ("the dream . . . is only a façade which conceals the real interior of the house"), and found himself drawn to attempt to improve on it. It is a sign, I think, of the spirit of cooperation in which he wrote the next two notes, that he adopts Jung's image of the house. "Would it be more true to say that in one's dreams one is constantly trying to <u>hide</u>, obliterate or overlay ones essential conflict by imposing a misleading symbolism? By insisting on dreaming of a body as a house one is concealing the body problem in an effort to keep it from being there. I feel sure that this is right. Have psychologists stated this view?" This idea, offered on page 21, is pursued in a longer note on page 23 in the form of a proposed revision to the text. White indicates that the text should be expanded after the comma in the middle of the sentence "As Freud says, dream analysis is the *via regia* to the unconscious." This is his proposed insertion: "A mind has a conflict. It endeavours to suppress it in dreams by imposing a symbolism—e.g. by trying to talk about houses instead of women. The psychoanalyst is presented with this symbolism (dream) and cunningly refuses to accept the mind's sleight of hand. He insists on re-substituting 'woman' for 'house'. Thus he gets down to the real conflict, through the deceitful dream. It is for <u>this</u> reason that" (and here the text would pick up again: dream analysis is the *via regia,* and so on).

There are only two more notes in the text. On page 36, White marks a passage that equates hell with the unconscious, and notes, "Cf. Dante's diagrams with Jung's in the A.B.C. book"—Joan Corrie's *ABC of Jung's Psychology* (1927)—thus making a connection between imaginative literature and the supposed science of psychoanalysis. And on page 48, he marks a speculative passage and puts it in his index ("48 Reason."): "But has it ever been shown, or shall it ever be, that life and destiny harmonize with our human reason—that they, too, are rational? On the contrary, there is good ground for conjecturing that they are irrational, or rather, that in the last resort, their meaning lies beyond human reason." White was prepared to accept this thought, but shortly afterward, faced with diminishing returns, he seems to have lost interest and stopped reading.

Any doubt about White's Freudian allegiances at this time would be dispelled by the remarkable note at the back of the book. He knew it was bound to occupy a lot of space, so he merely marked the place for it on page 7. Apparently he himself traced his troubles to an unresolved Oedipal complex and to a traumatic event of his early childhood. When he was only five, he had been ill with some stomach trouble and the doctor had decreed that he should be taken to England and given nothing but fluids during the voyage. Though his parents obeyed these instructions, he became progressively weaker, until another doctor overruled the first and had him fed solid foods again.[47] The note, which I quote in its entirety, is an exercise in free association alluding to that event. It falls into three parts, the second written as a marginal note to the first (fig. 6).

Conflict—Battle—Bottle. Pissing in a Bottle. Kissing in a bottle, in a B. Bottom (Bum) Rum (this made me laught) Pirates. 15 on d. man's chest. From Rumm to Bokhara one monarch the calif. Tried to write Bokk. Boc. A drink. We keep getting to drinks. Rum and milk. Milk bottle. Milk battle. Rattle. A conflict over milk silk. Sick. I evidently was in trouble before the age of six, for already at that time I tried to die of dysentery. Wine. Dis-entry. De sentry. To die of dis-entry. Failure to enter. Silk. Sick. Six. Beating. Carpets. To enter what? Car—Ker—K? My mother's name was K for Con. Failure to enter Con. What about the B. Bottom. Bum? Failure to materialise (state) here. Stale. Tail ('s tail).

why did I write "laught"?
Laughton
Lost-on
looked on
hooked on
Jews.
Circumcision.
Rum made me circumcised
Milk did.
Liquids did.
My penis was cut because I had liquids. Having liquids results in being cut.
Ostracised.
Dead end.

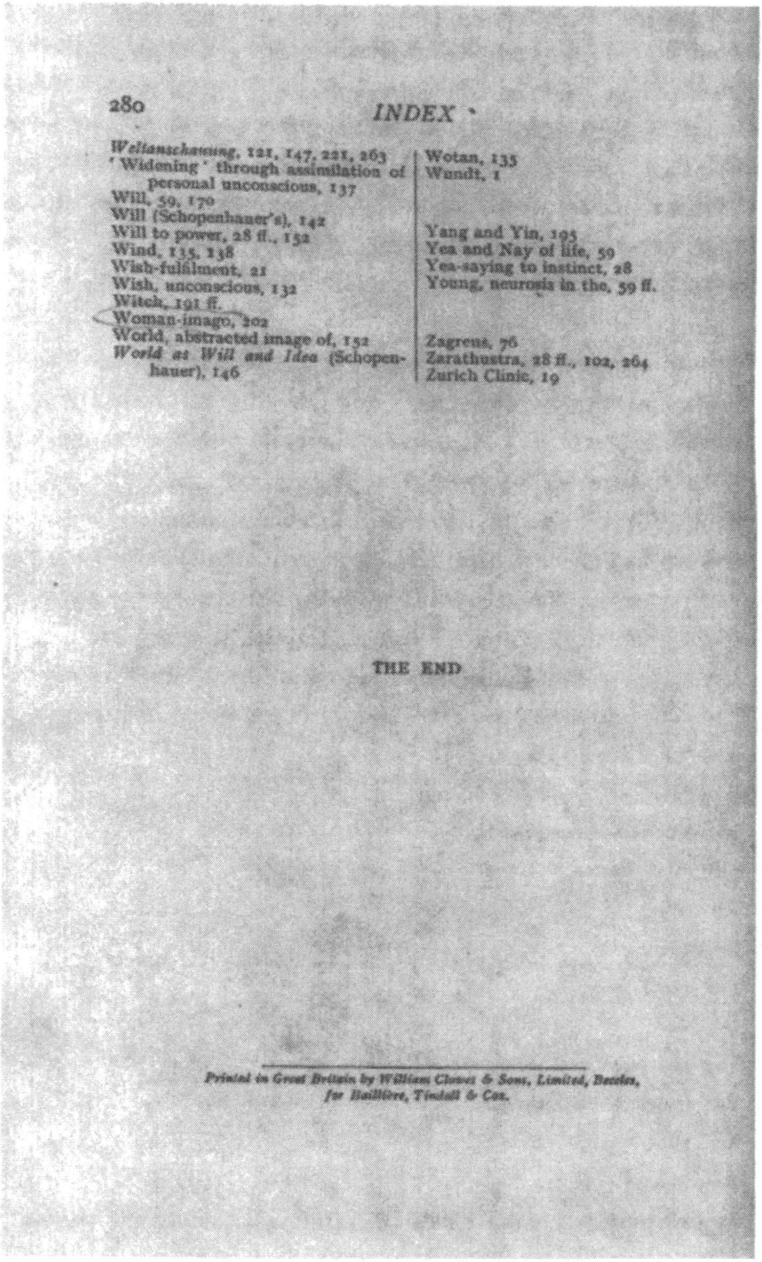

280 *INDEX*

Weltanschauung, 121, 147, 221, 263
'Widening' through assimilation of personal unconscious, 137
Will, 59, 170
Will (Schopenhauer's), 142
Will to power, 28 ff., 152
Wind, 135, 138
Wish-fulfilment, 21
Wish, unconscious, 132
Witch, 191 ff.
Woman-imago, 202
World, abstracted image of, 152
World as Will and Idea (Schopenhauer), 146
Wotan, 135
Wundt, 1
Yang and Yin, 195
Yea and Nay of life, 59
Yea-saying to instinct, 28
Young, neurosis in the, 59 ff.
Zagreus, 76
Zarathustra, 28 ff., 102, 264
Zurich Clinic, 19

THE END

Printed in Great Britain by William Clowes & Sons, Limited, Beccles, for Baillière, Tindall & Cox.

FIG. 6 C. G. Jung, *Two Essays on Analytical Psychology* (1928). Annotations by T. H. White. (Used by permission of David Higham Associates and the Harry Ransom Humanities Research Center, University of Texas at Austin)

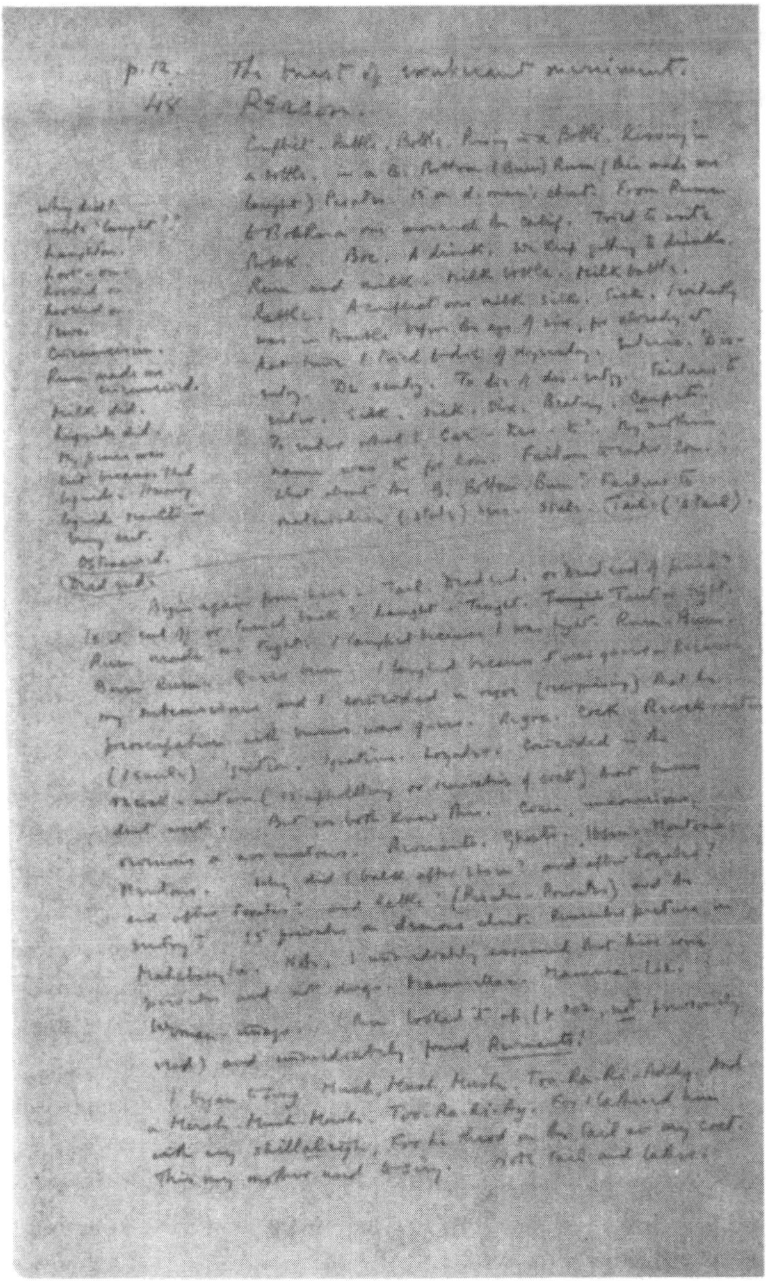

Begin again from here. Tail. Dead end. or Dead end of penis? Is it cut off or turned back? Laught—Taught. Taut or tight. Rum made me tight. I laughed because I was tight. Rum-Bum. Bum Rum. Queer bum. I laughed because it was queer—because my subconscious and I coincided in regoc (recognising) that the preoccupation with bums was queer. Regoc. Cock. Recock-nition. (I smile) Ignition. Ignatius. Loyaler. Coincided in the recock-nition (re-upholstering or renovation of cock) that bums dont work. But we both know this. Come, unconscious, revenons à nos moutons. Revenants. Ghosts. Ibsen. Moutons. Mentons. Why did I balk after Ibsen? and after Loyaler? and after Pirates? and Rattle? (Pirates—Privates) and the sentry? 15 privates on a demon's chest. Remember picture in Mahabaryta. Note: I understandably assumed that these were privates and not dogs. Mammiellar. Mamma-lie. Woman-imago. I then looked it up (p. 202, not previously read) and immediately found Revenants!

I began to sing Mush, Mush, Mush. Too-Ra-Ri-Addy. And a Mush-Mush-Mush. Too-Ra-Ri-Ay. For I lathered him with my shillaleigh. For he throd on the tail of my coat. This my mother used to sing. Note tail and lather.

I can only begin to unravel the connecting threads in this note. It *is* a genuine note, not just an emergency use of blank paper like some of the diaries we have seen written in margins without reference to the text. It constitutes White's response to Jung's rejection of the trauma theory: from what he believes to be his unconscious, White releases, by means of introspection and free association of ideas, residual evidence of his own inner conflict, which has to do with bums (bottoms, tails, dysentery, beating, lathering) and penises (cocks, privates, circumcision), his mother (Con, *mater*ialise, mamma and mammaries) and drinks (milk, bottle, boc, rum). Many of the associations are essentially verbal: "conflict" produces a synonym, "battle," which by the switch of a vowel becomes "bottle." Another small change turns "bottle" into "bottom," which is a genteel word for "bum"; "bum" generates the rhyming word "rum," and that makes White think of pirates, who drink rum, and hence of the famous pirate song in *Treasure Island*, but also of the secondary adjectival meaning, odd or "queer," which had in the twenties the same sexual connotations as it has now. Sound-patterns emerge— "silk / sick / six" for instance—and pass readily from one language to another. The French exhortation *revenons à nos moutons* ("let's come back to our sheep," that is, get down to business) morphs into revenants ("Ghosts") and lies (*mentons*, "let us tell lies"). Some words prompt bookish memories. Stevenson's song, "Fifteen men on the dead man's chest, / Yo-ho-ho and a bottle of rum," is easy, as is the clear reference to Ibsen's *Ghosts*, but I have not been able to trace the phrase "From Rumm to Bokhara one monarch the calif" or to locate the illustrated edition of the Indian epic *Mahabharata* in which White must have encountered an image of a figure with dogs lying on its chest which he at first mistook for breasts. The development of all this dense Joycean wordplay is dynamic in itself, and the dramatic immediacy of seeing it unfold is increased by White's own interruptions, for example his stopping to reflect upon his own reactions ("why did I write 'laught'?"), his turning aside to pursue a word he's just noticed—"woman-imago"—in the printed index, and his recording his own behavior (singing the Irish song).

Taking it slowly and accepting all sorts of associative links, we can begin to make sense of White's initially chaotic-looking note. Is it worth the trouble? Surely it is. White himself chose to preserve it along with the book. It meant something to him. The record of a dip into the contents of his unconscious mind, it acted at the same time as a vindication of his faith in Freud. His triumph over "revenants" indicates that he was pleased to find that the ostensibly random connections of the method of free association led him back repeatedly to the same few elements and confirmed his self-diagnosis. Freud's system and psychoanalytic techniques must at that time have appeared to White to have greater explanatory—and presumably consolatory—power than Jung's. For White, writing marginalia was definitely a form of therapy.

From the point of view of the biographer or biographical critic, a note like this is invaluable for the unusually direct access it provides to the author's thought processes and secret obsessions. Whether they were based on subjective inference or on statements made by White himself in conversation or correspondence, contemporary reports about White's personality had to be filtered through his relations with other people. Here, though he takes Jung as his starting point, he is addressing himself, his "unconscious" or "subconscious" self, in as unguarded a way as he can manage.

For both White and his critic, however, psychological revelation is only part of the story. These marginalia offer insight, no doubt, but insight that is restricted to the terms of one prevailing system. Fortunately they have other, more practical advantages. White may have suffered confusion over his sexuality, but he seems never to have doubted his vocation as a writer. Warner shrewdly observes that "White could scarcely take pen in hand without thinking of a book" (p. 87). Even a note that began in private anguish could be turned to professional account. In August 1928, White had filled eleven pages of a notebook with a plan for a pirate novel provisionally entitled "Skull and Cross Bones, or the World of Play."[48] Between then and August 1932—almost certainly while he was at Reigate in 1930–32—he turned it into a full-length Aston satire about a cruise organized by a mad psychiatrist who recruits a mad crew, who all turn to piracy. Title by then: "Rather Rum."[49] What had intervened between the first germ of the idea and its full development later was White's reading of Jung. As the dormant pirate project influenced the sequence of ideas in White's long note, so the note brought out personal associations and related ideas that could give the pirates life; one conditioned the other.

In thus exploring and exploiting the unconscious, White was reflecting the convictions of his age about the psychology of creativity.[50] The connection between the note and the finished manuscript also exposes the coded character of his fiction: just as First Lesson could be presented to the general public as the history of a frustrated heterosexual love but properly understood by initiates as a homosexual novel, so the high jinks of "Rather Rum" would disclose other levels of meaning to those in the know.

chapter five

Two Profiles

Case studies that present one annotated book in an appropriate historical context, establish the circumstances of annotation, and offer an estimate of the significance of the notes may be interesting in themselves, but historians don't like them much, and they may make even a committed layperson uneasy because they seem not to lead anywhere. Like the objects—the books—themselves, they appear self-contained, complete, and *singular*. How can the evidence of Brooke's *Introduction to Poetry* be used to explain anything else; how can you generalize on the basis of Hester Piozzi's *Rasselas*, let alone of T. H. White's extraordinary Jung? It can be done: the records of specific reading encounters can lead to legitimate historical generalizations. The previous chapter suggests some ways in which they might, and in Chapter Eight I shall be considering the role of marginalia in the new academic field of the history of reading. The present chapter aims to illustrate another way of moving forward from the case of the unique volume by studying annotated books en masse so as to build up a profile—first of an annotator, and then of a book.

The original and literal meaning of "profile" is the outline of something—a human face, a landform, a building. In the verbal "profile" of a public figure or place or institution we expect the outline to represent something substantial; at the same time, we look for a deliberate suppression of detail in the interest of prominent features and repeated patterns. To sketch out the profile of a book or a reader we need, accordingly, a sizeable mass of evidence from which to extract recurrent and characteristic qualities. Coleridge is a natural choice for the exemplary reader, both because of his pivotal place in the history of marginalia in English and because of the scale of the available archive; for the book I have settled on Boswell's *Life of Johnson* as one with a good long history of active readership from 1791 to the present.

Statistics about Coleridge's reading and his habit of annotation are now readily accessible in George Whalley's foreword and introduction to the edition of the *Marginalia,* and through the text of the edition itself, which publishes—in round figures—8,000 of Coleridge's notes from 450 titles (700 volumes) by 325 authors, and records 70 further "lost" books, that is, ones that are certified as having been annotated by him but of which the whereabouts are unknown. Books containing only "marks" of ownership—an autograph or presentation inscription, or passages marked without words—are not included. The range of reading is impressively broad and eclectic. Coleridge can be seen to have annotated books from the whole span of Western civilization and from every period of European publishing history to the time of his death. He annotated books in English, German, Italian, Latin, and Greek, with some excursions into French and Hebrew. He read knowledgeably in the areas of literature, theology, philosophy, science, and politics; he also enjoyed history, biography, and books of travels. Since he never acquired professional qualifications for the church or the university and struggled all his life to earn a living as a writer and occasional lecturer, he had plenty of time and incentive to read widely. Some categories of his reading, however, show more activity than others. A quick survey of the tables of contents of the volumes of the *Marginalia* puts contemporary German philosophy in the lead, with 63 titles, followed by current politics (54), religious controversy (52), and contemporary literature in English (48). The categories could be widened. English literature would be larger if 41 older works were added to the contemporary ones; on the other hand, religious *issues*—recent controversy plus 30 works of biblical scholarship plus 41 classic texts—account for the single largest category overall.

These figures may indicate a need for caution in the profiling project. Impressive, even formidable as the *Marginalia* may be, 52 works of religious controversy and 89 of literature in English are not many for a lifetime, and so we have to consider negative evidence, what is *not* there. Of course the record of reading can never be complete for Coleridge or for any other reader. Undoubtedly he read borrowed books, school textbooks, library books, reference books, periodicals and other ephemera, besides the books in his own library. We have no assurance that he read all the books that he did own, or that he read through all the ones he started. Until he was in his forties, he led a nomadic existence, picking up books as he could, and often having to leave them behind. Hence, in spite of the existence of letters and notebooks with detailed accounts of his reading, and of a large body of works providing internal evidence, it is impossible to reconstruct his reading history exactly.[1]

Up to a point the same holds true of the annotated books that represent a subset of his reading as a whole. Besides the registered "lost books," there were without question others never mentioned: they emerge in the salesrooms now and then. We have to postulate gaps in the record, and have really no way of knowing what kinds of gaps they might be, to what areas of the general literature those missing books might have belonged. Nevertheless, Coleridge's performance as an annotator is a less complicated subject than his history as a reader, and we have reason to believe that the group of just over five hundred books identified in the standard edition of the *Marginalia* includes most—at a guess, 80 percent—of the books that Coleridge annotated. At least we can say that the range of his activity as an annotating reader was not less than we find it there, and the existence of such a large body of writing makes it possible to identify patterns of use. I wish to concentrate on three of these: the biography of Coleridge as an annotator, the physical features typical of his work, and its distinctive style.

The surprising thing about Coleridge's career as a writer of marginalia is that it does not appear to have got off the ground until he was in his thirties. There are books with notes by him written before then, but those notes are invariably brief and sketchy. He did not mean to deface his books and, since he always used notebooks, he had no need to; only occasionally he would write himself a brief memorandum or, as in the case of the Voss cited in Chapter One, leave a warning for a future reader. The "future reader," indeed, is a key factor: virtually if not absolutely all the books annotated by Coleridge in a way that now seems to us characteristically *his* way—that is, with long, discursive comments and arguments—are associated with other readers, usually Coleridge's intimate friends. (This is one of the reasons for believing that most of his marginalia have in fact survived: the friends looked after the books and kept track of them. Coleridge also knew they were special, and made provision for them in his will.)[2]

A breakthrough seems to have occurred in November 1803, when Coleridge was thirty-one. Wordsworth had been reading Shakespeare's sonnets in Coleridge's copy of a set of *The Works of the British Poets,* in which both he and Coleridge's brother-in-law Robert Southey had made manuscript notes. Taking up the Shakespeare volume and coming upon a penciled note of Wordsworth's critical of the sonnets, Coleridge answered with a long note of his own, in ink. Wordsworth's remark was as follows: "These sonnets beginning at 127, to his Mistress, are worse than a puzzle-peg. They are abominably harsh obscure & worthless. The others are for the most part much better, have many fine lines & passages. They are also in places warm with passion. Their chief faults, and heavy ones they are, are sameness, tediousness, quaintness, & elaborate obscurity." Coleridge's response begins,

> With exception of the Sonnets to his Mistress (& even of these the expressions are unjustly harsh) I can by no means subscribe to the above pencil mark of W. Wordsworth; which however, it is my wish, should never be erased. It is *his:* & grievously am I mistaken, & deplorably will Englishmen have degenerated, if the being *his* will not, in times to come, give it a Value, as of a little reverential Relict—the rude mark of his Hand left by the Sweat of Haste in a St Veronica Handkerchief! And Robert Southey! My sweet Hartley! if thou livest, thou wilt not part with this Book without sad necessity & a pang at Heart.[3]

Coleridge's seven-year-old son Hartley was to be christened that day. Anticipating the time when Hartley would inherit the volume, Coleridge went on, in his note, to reflect upon the christening and upon his son's literary education. As an accompaniment to the sonnets of Shakespeare he recommends "the Chapter in Potter's Antiquities on the Greek Lovers," especially Potter's account of the "Theban Band of Brothers" wrongfully (according to Potter and Coleridge) suspected of having harbored sexual desires for one another. Coleridge thus obliquely acquits Shakespeare of having had such feelings, and himself of considering them as anything but the "very worst of all possible *Vices*." (Wordsworth had made no reference to homosexuality.)

This carefully dated note of Coleridge's is exceptionally complex, especially as it bears upon Coleridge's relationship to Wordsworth. Without probing psychological depths, however, and taking it simply as part of the story of his career as a writer of marginalia, it is still striking in a number of ways. This first known expansive note was a response, not to Shakespeare's text directly, but to a note by another reader. It followed the precedent of Wordsworth and Southey whose notes were already present in the volume. Coleridge chose to address it to young Hartley as though he were writing a letter, but he must have foreseen that Wordsworth and Southey were much more likely to read and understand it than Hartley would be for some years to come. Although the ostensible subject is literary evaluation, the motive for writing is transparently personal: Coleridge sought by these means to create or consolidate the attachments that bound them together—himself, Wordsworth, Southey, and Hartley. Finally, the note expresses Coleridge's veneration for Wordsworth and correctly predicts the future value of his friend's hastily scribbled remarks. Surely it crossed his mind that what could happen to Wordsworth's notes could happen to his own, that they would be treasured by a small circle and eventually achieve the recognition of a larger public. That, at any rate, is what came to pass.

In January 1804 Coleridge annotated heavily, in pencil, the first dozen or so pages of a copy of Thomas Malthus's *Essay on the Principle of Population* by way of assistance to Southey, who had to review it.[4] By then he had probably also begun to write brief notes, appreciative and explanatory, in copies of the works of Sir Thomas Browne destined for Sara Hutchinson, Wordsworth's sister-in-law, with whom he was hopelessly in love. On 10 March 1804, on the verge of embarking for Malta with no certainty of return, he used the front flyleaves of one of these volumes to write her a long letter by way of introduction to Browne, and it was this long note, carefully revised, that he chose to publish in *Blackwood's* magazine in 1819—the first sample of the marginalia published under his own authority.[5] (Instead of leaving the books with her, however, he appears to have kept them by him and to have continued the work of annotation off and on over many years.) From his departure in April 1804 until some months after his return in August 1806, there is little evidence of annotating activity, but in the summer of 1807 when he was staying with his old friend Thomas Poole in the country, he cheerfully annotated several of his host's books at their owner's explicit request—and also, accidentally, a book on loan from a Book Society that he had taken for one of Poole's own.[6] After that, it seems, there was no stopping him.

The next landmark is the copy of Samuel Daniel's *Poetical Works* that Coleridge borrowed from Charles Lamb while working as a journalist in London. Lamb must have spoken dismissively of Daniel's poem *The History of the Civil War,* but Coleridge, when he read it through, thought quite well of it, so he annotated it to try to win Lamb over. On the front flyleaves he wrote not one but two letters, a few hours apart, urging Daniel's cause. This is the first of them, written in the form of a letter:

> Dear Charles, I think more highly, far more, of the "Civil Wars," than you seemed to do (on Monday night, Feb. 9th 1808)—the Verse does not teize *me;* and all the while I am reading it, I cannot but fancy a plain England-loving English Country Gentleman, with only some dozen Books in his whole Library, and at a time when a "Mercury" or "Intelligencer" was seen by him once in a month or two, making this his Newspaper & political Bible at the same time / & reading it so often as to store his Memory with its aphorisms. Conceive a good man of that kind . . . & then read this poem assuming in your heart his Char-

acter. . . . Have I injur'd thy Book——? or wilt thou "like it the better therefore?" But I have done as I would gladly be done by——thee, at least.——[7]

Coleridge was in no more hurry in this case than in that of Sara Hutchinson to send the annotated book to its intended recipient. Lamb went in quest of it himself, over a year later, and recovered it at the newspaper office where Coleridge had left it: "I found two other volumes (you had three), the 'Arcadia,' and the 'Daniel,' enriched with manuscript notes. I wish every book I have were so noted. They have thoroughly converted me to relish Daniel, or to say I relish him, for, after all, I believe I did relish him. You well call him sober-minded. Your notes are excellent. Perhaps you've forgot them."[8]

Lamb went on to become the chief publicist of Coleridge's skills as an annotator, his generous response to the fate of his Daniel carrying over into the famous essay "The Two Races of Men" in 1820. And Coleridge from about this time (1808) became a serious writer of marginalia. The pattern of his practice was established in these early efforts: he seldom undertook to annotate a book except with the prospect of sharing it with someone, and the letter-like style of his notes reflects the quality of his relationship with the person for whom they were intended. After the Poole phase and the Lamb phase, he went to live with the Wordsworths and annotated some of their books; after that, some of Southey's. Among the later suppliers of books for annotation were John James Morgan, in whose family Coleridge lived for a few years; Henry Crabb Robinson, a lawyer and Germanist; James Gillman, the surgeon with whom Coleridge lodged from 1816 onward; and Joseph Henry Green, a young surgeon with whom Coleridge undertook a long and fruitful study of German post-Kantian thought. Green is the chief reason for the predominance of contemporary German philosophy in the *Marginalia*.[9]

Of course there are exceptions to the general rule that Coleridge annotated books for the benefit of other, familiar readers. The *Marginalia* demonstrate a spectrum of use, and even when other readers were at the back of his mind Coleridge sometimes forgot about them and wrote impulsively for his own satisfaction, or to challenge the author. A notebook entry of December 1804 acknowledges and analyzes that impulse: "It is often said, that Books are companions—they are so, dear, very dear, Companions! But I often when I read a book that delights me on the whole, feel a pang that the Author is not present—that I cannot *object* to him this & that—express my sympathy & gratitude for this part, & mention some fact that self-evidently oversets a second. Start a doubt about a third—or confirm & carry a fourth thought. At times, I become restless: for my nature is very social."[10] If it is true that Coleridge did not begin to annotate books extensively until he was in his thirties, then the writing of marginalia provided an outlet for the frustration that this observation of his expresses, as well as a way of involving absent friends in the reading process.

Multiple sets of works by Shakespeare and by Robert Leighton, the seventeenth-century archbishop of Glasgow who was enjoying a revival in the early nineteenth century, bear witness to the mixed motives of Coleridge's marginalia. Three of the four extant annotated Shakespeares are associated with the preparation of series of lectures, though two of them belonged to friends—the Morgans and the Gillmans—and also include notes written for them.[11] The first of the Leightons contains some painfully revealing personal notes that seem to have been wrenched from Coleridge by an irresistible impulse—one of them is signed "S. T. C. i.e. Sinful, tormented Culprit"—whereas the second is a distanced critical commentary written for James Gillman and the third a copy marked up for publication as part of a proposed edition of Leighton.[12] These marginalia exhibit a range of attitudes and purposes. And yet in every case there is an audience in view, albeit sometimes a faceless one. Even the first Leighton was not Coleridge's own but had been given to him on loan. He wrote his notes in pencil and could have rubbed them out himself before the book was returned to its owner, William Brame Elwyn; instead, he let Elwyn make the decision, choosing to leave the notes as they stood and adding a tribute to Leighton's spiritual power: "Surely if ever Work not in the sacred Canon might suggest a belief of Inspiration, of something more than human, this it is. When Mr. E. made this assertion, I took it as a hyperbole of affection, but now I subscribe to it seriously, & bless the Hour that introduced me to the knowledge of the evangelical apostolical Archbishop Leighton."[13] Elwyn was himself, it appears, struggling to reform, and Coleridge may have thought his example would be an encouragement to him; at all events, the record of an intensely personal reading was allowed out into the public sphere.

It is worth stressing that in the context of the early nineteenth century Coleridge's practice was not unusual and that his notes certainly were not unwelcome to the owners of the books. Even Robert Southey, who deplored Coleridge's way with books, having a fine collection himself and being particularly fastidious about it—his own marginalia are normally restricted to a tiny discreet "S" in pencil marking noteworthy passages—can in the end be found laboriously overtracing Coleridge's notes in ink "that nothing be lost." Coleridge himself gradually ceased to fear adverse reactions and confidently gave annotated books as presents: a good example is the copy of Richard Field's *Of the Church* inscribed for his son Derwent in 1819. As word got round, even comparative strangers would send books to Coleridge so as to secure his opinion in the form of marginalia, and Coleridge, obliging them, was well aware that the results would circulate. In the case of some new publications— Barry Cornwall's *Dramatic Scenes* and Charles Tennyson Turner's *Sonnets and Fugitive Pieces*, for instance—he knew or suspected that his comments would find their way back to the authors themselves.[14]

This possibility must have made him more guarded in the marginalia than he would otherwise have been. Of Isaac Taylor's anonymously published *Natural History of Enthusiasm* (1829), he scrupulously observed, "The name of the Author of the Natural History of Enthusiasm is unknown to me and unconjectured. It is evidently the work of a mind at once observant and meditative. And should these notes meet the Author's eye, let him be assured that I willingly give to his genius that respect which his intentions without it would secure for him, in the breast of every good man."[15] Actually this Taylor note is slightly suspect, for Coleridge published it himself and the published version is the only one we have, the original having been lost. It is not that there is any reason to doubt its having existed, just that it is very likely that Coleridge revised his words for publication as he had done with Browne earlier. By the time he published his notes about Taylor, he had been deliberately mining the marginalia for a decade or more, extracting good notes from previously annotated volumes and making more notes with possibilities of publication in mind.

The remarks with which Coleridge introduced the Taylor notes in his book *On the Constitution of the Church and State* (1829) are a typical piece of personal myth-making:

> And here . . . I transcribe two or three annotations which I had *penciled*, (for the book was lent to me by a friend who had himself borrowed it) on the margins of a volume, recently published, and entitled, "The Natural History of Enthusiasm." They will, at least, remind some of my old school-fellows of the habit for which I was even then noted: and for others they may serve, as a specimen of the Marginalia, which, if brought together from the various books, my own and those of a score others, would go near to form as bulky a volume as most of those old folios, through which the larger portion of them are dispersed.[16]

It is instructive to see how Coleridge, toward the end of his career, saw himself as an annotator and wanted to be remembered—namely, as having been considerate (the notes were "penciled"), precocious (he did this at school), industrious (his notes would make a bulky volume), popular (a score of friends support his habit), and learned (most of the notes are in old folios, and the use of the Latin term "marginalia" links his work with centuries of dusty scholarship). There is some foundation for all these claims, but Coleridge has also, naturally, left a lot out and embroidered what he chose to put in. He was in the public eye and had been suffering adverse publicity for many years, through reviews and gossip that represented him as dull, indolent, obscure, and immoral.

In self-defense, he kept struggling to reclaim his image. In his autobiography *Biographia Literaria* (1817) he had also emphasized erudition and precocity, taking some liberties with chronology to do so.[17] The *Biographia* opened with a lively account of Coleridge's experience at

Christ's Hospital, the distinguished charity-school founded by Edward VI, thereby establishing the image of the promising schoolboy Coleridge once had been. Lamb, who had entered the school at the same time as Coleridge though in a lower class, had also been writing about it, notably in "Recollections of Christ's Hospital," first published in 1813 and reprinted with this title in Lamb's *Works* in 1818. A month before the "Two Ages" essay, in November 1820, Lamb celebrated the school once more and affectionately reminisced about Coleridge as an "inspired charity-boy" spouting Greek in the cloisters.[18] But Lamb's tributes to Coleridge do not mention annotation as a habit dating from their school days, the physical evidence is against it, and it seems most likely that Coleridge was building upon a sentimental image created by himself and Lamb, and pushing the habit for which he was *then* known, in 1829, back to the days of childhood. The desire to be associated with "old folios" may also be connected with Lamb, who loved old English books and—as we have seen—shared them with his friend. Coleridge was accurate enough in calculating the quantity of his marginalia, but it is not strictly true that most of them are written in old folios; that part of his self-description seems also to be exaggerated for rhetorical effect. (He might simply have been carried away by the momentum of his sentence, which was leading in that direction.)

Coleridge's assessment of himself as an annotator was reinforced by his literary executors, who began shortly after his death to act on his hints and to publish substantial extracts from the marginalia, initially in the last two of the four volumes of *Literary Remains* (where the notes were selected mostly for their bearing on religious issues, since by then Coleridge's orthodoxy was being challenged) and then in separate collections of *Notes and Lectures upon Shakespeare and Some Other Old Poets and Dramatists* (1849), *Notes on English Divines* (1853), and *Notes, Theological, Political and Miscellaneous* (1853). Reprinted in Shedd's American edition of Coleridge's *Complete Works* (1853) and in various later selected editions, they were present—attractively accessible and comparatively informal—as an incentive to other amateur writers in margins throughout the Victorian period. With the waning of his influence in the early years of the twentieth century and the shift of attention toward the newly released notebooks (heralded by a selection, *Anima Poetae,* in 1895) and the letters (the first major edition appearing also in 1895), the marginalia went into limbo until the Bollingen Foundation announced the projected publication of a full-scale scholarly edition of the *Collected Works,* and the *Marginalia,* conceived as a coherent body of work, finally achieved the folio status that Coleridge had foreseen 130 years before.

The expectation of an audience accounts for nearly all the characteristic features, both physical and stylistic, of Coleridge's marginalia. They had to be legible; therefore they are generally written in a clear hand, and in ink (fig. 7). Coleridge may have made a conscious exception for Southey's books, and he certainly did for contemporary German books in which the paper was of such bad quality that ink ran and pencil was more reliable: "the paper retains the Ink but the Ink will not retain the Letters," he grumbled.[19] A free-standing note at the front of the book, such as the one quoted earlier from Lamb's Daniel, would serve as an introduction to the marginalia scattered through the volume as well as to the author of the volume. As for the notes inside, if they were to do justice to an idea and to be more than cryptic memoranda to the annotator alone, they were liable to grow long, and then if they could not be fitted into the margins of one page they would have to be allowed to run over into the next. Though Coleridge often complains about the restricting effect of narrow margins, they do not really seem to have presented a problem once the knot had been cut and the page turned: for example, the warning that "this is a subject delicate and dangerous—at all events, requiring a less scanty space than the margins of these *honestly* printed pages" comes at the end of a note of about 450 words covering the margins of six of the folio pages of Jeremy Taylor's *Polemicall Discourses,* the most heavily annotated of all the surviving annotated books.[20]

A single note from that copy of *Polemicall Discourses* may serve to illustrate the distinctive style of Coleridge's marginalia. It is not one of his showier notes, and its subject, the route to salvation, is not likely to be immediately appealing. It does not have the humor, the intellectual bravado, the dazzling erudition, or the personal revelations that give

No piecing or partial Cause (said *Luther*) approacheth thereunto; For Faith is powerfull continually without ceasing; otherwise, it is no Faith. Therefore what the works are, or of what value, the same they are through the Honor and Power of Faith, which undeniably is the Sun or Sun-beam of this shining.

Melanct. seventh Replie.

In *Austin* (said *Melancthon*) these words (*Sola fide*) excludeth directly the world.

Luthers Answer.

Whether it bee so or no: These words of *Austin* do sufficiently shew, that hee is of our opinion, where hee saith, Well may I bee afraid, but I do not therefore despair: For I think upon and remember the wounds of the Lord. And further, *in Libro Confessionis*, hee saith, Wo bee to the life of that humane Creature (bee it never so good and worthie of praise) that disregardeth God's Mercie.

Hereby (said *Luther*) hee sheweth plainly, that Faith is Active and powerful in the Beginning, Middle, and End, that is, continually. As also the *Psalm* saith, By Thee is forgiveness, &c. Also, *Enter not into judgment with thy servant*, &c.

Melanct. eighth Replie.

Is this saying true, The Righteousness of works is necessarie to Salvation?

Luthers Answer.

No, (said *Luther*) works do not procure nor obtain Salvation, but they are present by and with Faith, which obtaineth Righteousness; as I of necessitie must bee present at my salvation. The opinion of *Sadoleus* may bee this, that faith is a work required by God's Laws, as Love, Obedience, Chastitie, &c. Therefore, hee that believeth hath fulfilled the first part of the Law, and so hath a beginning to Righteousness, but when this beginning is present, then other works are required which are commanded in the Law, which must bee don after and besides Faith.

Hereby wee see (said *Luther*) that *Sadoleus* understandeth nothing in this Case: for if Faith were a commanded work, then his opinion were right, and faith in that sort would regenerate one in the beginning, as other good works would also renew one afterwards.

But wee saie, That Faith is a work of God's Promise, or a gift of the holie Spirit, which indeed is necessarie to the fulfilling of the Law, but it is not obtained by the Law nor by works. But this presented gift (Faith) regenerateth one continually without ceasing; nevertheless, the regenerated person doth new works; but new works do not make a new person. Insomuch now, wee see, that the works of St Paul were not therefore pleasing to God, becaus they were good works, but becaus they were don by *Paul*, who pleased God, which works had not been pleasing to God, if in case *Paul's* person had not been pleasing to God.

Therefore (said *Luther*) wee can attribute to works in themselves no righteousness before God, although they adorn the person accidentally, and make illustrious by certain and sure Recompence, but they justifie not the person: For wee are all justified after one kinde of sort in and by one Christ; wee are altogether acceptable and pleasing according to the person; yet one star excelleth another in brightness, but God loveth no less the star (*Saturnus*) then hee loveth the Sun and Moon.

To conclude, a faithful person is a new Creature, a new Tree. Therefore all these speeches which in the Law are usual, belong not to this Case: As to saie, *A faithful person must do good works*; neither were it rightly spoken, to saie, *The Sun shall shine*; *A good Tree shall bring forth good Fruit*: or, *Three and seven shall bee Ten*, &c. For the Sun shall not shine, but it doth shine by nature unbidden, it is thereunto created. Likewise; A good Tree bringeth forth good fruit without bidding: Three and seven are ten already, and shall not bee &c. Insomuch that wee speak not of what shall bee don, but

X 2 of

FIG. 7 Martin Luther, *Colloquia Mensalia* (1652). Annotations by S. T. Coleridge. (Used by permission of the British Library)

some of his notes their great charm. But it does have other qualities that are even more typical of him. Coleridge's annotations are not the systematic elucidations of an editor or the point-by-point confutations of a polemicist. They emerge and develop unpredictably, taking off with the impetus of a particular phrase or idea but wandering at will thereafter—or so it seems. Here Coleridge is reading through Jeremy Taylor's *Dissuasive from Popery*. The marginalia in the volume make it abundantly clear that he admired Taylor as a man, as a prose stylist, and as a defender of the Church of England and the *Book of Common Prayer* through the turmoil of the Civil War period, while at the same time regretting Taylor's High Church sympathies and the allegiance to the early Fathers of the Church that went with them. He thought Taylor had too much intellectually in common with his Roman Catholic opponents. At a certain point, Taylor is busy refuting the arguments of a Roman Catholic controversialist, John Sergeant, specifically his defense of the Catholic's reliance on Church tradition. Coleridge thinks he is splitting hairs and wasting energy. Taylor says, "When he talks of being infallible, if the notion be applied to his Church, then he means an infallibility, *antecedent, absolute, unconditionate,* such as will not permit the Church to erre." This is Coleridge's response, spelled out over two pages:

> Taylor himself was infected with the Spirit of Casuistry, by which saving Faith is placed in the Understanding, and the moral Act in the outward Deed. How infinitely safer the true *Lutheran* Doctrine, "God can not be mocked." Neither will Truth, as a mere conviction of the Understanding, save, nor Error condemn. To *love* Truth sincerely is spiritually to *have* Truth: and an Error becomes a personal error not by its aberration from Logic or History but so far as the causes of such error are in the Heart, or may be traced back to some antecedent unchristian Wish or Habit. To watch over the secret movements of the Heart, remembering ever how deceitful a thing it is, and that God can not be mocked tho' we may easily dupe ourselves; these as the *Groundwork;* with prayer, study of the Scriptures, and tenderness to all around us, as the *Consequents;* are the Christian's Rule & supersede all books of Casuistry: which latter serve only to harden our feelings and

pollute the imagination. To judge from the Roman Casuists, nay (I mourn to say) from T's own Ductor Dubitantium, one would suppose that a man's points of belief, and smallest determinations of outward conduct, however pure and charitable his intentions and however holy or blameless the inward source of those intentions or convictions in his past & present state of moral Being, were like the performance of an electrical experiment, and blow a man's salvation to atoms from a mere unconscious mistake in the arrangement of the apparatus.—See Livy's account of Tullus Hostilius's experiment to draw Lightning from the Clouds. *Ceremoniis* non rite peractis [because the *ceremonies* were not correctly performed] *Jupiter* enraged shot him dead. Before *God*, our Deeds (which for *him* can have no *value*) gain acceptance, in proportion as they are evolutions of our spiritual Life. He beholds our Deeds in our Principles. For *Men*, our Deeds have *value* as efficient causes, *worth* as symptoms. They infer our Principles from our Deeds. Now as Religion, = the Love of God, can not subsist apart from Charity = the Love of our Neighbor, our conduct must be con-formable to both.[21]

By the time he wrote this, Coleridge was aging, overweight, and chronically ill, but he was still nimble mentally, and in his notes he gives constantly the impression of someone running upstairs taking the steps two at a time. Instead of endorsing or qualifying Taylor's point about the alleged infallibility of the Church, he skips that step and goes on to the next, in which he explains the reason for his objection to Taylor's even stooping to debate such a question. By arguing with the Roman Catholic apologists on their terms, he has in Coleridge's opinion lost sight of much more fundamental issues. Coleridge cites scripture— "God is not mocked" (Galatians 6:7)—as a reminder that outward con-formity cannot be sufficient, and that if Christians have a role to play at all in their salvation it must go deeper than that. Developing these ideas, he jumps a step again and produces a scientific analogy to express his in-dignation; that in turn reminds him of a classical anecdote (the details are a bit muddled but the gist of it is correct), which leads him to contrast the vindictive pagan god with the loving god of Christian faith; and so he ends with a revised version of the proper relation between principles and conduct. Though his response may appear tangential to the text, it is actually a direct confrontation—not with the words of the passage in question, but with the state of mind that underlies them. Though it may appear to wander—what can electrical experiments and the history of Livy have to do with the debate over outward conformity?—it is actually highly focused, every statement working toward the solution of the problem at hand, though in a tentative, exploratory, non-dogmatic way.

Singly or in bulk as the set of notes belonging to a given volume, Coleridge's marginalia in their desultory way dramatize the process of reflective reading. They show the reader moving along without stopping, or with only brief moments of hesitation, until he is arrested by something that makes him take notice, at which point he settles down to deal with it. He is a good-natured, generous reader: his advice to Lamb about adopting the character of the author while reading was based on his own practice, and the irritable expostulations that are perhaps the commonest form of readerly intervention are very rare with him.[22] But he read intently, and where the text recalled him to himself by demonstrating that he and the author were not of one mind, he took the occasion to heart and dealt with it seriously.

These qualities in the marginalia have led to their being taken for spontaneous private utterances, and also for habitual behavior. Coleridge himself encouraged this impression. It would perhaps be more accurate, however, to say that they were not habitual but occasional, not spontaneous but deliberate *representations* of his reading. Coleridge did not invariably annotate as he read. He did it at first for professional purposes or to please his friends, and if it became a settled habit, it was one that crept up on him in middle age. His notes are unusually expansive because they were designed to make sense to other readers, and their desultory and mercurial character arises from their having been mentally addressed, like talk or correspondence, to an absent friend. Coleridge often cast his flyleaf notes as letters, and his marginal notes maintain the stance of the friendly letter writer. If he felt free to move abruptly from theological issues to electrical experiments and then to Livy, without formal transitions, in the note to Jeremy Taylor it was not—or not just—because that was the way he thought, but because the book belonged to Charles Lamb and the note was tacitly addressed to him. Between friends conversation is easy in part because there is so much that need not be said: hence the skipped steps. Lamb would have recognized and appreciated the allusion to Livy without having to have its relevance spelled out for him. To Lamb, furthermore, Coleridge knew he could be himself, earnestly striving to work out a problem of great practical consequence.

Given the circumstances of their composition, it is only to be expected that Coleridge's marginalia should have qualities in common with his celebrated conversation and his letters to friends. All are in a sense responsive and dependent modes: they require the stimulus of another mind. All ascribe high value to originality and sincerity. Coleridge was very good at them. He could take any topic offered by a fellow diner or a correspondent or a book and run with it before an audience; he cultivated the art of being delightfully erratic and unpredictable without losing the thread of discourse. It is a sign of the close proximity of these different forms of expression (the personal essay is another related one) that some of the marginalia were silently absorbed into the *Table Talk* published by his nephew in the year after his death.[23]

Coleridge's marginalia are therefore unlike the marginalia of Aquinas that he mentions in the *Biographia* (1:104). They reflect the standards of the period in which they were written as well as the personality of their author. They could be called *familiar* marginalia, as Cicero's letters home from his place of exile came to be known as letters "to his familiars," familiar letters. Though readers have sometimes complained that the effect of the standard scholarly edition of Coleridge's works is to dehumanize him and turn him into a walking library, the marginalia— bookish though they certainly are—work in the opposite direction, reminding us that books themselves can be used to serve the ends of friendship as well as those of learning and criticism.

A book that demonstrates almost the opposite effect—a book that has been taken for a man—is Boswell's *Life of Johnson,* which readers from the start have "loved, or loved to hate." The strong reactions that Johnson provoked in the press as well as in personal acquaintances in his lifetime were perpetuated afterward in reactions to the *Life*—involuntary tributes to Boswell's success in keeping Johnson from decay. "Had his other friends been as diligent and ardent as I was," Boswell declared, "he might have been almost entirely preserved. As it is, I will venture to say that he will be seen in this work more completely than any man who has ever yet lived."[24]

The key factor in Boswell's success at preservation, as he himself well knew, was the decision to allow Johnson to speak in his own voice through extensive quotations from his writings (especially letters) and carefully dramatized scenes and table-talk. A foreseeable consequence of this method of representation was that there would always be readers who found the impulse to talk back quite irresistible. Fulke Greville, whose marginalia have already been described, was only one of the earliest to do so. In the remainder of this chapter I undertake a profile of other marked and annotated Boswells.

Boswell's *Johnson* presented itself from the beginning as a multifaceted book and a bit of a hybrid—biography, but also history and archive. The full title when it was first published, though the running heads read simply "Life of Johnson," was *The Life of Samuel Johnson, LL.D. comprehending an Account of his Studies and Numerous Works, in Chronological Order; a Series of his Epistolary Correspondence and Conversations with Many Eminent Persons; and Various Original Pieces of his Composition, Never Before Published. The Whole Exhibiting a View of Literature and Literary Men in Great-Britain, for Near Half a Century, during which he Flourished.* Besides the documents, records of conversation, and connecting narrative, Boswell provided ample footnotes to incorporate further documentary evidence. In the revised second and third editions he added yet more, and the process was continued by later editors, starting with Boswell's collaborator Edmond Malone. In 1831, John Wilson Croker notoriously expanded the *Life* not only by increasing the amount of editorial commentary but also by interpolating other writers' accounts of Johnson's life to flesh out areas in which Boswell's records were sketchy. Later rearrangements tended to restore Boswell's text and to subordinate other accounts, but still the book continued to grow with the supplements of new Johnsoniana and increasing quantities of illustration.[25] The net effect of Boswell's plan and procedure, then, was and is a baggy monster of a book in anything from one to ten volumes—a lovable giant or an intimidating ogre, depending on your point of view.

Hoping to find out what marginalia might look like outside the fortresses of special collections, I decided to examine every copy of the *Life of Johnson* that crossed my path as I was engaged in the larger project of research for this book, spreading the net beyond the great rare-book libraries to include undergraduate collections and well-established public and private libraries. The eventual total of 386 copies included 126 editions (many of them really reprints with revised title pages) published between 1791 and 1994: 251 copies in university libraries, 54 in national libraries, 48 in public libraries, and 33 in private libraries. North American collections accounted for 241 copies, and libraries in the British Isles for 145.

Though most of the twentieth-century and many of the mid-to-late nineteenth-century editions were what I think of as career library books—that is, copies bought for the library in the first place, that have never had private owners and that would have been subject to prohibitions about marginalia—most of the earlier ones came by purchase or bequest from private collections and might be expected to contain readers' marks or notes. Predictably, some of the lifetime library books also turned out to have been annotated at some point, but I have to report, disappointing as it is in some ways, that on the whole library users are good citizens and for the most part copies that had always been housed in libraries remain unmarked. Roughly half of the total number contained readers' marks of some kind: 47, signs of ownership only (initials, bookplates, signatures); 72, marks without notes; 72, annotations brief or extensive; and 10, some form or other of extra-illustration, that is to say, portraits or other images supplied by a reader. So 201 could be counted as marked, and the remaining 185 as unmarked or "clean," but only about 40 percent are marked in a substantive way (that is, marked or annotated) and not quite half of those, slightly less than 20 percent, contain discursive marginalia. By comparison with Coleridge's five-hundred-odd titles these are modest results, not statistically significant, and discouraging to the profiler; still, there are lessons to be learned from them.

Individual copies are often preserved for their unique features. About a score of these books have association value, for example presentation copies of the first edition inscribed to Sir Joshua Reynolds (to whom the work was dedicated) and Warren Hastings; the second edition presented by Boswell's daughter Elizabeth to the surgeon who attended Boswell in his last illness; and copies known to have been owned by eminent persons from Boswell's time to our own—Edmond Malone, Hester Piozzi, Leigh Hunt, Thomas Carlyle, G. H. Lewes, Thomas Hardy, J. P. Morgan, C. S. Peirce, Willa Cather, Wallace Stevens, T. H. White, Elizabeth Bishop.[26] Some of these are unmarked or only vestigially marked, but others are valuable for the insight they give into the mind of the annotator.

Leigh Hunt's copy is a case in point; many books survive with his marginalia, and it is possible to see his Boswell as typical among them. Hunt was a heavy marker who used underlining, crosses, exclamation marks, and the rest of the standard armory to isolate passages he found significant in one way or another. These marks appear throughout the ten volumes of his Croker edition of Boswell, extending even into an appendix in the last volume. He freely sprinkled the text and footnotes with brief notes of approval or disapprobation: "Good," "Excellent," "Alas," et cetera. Longer notes are also quite common, and Hunt let them run over from one page to the next. He made the book a repository of information about Johnson from other sources, copying out Holcroft's opinion of Boswell and pasting in some clippings about Johnson from the periodical press; and he annotated the book on more than one reading, occasionally repeating himself. Though the notes appear to have been written for his own amusement as he communed with his books, the way in which he refers to his life and opinions suggests that he must have been conscious also of the likelihood that they would fall into other hands eventually. At some point either Hunt or a later owner overtraced many of his penciled notes to preserve them.

Like other readers, Hunt tested Johnson's opinions against his own and liked to record both agreement and disagreement—declaring the superiority of Thomas Gray to Mark Akenside, for example (6:150). He comments shrewdly on Boswell's interpretation of events, as when Boswell teases Johnson with an account of a Scotsman who speaks as ill of the English as Johnson was inclined to do of the Scots, and who would say of Johnson himself, "Damned rascal! to talk as he does of the Scotch" (6:313). Boswell observes that this report seemed to give Johnson pause; he speculates that it may have been because it "presented his extreme prejudice against the Scotch in a point of view somewhat new to him by the effect of contrast." Hunt underlined "contrast," and commented, "And similarity!—I have no doubt it struck him much;—made him suspect that obloquy was not a whit better thing in one man's mouth than in another's." This sort of comfortable moralizing is characteristic of Hunt's marginalia, which I always seem to feel I ought to like better than I do, since they are generally alert, appreciative, and reflective. Only they do seem glib.

Still more characteristic of Hunt is the response of personal reminiscence, which crops up in the most unlikely places. Of a commonplace little tailpiece in his copy of Abraham Cowley's *Works,* for instance, he says, "It is always delightful to me to meet with this picture of Venus, owing to its having been in some of my school-books" (1:lxviii). Coming upon a character called "examiner Li" in a "Chinese novel" by Yu Chiao Li, he recalls his glory days as editor of the controversial *Examiner* and exclaims, "Myself! by title and name" (1:120). Boswell's *Johnson* contains its share of such notes, for instance Hunt's reaction to the account of Johnson's melancholy in 1729, when he was an undergraduate between terms and suffered, as Boswell says, from "a horrible hypochondria, with perpetual irritation, fretfulness, and impatience; a dejection, gloom, and despair which made existence misery" (1:63). Hunt's note here runs on for four pages, revealing highly personal experiences and opinions (including a view of his time at Coleridge's and Lamb's old school):

I had it myself at the age of 21, not with irritation & fretfulness, but pure gloom & ultra-thoughtfulness,—constant dejection; during which however I could trifle & appear chearful to others. I got rid of it by horseback, as I did also of a beating of the heart. I had the same hypochondria afterwards for four years & a half together. In both cases I have no doubt that indigestion was at the bottom of the disease, aggravated by a timid ultra-temperance. I never practised the latter again, & the far greater part of life has been chearful in the midst of many troubles. I have however not been a great or luxurious feeder, & I have to be chearful upon system as well as inclination. My childhood was very chearful, filled with tenderness; & I had many illnesses during infancy. I think I owe my best health to the constant & temperate regimen of Christ-Hospital. During both my illnesses, the mystery of the universe sorely perplexed me; but I had not one melancholy thought on religion.

To Hunt admirers this sort of confession may be captivating; even to Hunt skeptics it is intriguing to see his analysis of his own case and refreshing to hear an aging man speak up against temperance. As we shall see, Boswell's *Life* provoked personal revelation in other readers besides the rather vain Hunt, so his use of the book can be seen both as individual and as part of a general pattern.

Although readers' notes from any period constitute evidence about the reception and reputation of a given work, the most valuable marginalia from the vantage point of the historian or biographer are normally the earliest, those written by contemporary witnesses. Fulke Greville's copy of Boswell stands out among individual copies annotated by readers who had known Boswell or Johnson or other members of their circle, but at the same time it stands for them all, offering facts or interpretations of events that may be at odds with the text and that supplement it in useful ways. Piozzi's two annotated copies of the *Life* were thought to contain enough substantive evidence in their marginalia to warrant separate publication in 1938.[27] After the marking of Johnsonian dicta with signs of approval or disapproval, the commonest kind of annotation to Boswell is the identification of persons whose names Boswell had been obliged to conceal or suppress; as a general rule, readers closer to the time of publication are in a better position to make accurate identifications than later readers, though of course historical critics may have special claims even at a considerable distance from the events recorded. Some of those contemporaries were like Piozzi in that they enjoyed exceptionally privileged positions in Johnson's life, without having the outlets for publication that were available to her; therefore their memories were entrusted to their books.

One fascinating copy that resembles Greville's in certain ways I should perhaps have disqualified on the ground that its notes are not strictly "marginalia": it contains negligible notes in the text itself but has reading notes keyed to the page numbers of the book at the back of each of its three volumes. These are not notes written on the endpapers but a sort of reading diary written up separately and added to the volumes when they went to be bound or rebound. The unidentified writer of the notes in this second edition (1793) now in the National Library of Scotland was a Lichfield man, twenty years younger than Johnson, who had gone like him to Lichfield Grammar School and then later to Pembroke College in Oxford. He was acquainted with the Garrick family and remembered David Garrick as one of the older boys at school; and he had known Johnson's stepdaughter Lucy Porter for forty years. One of his notes records a chance meeting with Johnson at Lucy Porter's house during Johnson's last visit to Lichfield in 1784, the year of his death: in this tragicomic scene the author presents himself in Boswellian mode fawning on the sick and irritable Johnson and being rebuked for his pains—"I think he said dont Sr talk childishly" (3:+3). Since he has Lucy Porter introduce him as "Mr L," I call him Mr. Lichfield. His copious notes, dated from 1793 with additions as late as 1800, are full of wonderful Lichfield gossip, such as the claim that Mr. Pearson, the much younger clergyman to whom "Lucy the Man-hater" left her estate, had been her "Cicisbeo" (meaning an attentive male companion, without implications of sexual impropriety), and that Johnson in his youth, according to the alderman William Webb, had had a reputation for fighting dogs and "woud conquer almost any Mastiff" saying that the secret was to "keep your eye steadily fixed on the Dogs Eye" (2:+13, 2:+9).[28]

Apart from the colorful testimony of Johnson's contemporaries, one finds incidental anecdotes and striking historical details in marginalia of every period. John Gibson Lockhart's copy of the five-volume Croker edition of 1831, for instance, frequently takes Boswell and Croker up on Scottish lore: Lockhart was Walter Scott's son-in-law and biographer, and an editor of the *Quarterly Review*. To the observation "that Glasgow University had fewer home students since trade increased, as learning was rather incompatible with it," he adds this remark: "It has chanced that I have of late years discovered two of my fellow-students at Glasgow College in the positions of their own fathers from which these worthy persons wd fain have endeavoured to make them rise—one I found a street porter in the town—another a ploughman in the neighborhood. What had they suffered by the experiment? On conversing with the ploughman I perceived great, very great soreness. The porter had become a bottlemad brute. 1834" (2:294).

Lockhart's testimony reflects social concerns of his time and place, but he seems to have kept his reflections to himself. Other annotated copies show readers socializing within the covers of the book. A copy of the first American edition of 1807 contains charming evidence of shared use in the Bradford family, two brothers and a sister writing notes for one another: "This man's [Boswell's] egotism is disgusting" (1:323); "If you should like a translation of this I will send it, Sarah" (1:222); "Do you Sarah approve of this [rising early on the sabbath]?" "Certainly!" (1:239); "Mind that John" (1:348). Then again, since many of these copies circulated in college libraries or public lending libraries, some of them naturally show readers reacting to other readers. In a Harvard copy of the scholarly Birkbeck Hill edition of 1887, typically, one reader was moved to mark Johnson's comment on hedonism—"A man may have a strong reason not to drink wine; and that may be greater than the pleasure" (3:327)—and to gloss it with "see Aristotle Eth. Nich. Book I," to which another reader retorted, "You don't have to brag about taking Phil. A. You aren't Samuel Johnson. L. S. K." Later, following Boswell's defense of Johnson's hobbies (such as pruning a vine, "at which those who may smile, should recollect that there are moments which admit of being soothed only by trifles"), which the Aristotle annotator dismisses as "Bull," L.S.K. bristles again: "The remark of an unobservant mind" (3:398).

Several copies show signs of having been worked on by generations of students, and even mere markings may be eloquent, as in the 1927 Oxford edition still on the shelves of the English Faculty Library at Cambridge, where besides a few headings and comments in several hands, one finds the following passage with penciled underlining and seven vertical lines in the margin: "Talking of education, 'People have now-a-days, (said he,) got <u>a strange opinion</u> that every thing ought to be taught by lectures. Now, I cannot see that lectures can do so much good as <u>reading the books from which the lectures are taken</u>. I know nothing that can be best taught by lectures, except where experiments are to be shown. You might teach chymistry by lectures.—You might teach making of shoes by lectures!'" (1:337). Seven lines in the margin indicate an unusual degree of astonishment and, presumably, agreement in the reader encountering a kindred thought across the centuries. All these are, admittedly, incidental—and not particularly brilliant—comments in unique copies. Is there any point in trying to shake them into patterns and make a profile out of them?

I believe there is. At the very least, it is possible to say that these marked and annotated Boswells conform to and corroborate patterns established by other means. On the evidence of this sample, scholars concerned with general trends in the reception of the *Life* and hence with the posthumous reputations of Boswell and Johnson are likely to find support for their conclusions in the responses of particular readers over the years. They will find Boswell censured for servility, especially in the first half of the nineteenth century, and Johnson loved or hated for his adages and opinions. Anyone tracing the work of a particular annotator, such as Hunt, would be able to compare his Boswell with his other books, and his practice with that of other readers. For those who take an interest in the way readers make use of their books, these Boswells exhibit the full range of familiar practices—subject headings and indexes, extra-illustration, minute correction, sociable exchange, et cetera—and can once again confirm patterns arrived at by wider study. But in addition to the modest reinforcement these copies of the *Life* may provide to histories of the book and reading, and to histories of *this* book, there is value in the way they may provisionally suggest new patterns to watch for. Though the numbers are small, they make a start.

To some book lovers it will appear to be only proof of the depravity of human nature that no physical properties, neither striking beauty nor repellent ugliness, appear to deter the driven annotator. No edition in this survey was spared, neither the spacious pages of the handsome first edition nor the narrow margins of the modern Everyman. The elegant 1826 Oxford English Classics and the cramped one-volume Routledge edition, the nasty double-columned Crokers of the 1840s and deluxe editions like the lavish Napier of 1884, the luxurious Reynolds Edition of 1885, and the fancy Navarre Society production of 1924—all attracted notes or marginal markings sooner or later. On the other hand, considering the scale of the work, a surprising proportion of the total set contained a very small number of notes or marks, sometimes only one or two all together. I can give only a few examples and hardly know how to account for this phenomenon, which runs counter to the prevailing image of the habitual annotator.

A copy of the first edition in the National Library of Scotland has only one real note, the correction of a biblical reference: the angel of the Lord smote in the night not "forty thousand" Assyrians, but "185,000 vide 19 to 2 kings [i.e., 2 Kings 19:35]" (1:370).

In another, in New York, Charlotte Beauclerk or a later owner made a few pencil marks but similarly wrote only one note, to identify "a very celebrated lady . . . then just come to London" as "Hannah More" (2:529).

In a copy of the Dublin edition of 1792 now in the Cambridge University Library I found only two signs of use apart from ownership marks, one the correction of a typo and the other the marking of a single passage about old men having to be governed like children.

There are several penciled marks but only one note—correcting a reference to Laurence Sterne in one of Boswell's footnotes—in a copy of the second edition of 1793 in Austin, Texas; and in their copy of 1824, many marked passages but no notes until the final volume, where there is a sudden flurry of disagreement sparked by a question of medical ethics. Was the reader a doctor? Johnson opposes telling soothing lies to the sick, saying that the truth might "bring his distemper to a crisis, and that may cure him" (5:189). The reader protests, "Dr. Johnson was decidedly wrong in this, the mind of an invalid is not always sufficiently strong enough to learn the whole of such a truth as that, & then you <u>must</u> of course feel yourself the <u>murderer</u> of that man whom with a little more caution you might have preserved—<u>all</u> <u>Medical</u> Men will agree in this."

In a copy of the uninviting one-volume edition of 1848 at the New York Public Library, there is very light underlining in one place only, marking a comment about "illicit commerce between the sexes"; and in an 1867 illustrated edition at Harvard likewise only one marked passage, this time an observation about the status of women—"Women have a great advantage that they may take up with little things, without disgracing themselves" (p. 327).

There is a note to one of Birkbeck Hill's footnotes about Goldsmith's way of working with proof-sheets in the Huntington copy of his standard edition (1887): the reader says, "This was Walter Pater's method" (2:15).

Elizabeth Bishop's Modern Library copy of 1931 contains many marked, checked, and underlined passages to show how the book interested her, but she was moved to words only once, when she observed that a particular paragraph ("Let me apologize," p. 255) "Sounds like a <u>note</u> for Proust."

Copies in which there are either very few marks or very few words are intriguing because they suggest the crossing of an invisible border. Of course it is possible that habitual markers were just passing through, dipping into the *Life,* haphazardly fetching up in Volume 3 or Volume 5 where they left their marks as usual; but it doesn't seem likely. In every case it looks as though readers who had been content to stay out of it for a long time suddenly felt impelled to pitch in. What pushes a hesitant or reluctant annotator over the brink? In the instances cited, there seem to be three motives: adding information or correcting an error, when the annotator has reason to be confident about the correction (Hannah More, Sterne, 2 Kings); taking note of a particularly salient observation that the reader feels strongly about (old men needing governing, women being privileged to deal with trivia, doctors keeping patients in the dark); and recording a personal insight (the links between Goldsmith and Pater or between Boswell and Proust). But there must be an additional criterion of strength of impulse and hence of degree of need for self-expression—a single drive underlying all three motives—when the reader has read so long in silence, and it might be that the clue to that impulse is also to be found in the set of Boswells.

I had been hoping, when I began this survey, that it would provide access to the articulate responses of the lay reader, that touchstone of criticism memorably invoked by Johnson himself when he asserted that "by the common sense of readers uncorrupted with literary prejudices, after all the refinements of subtilty and the dogmatism of learning, must be finally decided all claim to poetical honours."[29] And to a certain extent I found what I had hoped for—the comments of actual readers over a long stretch of time, with some consistent themes emerging. Many readers expressed their vexation about Boswell; several, especially in America, focused their comments on social and political issues about rank and deference. But the common denominator, the one consistent factor in virtually all the notes, is personal applicability. It is not only the one-time note writers who speak up because personal experience requires or authorizes them to do so. All corrections and disagreement display the reader's supposedly superior information or insight. Conversely, passages marked approvingly (such as the observation about women and little things, above) express points at which the reader feels entitled to endorse the author's views and to call upon them as reinforcement for his or her own. The book provides an occasion for the process of construction or monitoring of identity described in Chapter Three. Leigh Hunt's remarks about his own melancholy, the Cambridge student's opinion of lectures, Mr. Lichfield's revelations about Lucy Porter, Lockhart's contact with Glasgow alumni—all these notes designate points at which readers became aware that the subject matter of the book intersected their own lives and their own areas of competence.

A multitude of other notes to Boswell could be cited in the same vein, but I shall offer just a few. The philosopher C. S. Peirce (1839—1914) carefully dated one of the notes that he wrote in a copy that he had been given in 1854 so as to put the weight of many years' experience behind his challenge to Johnson's authority. Johnson contends that men who lay out their own time are bound to have "tedious hours," but Peirce cannot agree: "I never had <u>one</u> tedious hour under such conditions though they have long been usual with me. C. S. P. 1910 Jan 31" (2:127). T. H. White shows a kind of comic rivalry in his comment to one of Boswell's notes about drinking—itself a gloss on the report that Dr. John Campbell boasted of having drunk thirteen bottles of port at a sitting (p. 328). White's claim? "I once drank seven <u>bottles of champagne</u> between breakfast and midnight."

An unknown reader inclined to be sarcastic at Boswell's expense in a British Library copy of the 1829 edition goes to some pains to record a moment of agreement with Johnson's protest "Nay, Sir, how can you talk so? What is <u>climate</u> to happiness? place me in the heart of Asia, should I not be exiled?" This the reader confirms by his own example: "15th Novr on the Nile—how often have I found this realised" (p. 198). And to demonstrate that notes like these, prompted by a sense of personal engagement—almost, it would seem, of personal *responsibility*—are not all matters of great moment, let me end with one from another British Library copy, this time the voluminous ten-volume set of 1835. "A dog will take a small bit of meat as readily as a large, when both are before him," Johnson asserts, illustrating a point (3:97). Surely this is an innocuous statement? No. "He is quite wrong there." Was the reader a seasoned dog-handler? A veterinarian? Readers do not contradict without a conviction that they are entitled to do so, but such conviction will induce even a normally reticent reader to lay pen to paper.

I expected to find some of the more controversial passages in the *Life*—provocative statements about Scots, women, Whigs, and so on—regularly marked or protested against, but the only conspicuously singled-out passage that I am aware of in this set of copies is one that quotes Johnson's observation that the letter "*H* seldom, perhaps never, begins any but the first syllable" of a word, unless it is a compound. This passage I found the object of debate in two copies. A Cambridge University Library copy of the first edition annotated in at least four hands has in the margin at that point a list of words that would appear to refute Johnson's statement: "Shepherd | Cowherd | Abhor | Behave | Uphold | Exhaust" (1:166). Then a note by a later reader remarks, "N. B. All but one of these are <u>compound</u> words where h begins ye <u>first</u> syllable of ye simple word." Similarly, a copy of the eighth edition of 1816 at Victoria College in the University of Toronto, annotated by three or four hands, notes at that point—first underlining the "h" in "perhaps"—"An instance of it in his very assertion." In this edition the editor (Malone) had got involved in the dispute himself, and another reader marks his footnote ("sometimes . . . in words compounded, as *block-head*") with an approving "Good" (1:281).

What leads readers to ignore matters of generally acknowledged importance like politics and religion in favor of principles of language and the eating habits of dogs? The marked and annotated Boswells frustrate expectation but in a way that reveals the limitations of expectation and in fact vindicates the experiment. Boswell's alert, annotating readers respond to topics that touch them personally. Their selections of passages for marking and comment tend, in consequence, to be individual and idiosyncratic. If it seems perverse to say that idiosyncrasy constitutes a pattern, it must at least be acknowledged that on the evidence of these annotated copies of the *Life of Johnson,* Boswell's readers were looking for help with their own lives and were most struck by those places in which there was something at stake for them personally. If this is not the natural attitude of all "readers uncorrupted with literary prejudices," still it seems to have been consistently the main concern of readers of this great biography over two hundred years. Their collective profile can only be a group portrait of individuals.

chapter six

BOOKS FOR FANATICS

"She picks up the notebook that lies on the small table beside his bed. It is the book he brought with him through the fire—a copy of *The Histories* by Herodotus that he has added to, cutting and gluing in pages from other books or writing in his own observations—so they all are cradled within the text of Herodotus."[1]

The English patient's "notebook," elsewhere called his "common-place book," his "journal," and his "holy book," is a particularly fine fictional example of the kind of artifact that is the subject of this chapter: the book that has been chosen to protect and preserve the treasures of the owner's spiritual life. If I call such things "books for fanatics," it is with neither moralistic nor frivolous intent, but trusting that "fanatic" may be used neutrally and even admiringly to describe someone driven by intense, obsessive interest, the sort of passion that brings life into sharp focus. The truth of the matter is that no better word presents itself for such owners and such use; for the object itself I am still more at a loss. In the course of this chapter I shall be introducing terms that seem just about right for certain cases, but none that is adequate to the set as a whole. Among those rejected are fetish, icon, talisman, portfolio, album, scrapbook, and shrine. It might be that we need a new word altogether: bibliofile, perhaps, or BEPU—Book Enhanced for Personal Use. Or we may choose to adopt different names on separate occasions, as Michael Ondaatje does in *The English Patient,* to emphasize one aspect or another of a multi-purpose object.[2]

The enhanced Herodotus plays so central a role in *The English Patient* that the author was prepared to take risks for its sake. Readers of the late twentieth century apply certain standards of probability to even the most romantic narratives, and the image of a man escaping from a blazing plane in the desert, naked except for a leather helmet all aflame, but clutching a copy of the *Histories* of Herodotus, is a bit of a stretch for them. By the end of the novel, when the sapper Kip foresees that "they will bury everything except the book" (p. 286), its importance is well established, and bringing it through the fire seems a natural thing to have done, but early on it courts incredulity and ridicule. What is the Herodotus for? The English patient (actually a polymathic Hungarian, Count Almásy, who had worked for the Germans during World War II) is at first a mystery, for not even the patient himself appears to know who he is.

As his only possession, and one with his writing in it, the book contains clues to his identity—given the novelistic convention about annotated books and the aggravated circumstances in this case, it could be said to *contain* his identity. As a collection of ancient stories about the desert lands in which he is also a traveler, it is "his guidebook, ancient and modern, of supposed lies" (p. 246). Some of Almásy's work with the book is designed to vindicate Herodotus: when he comes upon evidence that lends support to the "supposed lies," he pastes it in. He also supplements the information that Herodotus provides with further facts and later histories—extensive notes about desert winds, for instance, and about the Renaissance in Italy.[3] And in the pages that he doesn't usually bother reading (pages about wars, appropriately), he inserts personal notes in the manner of a diarist: "He bought pale brown cigarette papers and glued them into sections of *The Histories* that recorded wars that were of no interest to him. He wrote down all her arguments against him. Glued into the book—giving himself only the voice of the watcher, the listener, 'he'" (p. 172).

The book goes everywhere with him; he reaches out to touch it in the night. Besides being the repository of his interests and secrets, it had also been an agent in his personal history. It was the source of the story of Candaules and Gyges that Katharine Clifton chose to read at the camp-fire, a story that anticipated and precipitated her affair with Almásy. When he had to leave her injured and immobilized in a cave to go for help, he painted her body according to traditions learned from Herodotus, and in parting he set the book beside her.[4] So the Herodotus fulfills for him several roles at once: it is a physical memento of his love, a journal of private thoughts and feelings, a commonplace book where specialized information can be collected and brought into order, and a notebook for miscellaneous discoveries and observations. Being all these things at once it is more than any one of them and greater than the sum of all; it is "his holy book."

Highly personalized and bizarre as it may seem to be, the Herodotus of *The English Patient* represents a not uncommon phenomenon in the book world. Finding a volume catalogued as having "copious" annotation quickens my pulse because there is always a chance that it will turn out to be just such an encyclopedic compendium. Books last. Readers know that. Almásy's book would not be buried with him. Nor is he the only member of his world to confide in books. His nurse Hana writes notes in books from the library of the ruined villa they inhabit, choosing them almost at random and hiding them on remote shelves.[5] (They are not her own books but after all she is suffering from shell-shock, the books have been abandoned, and the notes give us immediate access to her mind. We need them as much as she does.) For certain people it is easy and convenient and a sign of their confidence in books that they should adopt them as vehicles for ideas and concerns that require a less ephemeral medium than notepaper. As time passes and materials are accumulated, the composite volume becomes more and more precious. Adding to it is such a source of satisfaction that it may become exclusive and addictive. On the other hand, this process of book-expansion is related to quite ordinary and respectable forms of behavior, and it is not easy to tell, particularly if you are the owner, when a book has crossed the line between conventionality and fanaticism. I wish first of all to consider four traditionally acceptable activities related to the Almásy treatment—well, three that are acceptable and one that is sometimes controversial, the fascinating fad of extra-illustration—and then to describe a few books that strike me, at least, as being manifestly over the top.

The leading holy book of the English-speaking world in the period with which we are concerned has of course been the King James version of the Bible—significantly, after a century of religious controversy, a translation authorized explicitly on condition that it appear without printed commentary in the margins. Only explanations of Hebrew and Greek terms, and internal cross-references (to other passages in the Old or New Testament) were permitted.[6] In no time at all theologians, biblical scholars, and ordinary readers filled the gap with their own or others' explanations of difficult passages. Furthermore, since the Bible in English was likely to be the one book a Protestant household possessed if it possessed only one book, the Bible came to be used as the register of family records, especially but not exclusively births, marriages, and deaths. In these two functions, as object of study and repository of valuable documents, the Bible is a prototype of all especially treasured and pored-over volumes in the succeeding centuries. It *attracted* supplementary materials, almost as an act of worship, certainly in a spirit of reverence. In a pattern of events that we see repeatedly in the book trade— the market catching up with and capitalizing upon amateur activity— "illustrated" editions of the Bible began to be issued early in the eighteenth century, for example *The Sacred Books of the New Testament, Recited at Large: and Illustrated with Critical and Explanatory Annotations, Carefully Compiled from the Commentaries and Other Writings of Grotius, Lightfoot, Pool, Calmet, Le Clerc, Lock, Burkit, Sir Isaac Newton, and a Variety of Other Eminent Authors, Ancient and Modern. Embellished with Ornamental and Useful Representations, Curiously Design'd, and Engraven on Copper* (1739). This was what we would call a critical variorum edition—one that assembles the observations of various commentators—and one that interestingly combines verbal and visual additions to the text.

Of course the presence of voluminous printed commentary did not stop readers from creating their own personal copies. Of the many annotated Bibles that I have seen, one of the most beautiful—but in its method, at the same time, quite typical—is a famous one that belonged to Edmund Law, master of Peterhouse and bishop of Carlisle (1703–87), and that was passed down in his family. It contains the bookplate of his son George Henry Law, also a bishop, and some notes in other hands made both before and after the main body of notes by Law himself. It is a quarto edition, 1606, of the Geneva or "Breeches" Bible, interleaved with larger pages and bound in three big handsome folio volumes. The interleaved pages are ruled into two columns, like the printed text, to take the corresponding notes. In the text itself there is some underlining and there are a few notes, but for the most part marking of the text is keyed to notes on the interleaves. On a front flyleaf (1: −6), Law explains the purpose of the annotation: "This Book contains Remarks from various Authors in relation both to ye original Text & Versions, chiefly in ye New Testamt, by way of Materials towards a more perfect edition, as well as a more accurate Translation, wch is extremely wanted. E Law 1757[.] I made use of this <u>old</u> Translation as giving me an opportunity of comparing ye last with it, wch is often chang'd for ye worse: & took up with ye present interleav'd copy, tho' scribbled in by other hands[.]"

Annotation in the three volumes is uneven, some passages receiving a great deal more attention than others. Much of the work consists of extracts copied from other books, and as Law's introductory note indicates, the translation is his main concern. At the notorious verse (Gen. 3.7) that gave this translation its popular name—"they <u>sewed figge tree leaves together</u>, and made themselves <u>breeches</u>"—Law takes in the printed marginal gloss *"Ebr. things to gird about them to hide their privities"* and proposes alternative translations, "joined together fig branches" and "subligacula, <u>waist-clothes</u> or Girdles." Law's annotated Bible is a work of devotion as well as an exercise in professional scholarship, and there are many like it. It serves to represent two respectable readerly activities, note-taking and editing. Students were taught to copy glosses and commentary into their schoolbooks. Printed editions of the Bible and of classical and vernacular literature provided models of scholarly annotation that readers could extend to works of their own choosing. So

Law brought together in his Bible relevant materials from many other sources, the book itself providing the system of organization. This is an important principle: the text takes the lead. Whether the reader is copying in notes or preparing an edition, not only the individual marginal note but the whole enterprise of annotation is responsive, following and respecting the structure and sequence of the original.

The commonplace book is another matter altogether, for it imposes *its* structure without distinction on materials culled from various sources. As I pointed out in Chapter One, the relationship between the annotated book and the commonplace book is normally complementary: readers used to mark passages in a book with a line or a cross to show that those passages were later to be copied out into their commonplace books and disposed according to alphabetical or topical arrangements. In the copying process the transcribed passages would be cast adrift, though with the prospect of taking part in the construction of a new work eventually. This was a tested and reliable way of storing and retrieving potentially useful material. Students for centuries learned traditional systems of arrangement or adapted them to suit themselves. John Evelyn recommended a technique of his own to his friends; Piozzi had the "Thraliana" notebooks, and Virginia Woolf her reading notebooks. In the seventeenth century printers sold ready-made commonplace books with headings and blank spaces, reducing the need for spending lesson time on teaching a single system. Locke proposed his *New Method of a Common Place Book* in 1686, and his initiative may have extended the life of the uniform system perhaps a century longer, as students worked or tinkered with his ideas. But gradually it faded away.

The commonplace book is essentially a filing system, and it is simpler to keep the filing system separate from the library than to settle, as Almásy did, on a single work capacious and flexible enough to do double duty—even contradictory duty—as itself and as a warehouse for products from other places. A reader would need to know a book very well in order to be able to find the spot where he was keeping stuff about desert winds (not under "W," and not with index tabs). Of course that is part of the point about Almásy: he *is* a complicated character, and he does have an obsessive's grasp of the *Histories*.

Printed books doubling as commonplace books are unusual, but they turn up among annotated books from time to time. Bishop White Kennett's copy of the *Book of Common Prayer* is a case in point. Kennett, who died in 1728, made this book—interleaved, with the blank pages marked off in double columns as in Law's Bible—into a commonplace book by writing at the tops of the columns headings under which he would enter materials that came his way through books or conversation: "Translations of the Liturgy," "Church Musick," "Singing Psalms," "Set Forms of Prayer," "Reading Desk," and so on. On the flyleaf that contains his bookplate (p. −5), proud owners have added their own names and traced the pedigree of the volume from Kennett's family through five later hands to 1877. The first of these notes records the passing of the book out of the family: "J. West. Bought of Bp Kennets Sons Widow. July 2. 1737. with 64. volumes of MSS. wrote by the laborious hand of that Indefatigable and Zealous Collector of Ancient English History, Ecclesiastical & Civil." It is thus not unheard of that a book should serve also as a commonplace book. From the perspective of history of the book, however, Almásy's Herodotus sounds less like a commonplace book than like a case of extra-illustration. The practice referred to earlier as respectable but also controversial, extra-illustration is perhaps best understood as a way of describing a *collection* housed in a book, the book providing both the hard covers and the rationale for the collection.

In practical terms, an "extra-illustrated" book is one containing more illustrations than it came with from the publisher. Etymologically, it is one illustrated with materials brought in from outside. "Extra-illustrated" seems to have entered the language in the 1870s; the earliest example in the *OED* is dated 1889, but the word appeared in American sale catalogues at least as early as 1878.[7] It must have been introduced to avoid the ambiguities of the earlier term "illustrated" which could also refer to illustrations provided by the author or publisher as an integral part of the text, as in the 1739 edition of the Bible cited earlier. Cataloguers quite like it because it produces a catch-all classification for books with foreign elements ranging from a single additional plate presented as a frontispiece to the dozens or hundreds of miscellaneous bits and pieces that readers have been known to drop into their books—autographs, letters, photographs, pamphlets, newspaper clippings, twists of hair, pen-and-ink drawings, broadsheets, visiting cards, watercolors, envelopes, pressed flowers, maps, scraps of cloth, in short just about anything flat.

It is in many ways an unsatisfactory word, however, and its history is confusing. At some point late in the nineteenth century books began to advertise themselves on their title pages as "extra-illustrated" editions, meaning, apparently, that they contained more illustrations than you might expect (not merely a frontispiece); but all copies came from the publisher in the same state. What were you to call one of them that acquired other illustrations later? The word has had better success in North America, where it originated, than in Britain, but it has never really caught on, even in the specialized circles of librarians and connoisseurs. It is partly for this reason that it is hard to find out anything about extra-illustration—it's not a word that everyone uses—but also because the products of this activity, when they are preserved, have no obvious place to go to and are sometimes classified as books, at other times as albums or scrapbooks or, when they are very grand, as the responsibility of departments of prints and drawings.

The preferred term in British libraries is "grangerized": the two words emerged about the same time, and the *OED* treats them as synonyms. A "grangerized" book is one that has been supplemented with portraits and other images, often cannibalized from other books. (The grangerized book is the enriched one, not the mutilated victim.) Book lovers are united in condemning this pastime now.[8] The *OED* explains where the name came from: "In 1769 James Granger published a 'Biographical History of England', with blank leaves for the reception of engraved portraits or other pictorial illustrations of the text. The filling up of a 'Granger' became a favourite hobby, and afterwards other books were treated in the same manner." Up to the first comma this statement is correct; what follows, however, is misleading at best. Efforts have been made since 1809 to clear Granger's name from the slur perpetuated (not initiated) by the *OED,* so far to no avail; I mean to do my bit by attempting to sort out what really did happen, and by insisting on using "extra-illustrated" instead, for all its faults.

James Granger (1723–76), vicar of Shiplake, a print collector himself, conceived the idea of making a catalogue of extant engraved portraits of eminent figures in British history, organized according to the reigns in which they flourished, with subdivisions for different classes of persons from the monarchy down, by way of encouraging the collection of such portraits "to supply the Defect, and answer the various Purposes, of Medals."[9] Each entry describes the known prints and says where they can be found in this or that history, biography, or book of heraldry. To the entries in his catalogue Granger added biographical summaries, so that the end product was more than a catalogue: it was a prototype of the *Dictionary of National Biography*. Granger enjoyed the cooperation of several important collectors, and dedicated the work to Horace Walpole. Appearing with such patronage, in an age of comprehensive reference books that was also an age of national pride and self-definition, the work that Granger had intended as a modest handbook for a small group of antiquarian enthusiasts succeeded beyond all expectation. Granger himself published a supplementary volume in 1774 and a second edition in 1775; further revisions were made in posthumous editions by other hands. Later commentators attributed a rapid rise in the price of prints that occurred some time in the late eighteenth century, together with the roughly contemporaneous and obviously related fad of embellishing books with plates and cuttings, to the impact of Granger's work; but these are claims of at least forty years later, and solid evidence is wanting.[10]

Granger himself never published his work with blank spaces for portraits. The misconception reflected in the *OED* may have arisen from later practice and from the fact that some of the few extant copies of the first edition were printed on only one side of the leaf: both British Library copies, for example, appear in this state. But the blank pages were the publisher's substitute for interleaving in copies specially designed for a group of collectors who were asked to annotate the work, indicating additions that would then be incorporated in later editions.[11] Granger could therefore be said to have contributed to but not created the occupation to which his name was eventually attached a hundred years or more later.

The idea of extra-illustration was that the owner of the book would collect prints with which to embellish it and then have the book bound, when the collection was complete, with the plates inserted at the appropriate places. Depending on the owner's taste and budget, illustrative plates would be cut down to the size of the volume, or the pages of the volume and the smaller prints built up ("inlaid" in a larger sheet as in a frame) to the size of the largest print. To save time and money an owner might start out by having the book interleaved to receive prints as they came in; it would be cheaper still, though inadvisable, to paste the prints directly onto the pages of text. The fad could almost have been the result of a conspiracy in the book trade, for it called upon the combined resources of publishers, printers, booksellers, print dealers, inlayers, and binders. Grangers were popular subjects for illustration, but not more so than other historical, biographical, topographical, and theatrical subjects, and almost certainly not at or even close to the date of their first appearance in 1769.[12]

A copy of Colley Cibber's popular autobiography—*An Apology for the Life of Colley Cibber, Comedian*—extra-illustrated by Queen Charlotte, the consort of George III, is a model of its kind. The octavo pages of the original were inlaid in folio sheets and the queen's selection of prints bound in with them to make two handsome folio volumes. With a substantial collection to draw on, the queen was able to avoid the usual approach of theatrical portraits (actors in costume for celebrated roles) and take a more challenging route. In Chapter 1, "The Introduction," for example, there are four prints, at three points. On 1:5, Cibber describes what is to come: "This Work, I say, shall not only contain the various Impressions of my Mind, (as in *Louis the Fourteenth* his Cabinet you have seen the growing Medals of his Person from Infancy to Old Age,) but shall likewise include with them the *Theatrical History of my Own Time*, from my first Appearance on the Stage to my last *Exit*." Here a grand portrait of Louis XIV illustrates Cibber's parenthetical analogy, as opposed, say, to a portrait of Cibber in his final part. The other plates are also oddly incidental to the text but have the virtue of variety. Cibber identifies his father as a sculptor, saying, "The *Basso Relievo* on the Pedestal of the Great Column in the City, and the two Figures of the *Lunaticks*, the *Raving* and the *Melancholy*, over the Gates of *Bethlehem-Hospital*, are no ill Monuments of his Fame as an Artist" (1:6). To illustrate this sentence the queen used, not a portrait of Cibber the elder, but two prints, the first a picture of the asylum, "New Bedlam in Moorfields" (not one showing the famous statues), and the second a version of the allegorical design for the pillar commemorating the Great Fire. Continuing to shun obvious literal references, she chose for her last contribution in this chapter the image of a Roman emperor, Vespasian ("T. Flavius Vespasianus Augustus" on the caption), to go with another of Cibber's asides: "But farther; if even the great *Augustus*, to whose Reign such Praises are given, cou'd not enjoy his Days of Peace, free from the Terrors of repeated Conspiracies, which lost him more Quiet to suppress, than his Ambition cost him to provoke them" (1:22). Cibber alluded to a different Augustus, but the generic title goes with the generic problem of what Cibber refers to as "the Vanity of Greatness," so that Vespasian is perfectly relevant and not necessarily a blunder. The work as a whole displays an alertness to the text and an ingenuity in the matching of image to text that makes deliberate choice the more likely alternative.

It is difficult to ascertain exactly when illustration, as opposed to ordinary print collecting, became a fashionable pastime. It is even difficult to say, in most cases, when a particular book was illustrated, because the process could take years, the copy chosen was not necessarily the latest edition, and unlike annotators the collectors seldom sign or date their work. The earliest datable examples I have encountered belong to the 1790s, and the first serious notice of the phenomenon—in Dibdin's prose treatise *The Bibliomania* (1809)—does not name any that are definitely earlier than that. (Dibdin not very helpfully describes "illustration" as a development of "within the last half century." He formally absolves Granger of sole responsibility for "the mischief which this passion for collecting prints has occasioned.") The practice seems to have begun among wealthy and aristocratic collectors and to have spread gradually to the middle classes. Daniel M. Tredwell says that when he started doing it in the 1840s it was practically unknown in America, but that it rapidly became popular there too.[13] The rage seems to have died about 1900, though later examples surface occasionally and the Berg Collection has at least one book—Buxton Forman's copy of John Nichols's *Byron* (1883)—that was still in progress, collecting twentieth-century plates and clippings, when the last owner died. (It may, however, simply have been abandoned in that state shortly after the turn of the century by Buxton Forman himself; he died in 1917.) A 1907 edition of Boswell's *Life of Johnson* at the Huntington is extra-illustrated with colored magazine clippings of perhaps the 1930s.

If commercial interest is a good indicator of a growing market, 1790 may be a significant date. The first illustrators had to use money and ingenuity to collect existing prints or books with prints, but the book trade soon took notice and simplified the process. It was in 1790 that a publisher, William Richardson, decided to commission a series of prints specifically designed to illustrate Granger's *History;* by 1812 copies of Granger were being made available with additional, pre-printed title pages with the volume and part numbers left blank for owners to fill in when they were ready to take their sets to the binder. Other frequent subjects received similar attention—a limited edition of Byron's *English Bards and Scotch Reviewers* (1865), for example, advertised its "ample quarto page" as being especially suitable for "illustrators." Booksellers also assembled extra-illustrated copies for sale ready-made to collectors who lacked the time or expertise to hunt down prints for themselves: several of the early "illustrators" named by Dibdin were booksellers.[14]

The most famous and most sumptuous of all British extra-illustrated books, the one that set a standard early on, is the Sutherland Collection, now kept in a special cabinet in the Print Room of the Ashmolean Museum in Oxford. In 1795, Alexander Hendras Sutherland began collecting prints and drawings relating to the Civil War period to illustrate the Earl of Clarendon's and Gilbert Burnet's histories—Clarendon's *History of the Rebellion,* his *Life,* and the *Continuation of the History,* and Burnet's *History of His Own Time.* By 1819 he had assembled 10,000 items. After his death in 1820, his widow continued the work: the publisher's advertisement to the 1824 edition of Granger mentions that she had recently paid the highest price ever known to have been given for a single print, eighty guineas for a portrait of James I and his queen.[15] By the time she called a halt, published a catalogue of all the plates by subject (1837), and had the whole set bound in 57 elephant folio volumes, the collection contained 18,742 prints and drawings by 1,457 known artists. There are many huge leaves of plates to every inlaid leaf of text; some are duplicates, representing more than one state of the print in question. Besides portraits and topographical scenes (London, Westminster, Paris, etc.), there are images of medals, inscriptions, events (the Spanish Armada, the Gunpowder Plot), and monuments; sheets of letterpress such as proclamations and the title pages of books; caricatures; maps; and original drawings and watercolors. The fact that this is collecting on a Guinness Book of World Records scale no doubt enhances its value as a historical resource, but it does rather overwhelm Clarendon and Burnet. The Sutherland Collection is aptly named; it is a collection, a picture archive that has left extra-illustration far behind. Richard Bull's roughly contemporaneous Granger went farther still and actually sacrificed the text to the prints, using the pages of the book for captions that are pasted directly onto the plates. These are no longer even held in volumes but are disbound and stored in boxes.

A bookish person is likely to regret the effacing of the text in such extreme cases, and to take pleasure in less ambitious, less expensive, and more typical examples of extra-illustration. The simple way to choose a subject for extra-illustration during the Victorian period when the craze was at its height was to take into account the standard offerings of the print market and to buy a book with an index. (The index acts as a guide to the binder for the placing of prints, and before that as a finding-list for the collector; owners checked entries off as they acquired the prints. The most basic sort of index would list proper names only, but then portraits were the type of print most readily available.) The harder way was to take a beloved book and work with it, getting to know it still more intimately in the process. A suppressed edition of letters by Charlotte Brontë, including all her letters to her friend Ellen Nussey, was rescued by someone—just possibly Nussey herself—who had it interleaved and proceeded to extra-illustrate it with autographs, envelopes, visiting cards, pictures cut from books and magazines, manuscript notes about Brontë, a scrap of silk from the dress she wore on her honeymoon, an advertisement for the Brontës' abortive school, a family tree, and a few other relevant odds and ends.[16] This book, now in the Houghton Library at Harvard, is a minor treasure-trove, but whoever made it up was only doing what many of his or her contemporaries did, keeping an album based on a printed book.

In a similar way, an unidentified follower of the Romantic poets filled a copy of Margaret Sandford's *Thomas Poole and His Friends* (1888), now at the Huntington, with 134 extra plates and souvenirs, including autograph letters and a flower taken from Wordsworth's garden in 1844. The insertions were prompted by the text and do not overwhelm it; the work is still a book in two volumes. A fine twentieth-century example is the family record maintained by Philip Gosse and eventually donated to the Cambridge University Library as an extra-illustrated copy of his father's biography of his grandfather, Edmund Gosse's *Life of Philip Henry Gosse F.R.S.* (1890). The narrative stretches back to the birth of Thomas Gosse in 1765; the documents added by Philip Gosse include original letters dating from 1839 to 1931, drawings, watercolors, photographs, a marriage certificate, a school schedule, a family tree, newspaper clippings, and advertisements.

Personal involvement was not the only motive for extra-illustration, and the range of subjects seems to have been limited only by the imagination and diligence of the collectors. The best of them exhibit profound knowledge of and fidelity to the text, and resourcefulness in the collection. The original owner of the copy of Samuel Smiles's *Lives of the Engineers* (1861–68) now at the University of Toronto might have found portraits of the engineers fairly easily, but he or she did not stop at that, and as a result the work now contains 697 extra illustrations representing not only technical challenges and triumphs mentioned in the text (the Thames tunnel, for instance, 5:48) but also minor details from the text and footnotes: for instance, the phrase "rude tracks" in 1:160 justifies a pretty picture of a country path. There are extra-illustrated travel books, local histories, nature studies, and bibliographies. There is a mildly pornographic copy of Count Gamba's *Amours, Intrigues, and Adventures of Lord Byron* in the Houghton; the Berg contains a copy of Nathaniel Hawthorne's novel *Transformation* (titled *The Marble Faun* in America) for which some enthusiast arranged to have dozens of photographs taken in Rome, perhaps in the 1870s or '80s.

What do extra-illustrated books like these, strange and wonderful as they may be, have to do with marginalia? There are remote resemblances: like marginalia of the same period, extra-illustration can be thought of as a reader's personal contribution to a book, and as constituting a form of comment and evaluation. Extra-illustrated books like annotated ones afford later readers not only incidental rewards in the way of unpredictable connections and rare or unique documentation, but also a detailed guide to what attracted readers' attention long ago. There are, in addition, closer links. Many extra-illustrated books also contain readers' notes; many annotated books are also extra-illustrated. Roger Stoddard describes "marginal extra illustration" (meaning "watercolors in the text block and margin") as a practice associated with the late nineteenth century.[17] The Thorn-Drury collection acquired by the Bodleian Library in 1931 and described by B. C. Bloomfield (p. 449) as "a mine of information" about seventeenth-century poetry consists of seventy volumes—"interleaved and annotated," according to the library catalogue, but perhaps better referred to as extra-illustrated— that are essentially scrapbooks based on editions of the poets' works. A copy of William Mason's edition of Gray (with Mason's memoir of his friend) was handsomely extra-illustrated by its Victorian owner George Daniel, but before his time it had already been annotated by previous owners, Isaac Reed and Reginald Heber; and after Daniel had his prints and manuscripts bound in, in 1835, it continued to attract contributions by later owners into the twentieth century.[18]

The two categories overlap and can be hard to disentangle. Historically, furthermore, they have not always been distinct. Today "extra-illustration" is generally reserved for illustration by pictures and material objects, "annotation" and "marginalia" for written words. But in the eighteenth century, as we see in the example of the Bible, "illustration" could be and normally was achieved by words. Even in 1809 Dibdin included illustration by the written word in the same category as illustration by prints:

> There is another mode of illustrating copies by which this symptom of the Bibliomania may be known: it consists in bringing together, from different works, (by means of the scissars, or otherwise by transcription) every page or paragraph which has any connection with the character or subject under discussion. This is a useful and entertaining mode of illustrating a favourite author; and copies of works of this nature, when executed by skilful hands, should be preserved in public repositories. I almost ridiculed the idea of an ILLUSTRATED CHATTERTON, in this way, till I saw Mr. Haslewood's copy, in twenty-one volumes, which riveted me to my seat! (pp. 64–65)

Dibdin's wish was granted: many books illustrated in this way are now "preserved in public repositories," and many annotators must have been spurred on by the hope that their own would qualify. Although the procedure of transferring information and commentary by copying them from one book into another had been going on for a long time, unlike the new way of combining text and prints, Dibdin helped to legitimize and regularize the scissors-and-paste method.

Knowing that this kind of extra-illustration was common practice throughout the nineteenth century helps us to understand what certain forms of annotation were about. Richard Woodhouse's copies of Keats's *Endymion* and *Poems,* mentioned earlier, fall into this category, as do many books from the working libraries of scholars and editors. A volume of Alfred, Lord Tennyson that once belonged to James Dykes Campbell, for example, actually contains three titles: Tennyson's *In Memoriam,* Frederick W. Robertson's *Analysis of Mr. Tennyson's "In Memoriam,"* and *An Index to "In Memoriam,"* all of them annotated and the first interleaved to take variant readings and a collection of parallel passages from other poets, English and classical. Into this carefully compiled work someone else has copied, from a published report, Tennyson's own marginalia to *In Memoriam.*[19] The creation of such a book is a mark of respect and not just a matter of scholarly convenience:

Dykes Campbell paid Tennyson's poem the tribute of his focused attention, and the later annotator paid Campbell a tribute in turn by carrying on his work.

Not all the books thus richly and industriously illustrated by their readers and passed on for the public good were "executed by skilful hands," as Dibdin optimistically put it, but with the passing of time even those that were not may be of considerable interest. The British Library copy of Richard Clark's *Reminiscences of Handel*, extra-illustrated by the author between 1836 and 1853 or later (Clark died in 1856), is—not to put too fine a point on it—the work of a nutter; but it represents the Victorian love of trivial particulars and is in any case a captivating monument to the intractability of folly. A reputable musician, Clark has gone down in history as the perpetrator of two erroneous but tenacious ideas—first, that the Elizabethan John Bull composed "God Save the King," and second, that Handel composed "The Harmonious Blacksmith" after hearing an actual blacksmith, William Powell of Cannons (or Canons), Whitchurch, singing a song by Wagenseil. Clark aired the latter theory in 1836 along with miscellaneous other bits and pieces in an eighteen-page pamphlet, published by subscription and dedicated to the queen. The full title may be helpful: it is *Reminiscences of Handel, His Grace the Duke of Chandos, Powells the Harpers [i.e., Harper], The Harmonious Blacksmith, and Others. With a List of the Anthems composed at Cannons, by Handel, for the Duke of Chandos. And an Appendix, Containing Some Extracts from the Wills of the Duke and Second Duchess of Chandos, and a Copy of the Will of G. F. Handel.*

The British Library volume, a large folio bound in red velvet, contains two copies of Clark's pamphlet, one of them printed on pink paper, and a copy of *How to be Rid of a Wife* (1823) by Isabella Spence—a fictional account of wife-selling supposed to have been based on the true story of the Duke of Chandos. Clark annotated both works and bound in a variety of extra material to support his views: portraits, letters, reviews, clippings, and music, including his own published arrangement of "A Favourite Air by Wagenseil with Variations by G. F. Handel." On page 8 of the pamphlet he had given the text inscribed on the memorial that he had himself had erected for the blacksmith; his manuscript note

says, "Rd. Clark possesses the very Anvil at this time August 8th. 1849."
In a further note he adds, "*NB*. It did not fetch 5£ at the sale in 1853."
Spence's narrative he describes in his appendix as very scarce, but valuable for providing "many particulars of Cannons, Whitchurch, and of Handel's masterly performance on the Organ at Whitchurch." Unluckily, Clark appears to have confused the first Duke of Chandos, who had been Handel's patron, with the second, who was alleged to have rescued Anne Wells by purchasing her from her ostler husband and subsequently marrying her himself. Under this misconception Clark "corrects" some of the clippings and other documents in his collection. The confusion is compounded in his extremely circumstantial account (p. −17) of the fabric used for binding the volume, which Clark associated with the wife-selling story:

> The History of the Velvet is as follows.
> The Duchess of Chandos died 1750 and was buried at Stowe in Buckinghamshire contrary to the wish and Will of her Lord [the first Duke], because she and the then Duke [the second] did not agree. She was however removed in the next year 1751, to Whitchurch Cannons, according to her Lords Will.—This velvet was used on that occasion and afterwards purchased by the Governors of the Foundling Hospital. I however obtained the same Velvet as will be seen by the following letter from Mr. Brownlow and I have great pleasure in returning a piece of the same to the Revd. G: Mutter, Incumbent, there to be used again in that Church after a lapse of 86 years on the Pulpit. Rd. Clark <u>This book is bound with the Velvet.</u>

This odd relic, red velvet and all, bears witness to the obsessions of an energetic eccentric. But it does have historical value as well as human interest, for it preserves a number of ephemeral publications, shows how in that period a book might be used as a cache for items relating to a particular person or subject, and enables us to trace an error to its source. Indeed it would be wrong to disparage "human interest" and suggest that it is not valuable in itself, for handling an object like this book of Clark's brings the past into the present, making it tangible and complicated again.

Though it is physically very different from the Clark volume, a collection of pamphlets by or about Joanna Southcott, also in the British Library, helps us to see another obsessive character sympathetically, as from the inside, at a specific point in time. Southcott, the daughter of a farmer and in early life a Methodist, emerged as a prophet at the end of the eighteenth century, declared herself the "woman clothed with the sun" of Revelation 12, and attracted a considerable following. She died in 1814, having literally failed to deliver—she announced herself, in her sixties, as about to give birth to Shiloh, the promised "man-child" of the Book of Revelation, but he never appeared—and she is now simply written off as a religious maniac. She must have transformed lives at the time, however, and the movement that she founded persisted to the end of the nineteenth century. Before the Shiloh fiasco a young man named William George Thompson, one of her adherents, undertook to annotate her writings and pamphlets written about her. He did it in a distinctive way, systematically and laboriously recording parallels between her text and the Bible, in particular glossing allusions and echoes (fig. 8). At every such point, he inserts a neat little superscript italic letter, usually in red, within the text, and the reference to the Bible, correspondingly marked, in black in the margin. He made Southcott's text look like the King James Bible, as though her work as much deserved to be a part of it as any of the canonical prophetic books. His close comparison of Southcott and the Bible would to a partisan like himself appear to support her claims to supernatural inspiration (she and the Bible sound amazingly alike), whereas a skeptic would see it only as proof of her prior knowledge of the language of the Bible (she was inspired *by* the Bible).

The British Library collection consists of five volumes of these tracts, all annotated in the same way. The first volume, starting with Southcott's *Strange Effects of Faith* (3rd ed., 1801), is signed and dated Easter Day, April 14th, 1811. On a back flyleaf, Thompson addresses the reader directly in a rather remarkable note that makes it clear that he was struggling with his own uncertainties and not merely proselytizing:

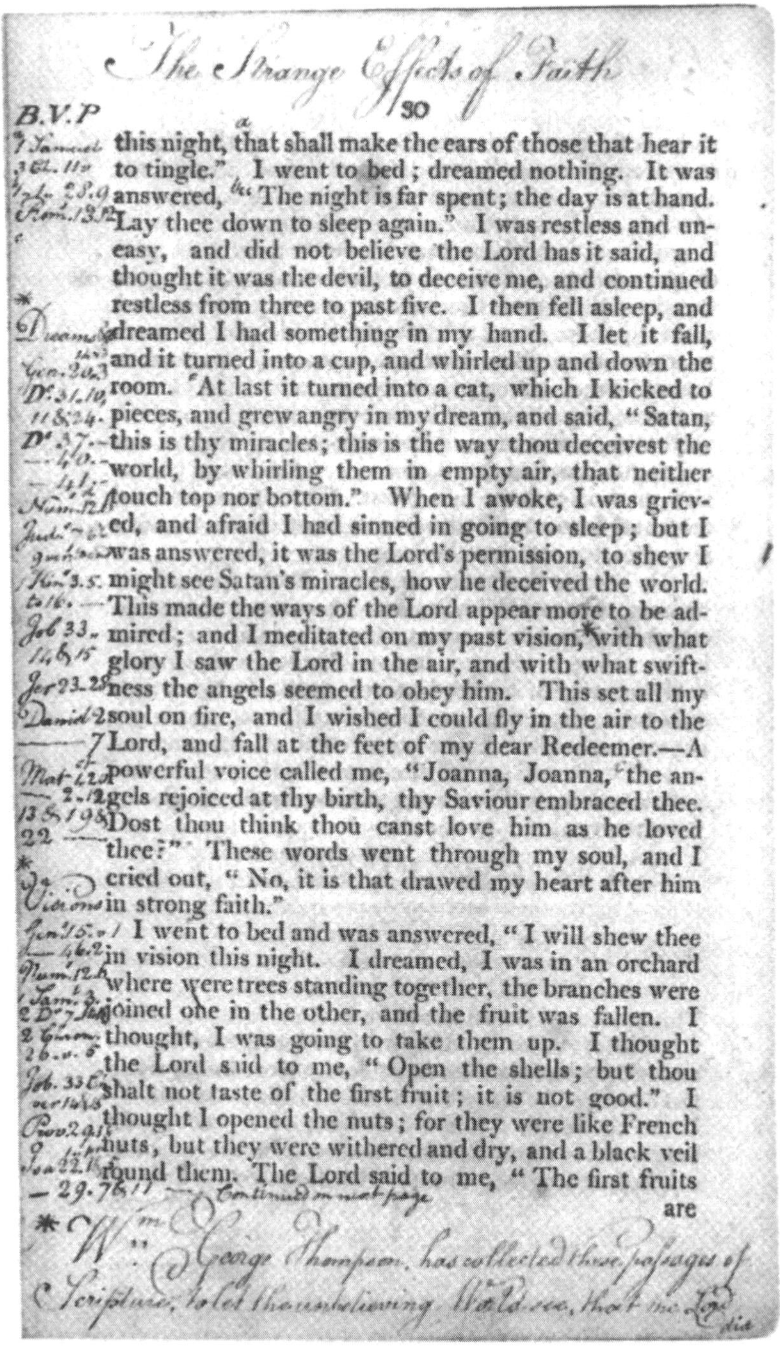
The Strange Effects of Faith

B.V.P 30

this night, that shall make the ears of those that hear it to tingle." I went to bed; dreamed nothing. It was answered, "The night is far spent; the day is at hand. Lay thee down to sleep again." I was restless and uneasy, and did not believe the Lord has it said, and thought it was the devil, to deceive me, and continued restless from three to past five. I then fell asleep, and dreamed I had something in my hand. I let it fall, and it turned into a cup, and whirled up and down the room. At last it turned into a cat, which I kicked to pieces, and grew angry in my dream, and said, "Satan, this is thy miracles; this is the way thou deceivest the world, by whirling them in empty air, that neither touch top nor bottom." When I awoke, I was grieved, and afraid I had sinned in going to sleep; but I was answered, it was the Lord's permission, to shew I might see Satan's miracles, how he deceived the world. This made the ways of the Lord appear more to be admired; and I meditated on my past vision, with what glory I saw the Lord in the air, and with what swiftness the angels seemed to obey him. This set all my soul on fire, and I wished I could fly in the air to the Lord, and fall at the feet of my dear Redeemer.—A powerful voice called me, "Joanna, Joanna, the angels rejoiced at thy birth, thy Saviour embraced thee. Dost thou think thou canst love him as he loved thee?" These words went through my soul, and I cried out, "No, it is that drawed my heart after him in strong faith."

I went to bed and was answered, "I will shew thee in vision this night. I dreamed, I was in an orchard where were trees standing together, the branches were joined one in the other, and the fruit was fallen. I thought, I was going to take them up. I thought the Lord said to me, "Open the shells; but thou shalt not taste of the first fruit; it is not good." I thought I opened the nuts; for they were like French nuts, but they were withered and dry, and a black veil round them. The Lord said to me, "The first fruits are

Continued on next page

Wm. George Thompson, has collected these passages of Scripture, to let the unbelieving World see, that the Lord ...

FIG. 8 Joanna Southcott, *The Strange Effects of Faith* (Exeter, 1801). (Used by permission of the British Library)

B.V.P 31 Scripture Comet Visions Continued

are fallen ; they are not good. Look up, and thou
wilt see berries ; and when they are ripe, they will be
good." I looked up, and saw berries like the berries
of potatoes ; and went to a house, where I saw the
Lord. He rose up, as one out of sleep, and told me
to go, and mind all I had seen. I awaked.

The same night, I dreamed I was on the sea ; and
I saw a large oven full of meat ; and the stopper
broke, and the meat swam on the sea in abundance.
When I awoke, I was answered. " Thy dreams puz-
zle thee ; but wars and tumults shall arise from
abroad and at home. The sea shall be laden with
ships, many shall break in pieces, and thousands shall
launch in the deep. As to the dream of the fruit,
couldest thou look into the hearts of men, thou
wouldest see them as the fruit, withered."

Another night, I dreamed I saw my father sweeping
out the barn floor clean, and would not suffer the
wheat to be brought in the barn. He appeared to me
to be in anger. When I awaked, I was answered, " It
is thy Heavenly Father is angry with the land ; and
if they do not repent, as Nineveh did, they shall sow,
but they shall not reap ; neither shall they gather into their barns. There shall come three years, wherein
there shall be neither earing nor harvest."

Another night, it was said unto me, " I will shew
thee in dreams, of my anger against the nations."—
I dreamed I had a dish in my hand, with dirt in it ;
and some one throwed honey over it ; and the children
eat it, for the sake of the honey, which made me
sick. I awoke with my dream. I was answered,
" So sick is the Lord of the world. They eat the
honey and the poison together."

Another night, I dreamed I heard heavenly music
sounding in my ears, and a flock of sheep was gather-
ing round it. When the music ceased, the sheep leaped
for joy, and ran together, shaking their heads ; and
one shook his head almost off, and seemed to have
nothing but ears. I went towards them, and awoke.

I was

did reveal his Will to Men, (but particularly to his servants
the Prophets) by Dreams & Visions of the Night. (D.)

It is hoped the reader of this Volume will follow my humble entreaties—First, to read this through and if they can see nothing in this Vol. have another, which I am willing to lend, provided their return'd safe. This caution I took, because I am aware the persecution I must undergo, in believing these writings to be indicted by the same Spirit, that inspired those men that wrote the old and new Testament—

I have the natural pride of mankind, and have no desire to be an object of ridicule; but whatever pain or mortification the pride of Character, or reputation, may produce in me, it is my superior duty to adhere to truth. The mockery of the World I must endure; the pity of my Friends, who would promote every worldly advantage for my interest, I must feel, and many I know are sorry for me, believing me to be a deluded Youth. It is my sincere wish that they may throw aside their prejudice as I have done, and endeavour at least to prove me in error. (p. +1)

Thompson's work seems to me honorable though deluded: it is clear from this dignified statement and his conscientious annotation of the Southcott tracts that he really was doing everything he could to come at the truth, and that he understood that it was as possible that he was carried away by enthusiasm as that his friends were blinded by prejudice. Allowing his precious books to circulate was not a vain but a courageous gesture.

My last example of a customized book of the Herodotus type is courageous in a different way. It is a copy of the 1798 first edition of William Godwin's *Memoirs of the Author of A Vindication of the Rights of Woman,* that is, his biography of his wife Mary Wollstonecraft, who had died after giving birth to their daughter, later Mary Shelley. Godwin challenged convention by revealing aspects of Wollstonecraft's life that most biographers would have chosen to conceal, notably her extramarital love affairs with Gilbert Imlay and with himself, her attempt to kill herself over Imlay's infidelity, and the protracted suffering of her last illness. The plain speaking, naming of names, and overall indiscretion of the first edition caused such an uproar that Godwin was persuaded to make substantial revisions in the second; but it was the first edition that John Horseman, one of Godwin's many young admirers, acquired in 1798 and stuck to for the rest of his life. The book is now in the Pforzheimer Collection of the New York Public Library, having had a new spine and endpapers since Horseman's day.

Horseman (1776–1844), who eventually took orders and became a fellow of Corpus Christi College in Oxford, had given it hard use. None of the endpapers available to him was left blank, and most pages of the text are so filled with notes (in ink) in his tiny hand that he had to number the margins to show the proper sequence for reading. The front flyleaves hold a few pasted-in clippings from periodicals. Here and there a few words or phrases are blacked out, and two notes are covered over with slips of paper on page 133, which is concerned with the attempted suicide. Horseman's name is written on a loose page (probably one of the original endpapers) pasted onto the first page of text, together with the following note: "This book is treated with delicacy in the Analytical Review; and with scurrility in the British Critic. The Revd. Wm. Beloe is the writer of the criticism in the British Critic.—In the Monthly, with more candour than in the British Critic.—G. got 100 gs per vol. for Mem. &c. Underwood—N.B. The B.C.s (rather Beloe) vindicate Imlay!!—How detestable!! Bah!" ("Underwood" was perhaps the source from whom Horseman found out what Godwin was paid for the memoirs and the Wollstonecraft manuscripts that were published at the same time.) This early note sets a tone for Horseman's work with the *Memoirs,* though it is not typical of his method, which is normally pasting-in and transcription of the kind recommended by Dibdin.

Dibdin's explanation of illustration as an assembling of "every page or paragraph which has any connection with the character or subject under discussion" is cheerfully vague. What principles of connection are appropriate, what are not, and who is to judge? Most readers seem to have been satisfied with traditional bibliographical and biographical evidence: they collected references to their book or edition and published opinions about their author or subject. As a further step, they might take note of parallel passages in other authors: Charles Lamb's Milton typically contains quotations from earlier poets, as do Woodhouse's Keats,

John James Raven's Macaulay, and many others among the annotated books I have been describing. This approach was so well established that John Ferriar was able to publish his collected *Illustrations of Sterne* as a study of Sterne's literary sources in 1798. But even the decision as to what makes a passage "parallel" is a personal decision, and the farther removed annotators became from the routine course of biographical and bibliographical matters of fact, the more distinctively their own their collections were likely to be.

Horseman's Godwin is decidedly personal in spite of its being mostly a compendium of quotations. For forty years or more, Horseman made this little volume an object of devoted attention and the repository of everything he considered relevant from his reading.[20] His notes eclectically draw upon the works of Godwin, Wollstonecraft, and P. B. Shelley; periodicals from 1770 to 1838; essays and fiction; and published letters and memoirs. On the title page, between the title and the author's name, he proposes an epigraph from Dryden: "A female softness with a manly mind." Biographical information is included for members of the family who were not part of the narrative or even born at the time of publication—William Godwin Jr., for example, who died in 1832. Only the pages concerned with Imlay are left blank and eloquently silent. With this exception, no information, it seems, is too trivial: Horseman for instance takes the trouble to identify a woman present at Wollstonecraft's deathbed whom Godwin refers to merely as "another very kind and judicious lady" as "Miss Jones" (p. 187). But the most common sort of addition to the text consists of reflections on ideas, especially controversial issues such as suicide, the case against matrimony, and the education of women. Some of the extracts on these topics are so long and the book so crowded that the notes carry over from one page to the next. Horseman quotes a great variety of authorities—Samuel Johnson, Tom Paine, Anna Jameson, Bulwer-Lytton, and even (on suicide, pp. 134–35) J. C. Morgan's 1822 *Sketches of the Philosophy of Morals.*

This book gives a clear impression of the range of Horseman's reading and the nature of his opinions (he would not have transcribed passages he did not agree with); it also suggests that his reading and his opinions were formed and directed by the *Memoirs* in the first place.

Thus the illustrated book (which initiates the search) and the common-place book (which ends it) overlap again. Horseman's Godwin resembles Almásy's Herodotus more closely than does any of the other works I have surveyed. In both cases an enterprising reader establishes a special relationship with a particular book, making one copy distinctively his own by investing labor and imagination in it. The larger the investment, the more personal the book becomes, and the process is potentially unending. If this activity sounds dangerously emotional—well, it might be, but it fills a need and Horseman does not seem to have come to any harm by it. Clark and Thompson may have been confirmed in erroneous convictions or, since in both cases they made their work public, may have been talked out of them. From the point of view of readerly behavior, extremists like these only define the outer limits of common usage.

chapter seven

POETICS

Somewhere, sometime, I came upon the published opinion that Horace Walpole is "the prince of annotators." I can't now lay my hands on it. Wilmarth Lewis's authoritative, affectionate account of Walpole as an annotator does not go in for large claims. The closest I have been able to get to that extravagant statement is Morris R. Brownell's more restrained remark, "Perhaps only Horace Walpole can rival Mrs. Piozzi as an annotator of books" (p. 99). These two do indeed make a legitimate and interesting pair for comparison because they wrote about the same time and in rather similar ways, and because there is a fairly substantial body of marginalia by each of them available for study. Both are fascinating, but in my opinion both are outclassed by other writers of marginalia. Comparisons and preferences like these are based on implicit standards of measurement; and yet where marginalia are concerned, those standards are makeshift at best. This chapter aims to define the qualities that make for good marginalia; it is offered as a user's guide to the writing as well as the interpreting of readers' notes in books. I shall be describing and quoting marginalia I enjoy and annotators whose work I always look forward to seeing more of, as well as a few I have found myself trying to avoid—for standards are established by rejection as well as by approval. The criteria I propose unavoidably include an element of subjectivity, but I hope they may be persuasive and useful for all that.

As with any human activity, in marginalia it is possible to distinguish between a basic standard of competence and a higher standard of artistry or excellence. As with any kind of *writing*, it is reasonable to expect that some of our requirements will be common to many forms, but others peculiar to the one under discussion. Readers' notes, responsive by nature, must be judged partly by the standards that apply to the original or host genre (good recipes in cookbooks, up-to-date addresses in directories), partly by the general rules of composition, and partly by special laws of their own. I plan to concentrate on the last of these three categories, and to work up from the basics. The first phase may appear to belabor the obvious.

As a minimum, notes should be intelligible. Even supposing that some marginalia are intended for the owner's eye alone, still the owner may need to be able to make sense of them years later, and they ought therefore to be reasonably legible and coherent. If they depend on a shorthand system of marks, or on actual shorthand, then it should be an established system and not one custom made for a single occasion. (The latter, even if it comes with a key to the code, generally turns out hardly to be worth the trouble, as I pointed out in Chapter One.) Darwin, Melville, and no doubt thousands unknown to fame before and after them developed time-saving systems of marking that they found convenient and intelligible, and that a third party can generally understand with little effort, because they fall into regular patterns.

Marginalia should be relevant to the work they appear in. To start with deliberately modest examples, a tourist guide to Salisbury Cathedral, published about 1800 and acquired by the British Library in 1874, contains notes made by an unidentified annotator who supplemented the guide by registering changes made in the cathedral since the time of printing, such as "Both are now (1810) in the Nave," for instance; adding statements made by authorities who contradict assertions in the text; and providing neat little sketches of architectural details. All these additions would have helped the annotator to recall the visit to the cathedral; over time this copy became a useful historical record because the supplementary notes have a direct bearing on the subject of the pamphlet, freezing the cathedral as it was in 1810. Of a different but likewise common kind, Sophia Banks's bibliographical annotations to her books about archery, which usually provide factual information about provenance, have less to do with the subject of archery itself than with the business of collecting and organizing a specialized library, but they are still entirely relevant to the copies at hand.[1]

And marginalia should be honest—preferably correct also, but at least truthful as far as the annotator was concerned at the time of annotation. There are accounts of hoax, or cod, marginalia. Legends (or fantasies) circulate among graduate students of false or obscene notes signed with the initials of notoriously pedantic professors. Max Beerbohm made a hobby of this sort of thing, as we shall see. But by and large, as the violation itself suggests, we rely on the honesty of readers' notes: what would be the use of the Salisbury guide or of Sophia Banks's library notes to anybody at all, otherwise? The honesty convention, perhaps based on the assumption that notes are a private matter between the reader and the text—or rather, a private matter for the reader who has no reason to lie to him- or herself—has to be qualified by the realization that notes are in fact often written, consciously or not, for a third party; but it remains a central characteristic of the marginal note and a key element in the reader's attitude toward it.

Over and above these minimal requirements, there are many features to admire in even very ordinary marginalia. The later reader is grateful for *certified* expertise. That means that when annotators take material from another book to illuminate their own, the source should be identified; and if the ideas are the annotators' own, they should take responsibility for them by writing their names on the flyleaves or by signing the notes that are theirs. (A friend who works on Blake, with whom there is some risk of confusion if not of fraud, goes further: he says marginalia ought to be signed, dated, and notarized.) Many books containing potentially valuable historical evidence have to be ignored or treated with great caution because we have no way of assessing the authority of the annotator.

On the other hand, anything that allows a later reader to reconstruct the circumstances of composition will contribute to a better understanding and a better judgment in the end, as in the case studies of Chapter Four. A simple example better suited to this discussion of basic requirements might be the copy of John Clare's *Poems Descriptive of Rural Life and Scenery* (1820) in the Berg Collection of the New York Public Library. This publication was a milestone in Clare's career, and the copy is of interest because the annotator, Eliza Louisa Emmerson, a poet herself, became one of Clare's middle-class backers and edited some of his later work. The notes include a verse tribute to him (dated 16 February 1820) and comments on individual poems, for instance "This Song is tenderly sweet, and poetically beautiful" (p. xxiii). That these are not spontaneous expressions of delight upon the discovery of a new poetic genius, however, becomes apparent from the inscription to the volume: "To, The Right Honorable Admiral Lord Radstock—this little volume is most respectfully presented—anxiously entreating his Lordships benevolent patronage, and protection of the humble, but extraordinary Poet Clare—and his productions!" (p. −3). It is signed "Incognita" but that word has been crossed out and Mrs. Emmerson's full name given instead. So it appears that Mrs. Emmerson prepared this copy specially, with notes to encourage an enthusiastic reading, in the hope of securing Lord Radstock's patronage, as she successfully did—all too successfully in the opinion of modern critics who deplore the repressive influence of Clare's well-meaning supporters.[2]

With a form of writing that by its nature displays the work of two writers at once, it is encouraging to see as good a match as possible. This principle might operate in one or more of many possible ways, as with all matchmaking. The author and the annotator might be a good fit intellectually, for example; or they might be contemporaries with comparable social backgrounds; or they might be experts in the same field. The common features themselves are less important than the ends that common features are expected to achieve, namely a competent and fair reading, or what Coleridge called "genial" criticism—criticism written in the spirit of the original.[3] Denis Johnston's notes on James Joyce and

Northrop Frye's on John Bunyan are fine modern examples. I believe it is for this reason that Anna Seward's comments on William Cowper's poem *The Task,* in the British Library, seem to me better than Eliza Emmerson's comments on Clare: although she is not shy about expressing disagreement, Seward's response displays political as well as poetic sympathies—a double match. But it may be only that the circumstances of the Clare volume violate the honesty principle.

A modern illustration of the effect of a good match is the pair of copies of Marianne Moore's *Selected Poems* (1935), also in the Berg Collection. One contains notes by John St. Edmunds (or Edmunds), the other by May Lewis. Edmunds is described in a bookseller's or librarian's note as "one of those correcting the text of this book." His ownership inscription is dated 12 September 1938. Edmunds was only twenty-two or twenty-three when the book appeared, and what is meant by "correcting the text" is not clear. His name does not appear in the published letters or the biographies. Could he have been an employee of the publisher? Could the description of him be merely an inference from the marginalia themselves? Whatever his status, Edmunds took a lively interest in Moore's work. His notes contain brief evaluations of many individual poems: "This is a marvelous poem" (p. 1), "there are good things here" (p. 22), "one of the best" (p. 29). He also marks and comments on Moore's diction frequently. On page 7 alone, he says that *hard* is the "vital word," *indigo* "in place," *ichneumon* "over intellectual," and *pivoting* "the adequate word." Elsewhere, words are "delicious" (p. 5), "silly" (p. 9), "rather trifling" (p. 11), "horrible" (*gondoliering*, p. 15). Since Moore's vocabulary is striking and readers do love or hate it, it is useful to see what a contemporary, perhaps an insider, chose to focus on. But Edmunds was a musician by profession, and although he declares his opinions he does not elaborate on them.

May Lewis was a fellow poet. Her annotations stem from her reading of the book for review. There are penciled marks in the margins and underlining here and there throughout the volume, and in some of the larger blank spaces there are fuller notes that mark her progress, such as this one at page 45. (I have started new lines where she did, to allow ambiguities to stand.)

out of the minutiae come big things

she seems able to get outside stand off see earth from another planet

Poetry is everything if we go deep enough

What repetitious emptiness it runs through

the hand like water nothing remains. But hold

M. M. prickly product and there is a kernel to grasp

These are half-formed thoughts that seem to have been jotted down in haste and excitement. On an endpaper (p. +2) there is a more settled judgment: "I did not like her at first[.] I said to myself all the banal things: Is this poetry? These rigid brittle intellectual splinters? 'The poetry is in the pity[.]' The poetry may not be floating oil on the surface; it may be in other aspects so taking that thought: The p. is in the p., like a staff in the hand I went on and on, deeper and deeper in the book. I found the p."

May Lewis's notes on Moore's poems reveal a markedly deeper quality of sympathetic understanding than that displayed in the other copy. I take it to be a sign of the more perfect match between the author and the annotator in her case. Whereas Edmunds was satisfied with brief and brisk judgments expressed in conventional language, Lewis seems to have been spurred by Moore's poems to write at greater length, exploring her reactions and trying to find exactly the right words for them. She did eventually use some of her first thoughts, originally recorded as marginalia, in an article for *Forum and Century* in July 1936. She called it "an appreciation." From Moore it drew a grateful acknowledgment in the form of an inscription she wrote on the half-title page of this copy: *Selected Poems* "of Marianne Moore who is well aware of a good interpreter—February 8, 1938."

The contrast between these two copies of the same work leads to another point. We relish good writing in marginal notes, especially so because in a provisional and informal genre we have little reason to expect it. Among the universally recognized signs of good writing (avoidance of cliché, mastery of metaphor, and so forth), there are a few that seem particularly appropriate to the conditions of marginalia: economy, because of constraints of space, and wit, for related reasons; an individual voice, because marginalia in the past few centuries have become increasingly personal; an air of spontaneity, reinforcing the honesty convention; and passionate expression, as proof of engagement. Perhaps the most elusive of these is "voice," and yet we would probably agree that we seem to "hear" the tones of distinct characters when we read Greville (Scriblerus) as opposed to Pound or Twain or Piozzi or Blake. Of course our sensitivity to individual speech patterns builds up with exposure. But even small things, like the little interjection of surprise— "Hullo!"—in Webb's Rousseau, give a vivid impression of personal voice. For a concise example, I propose the only note by Gertrude Stein in a copy of the autobiography that she wrote in the guise and under the name of her companion. The note, though short, is bafflingly gnomic and involuted. It sounds just like her. On the title page, immediately under the title, *The Autobiography of Alice B. Toklas*, Stein wrote, "I am very pleased with myself for having done so."

Finally, we hope to see signs of mental life in the annotator. It may be the absence of vital signs, not just unsightliness, that makes yellow highlighter so discouraging. Personally I find Mitford's mechanical sticking-in and copying-out of bits of bibliographical lore nearly as bad. In a form that records a transaction between two minds, it is reasonable to suppose that they will differ from each other and that differences will show. ("Without contraries is no progression," as Blake says.) In a dynamic form—for notes tend to be written while reading is in progress, and to reflect fluctuations of response—there may well be changes in the reader's point of view, such as we saw in May Lewis's copy of Marianne Moore's poems. At even a basic level in everyday annotation, therefore, it is good to see proofs of the independence of the reader, as opposed to merely dutiful marking, noting-down of subject headings, and transcribing of ready-made materials from elsewhere. Independence assumes a measure of originality. As the reader evolves ideas of his or her own out of the material of the text, registering the process step by step in marginalia, we seem to be witnessing—albeit on a small scale—a dramatic event.

Fiction is seldom annotated except by teachers, so I was drawn to an item in the Beinecke Library catalogue, a copy of George Eliot's *Mid-*

dlemarch described as containing "pencil notes throughout" by an unidentified reader. The book was probably preserved for its association value: it also contains an inscription dated 1873, written and signed by George Eliot's common law husband, George Henry Lewes. The notes are not many but they do continue throughout the book, showing that the reader persisted to the end. For the most part, they register moments of resistance—and it is interesting to see what those points were for a contemporary reader—but they soften into approval toward the end, and the overall impression is that this first-time reader, initially repelled by the book, was gradually won over. It seems very likely that the notes were in fact written by the original recipient, Mrs. Trübner, to whom Lewes inscribed it in French as a "souvenir d'amitié."[4] One of the notes is also in French (4:6); the reader expresses bewilderment about some words and names that would not have troubled an English reader (White of Selborne, for instance, 4:275); and some of the notes are unidiomatic, for instance "It is very unnatural that an impatient man like Ladislaw would have lissening to this long speech" (3:336). Part of Mrs. Trübner's difficulty—assuming that she was the annotator—arose from difficulties with the language. But she also notes what appear to be inconsistencies or implausibilities of characterization: of Fred Vincy's abrupt departure she says, "this leave-taking is very inartistic and clumsy" (2:42), and upon Dorothea's understanding of Casaubon's dependence, "these reflexions are a great deal to[o] subtle for Dorothea" (3:93). Toward the end, though, there are some positive remarks and warm appreciation. She describes Lydgate's thoughts about Rosamund as "wonderfully clever, but very depressing" (3:290); and against Rosamund's quavering question, "What can *I* do?" she writes "deep thought beautifully expressed" (3:304). Whoever made them, these notes express both independence and a capacity for development.

Francis Palgrave's copy of Alfred Russel Wallace's *Contributions to the Theory of Natural Selection* (1870), annotated in 1871, shows development of a different kind. In this case, the notes exhibit a reader taking in an argument as a chameleon takes in a fly. For a while he watches to see where it's going, then he begins to pay close attention, then he attacks, then he digests. Wallace's book is a varied collection of essays on natural history; it contains one, for instance, titled "The Philosophy of Birds' Nests." In the paper "Mimicry and Other Protective Resemblances among Animals," Wallace promotes the idea of a "special creation" of "mimicking species." To strengthen his case, he attempts to anticipate objections. Palgrave underlines a few words and raises an objection. First Wallace: "Against the special creation of mimicking species there are all the objections and difficulties in the way of special creation in other cases, with the addition of a few that are peculiar to it. The <u>most obvious</u> is, that we have gradations of mimicry and of protective resemblance—a fact which is strongly suggestive of a <u>natural process</u> having been at work." Then Palgrave: "'Special creation' is not a probable or very intelligible thing: but it is meant to imply a process contradictory to 'nature,' & hence an argt. from natural process does not touch it at all as a general postulate—" (p. 108). Wallace: "Another very serious objection is, that as mimicry has been shown to be useful only to those species and groups which are rare and <u>probably dying out</u>. . . ." And Palgrave: "How shown? the only fact is, that mimicry is confined to a few individuals" (p. 109).

Eventually, when Wallace maintains that in insects only females exhibit mimicry, Palgrave shows his exasperation with the essayist's logic and casts up to him a contradiction from an earlier page: "This argument seems to me to involve the idea of special creation in a very specialized form. Unless the variable tendency be confined to the female, the male would also vary into a 'protected' form: and though the female, Nature, may be the most valuable, yet the male (for his own sake) wd be glad of protection & would survive the more for it. Or, the argt wh. here accounts for 'protected' females annihilates the argument on nymphelides of <u>both</u> sexes" (p. 78). As notes of this sort multiply, Palgrave gradually loses faith in his author, observing at the end of an essay on instinct, "This is an excellent example of Mr. W's curious combination of fine individual observation & defective powers of reasoning . . . " (p. 210). Palgrave was a man of letters, not a biologist; he later became professor of poetry at Oxford and is best known for his *Golden Treasury*. He is not an expert reader, nor an especially good match for Wallace, but he is a *good* reader, alert and open-minded. Even a small sample from his notes shows that he was thinking independently and critically as he read, testing and adjusting his own position before coming to a settled view.

At a higher level, with marginalia that are out of the ordinary and annotators who are artists in the genre, all the basic criteria apply but there needs to be also something more (a heightened degree of honesty, erudition, good match, and so forth) or else something unexpected—such as the drawing of a home-made fox trap, among the planting schedules in Cooke's *Complete English Gardener*—that lifts a set of notes above the merely acceptable.

Intelligibility itself is susceptible of art. At the University of Texas, I called up several books from the collection of a former professor of philosophy there, Oets Kolk Bouwsma, and was impressed by the simple system he had devised for annotation. It must have made his books lastingly useful to him, and because the system is transparent, the same is true for later readers. Bouwsma's system has several commonplace features. He uses ink, keeps a running index at the back, underlines text and makes lines down the side of the page, and writes subject headings in the margins. Less conventionally, he reserves the top of the page and occasionally the foot also for reflections of his own, thereby recording his progress through the book stage by stage in a direct and easily accessible way. The deeper margins top and bottom give him space to stop and think in.

A small sampling of notes from Bouwsma's copy of the classic American autobiography *The Education of Henry Adams,* for example, shows him gradually working out the roots of the personal and social problems that Adams describes by tracing them to Adams's confused concept of education itself. On page 44, he underlined the sentence "The more he was educated, the less he understood." His comment at the top reads, "How analyze—an understanding of oneself? Such understanding may be impossible, of course, if it implies a self which can be understood." An underlined passage on page 53—"the American boy of 1854 stood nearer the year 1 than to the year 1900"—provokes a longer observation: "This idea of being educated for one's time—this sounds like Dewey—being educated for comfort in one's time. One might suggest that one's education should fit one for living in any time—Socrates, perhaps. Education should prepare one to meet those problems which are enduring, and which recur in every time. For right action, for overcoming temptation, for driving on to the thing needful. Adams certainly sought what only religious education could provide." When Adams deplores the fact that social snobbery infected the academy of his day, Bouwsma again underlines a phrase and questions his assumptions. This is the text: "If parents went on, generation after generation, sending their children to Harvard College for the sake of its social advantages, they perpetuated an inferior social type, quite as ill-fitted as the Oxford type for success in the next generation." Bouwsma comments, "Here Adams suggests what he might have obtained. Is it Dewey again? For 'success in the next generation'—success!" (p. 65).

And so Bouwsma continues, as he reads, to notice relevant passages and to register significant reactions, steadily sorting out his own ideas. On page 242, when Adams complains that "Newport was charming, but it asked for no education and gave none," he notes, "Isn't it that in Adams' sense of education, no man ever is educated. He expects the world not only to furnish an environment, but also to furnish the ideals. That it never does." His distaste for Adams seems to increase toward the end of the book, until finally he marks another passage and makes his judgment explicit. The text reads, "To one who, at past sixty years old, is still passionately seeking education, these small, or large, annoyances had no great value except as measures of mass and motion." Bouwsma sharply responds, "When after sixty Adams still writes in this way about education, it seems a little silly, much silly in fact" (p. 395).

Though I mention him as a model of intelligibility, like other skilled annotators Bouwsma actually displays a combination of desirable qualities: an elegant adaptation of traditional techniques, serious engagement with the text, clear expression, and a convincing personal voice. Though it is difficult to document because of space constraints, he also provides a reasonably good example of the distinctive advantage of the marginal form, scope for debate, and hence of the advantage of the debating talents of sharp intelligence and forceful expression.

I hesitate over the word "debate" since, as I pointed out earlier, authors cannot respond to defend themselves. "Minute criticism" might be more exact. But when the annotator's words are on the page along with the author's, the author's words constitute a check on the annotator. Then the comment can be seen by a later reader to be valid or not, and so to that reader at least, the exchange has the *effect* of debate. It is a very common effect, especially with marginalia attached to polemical books. The anonymous critic of Bishop Watson's *Letter to the Archbishop of Canterbury*, quoted in Chapter One, behaves for his few pages like a debater hounding his opponent point by point. Blake's and Macaulay's marginalia are unsparing in rebuttal when the annotators think the authors in the wrong. Alert readers like John Horne Tooke and Augustus Frederick, Duke of Sussex, whose work is well represented in the British Library, pounce on careless or inaccurate remarks with obvious relish— it's all part of the intellectual contest between them and the authors. (When Tooke's library went on sale after his death in 1812, the catalogue singled out the annotated volumes as of special value.)[5]

Up to a point, prickly marginalia fired by indignation can be stimulating in the way that lively debate is stimulating. To this day, negative reactions of resistance, anger, even outrage, probably inspire the majority of readers' notes. But marginalia that are unremittingly angry or contemptuous only become tedious and put the annotator, rather than the text, in a bad light. Macaulay himself goes too far sometimes, for example in his comments on T. J. Mathias's *Pursuits of Literature:* "Bah!" (p. vii); "A contemptible heap of rant & twaddle" (p. xx); "Senseless trash" (p. 4); "Stuff" (p. 17); "Fool!" (p. 26); "Noisome pedantry" (p. 27); "Trash" (p. 34); "A good line for a wonder" (p. 51); "Stupid pompous nothingness" (p. 178); and so on.

Thackeray's caricature of the annotator as Jones at his club, scoffing at his book after dinner, is so true to life that we are likely to be quite impressed by marginalia that are not like that—that take the book seriously, that take care with it, above all those that adopt a charitable attitude toward it. The patient scholarship of Francis Hargrave is a model in this respect. He is seldom—I think, in fact, never—colorful or passionate, but he is exact and reliable. He takes the trouble to explain himself. In his own edition of *Coke upon Littleton* (1775), to draw on a microscopic sample, he noticed an error that would have to be put right at the next opportunity; instead of just changing the word he made a memorandum justifying the change. He had said that the text would "be collated with the *Rohan* edition, which was preferred by Sir Edward Coke," but as he notes, "<u>Rouen</u> is the proper word. Lord Coke calls it <u>Roan</u>. I was led into ye error of calling it <u>Rohan</u> by the editor of the 11th edition, who in his notes to ye preface so spells ye word."[6] A few pages farther on, having added to his printed footnote a reference to a recent ruling that a borrower "may be a witness in an information for usury" whether the debt has been repaid or not, he adds yet another manuscript note in the margin: "On reading Abraham & Bunn a 2d. time, I doubt, whether the case proves more, than that the borrower may qualify himself as a witness by proving payment of the debt" (fol. 6v). Of course Hargrave's precision, misapplied or in less capable hands, runs the risk of pedantry. Some of the best kinds of marginalia have less appealing counterparts and imitators. Coleridge's son Hartley, perhaps oppressed by his models, turned the marginal note into a miniature essay and thereby bled most of the vitality out of it.

As Hargrave raises the standard for certified expertise, so a minor Victorian writer shows what can be done with an unusual level of "genial" receptivity. William Godwin's tribute to Mary Wollstonecraft, *Memoirs of the Author of A Vindication of the Rights of Woman* has come up before, in Chapter Six, as the subject of the attentions of John Horseman. It would be an understatement to say that it was a controversial book when it was published in 1798. It was scandalous then and if anything it became more so as times changed and Wollstonecraft and Godwin faded from the memory of the living. Benjamin Dockray, author of brief reflections on moral and topical subjects that were collected under the title *Egeria* in the 1840s, acquired a copy of Godwin's *Memoirs* secondhand in 1860 and settled down to read it for the first time. His ownership inscription is dated 16 August 1860. He was a methodical reader who recorded on the first page the date at which he began reading (18 August) and on the last page, page 206, the date of finishing (24 September). All the notes are in pencil. Dockray's routine annotation includes plentiful underlining, setting-off of passages with lines and exclamation marks, small stylistic corrections, and cross-references of two kinds, internal cross-references to other places in the book where a given topic had come up, and external ones to other books in his own library. He made up an index at the back of the book, starting on the back flyleaf (p. +4) and working inward to the first blank page at the back (p. +1). Most of the subject headings in that index are his own words, for example, "Alternatives—determined by slightest causes"; but many are just the obvious, such as "Fuseli 85+: 89. 90+: 101–113." (The cross indicates that there is a manuscript note on the same page.)

Dockray ranks high on the intelligibility scale, but that is the least of his virtues as an annotator. His notes, which do not appear to have been written with any later reader in mind, show him thinking aloud as he reads. Above all, they show him making connections. Moving back and forth in the book, he keeps track of recurrent topics by recording pages on which they have appeared before or will appear later. He identifies literary allusions and notes other parallel passages as they occur to him, citing for example Isaac D'Israeli, Goethe, Goldsmith, and Rousseau, and thereby setting the work in an expanding context of significance. Most important of all, like Mrs. Piozzi he brings personal experience to bear, testing Godwin's interpretation of the story by reference to his own life. Some of these points of connection are trivial, but they have a cumulative effect, and in any case the effort of sympathetic understanding is the main thing. On page 106, for instance, when Godwin builds up to the introduction of Imlay by saying, "It was about four months after her arrival at Paris, that she entered into that connection, from which the tranquillity and the sorrows of the immediately succeeding years of her life were solely derived," Dockray merely underlines "Paris" and observes, "Aug 30[/]60 I am copying at present the pencil Notes of my last visit to Paris 1843"—as though the tranquillity and sorrows of Wollstonecraft's life were less interesting to him than the adventitious bond of their both having once been to Paris. When he hears of her first novel, similarly, the pencil comes out to underline words that create a link between them: "At Bristol Hot-Wells she composed the little book which bears the title of *Mary, a Fiction*. A considerable part of this story consists, with certain modifications, of the incidents of her own friendship with Fanny." Dockray writes, hardly dispassionately, "This is a very effective plan of Novel-writing:—imagination & memory reciprocate; the affections mingling, the real & the ideal take from this combination new beauty & new force—Egeria Vol page ('The episode of Nisus and Euryalus & that of Pallas in the Aeneid')" (p. 60).

Under these circumstances, it is not surprising that his reactions to Wollstonecraft's words and actions err, if they err, on the side of charity. He responds empathetically. When Godwin quotes her account of her feelings upon the death of her friend Fanny Blood ("still she is present with me, and I hear her soft voice warbling as I stray over the heath"), Dockray responds, "The phraseology here, shows that the memory of facts had risen to the Ideal, & taken the colours of Poetry: but they were not therefore less sincere,—for, this was the natural result for a mind like hers" (p. 48). And when Godwin tersely refers to her attempt at suicide ("she formed a desperate purpose to die"), Dockray, though conventionally religious himself, casts her in heroic terms: "That she could disengage herself from the purpose of suicide,—to go to Norway for Imlay, is wonderful. But it is possible that her contemplation of suicide presented that event as a refuge always in her power; as Cleopatra in Shakespere 'Now am I marble-constant &c'" (p. 131).

Dockray's sympathetic attitude in fact extends beyond Wollstonecraft to Godwin and, more remarkably, to the social group that ostracized them after their marriage. Their relationship had been an open secret, and Godwin represents Wollstonecraft as having been betrayed by one-time friends who ceased to see her once it was legitimated. His indignation is scathing: "She was of too proud and generous a spirit to stoop to hypocrisy. These persons, however, in spite of all that could be said, persisted in shutting their eyes, and pretending they took her for a married woman. . . . The moment she acknowledged herself a wife, the case was altered." Dockray tries to put the case for the defense, imagining the awkward position even of those who had wished her well: "Till then—the charity of her acquaintance could employ a kind pretence; afterwards this pretence was taken from them by the marriage with Godwin. They would have been glad of another,—but none was possible" (p. 165).

Godwin's final flourish implies a philosophical position Dockray could not share. Instead of shouting "Blockhead!" or "Atheist!" in the margin, however, he responds mildly. Godwin describes how "a fatal event, hostile to the moral interests of mankind, ravished from me the light of my steps, and left to me nothing but the consciousness of what I had possessed, and must now possess no more." Dockray marks off the phrase "hostile to the moral interests of mankind" and questions the text, "Does Godwin mean death? I think it very likely that Godwin's early & life-long reading was very much confined to the doubting order of minds; that he was really very uninformed as to the other aspects & the positive resources of Our Human Nature" (p. 205). These are the words of a reader who disagrees but who, instead of condemning the book and the author, makes an effort to understand and allow for a position different from his own.

Not so kind, generally, but sharing some of Dockray's warmth is the annotator who sees the comical side of a book and knows how to bring it out. Humor is generally welcome in marginalia. Many of Thackeray's books contain engaging little sketches that illustrate the text and at the same time, albeit in a wordless way, express his delight in it. Another caricaturist, Max Beerbohm, always fond of practical jokes, not only wrote comments occasionally in his books but also "improved" a few favorites with fraudulent inscriptions, captions, blurbs, and illustrations. One of the most complicated was his doctored copy of Queen Victoria's *More Leaves from the Journal of a Life in the Highlands,* with playfully-intended forgeries of her handwriting in annotations, captions, and a dedicatory inscription "for Mr Beerbohm | the never-sufficiently-to-be-studied writer | whom Albert looks down on affectionately." S. N. Behrman calls this "his collaboration with the Queen" (p. 102); hyperbolic as it is, the phrase has some truth to it. A picture of one of the queen's dogs carries the manuscript note, "Such a dear, faithful, noble *friend* and companion, and for whom Albert had the *greatest* respect also. Victoria R." Beerbohm's parody is absurd because it is almost credible: it only exaggerates qualities already present in the book. Other exercises of this hobby of his are less elaborate and more straightforwardly satirical (fig. 9).[7]

Indeed satire and ridicule, adversarial forms of humor, are more

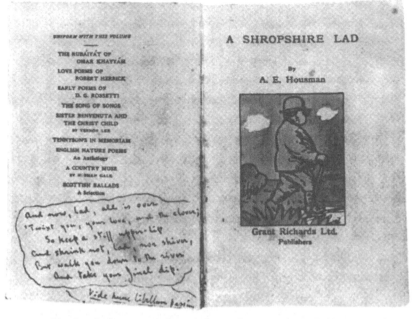

FIG. 9 Max Beerbohm, watercolor painting and ms. note in A. E. Housman, *A Shropshire Lad* (1920). The ribald verse parody reads, "And now, lad, all is over, / 'Twixt you, your love, and the clover; / So keep a stiff upper-lip / And shrink not, lad, nor shiver, / But walk you down to the river / And take your final dip." (Used by permission of the Warden and Fellows of Merton College, Oxford)

common among annotators than Thackeray's genial behavior. Samuel Parr's copy of *Poems by Mrs. Pickering* (1794), for example, is thickly peppered with sarcastic remarks. The fun starts on the title page, where Parr mocks the rather pompous crediting of other contributors (besides Mrs. Pickering's, the volume includes poems by John Morfitt and Joseph Weston, "the Author, and Translator of *Philotoxi Ardenae*") by adding himself: "with notes explanatory and ornamental by Philononsensicus." There were personal reasons for his reacting as he did and wishing to dissociate himself from the book. A fine Latin scholar, but a prickly person and an outspoken Whig, Parr had settled in Hatton as parson and schoolmaster. One of Morfitt's pieces, "Lines on Hatton," includes a verse portrait of him, so when Morfitt introduces Hatton as "A Village near Warwick; the Residence of Dr. Parr," Parr crosses out the last five words and writes, "blot it out for shame—."[8]

Parr appears to have objected mostly to Morfitt's poems, and especially to Morfitt's high-toned cant (what we might now call "political correctness"), though the root of the problem may have been political differences. Parr was a friend and defender of Joseph Priestley, who had not long before been driven out of the country by Church-and-King rioters in Birmingham. Morfitt wrote against him in "A Poetical Effusion, on the Religious and Political Character of Dr. P——y" (pp. 68–70); the editor, Weston, anticipating trouble, tried to placate Parr in a prefatory note in which he quotes Parr's tribute to Priestley and unctuously praises Parr himself. Parr naturally sees through this maneuver and interprets the editor's words in parallel marginalia: "I will please my Church and King friends, but I dare not offend Dr Parr . . . I hope that is laid on thick enough, bravo, bravissimo" (p. iv). His reactions throughout are fairly brutal. He subjects Morfitt's lines "To Miss Wilson, of Hatton"—"What blissful moments have I spent with thee, / Friend of my soul!"—to systematic double-entendre (pp. 45–47). When Morfitt, in delicate allusion to her blindness, begins his poem "To Mrs. Pickering" by addressing her as "Sweet *Philomela,* warbling in the shade!" Parr turns her back from a nightingale to a woman by putting in one of his "ornamental notes," a drawing of a lady sitting under a tree with her legs straight out before her.

After Weston has the temerity to print "Sonnets; in Imitation of Milton" (p. 25), Parr attacks his poem "Written on Returning from Lichfield" (p. 27)—a thank-you note to his hostess there, lamenting the loss of bright rooms and lively conversation—by adding to the closing stanza. Weston's poem ends with a pathetic comparison between himself and the native Tahitian Omai, who had been a celebrated visitor in England twenty years earlier.

Amaz'd, FATIGU'D, I seek my joyless Dome;
No LARES *there,* alas! propitious shine!
Illum'd—then *banish'd*—to thy hateful HOME—
Poor, poor OMAI—what a Fate was *thine!*

But Parr finishes it off, suggesting that Weston must be out of touch with reality even to hint at a comparison between his situation and that of Omai:

> Not half so bad alas as mine!
> Shut up at home all in the dark
> As if they thought that I was stark.
> The last lines are in Imitation of Weston—

Finally, he marks and comments upon the last stanza of the last poem by Weston, "The Execution of the Queen of France":

> "Princess, rejoice! The awful moment's nigh,
> "That ends thy tortures—that rewards thy woes!
> "Yon S T E E L exalts thee to th'expecting sky,
> "And for perdition seals thy impious foes!"

The comment? "By ending this Book you end mine." Not yet fifty, Parr already had the reputation of a testy old codger. One can see why. But in this book at least there is ample evidence of mental vigor, and Parr's jokes are an effective antidote to the saccharine excesses of the verse. Though it is far from a "genial" response, it is relevant, witty, and justifiable.

Better than Parr on Pickering by quite a long shot is Keats on Milton. At this point we leave the masters of the art and enter the realm of the transcendent, where rules are cast aside. The copy of *Paradise Lost* annotated by Keats is not a showy object, just a neat pocket copy of an edition of no special authority in two little leather-bound volumes. It contains a great deal of underlining; one long introductory note on a flyleaf at the front of the first volume; eighteen further notes, most of them several sentences long, in the remainder of the work; and a draft version of a poem, "To Sleep." The whole set of notes has been published, and I select just two to represent them all.[9] A passage describing the palace in Hell is underlined throughout:

Anon out of the earth a fabric huge
Rose like an exhalation, with the sound
Of dulcet symphonies and voices sweet,
   . . . and straight the doors,
Opening their brazen folds, discover, wide
Within, her ample spaces, o'er the smooth
And level pavement: from the arched roof,
Pendent by subtle magic many a row
Of starry lamps and blazing cressets, fed
With Naphtha and Asphaltus, yielded light
As from a sky. (1:23; *PL* 1:710–30)

Keats comments, "What creates the intense pleasure of not knowing? A sense of independence, of power, from the fancy's creating a world of its own by the sense of probabilities. We have read the Arabian Nights and hear there are thousands of those sort of Romances lost—we imagine after them—but not their realities if we had them nor our fancies in their strength can go further than this Pandemonium—'Straight the doors opening' &c. 'rose like an exhalation—[.]'" Both Milton and Keats now arouse such automatic reverence that it is difficult for many of us to write and even to think straight about them. Had this note, with its fellows, been attributed to an unknown annotator, would it have seemed at all remarkable? I think so. It is "genial" and admiring. It conveys a complex idea (satisfying the criterion of "mental life") in an economical but still sufficiently developed way. And it is strikingly well written, from the provocative opening to the grand climax of parallel phrasing, "not their realities . . . nor our fancies."

A second sample confirms the impression of critical authority. It occurs at the moment when Satan enters the body of the sleeping serpent—another underlined passage of which I quote just a few lines.

   Him fast sleeping soon he found
In labyrinth of many a round self-roll'd,
His head the midst, well stored with subtle wiles.
   . . . in at his mouth

The Devil enter'd, and his brutal sense,
In heart or head, possessing, soon inspired
With act intelligential; but his sleep
Disturbed not, waiting close at the approach of morn. (2:80–81; *PL*
9:179–91)

Keats's comment here displays professional appreciation of fine detail but also an acute sensitivity that amounts to empathetic identification with both the author and the subject: "Satan having entered the Serpent, and inform'd his brutal sense—might seem sufficient—but Milton goes on 'but his sleep disturb'd not.' Whose spirit does not ache at the smothering and confinement—the unwilling stillness—the 'waiting close'? Whose head is not dizzy at the possible speculations of Satan in this serpent prison—no passage of poetry ever can give a greater pain of suffocation."

Had it been the work of an unidentified reader of the Romantic period, this copy of Milton might have been of interest to Miltonists following the course of the interpretation of his work and the development of his reputation, and to the new breed of historians of reading who want to know what the experience of reading can have been like in earlier generations. An inscription informs us that it was Keats's gift to Mrs. Dilke, so we realize that the notes are not a reader's private memoranda but a guide prepared for a friend, like many other annotated books of the time. But of course we do know that the notes are by Keats, not by just any ambitious young writer, and that in this case we are experiencing the conjunction of two extraordinary talents. Our reading of the text with the accompanying notes is mediated by what we already know about each of them and about the connection between them—particularly, by our awareness of Keats's awe of Milton and his efforts to learn from him. Furthermore we are conscious that both parties were changed by the encounter, that Keats's observations affect the way we now read Milton and that his attention to Milton had consequences for his own work. Besides the satisfaction of good criticism, Keats's copy of Milton conveys the thrill of genesis.

The conviction that Keats's notes on Milton, like Blake's on Reynolds, are of a different order from Parr's on Pickering does not depend on the seductiveness of great names alone. On the other hand, it would be wrong to disregard the influence of great names. A famous name (book, author, or annotator) ratchets up the standard: a great book may evoke better than usual notes from an ordinary reader, and a great annotator may work wonders with an ordinary book. For a while, not for long, I entertained the rule of thumb that one great name could lift marginalia above the level of basic competence, but that it took two to achieve transcendence. Then I thought of some of the promising combinations that had let me down.

The Berg Collection in New York contains many books annotated by Vladimir Nabokov, some of them by famous authors—the Freud-Jung letters, for instance, and translations of Proust, Tolstoy, Kafka, and Flaubert. Most of these great works were annotated to teach from. Where that is not the case, the notes tend to be brief and not very revealing. In the teaching texts, Nabokov puts considerable effort into comment on the translations, and it is sometimes possible to see the outlines of a lecture in the selection of passages and in Nabokov's instructions to himself on the flyleaves, so these notes are potentially valuable to followers either of Nabokov or of his subjects, as the notes on Milton by Keats might be to Miltonists or Romanticists. Perhaps the most striking is one on Kafka's *Metamorphosis* that brings together Nabokov's literary and scientific interests. Nabokov revised this note carefully and marked the pronunciation of the technical terms in a way that suggests that he may actually have read it out loud in class:

> What is the "vermin" into which poor Gregor is transformed? It obviously belongs to the phylum Arthropod but does this arthropod belong to the class "insect" or to that of "spiderlike creatures" or "centipedes" or even "crustaceans"? Critics have assumed it to be a cockroach (see 78) but this is an insect of flattened form (i.e. not with a round back and a tremendous convex belly as Gregor has) and one with six comparatively large legs (not the "numerous little legs" of Gregor). The "numerous" if meaning more than *six* would put it into another class of arthropods—not insects. However, six may seem

numerous to a transform man. Wing cases? It is brown. He had mandibles (p. 27). The old charwoman calls him "dung beetle" (not "cockroach" as in this idiotic translation). About 3 feet long. He never found out that there were wings under the hard covering of his back (the "wing cases" under which a beetles flimsy little wings are concealed).[10]

This is a helpful note, well developed and with some authority, but it is not what we might have hoped for from the combination of Kafka and Nabokov. I suspect that our disappointment arises from the fact that Nabokov is not actually engaged with Kafka in this note, but with his translators and commentators; also that he was doing what he thought appropriate for an academic audience, not pursuing his thoughts in an uninhibited manner.

Jeremy Bentham on Edmund Burke is another disappointment. One volume in the British Library contains eight pamphlets by Burke with Bentham's annotations. In this case there is no apparent expectation of the notes' being shared with any other reader. Bentham systematically marks passages with underlining or lines in the margin, and writes in subject headings; sometimes he keeps a separate index as well, listing key points with page references, or writes a general appraisal at the end of the work. Now and then he argues with Burke in the margin, as when Burke defends an unpopular tax on breweries. Burke puts his case: "Here is the effect of two such daring taxes as 3d. by the bushel additional on malt, and 3s. by the barrel additional on beer. Two impositions laid without remission one upon the neck of the other; and laid upon an object which had before been immensely loaded. They did not in the least impair the consumption: it has grown under them. It appears that, upon the whole, the people did not feel so much inconvenience from the new duties as to oblige them to take refuge in the private brewery."[11] Bentham's response? "It only proves that they like beer better than other things, which they must have deprived themselves of to procure the Beer." His remark is reasonable and salutary, but very few notes in the volume are even as remarkable as this; for the most part, Bentham is just another methodical reader.

Gibbon on Herodotus? Revision of his own work aside, Gibbon was not habitually an annotator, but there is an annotated Herodotus in the Rothschild Collection at Cambridge.[12] It is a magnificent vellum-bound folio of over a thousand pages, a scholarly edition with the Greek text and Latin translation in parallel columns together with a band of textual notes and two columns of footnotes on every page, the text proper being followed by almost two hundred pages of commentary. Gibbon's notes—about thirty-five of them, all in ink, in a big, even hand—occur fairly regularly up to page 173 and rarely thereafter; the last note appears on page 519. There is no sign of their having been prepared for someone else to read, but given that it was unusual for Gibbon to annotate books in this way, a silent audience remains a possibility. The conventional thing for a scholar like Gibbon to have done with a book like this would have been to subject the text to close scrutiny, collating it with other editions and comparing Herodotus's version of events with other accounts. Gibbon does correct the Greek once or twice, and he questions or clarifies statements in the text. When he cites an ancient or modern authority, he gives chapter and verse, that is, name and page reference. By and large, however, his notes are the notes not of a classical scholar but of a fellow historian. Though he calls Herodotus to task for occasional lapses, he observes approvingly that after all he had "a philosophic mind" (p. 173). He writes as though he enjoyed the reading and was being stimulated to think about history-writing in general. With the encouragement of vast margins, he takes the time to enlarge upon his impressions; his expansiveness requires a slightly larger than usual sampling.

On the story of Arion, the singer who was saved from drowning by a dolphin that let him ride on its back, Gibbon comments skeptically, "An odd digression, and most unphilosophical fable! Since it supposes the friendship of a man and a Sea-fish (a sort of porpess Pennant's British Zoology Vol iii p 48), and the exquisite sensibility of a <u>deaf</u> animal to the sound of the Lyre" (*History* 1.24; p. 11). The account of the Medes, who were tricked into making Deioces their king, shows how smoothly Gibbon's mind moved between narrative particulars and historical generalizations: "Rousseau has wisely observed (Emile, Part 1 p 281) that the most incredible narratives of Herodotus may be esteemed as moral lessons. In this doubtful history of the Medes we may trace the progress of Civil society. They renounced their freedom to escape the evils of anarchy: their slavery was confirmed and alleviated by the selfish arts, and specious virtues of their first king; but his son was a conqueror, and his great-grandson a tyrant" (1.95; p. 49). The marvelous story of Rhampsinitus, who robbed and outwitted the king and was eventually married to his daughter, provokes censure but also admiration: "This foolish story, so unworthy of a grave historian, is neatly and agreeably told; and the reader is tempted to forget, that this first of men is no more than a paltry thief, whose boldness and cunning might be easily matched or surpassed in the annals of the Old Bailey" (2.121, p. 159).

Two longer notes offer more insight into Gibbon's thought processes. In the first passage, Herodotus shows how Croesus had been partly to blame for his own fall: though he took the precaution of consulting the oracle of Apollo at Delphi (and rewarding it richly), he was too quick to interpret its responses in his favor. Notably, when he was advised that if he led an army against the Persians, he would destroy a great empire, he failed to consider the possibility that the oracle might refer to *his own* empire (1.91). In defense of the oracle, the priestess explains in the first place that no one can escape his destined lot, but secondly that Croesus should have made further enquiry to find out which empire had been meant. Gibbon's complex response combines scholarship, philosophy, and political pragmatism:

> A dangerous mode of defence! Neither Philosophy nor Religion will admit this mixture of necessary and contingent events. If the fall of Croesus was irrevocably decreed, the time and manner must have been equally determined. The smallest links are essential to form the perfect continuity of the great chain. The words of the Oracles themselves have been attacked with irresistible impudence by Oenamaus the Cynic (Vandal. de Oraculis p 330 &c), who demonstrates that such fatal ambiguity to a generous benefactor must have proceeded, either from the ignorance, or the malice of Apollo. I should like to know, how much Herodotus received from the priests of Delphi. (p. 46)

Finally, Gibbon takes exception to Herodotus's account of the assembly at which Xerxes put forward his proposal to lead an expedition against Athens (7.8–10; p. 509). The debate is covered in detail, with long harangues by Xerxes, Mardonius, and Artabanus given in full as direct quotations. Gibbon's statement not only exposes a technical problem that continues to plague historians and biographers; it also articulates a general rule for solving it:

> Without absolutely condemning the composition of speeches so familiar to the ancients, I shall presume to impose the three following laws on this species of historical fiction. 1 That the truth of the leading fact, of the council debate, orations &c be positively ascertained. 2. That some natural means be suggested through which, the historian (who cannot plead the inspiration of the Muse,) might derive his intelligence. 3. That the language and ideas be strictly adapted to the national and personal characters of his Dramatic speakers. On these principles it would not be easy to justify the orations of Xerxes, Mardonius, and Artabanus.

Gibbon's notes on Herodotus are quite as extraordinary as Keats's on Milton, and for similar reasons. Both display a high degree of mental life, intelligibility, certified authority, fine style, and good match. Over and above these estimable qualities, however, they represent something much more elusive. The words of Milton and Herodotus inspired these particularly gifted readers to creative acts of understanding and were in turn illuminated by them. Both parties were changed by the encounter. The only word that seems to offer itself to describe such significant and constructive events is "symbiosis," which denotes not a property of either player but a consequence of their coming together. The effect is unpredictable, and although a great name may be a contributing factor, it is no guarantee of great results.[13]

Historical accident may also play a part in producing what come to be seen as sensational marginalia. Suppose Keats had never become a household name? As I was writing this chapter, newspapers carried an account of an annotated Latin Bible that was expected to raise an enormous sum at auction. Six hundred English words and phrases written in the margins by an unknown scribe had been discovered to have been the work of a member of the team that produced the Geneva Bible in English, and they thus constitute "unique manuscript evidence" of the process of translation.[14] But suppose the Geneva Bible had sunk without a trace like some other early English Bibles? Then this copy would be just a glossed working copy like thousands of others. Under these circumstances, historical importance makes the difference between an interesting annotated book and an astonishing one.

A final example is the Beinecke copy of a pamphlet written by a West Indian plantation-owner named Estwick, published anonymously in London in 1772 to defend slavery. The annotator, Granville Sharp, opposes the author point by point in an exceptionally tenacious, rigorous, and expansive way. Even a relatively minor point like the analogy between slavery and the more widely accepted "pressing," or forced recruitment, of sailors has his full attention. Estwick formally addresses his remarks to Lord Mansfield: "The impressing of seamen, my Lord, is an idea as heterogeneous to the nature and essence of this government, as slavery painted on the blackest ground can be. It is slavery itself in its very definition; and what signifies the name, says Hudibras, since the thing is the same?" In the margin, Sharp objects, "One injustice cannot justify another!" But then Estwick goes on, and Sharp continues his underlining: "But the indispensableness of the measure has nevertheless (to continue the metaphor) given colour to the practice, and it is now seen in another light and view." At this point, Sharp finds it necessary to spell out the reasons for his rejection of the argument as it applies both to pressing and to slavery:

> Neither is pressing indispensible any more than the Slave Trade, because the imaginary necessity of pressing is occasioned merely by an unpardonable neglect of the Marine Department in time of Peace. For if all idle Persons that are fairly proved to be Vagabonds according to Law were sent on board the King's Ships & there maintained and instructed till they should be able to undertake the duty of Ordinary or professed Seamen there would be no want of Hands. Besides the pro-

fessed Seamen ought by way of encouragement to be ranked in a superior Class from the Probationers with some honourable mark of distinction; neither should they be subjected in like manner to ill treatment from their superiors (which is one of the greatest discouragements to the Sea Service) nor be liable to any punishment whatever until convicted before a Court Martial. This would render their profession honourable & their Condition, not only comfortable but even desirable to all active persons who want employment, instead of being shunned like a <u>Hell upon Earth</u> which is at present (and but too justly, I fear) a common Phrase to express the Hardship of the Sea Service. (pp. 6–7)

These are excellent notes, working out an intellectual position by reasoned opposition. What sets them apart from others of a similar kind is historical circumstance. Estwick was a contributor to the pamphlet war raging around the case of James Sommersett (or Somerset or Somersett), an American slave. Sommersett had escaped from his owner in England and claimed his freedom. His master had him retaken and confined on a ship bound for Jamaica, where he would be sold again. Lord Mansfield, as chief justice of the Court of King's Bench where the case was heard, ruled in Sommersett's favor and released him. The prime mover behind the case, however, was Granville Sharp, a largely self-educated clerk who devoted his free time, energy, and limited financial resources to philanthropic causes, especially the abolition of slavery. Upon the failure of a similar case a few years earlier, he had made a thorough study of the laws concerned with personal liberty and on that basis had written and published *A Representation of the Injustice and Dangerous Tendency of Admitting the Least Claim of Private Property in the Persons of Men, in England* (1769).[15] The entry on him in the *Dictionary of National Biography* says of the Sommersett case, "This first great victory in the struggle for the emancipation of slaves was entirely due to Sharp." A pamphlet annotated by Sharp in the course of the public debate thus recreates the process by which history was made. It is set apart by special circumstances from other polemical marginalia.

Although it is not possible to foresee special circumstances or to write a formula for producing superlative marginalia, it is possible with hindsight to identify some of their recurrent features: association with greatness (or at least with fame), historical significance, and creative symbiosis. In the scale of annotators—the adequate, the masterful, and the transcendent—where does Walpole stand? We are now in a position to reflect upon the opinion delivered at the opening of this chapter. Walpole was a lifelong book collector and annotator; his sympathetic biographer, Wilmarth Lewis, explains that his "early habit of writing in his books became so strong that in his old age he forced his gouty hand to write, no matter how tightly a book was bound or how cramped were its margins; his small left hand pressed painfully down to hold it open and steady while his right carved out a note" (p. lxiii). His ambition was to become the historian of his age through the posthumous publication of his memoirs and letters. He put his books to work. Some of them he extra-illustrated; others he kept as reference books in which his own notes acted simultaneously as memoranda for himself and as corrigenda for posterity. Walpole typically marked passages that interested him, filled in names where discretion had imposed silence, and added information from other sources or from private knowledge—frequently initialing the notes by way of endorsement. He often lent his books to friends, without seeming to have annotated them for anyone in particular. I have never encountered a personally revealing note in one of Walpole's books, or one that you could imagine he would object to seeing widely distributed once he was gone. This is not to say that his marginalia are cautious about other people's reputations—far from it—but they are calculated to enhance *his* reputation as judge and chronicler.

The scale of Walpole's corpus of marginalia is part of its strength, for he comments through his books on many facets of the life of his time, notably literature, the visual arts, politics, and antiquarianism. The same quality makes it folly even to attempt to represent him faithfully in a short space. On the other hand, the role he saw for himself as an annotator was quite consistently that of the corrector. His mandate was to set the record straight, to the best of his ability. He did not pretend to be impartial. He loved anecdote and must have particularly relished being in a position to expose the self-seeking or hypocritical statements of his rivals. Again and again, he punctures po-faced official history with delicious Aubrey-like detail. Of the Earl of Oxford's second wife, Sarah Middleton, for instance, Walpole recalls, "This Lady was a Rigid Presbyterian: the Italian Duchess of Shrewsbury asking Her if her Lord was restless & tumbled & tost about in the night like her Duke, She replied, I trouble my Head about no Lord but the Lord Jehovah—the Lord Jehovah, cried the duchess, pray who be dat? is dat one of de Queen's new Lords?"[16] When Walpole writes in such a vein from personal experience, his evidence must be taken seriously; often, however, he merely repeats unattributed gossip (as in Lady Oxford's case) because it is amusing and discreditable to his enemies or the enemies of his friends. So one is grateful for improved information—and Walpole's marginalia contain masses of it—and entertained by his stories, but suspicious of his motives. As an annotator, he ranks high for intelligibility, wit, and certified authority, but low for geniality, capacity for development, and creative symbiosis. He set out to correct and control his books; he was not to be caught off guard by them. He is a master, not a prince, among annotators.

chapter eight

Book Use or Book Abuse

Coleridge's marginalia converted me to writing in books. The annotated books that I studied afterward went further, making me into an advocate by showing me that this practice, sanctioned for centuries, could help readers to focus their attention and to recall what they had read more exactly, supplement and improve the books themselves, and provide evidence not available elsewhere. A new batch of "books with manuscript," as Robin Alston calls them, to me is like a heap of birthday presents waiting to be opened: they might contain almost anything, and there are bound to be surprises among them. A habit that has proved useful to many readers turns out to have incidental benefits also for the historical record. This being so, to quote the best administrator I know, "What's the downside?" Sad to say, there are good reasons for objecting to readers' notes in books. The first part of this chapter is devoted to the case *against*—not as in a trial, but as in a hearing. After that I go on to outline potential uses for marginalia, and in particular to consider the role marginalia might have in developing the history of reading. For obvious reasons the point of view throughout is that of the third party (neither the annotator nor the annotated author) contemplating a book already written in; and the judgment as to whether marginalia constitute use or abuse is a matter for the eye of the beholder. Our own notes we like, or have learned to live with; those we resist are always written by somebody else.

The first witness is a small boy taken against his will by his father to one of Maurice Sendak's book signings. Pushed forward to get his book signed, the boy looked at Sendak imploringly and said, "Please don't crap up my book!" And Sendak, sensibly, didn't.[1] This is an Emperor's New Clothes story: the child has a license to say what others think but dare not articulate. Marginalia are untidy. Books are no longer designed to incorporate them (though the electronic book may change that); the better produced and more beautiful the book is, the less hospitable it is likely to be to manuscript additions. Even in older books more closely modeled on glossed manuscripts, the handwritten note stands in glaring contrast to the printed text, and there is no note so neatly written as to be unobtrusive. Therefore the value of the notes has somehow to outweigh the intrusion. But connoisseurs and collectors throughout this century have been biased in favor of "clean" copies. There may well be rare-book collections that would show a book the door if they found a note in it. Readers vary in their willingness to entertain marginalia and zero tolerance is not unusual. The custodian of a private library once told me, bursting out like the little boy, that "Coleridge would spoil anyone's books if he could get his hands on them." Never mind that customs were different in Coleridge's day, never mind that the owners begged him to do it, never mind that the notes enhance the book and greatly increase its value—writing in books spoils them. As a professional, that librarian might be brought to admit some exceptions to the general rule, but in his heart he will probably always believe that it is absolutely, unconditionally wrong to write in books.

As both anecdotes indicate, marginalia arouse strong feelings. We seem lately to have made them taboo—a point I shall come back to shortly. The root of the hostility in these two cases at first appears to be aesthetic: marginalia are messy, and for the boy and the librarian nothing can make up for the loss of the unsullied page. Taste is not a trivial matter; wars have been fought over it. But there are other concerns here besides taste. Among them are property rights and proprietariness. It's "my book" that the boy strives to protect and to keep for himself. Not even the author is entitled to change it without his consent. Throughout the period we are concerned with, annotators themselves have remarked on and respected this principle. Their own behavior reinforces it, for just as they feel entitled to write what they please in their own books, so they are inclined to apologize when they do it to books that are not their own.[2]

The librarian's defense of other people's books is on the face of it quite different from the child's instinctive possessiveness toward his own. In the eighteenth century, book clubs and circulating libraries, where books were shared about, led the mounting opposition to marginalia. One of Coleridge's annotated books, Claude Fleury's *Ecclesiastical History,* still contains a label explaining the rules of the typical subscription library from which he obtained it, possibly under duress: "5. If any book is written in . . . while in the possession of a Subscriber, the same (or, if it belongs to a set, that set of books) to be paid for."[3] The London Library, founded in 1841 and still going strong, likewise includes a prim reminder in all its books: "It is hardly necessary to add that it is a serious infringement of the Rules of the Society to make pencil or other marks in the books of the Library." The book label for the library of the English faculty at Cambridge says, "You are requested not to mark this book IN ANY WAY."

Nowadays all public and institutional libraries more or less politely require that readers observe this basic civility. Their policy rests on widely shared assumptions about the superiority of the general good to the wishes of individuals and the tacit conventions that govern common (as opposed to private) property. The affronted custodian of Coleridge's annotated books could hardly invoke common interest or general good, however, since the books in his collection were not library books when Coleridge wrote in them. Would he argue that libraries ought not to acquire annotated books, or that the original owners should have done a better job of protecting them? There is probably not much point in pressing for a rational explanation in this case, where the librarian finds himself saddled with what he regards as damaged goods. His reaction is very like the child's response of revulsion and outrage: somebody else has got into *his* books.

Pride of ownership, which leads readers initially to write their names in their books, carries through for some of them into marginalia, further acts of self-assertive appropriation. Others, however, admit only the ownership or presentation inscription and reject marginalia as desecration. They consider it their responsibility to keep the book intact and unaltered. For most of the twentieth century, these two groups—call them A for Annotator and B for Bibliophile—have existed in a state of mutual incomprehension. (A thinks that B might as well stand for Bore, and B that A is for Anarchist.) B as a matter of course considers A to be slovenly, irresponsible, and self-indulgent. (See fig. 10.) The essayist Anne Fadiman, speaking up recently for the As, tries to collapse the distinction by arguing that As are book lovers too, only in a different way. Bs, she suggests, are "courtly" lovers who approach a book with "Platonic adoration, a noble but doomed attempt to conserve forever the state of perfect chastity in which it had left the bookseller." For them marginalia are anathema: "The most permanent, and thus to a courtly lover the most terrible, thing one can leave in a book is one's own words." The uninhibited As, on the other hand, are "carnal" lovers to whom "a book's *words* were holy, but the paper, cloth, cardboard, glue, thread, and ink that contained it were a mere vessel, and it was no sacrilege to treat them as wantonly as desire and pragmatism dictated. Hard use was a sign not of disrespect but of intimacy."[4] Fadiman writes on the defensive, using wit and exaggeration; her views may bring comfort to unregenerate As but will probably only stiffen the resolve of the courtly party.

Virginia Woolf, a B living among As, developed a system of reading-notebooks in order to avoid having to mark up her books. She also sketched out a satirical essay about marginalia, imagining a crusty Colonel venting his rage in the "violated margin" of a book; a timid clergyman contributing literary parallels; a sentimental lady making "thick lachrymose lines" against poems about early death, and pressing flowers between the pages; and a pedant correcting typographical errors.[5] Woolf's stereotypes raise a new objection: marginalia that were full of meaning for the original owners of the books are often of little or no interest to later ones. In that case, the notes no longer pay their way;

4 Underlining and Marginal Notations
Underlining and marginal notations not only disfigure documents, but change their original meaning.

Soulignements et notes marginales
Les traits de soulignement et les notes marginales non seulement abiment les documents, mais aussi changent leur signification originale.

FIG. 10 "Underlining and Marginal Annotations," from *A Guide to the Preservation of Archival Materials,* published for the National Archives of Canada (1981).

their quality is not high enough to warrant the violation of the text. This is a legitimate objection. Anyone who has handled large numbers of annotated books can vouch for the banality and predictability of a great proportion of the notes in them.

It is undoubtedly significant that Woolf's examples are all Victorian. There is no denying that some of the fears of educators and connoisseurs about the effect of the mass market in books after about 1820 were realized during the nineteenth century.[6] Standards of production did drop. Ill-prepared readers got their hands on materials not intended for them. Besides the learned, the Aquinases and Casaubons and Bentleys of their day, readers with no special competence took it upon themselves to criticize their books from the margins in annotations that are pedestrian for the most part, and sometimes worse—careless, ignorant, or abusive. Once outside the annotator's own collection and deprived of their connection with a known reader, such books are unremarkable except in bulk, as with the survey of annotated Boswells. To a book lover like Woolf they can be intensely irritating. So it may well be that Bloomsbury's anti-Victorian bias played a part in her general response to annotated books. But there is more to it than that.

Hermione Lee concludes her account of Woolf's essay by asserting, "What all these addicted annotators have in common is that they are forcing their readings on her."[7] This seems at first a heavy weight of significance to hang on a jeu d'esprit. In the manner of Charles Lamb in his Elia essays, Woolf takes a trifling pastime and playfully affects to prove that it discloses a basic human instinct and supplies a key to the labyrinths of the soul. Her subject is the annotator of library books who yields to the impulse to write in spite of printed prohibitions and fines: "this anonymous commentator must scrawl his O, or his Pooh, or his Beautiful upon the unresisting sheet, as though the author received this mark upon his flesh."[8] She speculates about the prospective audience— is it the author to whom these remarks are addressed, or is it the next borrower who needs to be prompted to share the experience and the opinions of "the Unknown"? For all her efforts to maintain a light touch, however, raw feelings show through in the language of the draft essay, as in the image of branding just cited and in pervasive sexual metaphors—

violation (of the margin), ejaculation ("of praise or disapproval": the Colonel's, in the presence of a lady reader), dissemination (of the clergyman's ideas). Lee responds sympathetically in kind, with her own vocabulary of addiction and forcing. Upon reflection her analysis can be seen to be justified, for Woolf does represent marginalia as an assault upon books, authors, and other readers.

Biographical and critical investigations of Woolf are bedeviled by speculation about sexual trauma, but I do not see personal revelations in this slight exercise, only strong language conventionally deployed to support deeply felt values. Woolf is not alone in using what may seem to be disproportionate analogies to express her disgust at the practice of annotation. Those opposed regularly describe notes in books as rape, addiction, sacrilege, "crap," noise, invasion, parasitism.[9] In this sort of intemperate language we hear undercurrents of fear comparable to the alarm expressed by the authorities at the possible consequences of "the private readings of particular readers" at the Reformation and of the rapid expansion of the reading market at the end of the eighteenth century, especially in the wake of the American and French Revolutions.[10] The great divide between As and Bs is no doubt also at some level political, the conservative force of the Bs seeking to restrain dissent, the As to incite it. (The unregulated growth of the Internet today prompts similar reactions.) But what are they afraid of, the opponents of readers' notes? Woolf's essay provides some clues.

Authority itself is at stake. Readers' notes are unpredictable and unanswerable. As a writer and publisher, Woolf was bound to be disturbed by them. The annotating reader always has the last word and the author has no recourse. If the annotator is identified, other users may be able to assess the reliability of the notes, but that is not possible with the anonymous annotators of whom Woolf specifically complains. And though her examples are relatively dull and harmless, marginalia can do serious damage. The most unpleasant ones that I have seen were contained in books written by colleagues of mine at the University of Toronto. An angry student had borrowed them from the library and returned them full of hate-marginalia, which then went into circulation along with the books. Somebody noticed, perhaps a later reader complained, and the books were withdrawn as mutilated copies ("mutilation"—another violent metaphor); but, for a time, this scheme of revenge did its work and who knows whether all the books subjected to this treatment have been recovered? Even innocuous notes—even helpful, accurate notes—are unanticipated and unauthorized additions. Those who aim to control the presentation and reception of the text are thwarted by readers who write in their books.

Renaissance scholars have long been aware that, as Slights says, "marginal annotation, whether printed or handwritten, can radically alter a reader's perception of the centred text."[11] The phrasing here is exactly right. Though the claim is sometimes made that marginal notes in books or documents "change their original meaning" (as in fig. 10), they don't, though they "can"—not "must"—change the reader's "perception" of their meaning. They introduce other facts and contrary opinions, the facts and opinions themselves being less significant than the demonstrated possibility of alternatives and opinions. They impose not just criticism but a critical attitude upon all following readers. Naturally book producers resent them. The core of Woolf's objection, however, is not so much the insult to the book, author, or publisher as the imposition upon the reader. This itself is a complicated affair.

Woolf's portraits of the imaginary Colonel and his ilk indicate that she hates to have a stranger tell her what to notice and what to think about a book. Alan Bennett's experience with the hair, cited in a note to Chapter One (p. 269, n. 8), shows how it works. Another reader has been there before you and marked a passage as particularly significant; that passage then stands out from the rest and you find yourself trying to figure out why it deserves such prominence. What might be called mental ownership thereby becomes an issue: it is not your own but A's book that you are reading, A's emphasis that you are obliged to adopt. Or you are involuntarily engaged with the earlier reader, agreeing or quarreling with "his O, or his Pooh, or his Beautiful" instead of getting on nicely with the author. Many of the readers who have talked to me about marginalia experience the encounter with other people's notes as a curtailment of their accustomed readerly freedom—a "forcing" (to use Lee's word) or coercion. They see annotators as aggressive bullies.

This harsh impression would no doubt astonish mild Anne Fadiman, for whom annotating books is an act of love, "transforming monologues into dialogues" (p. 34). But that is precisely the point. Set aside for the moment the scruple that annotation is not dialogue since the author cannot (normally) reply. Annotation introduces a second voice where writers and publishers intended only one; the reader talks to the book. For the initial annotating reader, marginalia articulate some of the thoughts stimulated by the act of reading. The second voice is his or her own, and the "dialogue" is a partial record of the reader's participation in the book, the naturally occurring transaction between text and reader. But when another reader butts in, the two-way relationship becomes an uncomfortable threesome. Virginia Woolf wrote frequently and eloquently about the spell of reading—the desirability and the pure pleasure of surrendering to the book, merging one's identity temporarily with that of the author—but also about the impossibility of total surrender: "We may stress the value of sympathy; we may try to sink our own identity as we read. But we know that we cannot sympathize wholly or immerse ourselves wholly; there is always a demon who whispers, 'I hate, I love', and we cannot silence him. Indeed, it is precisely because we hate and we love that our relation with the poets and novelists is so intimate that we find the presence of another person intolerable."[12] It is not clear from the context—Woolf's essay "How Should One Read a Book?"—whether she means that it is intolerable to feel the presence of another reader through notes in the book or to have another person literally in the room where reading is going on, but many readers testify like her to the extraordinary intimacy of reading, which for them is an intensely private act.

For readers who cherish the intimacy of reading, who hear only one voice at a time and cannot selectively shut out another, annotations in a book are not merely a distraction, they are a disaster. This attitude is understandable but, insofar as it is inflexible, not enviable. If we were dealing with intractable personality traits—a Fadiman gene for book abuse, say—we would have to accept the As and Bs as distinct types with no common ground between them. Evidence indicates, however, that the extreme B position is a latecomer to the history of the book. At a certain point, after centuries of acceptance, the practice of annotation crossed over into the realm of the taboo where we find it today. It seems to have been a gradual development, a shift of balance rather than a sudden movement. The necessary and successful campaign of the public libraries to control the behavior of readers played a part, as did the expansion of public schooling in the English-speaking world and the state provision of textbooks, which, like the library books, were going to have to be passed on through several generations of users. Teachers stopped advising students to make notes in their books—instead, they punished them for doing it. So a positive incentive was removed, and prohibitions were strengthened. These lessons, taught early, strenuously enforced, and internalized so that they were applied also to privately owned books, did not eradicate marginalia but they made annotators feel guilty about what they were doing and led collectors to shun marked books apart from association copies. Increasing prosperity and lower prices also meant that more and more readers could enjoy the luxury of getting books new.

There are good reasons for objecting to readers' notes in books, but they are not good enough to support a complete ban, let alone the sort of retrospective policy that has induced some collectors to erase marginalia. It would be equally inadvisable to take advantage of the politicized language of marginality, diversity, inclusivity, multivocality, interactivity, destabilizing, contestation, and so on to recommend a universal license to scribble. The way to resolve the conflict between As and Bs is not by choosing one entrenched position or the other, but by making an effort to understand the historical conditions that govern and have governed practices of annotation and considering actual cases one by one. Once let go the automatic partisanship, and it is possible to see that not all marginalia are worth having; by the same token, that not all marginalia are the same. They come, as we have seen, in various forms: authors' notes, students' notes, friends' notes, teachers' notes, and many others. Even from the third-party point of view, there is much to be gained from them—at the very least, a connection with the past and a sense of camaraderie among readers. (Gore Vidal quotes Princess Margaret on an attempt to read *The Decline and Fall of the Roman Empire:* "I even got

Gibbon out of the library. Didn't do so well with him. But the marginal notes of some old dean were fascinating. Every time there was an attack on the Christians he would write, 'Not true!' or 'Too vile!'")

It is hard to know just where to begin classifying potential uses of other readers' marginalia; if this book has been doing its job, it should be obvious already that such notes have a lot to offer, especially to historians, editors, bibliographers, collectors, and biographers. For now I shall follow my own advice and put forward a few new examples, not ones that are of especially striking importance (like Blake's notes on Reynolds) or immediately prepossessing (like *Tommy Trip's Valentine Gift*), but reasonably representative cases.

In the Berg Collection of the New York Public Library there is a hard-used little copy of *Plays* by William Wycherley, published in 1735. It was one of Charles Lamb's ragged books, acquired by him at second hand and given as a present to Leigh Hunt who later gave it to Charles Smith Cheltnam. There are three owners' signatures (but not Lamb's) on the title page; some observations by Hunt on the paste-down at the back; a bibliographical note by Lamb, attested by Hunt, on the title-page verso; ink lines and check marks (apparently Hunt's) intermittently through the text; and one other short note that I shall come to in a moment. The last leaf of *The Gentleman Dancing-Master* has a hole about the size of a quarter burned in it. None of these features is particularly remarkable; only the solid pedigree of the volume, guaranteeing its association with two well-known literary figures, has brought it safely through the salerooms to its present haven. Association has for a long time been the chief justification for the preservation of readers' notes. Holbrook Jackson, who declares that he loves annotated books "above all other *association copies*" nevertheless concedes that "books of this class must, in the main, justify their existence by the prestige of their commentating owners."[13]

In this context especially, prestige is a mysterious quality. It does not ultimately depend upon the authority or expertise of the annotator, nor upon the brilliance or copiousness of the notes themselves, but upon a sentimental and quasi-religious reverence in the later reader. (Lamb held this very volume in his hands, perhaps as he smoked a pipe at the fireside; these are words he himself wrote in it.) Commercial considerations aside, the feelings aroused by such a book are not to be mocked or dismissed, for it has talismanic value. The one other hastily written note in the Wycherley volume, unattributed and unpublicized, made the hair on the back of my neck stand on end, as it would not have done had the volume not already had this mysterious power. The hand is not Hunt's or Cheltnam's; it could be Lamb's. The key word, the name I read as "Downings," is not indexed in the Lamb letters, however, so it might antedate the period of Lamb's ownership. After his time the book was treated with respect, but at a certain moment, whether by him or by someone else, it was used as a memo pad: somebody opened the book at the blank back of the frontispiece, turned it sideways, and scribbled a note in ink, "MOTHER, I am gone to Downings for a little wile." Lamb's sister Mary killed their mother with a knife in a fit of insanity when Lamb was twenty-one. The idea that the note might be Lamb's or Mary's explains the frisson. Even if it isn't by one of them, it makes a curious addition to the other notes in the volume, showing the mixed use and mixed fortunes of this particular copy—as of many association copies. Though they tend to be valued more for the *presence* than for the content of their notes, they are nearly always worthy of attention on other accounts besides—in this case, not the memo only (whether authentic or not), but also the evidence of use and of ownership, and the nature of the comments on the plays as a guide to their reception by different readers at different periods.

Reception is one of the areas of study in which access to marginalia might be most profitable, since annotation for any purpose whatever gives evidence of the nature of the reader's interest and approach, and usually conveys an opinion about the value of the work. Examples given hitherto have tended to concentrate on the views of contemporaries of the author (as with Greville's Boswell and Piozzi's *Rasselas*), and such cases are likely to be especially prized because they are more remote from our own time, and less tainted by established reputation; but if the book itself merits study, the views of readers of any period have a contribution to make, even when they are not altogether original.

These views take a great variety of forms. William Beckford, methodical annotator that he was, usually copied extracts from the books themselves and let them speak for themselves, only occasionally adding a direct comment of his own. His copy of an 1816 edition of Samuel Johnson's *Diary of a Journey into North Wales* follows the general pattern, but by the time he was through with it, Beckford was sufficiently annoyed to include a long summary note, signed with his initials. His extract from page 41, for instance, begins by quoting Johnson's words and then adding a comment: "41 [']the ideas which it forces upon the mind are the sublime, the dreadful & the vast[.] Above is inaccessible Altitude, below is horrible profundity—He that mounts the precipices of Hawkestone wonders how he came thither & doubts how he shall return—his walk is an adventure & his departure is an escape'—These are indeed most precious specimens of Johnsonian pomposity—One would really think this Doctor mirabilis had been describing his ascent to the Shreikhorn or the San Gothard!—" Here Beckford's resistance is both literary and social: he sneers at Johnson's exaggerated language and at the insularity or provincialism that underwrites it, Johnson having never seen the Alps, as Beckford had, so as to gain a sense of perspective. From a sequence of such passages as this, particularly from Johnson's having disparaged several country seats on his route (thereby exhibiting, to Beckford's mind as to Greville's earlier, not honesty but ingratitude), Beckford comes to a final judgment:

The Doctor not having fared so sumptuously as he wished in Wales appears to have gone considerably out of tune & to have maintained but a half suppressed growl during the whole excursion. Pampered & extolled far beyond his deserts by a succession of gossiping Flatterers Male & Female who chose to believe in him as they did in the Gospel & in the Gospel through him, he seems to have set no bounds to his Conceit & arrogance, and to have looked down upon most of his Entertainers and their dinners with acrimonious contempt—I wonder the power of Fashion itself could have set up as a Demigod a more than Demi-brute & that such a number of Lords Ladies & Gentlemen were continually found pushing themselves in his way with their pans of Incense at the risk of having them all overturned & themselves tossed into the bargain—W B—

This acrimonious and colorful expression of opinion shows Beckford, in the aftermath of decades of Johnsonian biography and in the company of many of his generation, turning decidedly against Johnson as a personality and reading his minor works accordingly.

Edmund Ferrars's copy of Laurence Sterne's *Sentimental Journey*, in the British Library, is a somewhat similar case. A note on the title page indicates that Ferrars acquired this two-volume set in 1772. He annotated it very heavily, marking some passages, keeping an index on the flyleaves, introducing biographical and bibliographical information on the title page, and recording cross-references to works by Sterne and many other writers within the text. The great majority of his notes are concerned with Sterne's sources, dozens of them: Lucian, Burton, Swift, Scarron, *Don Quixote,* Ward's *London Spy,* and so on. The drift of this elaborate exercise is to prove Sterne's indebtedness to other writers and to raise the specter of plagiarism, as in Ferrars's observation, "The Materials of the last, this & the next Chapter are stolen from the Chinese Spy. V 2 & 3d—printed in 1762" (1:187). Ferrars's work might appear to be a project contemporaneous with publication, but the fact that many discoveries of parallel passages are attributed to John Ferriar's *Illustrations of Sterne* (1798) suggests otherwise. Most, though not all, of the materials in Ferrars's notes were derived at second hand from Ferriar and his followers and collated, for convenience, in this single copy. So what Ferrars did, perhaps thirty years after acquiring his copy of *A Sentimental Journey,* was "illustrate" it with references to earlier works in the manner exemplified by Ferriar (and later commended, as we have seen, by Dibdin in *Bibliomania*). His book bears witness to the way Sterne was being read by the early nineteenth century and contains some original contributions to a scholarly debate that continues to this day.

Another reader whose attitude toward his book changed over the course of time was John James Raven, whose father gave him an inscribed copy of Macaulay's *Lays of Ancient Rome* in 1848, when Raven was a schoolboy of fifteen. It now contains annotations in the margin and on interleaved pages, as well as having supplementary materials slipped in. Not all the notes are Raven's, but it is possible to distinguish two phases of annotation by him forty or fifty years apart. The first layer of annotation is classical and literary; it may have been accumulating for several years. Typically, the phrase "Her diadem of towers" on page 38 has three glosses: a parallel in Greek from Sophocles and two in English, one from Byron and one from John Keble. The second layer is no less a tribute in its own way, but it is quite different: it consists of parodies of Macaulay's work, dating from 1850 to the late 1880s. A note by Raven mentions his collection of these parodies and a paper based on them that he delivered in 1895 (p. −6); an offprint of that paper is kept loose in the volume. This copy is an object lesson in the complexities of audience response and reputation, as it shows a single reader adopting different attitudes under changing circumstances.

Writing in books has this in common with writing to the newspaper, that many more people experience the urge than actually go on to do it. The final incentive often comes from the annotator's confidence that he or she knows more than the author did about a particular matter and is therefore in a position to make a correction. (This may be another reason for the relatively light annotation of fiction by comparison with nonfiction.) From the point of view of the historian or biographer, eyewitness recollections—subject of course to the usual reservations about memory and motive—may be the most valuable kind of information annotated books can have to offer, supplementing or displacing official documents. Horatio Nelson's copy of Helen Maria Williams's *Sketches of the State of Manners and Opinions in the French Republic Towards the Close of the Eighteenth Century* (1801), for instance, has very little marking and only a few actual notes in it, but all his notes correct the author on matters of fact: Nelson did not cast anchor in the "road" of Pozzuoli (1:129); the Neapolitans did not send out pilots for the British ships, nor were pilots requested (1:129); Nelson at Malta was not informed that the French had set their course for Egypt (1:129); his fleet experienced not "a month's delay," but "five days" (1:130); not the "English fleet" but "3 sail of the Line" were involved in a particular action (1:131). Such corrections as these may or may not be significant and may or may not be corroborated by other evidence, but besides easing Nelson's mind and helping to get facts sorted out, the presence of five even petty corrections in three pages casts some doubt on the reliability of the work as a whole. Nelson certainly had his doubts: on 1:122–23, he wryly underlined the words, "it is no easy task to distinguish between the simple truth of historical fact, and the exaggerated features of an heated imagination."

Toward the end of his life, Graham Greene found himself beginning to be mentioned in memoirs and histories; some of the notes in his copies of these books make an effort to refine and control the way he was being represented. For example, when Christopher Andrew's *Secret Service* comes to the recruiting of Guy Burgess as a spy, probably by David Footman, Greene deliberately distances himself: "The only time I met Burgess during the war was when he joined Footman and myself for coffee" (p. 408). Greene's natural impulse is echoed in the behavior of major and minor players alike when they come to read about events in which they had participated. British Library copies of Richard Chandler's books about his travels in Greece and Asia Minor contain annotations by a member of the expedition, Nicholas Revett, who both directly and obliquely criticizes Chandler's leadership. An account of the Siege of Gibraltar contains additional manuscript information by someone named Booth who appears to have been an army engineer with a role in the siege that had gone unnoticed by the author, John Heriot. P. J. O. Taylor has recently uncovered annotations in an account of the Indian Mutiny of 1857; written by a lieutenant in the Allahabad Field Force named William Bayley, they constitute, according to Taylor, "the best and fullest account of that heroic advance of a tiny army surrounded by a rebel force outnumbering it by ten, or even twenty, to one."[14]

Unless the annotator is someone of considerable prominence, or the cataloguers (for bookseller or library) are exceptionally painstaking, however, first-hand information of this kind is liable to be overlooked. And that is a pity, because a new scrap of information or a different perspective will often fill out or freshen up an old story. *Pace* Holbrook Jackson, a case could be made for annotated books being all the more valuable when their owners are *not* eminent figures: a Nelson or Greene wanting to tell his own version and correct the record could have commanded other means of doing it, but a Revett, Booth, or Bayley probably could not. And if we are serious about recovering the views of disenfranchised groups like servants and women and prisoners, we should be looking at books as well as at letters and diaries.

Annotated books are for several reasons a goldmine for biographers. There is a convention in biography that books make the man, therefore that the catalogue of a subject's reading provides access to his or her inner life. But the presence of books on the shelf does not prove that they were read, nor that books from other sources, such as lending libraries, were not. It is probably more often than not the case that the crucial books, the character-forming ones, are not the ones found by the deathbed at the end. Among the books that survive, however, annotated ones are especially prized because marginalia do prove that those books were read. They generally also give some signs of how and why—for review or research or recreation, with great interest or not, with approval or not. With a sufficient number of books, as in the case of Coleridge, patterns of use may be identified and significant deviations observed; but even slight evidence may be significant. The American naturalist John Muir paid his tribute to Ralph Waldo Emerson's essay "Nature" with an exquisite little colored drawing of a tree (p. 509). The only extended remark in Wallace Stevens's annotated copy of Wordsworth's *Lyric Poems* comes at the end of the sonnet, "A Stream, to Mingle with your Favourite Dee" (p. 215), where he observes, "Final couplet. Unusual in W."—disappointingly spare annotation in one way, but still a sign of respectful attention and technical awareness.

Biographers have reason to be particularly grateful to subjects like Macaulay who regularly date their notes, and to books that encourage the recording of dates. Many family Bibles contain dates not otherwise available. Thomas Hardy's pocket-sized copy of *The Cathedral Psalter* registers his attendance at certain services, and sometimes his company: "Bonchurch 23.3.10"; "St Paul's 7 Nov. 11"; "Aug 11. 1897 Salisbury Cathl with E." John Keble's phenomenally popular *Christian Year*, a collection of his poems organized to accompany the sequence of Sundays and holy days throughout the year, served a similar function for at least one reader, Henry Shorthouse, who acquired the work as a present from his wife in September 1874 and proceeded to record readings and rereadings to the end of the century: the poem for the seventeenth Sunday after Trinity, for instance, he read at Hanfairfechan in 1894, at Lansdowne in 1898, and at Exmouth in 1899. James Stephens's copy of William Gemmell's *Diamond Sutra* at Trinity College Dublin shows that he started to read it on eighteen occasions between March 1937 and February 1948, and that he finished it fourteen times. Dates belong to the set of hard facts that form the backbone of the biographer's work. More subjective kinds of notes are liable to be more equivocal, for reasons that have been canvassed earlier, but biographers and readers alike can learn to make allowances as they do for direct quotation from journals and correspondence. The obvious advantage is the enrichment of the record: by casual remarks in the margins of their books we may find out what Gibbon thought of Herodotus, what Waugh thought of Connolly, what Stevens thought of Harvard, what Hardy thought of billiards (indeed, that Hardy thought about billiards at all).[15]

Not only the subjects' own books, but books by or about them, annotated by readers of their time—ideally, by readers from their own circles—can be grist to the biographer's mill; in fact any books at all read and annotated by their contemporaries might be relevant, though with diminishing probability as one moves outward from the subject. Because of the mixed motives and mixed use characteristic of marginalia, it is impossible to predict what will turn up where. If time permits, serendipity has profits and delights of its own for any reader curious about the past. A collection of books mostly on issues of birth control, from the library of Marie Stopes, incidentally includes her views on Oscar Wilde's libel suit against the Marquess of Queensberry.[16] Thomas Gray's copy of William Verral's *Complete System of Cookery* contains several marks and additions, allegedly in Gray's hand (I find it hard to imagine how he ever got access to a stove). Gray, or whoever it was, marked a recipe for anchovies with Parmesan cheese that I mean to try some day, on the author's particular recommendation: "This seems to be but a trifling thing, but I never saw it come whole from table" (pp. 219–20). The annotator also offers new recipes, including a "Stuffing for Veal or Calve's-heart" (p. +1) that is rather less appealing: it involves suet and a pickled herring, and the final judgment is, "tried, and found bad."

Hester Piozzi's annotations are full of reminiscence and minute detail: how an Irish lady of her acquaintance used to win at cards with the help of a leprechaun ("a Lypercorn Fairy"); how people dressed and what children felt at early performances of Handel; what unprintable quip Johnson made about Lord Bolingbroke; how the Easter custom of "lifting" persisted in North Wales in 1814; and how the courtiers of the Prince of Wales during his regency used to joke that his German motto, *Ich Dien,* referred to venereal disease, "Dying of the Itch."[17] (Is it possible that the last example accurately reflects court pronunciation of German at the time?) Practically all such readerly interventions enjoy an immediacy and directness lacking in secondary studies, and confirm Cathy Davidson's observation about heavily used old books: "Broken boards, turned-down pages, and abounding marginalia do not make for a place of honor in an early American book collection, but they do reveal patterns of reading, patterns of use, the surviving traces of an interpretive community long-since gone. But through these traces, some of the early readers remain surprisingly vivid even after nearly two centuries."[18]

One recently evolved area of scholarly interest for which marginalia might appear to be of great potential benefit is the history of reading, in the sense of the record of the reading experience. What more obvious place to look, you might think, than in the margins and on the endpapers of books, where readers have set down their first thoughts? This turns out to be a fraught subject, however.

For reasons of their own, historians—even historians of the book—appear, on the whole, to be Bs; they don't like marginalia. Davidson is unusual in her readiness to include the physical evidence of particular copies (including marginalia) among her source materials. What's wrong with it, and what are the alternatives? Eugene Kintgen explains, writing about the Renaissance and citing "a mass of anecdotal information about examples of reading" such as Gabriel Harvey's marginalia: "first, they are products of reading rather than the process that led to those products, and thus provide only indirect evidence about the process. . . . And they are not even products in the sense of veridical reports of the process, for constraints of various kinds (including the space available in margins) affect their form and content. Second, they are *merely* anecdotal, intriguing and illuminating to be sure, but suspect in their typicality."[19] The first objection might perhaps be got round: as reports subject to conventional restraints, readers' notes are no different from all the other kinds of documents that historians are accustomed to dealing with. But the second charge, that they are "anecdotal" and possibly not typical, is damning. Kintgen therefore, while he does not ignore these sources, allows them only a supporting role as "tests or illustrations of a theoretical practice of reading drawn from other sources."

Jonathan Rose *does* ignore them; his vision of the future of the history of reader response has no place for readers' notes. Reacting, understandably, against theorists who attempt to work with internal evidence (the text alone) and who exhibit what he calls "the receptive fallacy," Rose proposes best-seller lists, reader surveys, and autobiographies, assembled and analyzed by "the cooperative efforts of an organized body of scholars," as the only way to recover "the response of the actual ordinary reader in history."[20] The best best-seller lists, however, can only tell you what is sold, not what is read, nor how it is read. Surveys are liable to be haphazard, and the conditions of the survey compromise its results. Autobiographies, written from a retrospective viewpoint, have a vested interest in presenting a positive and consistent image of the subject. Finally, the "actual ordinary reader" derived from the averaging out of such sources can be guaranteed not to correspond to any actual ordinary reader whatever: Statistical Man is a robot. At least marginalia represent the actual responses of actual readers, and presumably they are no more compromised than autobiographies.

Other historians express reservations not merely about the use of readers' notes but about the project of recovery itself. Kintgen quotes Jon Klancher's advice to stop trying because reading cultures of the past are irretrievable: "we cannot penetrate the minds of all those readers who left no mark of their understandings, no trace of the doubtless ingenious ways they must have recombined, retranslated, or simply resisted the interpretive and ideological patterns framed by their texts."

Henri-Jean Martin points out, unexceptionably, that "Historians can never be sure that they understand exactly how their ancestors read any given text in an environment that is—to say the least—difficult to reconstruct." James Machor agrees: History of the Book, he says, has proven good at showing "how readers *used* reading materials." But it has its limits: "it has been able to reveal little if anything about the process of response and the dynamics of audience engagement in earlier periods—little, in other words, about *how* people read and how texts semantically delivered themselves to historically specific audiences." The essays published in Machor's collection do not even try to reconstruct "actual reading experiences" for nineteenth-century American readers because, in the first place, there is little documentation to go on, and, in the second place, such experiences are by their nature inaccessible: "[R]eading in the nineteenth century already had become, in one sense, what it largely is today: an extremely private activity that can never be fully recorded in performance because such a 'recording' is always selective, always a reconstruction, and hence always a reconstitution." Machor thus repeats the now familiar reservations about the fundamental unknowability of the mental process accompanying reading and the inadequacy of the documentary record, and like Klancher he abandons the idea of even trying to reconstruct the experiences of readers from the past.[21]

Robert Darnton, to his credit, stakes out a position on both sides of the fence. On one hand he expresses clearly and forcefully the difficulty of doing anything at all; on the other hand, he refuses to give up hope. "The difficulty," he says,

> lies with reading itself. We hardly know what it is when it takes place under our nose, much less what it was two centuries ago when readers inhabited a different mental universe. Nothing could be more misleading than the assumption that they made sense of typographical signs in the same way that we do. But they left little record of how they performed that feat. Although we have some information about the external circumstances of eighteenth-century reading, we can only guess at its effects on the hearts and minds of readers. Inner appropriation— the ultimate stage in the communication circuit that linked authors and

publishers with booksellers and readers—may remain beyond the range of research.[22]

Darnton's escape hatches are to be found, as is often the case, in the qualifiers: his readers left "little record" but not "no record"; and appropriation "may" but need not necessarily "remain beyond the range of research." In "First Steps Towards a History of Reading," he shifts the emphasis, declaring, "If the experience of the great mass of readers lies beyond the range of historical research, historians should be able to capture something of what reading meant for the few persons who left a record of it." He singles out "margins themselves" as good places to start out from.[23]

I think Darnton is right on both counts, only too cautious. Like Kintgen and Davidson, he refuses to accept his colleagues' counsel of despair and, for want of better, is prepared to consider the evidence of readers' notes. I would go farther than he does and say that from those notes we should be able to capture not just "something" but *quite a lot* "of what reading meant for the few persons who left a record of it"—and for others besides. The issue here is not a general question about the value of marginalia; no doubt all historians would agree that they might be a useful source of hard data like dates and opinions, and as reliable on these matters as any personal document is likely to be. The question is whether they give us any useful kind of access to the mental processes of readers. Doubts focus on the privacy of the experience and the typicality of the surviving records. Is the experience itself by its nature unknowable? Is the testimony of a single reader anecdotal and unusable? No doubt the experience *is* ultimately unknowable—we are incapable of capturing our own experience as we read, without spoiling it—but not being able to know everything about it does not mean that we can know nothing about it. We have readers' own records, written under varying conditions but all close to the moment of apprehension of the text; from them, sometimes with the support of information from other sources, we can learn much and infer more. The case studies in this volume were designed to illustrate the way in which the record of marginalia could be used to reveal not only the circumstances in which the notes were composed but also the frame of mind of the reader and the course of his or her progress through the book. Marginalia for all their faults stay about as close to the running mental discourse that accompanies reading as it is possible to be, and if we want to understand that process we are better off with them than without them. The reading experience since 1700 (by no means monolithic) may have been private but in many, many cases it is neither unknowable nor irretrievable.

That granted, the skeptic will ask how to get from the individual case to the generalizations that make up "proper" history. I propose two answers, leaving the problem of what constitutes proper history to the historians to thrash out among themselves. First, empirical methods encourage the mounting up of individual cases to a point at which they become susceptible of legitimate generalization. The Reading Experience Database, promoted by the Open University and the British Library, was founded on this familiar principle. My own profiles of Coleridge and of Boswell's *Life* could be taken as examples of an intermediate stage at which several hundred annotated books with something in common—a particular reader in one case, the same text in the other—may be analyzed to reveal larger patterns than can be found in a single exemplar. Historically discrete collections such as mechanics' institute libraries, clerical libraries, and family libraries could be studied for marginalia in a similar way. I have had the benefit of many narrower studies before me; that's the way scholarship grows. With a broader base of case studies of individual books, readers, and collections, historians of the book would be better placed than they are at the moment to decide whether or not it is possible to discover how readers of earlier periods approached their books, and what they got out of them; also what role marginalia have to play in the effort.

To the critics who argue that reading in the modern world is so private an affair that we will never be able to find out how our ancestors read their books, and that the record of the "few persons" (Darnton's words) who did leave traces of their experience has to be discounted because they may not have been "typical" readers, I reply that if "private" means exclusive to oneself, then reading is not a private but a social experience and practically any reader of a given time and place is as typical as any other. I do not refer merely to the sociable annotators of the eighteenth century and thereabouts. Reading had been an "interactive" experience for thousands of years before that convenient though ungainly word was coined. The whole reader-response movement is based on the axiom that "meaning is not something to be found *in* a text. It is, rather, an entity produced by the reader in conjunction with the text's verbal structure."[24] What that principle entails, as generations of critics have now demonstrated, is an acknowledgment that learning to read and write involves more than mastery of the alphabet; it is an initiation into a set of shared codes of communication. Readers are obliged to recognize and negotiate their way around the conventions of writing, just as writers are obliged to work within the structure of conventions that their readers understand. Although levels of proficiency vary, the basics are indispensable to all readers trained under the same system: they could scarcely be said to be making sense of a text otherwise, let alone talking to one another about it.

Many of these tacit codes can be inferred from readers' marginalia, addressed as they are to the author or to another reader. The slightest marks can tell us something. The name on the title page says, This book belongs to me and I expect it back if I lend it to you. Lines down the margin say, These are especially pertinent passages. Crosses at the beginning of a paragraph say, Take note of this—or perhaps, depending on the period, Copy this passage into your commonplace book under the following head. And discursive notes give us some insight into what the reader was thinking while in the process of reading. They are not perfectly transparent, they do not give us direct access to the complex motions of the reader's mind, but they do provide glimpses and from the glimpses we may begin to build up a reasonably reliable reconstruction of the process itself. In computer-speak, we could say that marginalia reveal the codes.

When Piozzi annotated *Rasselas,* she read both as a particular reader under special circumstances and as a typical reader of her time, governed and constrained by deep structures common to all. Her situation was unique but her assumptions were routine. The deep structures that can be inferred from the reader's comments, as the Piozzi case demonstrates, are the shared and in that sense the typical ones. Kintgen's point is well taken: "While it is undoubtedly true that circumstances affect the course of a reading, lending greater salience to some aspects of a text than others, their effect is distinctly limited, simply because readers can only deploy interpretive strategies they have already learned" (pp. 216–17). In as simple a case as General Wolfe's annotated copy of Gray's *Elegy* we can see not just how Wolfe used his book and what he thought of it, but how he and his contemporaries read it—namely, with attention to particular words and lines. For Wolfe, the *Elegy* was not something to be grasped as a whole but something to be appreciated for the nuggets of wisdom it contained. By his notes it appears, furthermore, that he was able to take it for granted that his was the natural way to read, and that another reader of his generation would understand what he was doing. From the record of a marked volume may be discovered, then, either or both of individual circumstances and shared reading practices.

With the second argument as with the first, multiple instances make a stronger case than single ones. It would be prudent to test the impression that this one copy gives us by seeking out marginalia in other copies of the *Elegy* or in other volumes of poetry. The remarks of reviewers and essayists might or might not confirm the observable practice of actual readers. Annotated books have a contribution to make in this growth area of modern scholarship, and the fact that they may be exceptional survivors hardly justifies avoiding them. They have, however, been hard to get hold of; so in the Afterword that follows, I have some proposals to make.

Afterword

By argument and example this book endeavors to establish the value of readers' notes—their value to the annotator in the first instance, and potentially also to the work and to the critic or cultural historian later on. Yet writing in books is on the wane and we are at risk of losing both the art and the artifacts. We cannot turn back the clock, but we ought to be capable of learning from the past and adapting traditional practices to meet present needs. How are we to proceed?

The first step surely has to be to bring more marginalia to light, for the couple of thousand annotated books that I have drawn from represent only a tiny fraction of the number that must be out there. This goal could be achieved little by little without calling on the heavy machinery of grants, societies, conferences, databases, and journals. Marginalia are not in that league and even if funding grew on trees, I doubt that the cast-of-thousands approach would work for this subject, which requires patience, time, a sort of tact, and informed sympathy. Ideally, as it seems to me, the work would be done piecemeal in response to the desires and discoveries of book users. Since there is no telling what may strike someone as significant fifty or a hundred or two hundred years from now, the minimum requirement must be a conservative approach, that is, doing nothing to eliminate marginalia in books or to impede access to them, and leaving intact all such signs of use. But it would positively speed things up if action were taken on several fronts at once, so for those who are interested I have the following practical suggestions.

Booksellers and the library workers who order, catalogue, and circulate books are in the front lines. I encourage them to be alert to the potential of annotated books, and to consider what might be done to accommodate them and make them more visible. Far from disparaging or concealing or erasing marginalia, booksellers used to make a point of mentioning readers' notes even when they were by unknown hands, and that could happen again. Who is to say that there would not be a market for annotated books, even anonymously annotated books, if only buyers were offered them? In a group of columns for *The Irish Times*, Flann O'Brien once proposed a book-handling service for the nouveaux riches, to make their libraries look used; this idea, introduced facetiously, nonetheless serves to remind us that books, unlike clothing, can acquire status from having passed through many hands.[1] Then again, though most first-time readers probably prefer to have a book to themselves, further experience can make company welcome and an annotated book allows the owner to read along with someone else. The copy of Fletcher's *Situation Ethics* described in the Introduction was discarded from a college booksale: perhaps it should have been set aside for a table of annotated books. If book dealers intended to cultivate demand, however, they would have to be prepared to devote more care to the cataloguing of the books in the first place. From the scholar's point of view it would be particularly helpful to have collections of long standing— private libraries, libraries of defunct societies, and so on—scrutinized when they are sold off, with special attention given to volumes containing marginalia.

Cataloguing is also crucial for the library user. Though electronic catalogues have gone a long way toward making readers' notes accessible, the system is still far from perfect. Retrospective electronic cataloguing does not usually mean a fresh look at the volume: it merely repeats the entry made by the original cataloguer and preserves the original selection, which will almost certainly have been haphazard. Furthermore it must use the words available to the earlier cataloguer, which may be "annotations" or "ms. notes" or "manuscript notes" or "reader's notes" or "adversaria" or any one of a dozen such headings. And cataloguing at this level has in the past generally been possible only for well-endowed special collections. If copy-specific cataloguing could be introduced for all second-hand purchases and not merely for rare books, that would be splendid; but at the very least, wherever copy-specific features are registered, marginalia should be recorded by a single, consistent, generic code, "ms. notes," and over time the outdated synonyms should be retrospectively converted—not a major chore once the catalogue is fully electronic. Reliance on a single code will make all examples of readerly participation instantly accessible, and that's the main thing.

If libraries had the resources to do more, I would ask for further discrimination: "ms. notes" that consist of a "presentation inscription" for example, being distinguished from "authorial revisions," "owner's signature," "typographical corrections," and so on. Anything that gives a general indication of scale of annotation is a godsend, and it would be particularly useful to retain the word "copious" because quantity of annotation is often the sign of an unusual situation. Greville's and Mr. Lichfield's Boswells were described as "copiously" annotated, as were several of the strange objects in Chapter Six. Categories at this point need not be rigorously defined since the main heading "ms. notes" will have already brought all the relevant works together; further discrimination is a refinement that could be left to the discretion of the cataloguer.

When the marginalia in them are thought to be significant, annotated books are sometimes left stored with other books in libraries and sometimes transferred to departments of manuscripts: this is one reason among many for neglect, as they may be caught between two jurisdictions. It does not much matter where they are housed so long as cross-referencing is possible and both the book and the presence of manuscript notes are entered in the records for both divisions. As an extension of the cataloguing of copy-specific features, however, I strongly urge as a matter of policy that bibliographers include marginalia in printed and electronic manuscript catalogues, whether they are catalogues of the manuscripts of a single author or of a collection or archive. The *Index of English Literary Manuscripts* sets a good example in this regard.

To readers and scholars using library books I say only, given the choice, take an annotated copy and see what the notes are about. If you happen upon a book with unrecorded notes, try not to be nettled, give them a hearing. You may be the first person since the writer to have read them. If they are of no interest, you can ignore them and get on with your work. If they *do* look interesting, they may be worth pursuing.[2] At least you can draw the marginalia to the attention of the library so that their existence is registered in the catalogue. With a little effort it may be possible to identify the annotator or the date or occasion of annotation, and these facts may contribute to your project: if so, incorporate the evidence of the annotated copy among your results and give this kind of book some positive publicity. (Better still, get the word "marginalia" into the title.) A particularly exciting or impressive discovery may warrant a case study or a profile. There are some fine models available: to name a few, Anthony Grafton on Budé, Wilmarth Lewis on Walpole, John Powell on Gladstone, Richard Sewell and Michael West on Emily Dickinson, Alan Gribben on Mark Twain, Alan Macdonald on T. H. White, and Cathy Davidson on unnamed early American readers. These scholars all show how marginalia can be used with sensitivity and intelligence either as a subject in themselves or in a supporting role, and this, for the present, seems to me the right way to go, to bring marginalia into the open without undertaking large-scale publication.

From time to time, for one reason or another, a body of notes will seem to cry out for publication; then the would-be editor will have to be prepared to face difficult decisions about physical presentation. The editing of marginalia presents problems that have really never been satisfactorily resolved, though we now have a history of publication of readers' notes in the vernacular going back two hundred years. Basically they are intellectual problems with physical consequences, like elusive psychosomatic diseases. Marginalia are responsive. They arise out of a reader's reaction to a prior printed text and are by definition dependent upon that text for their meaning. With rare exceptions they cannot be reproduced as free-standing utterances. Therefore editors find themselves having somehow to juggle two texts and book designers have technical complications to deal with. Even the selection of source text—the passage that prompted the reader's note in the first place—is often not easy, since the source text had a context of its own (how much of that needs to be included?) and the note may refer to a whole chapter and not just to the sentence it appears beside. Thus although the marginalia may be published in full, the source text is represented only through extracts. And how are the marginalia to be arranged: sequentially in page order, chronologically in order of writing, topically by the subject of the note or by the subject of the book?

Questions like these fade in comparison with the issue of precedence or relative status. Marginalia are responsive, but if the editor's goal is to present previously unpublished notes, they become primary and the source text secondary, in a reversal and at some level a falsification of the original relationship. Marginalia cannot become "central," it seems, without relegating the source text to the margins. As far as layout is concerned, this is never literally the solution: no one prints marginalia in the middle of a page with source text as a gloss. What we do instead is print the source text first in a smaller font, or in brackets, with the marginalia following in the standard font size, as in the cases of Keats and Blake, and of Coleridge in the *Literary Remains*. Editors bothered by the demotion of the source text may choose a method that gives it more equal billing, such as using the same print size but different colors to distinguish the one from the other (as in the Bollingen Coleridge), or the same size in double columns (as for Swift, in either Scott's or Davis's edition).[3] They may try a facsimile or semi-facsimile format: Fletcher's edition of Piozzi's notes in two copies of Boswell, for example, prints the whole Boswell text with the marginalia of both copies printed like old-fashioned glosses in the margins. Or they may go to the opposite extreme (as in Edward O'Shea's Yeats and Gribben's Twain) and eliminate the text altogether—a radical procedure that saves space, avoids misrepresentation, and leaves the reader free to seek out a copy of the book as a companion volume.

Of all these methods, the one that comes closest to reproducing the physical features and effect of an annotated book, short of photo-facsimile, is liable to be the most expensive, namely reprinting the full text of the book with the annotator's commentary as printed commentary. Unless the commentary is very extensive, this would be a wasteful choice, though economies might be made by printing the notes of more than one reader simultaneously. But this form of publication runs afoul of another characteristic feature of the genre. Marginalia written in books since 1700 are responsive. They are also *unauthorized,* and in this important respect they differ fundamentally from both the manuscript commentaries of manuscript books and the printed glosses of early printed books. However much friction there might have been between the central text and the side-notes in those cases, they were officially approved by somebody—author or editor or printer—prior to publication and as part of a supposedly coherent package. In a printed book with manuscript marks and notes, the gulf between the author and the annotating reader is immediately and visually apparent. Printing marginalia tends to eliminate the gulf. Until a cheap method of facsimile reproduction becomes available, marginalia are perhaps best dealt with selectively and as part of a critical or historical—as opposed to an editorial—enterprise.

Although publishers might be thought to have a role to play in the revival of marginalia, the surviving evidence suggests that annotators never have been deterred by narrow margins and that, on the contrary, official forms of encouragement such as ready-made interleaving fail to inspire them. Far more important are the education and example offered at home and school—including school libraries. The current blanket prohibition against writing in books is unnecessarily repressive, and it is not much comfort to know that it is bound to be ineffectual. We would surely be better off approaching the subject with understanding and discrimination. Of course children should be taught not to write in other people's books; but why should they be denied the outlet of writing in their own? Indeed, as I hope this book has shown, for many, many readers writing in books has over the centuries been more than an outlet for self-expression; it is—or can be—a discipline that fosters attentive reading, intellectual self-awareness, and incisive writing. Although it is impossible to know exactly why it is so commonly the marginalia of professional writers that came to be preserved and collected in special archives, there does seem to be historically a high incidence of the annotating habit in the community of writers, therefore perhaps a causal connection between the habit and the vocation. Parents and teachers could be taking advantage of this established link instead of trying to suppress it. Of course some parents and teachers, to this day, do: witness the Fadimans, Leavis, and Nabokov.

Ultimately, the future of marginalia rests with readers, and to readers I say (with William Blake), throw off the mind-forged manacles and take a pencil to your books. It is difficult to think of any kind of value attached to books that is not increased by the addition of notes. If it is only by the souvenir value of a presentation inscription, notes personalize our books. (A surprising but charming case is the copy of Kenneth Burke's *Grammar of Motives* in the Beinecke Library, autographed in ballpoint pen by Burke and a group of friends to celebrate a party in August 1965. One of them, Robert Osborn, added a drawing with a caption, "The man who, at that splendid luncheon party, juggled 8 balls including his own.") The example of Beckford shows how methodical dating and indexing can create a convenient reading record and filing system. Minute criticism in the margins at the very least allows a reader to let off steam; at its best, as with Keats on Milton or Blake on Reynolds, it is a vital part of the process by which the reader works out an independent position. For my money annotating books is a more profitable because less narcissistic exercise than keeping a diary. And it increases our satisfaction in our books if we know that they contain—like Woodhouse's Keats, Law's Bible, and Douce's Whitaker—useful supplementary materials and better or fuller information than other copies have.

We would do well to consider the example of the sociable readers of the eighteenth century and later who shared their annotated books and looked on readers' notes as value added. Whether for a network of scholars like that of William Oldys or Thomas Percy, a circle of friends like Coleridge's or of family like Mark Twain's, or an intimacy of two as with Hester Piozzi and Augustus Conway or James Wolfe and Katherine Lowther, annotated books bring pleasure by association every time they are taken up. It could be argued, indeed, that they make better tributes to friendship than letters do in proportion as the contents of carefully chosen books are more exciting than the details of people's home lives.

It may be objected that books are passé and readers' notes ipso facto things of the past. As evidence to the contrary, however, we see that interactivity is in its heyday and that the proponents of the electronic book seem to be keen to accommodate the desire of readers to be involved through annotation. Even if the format of books changes dramatically, readers will probably still be able to talk to them through some form of note-making. (Software for one of the e-books that I have been sampling, before it lets you write a "marginal" note, shrewdly asks whether you want it to be "public" or "private.") If things carry on much as they are now—and the consensus of predictions seems to be that books and monitors will continue to be complementary vehicles for the transmission of text—then steadily growing supplies of books old and new and nearly universal opportunities of private ownership will, I hope, guarantee the survival of these extraordinary glosses.

Notes

Introduction

1. Sampson, *Mandela,* pp. 233–34; Arts Section, *New York Times,* 26 September 1999, pp. 41, 43.
2. For full publication details of works referred to in notes, see the Bibliography of Secondary Works Cited. Bibliographical resources include *The Rothschild Library* (1954), Stoddard's *Marks in Books* (1985), Alston's *Books with Manuscript* (1994), and Rosenthal's *The Rosenthal Collection* (1997). Historical studies to date emphasize *printed* glosses, which overlap in many ways with glosses in manuscript: see especially Slights (1989, 1992), Tribble (1993), and the essays collected in Barney (1991) and Greetham (1997). Grafton is a notable contributor to the case study, with essays and chapters on manuscript notes by Casaubon (in *Joseph Scaliger*), Budé, and Harvey. Selections from Harvey's marginalia were published as long ago as 1913, but for a comprehensive recent reassessment see Stern (1979). For full-scale treatment of John Dee's library, see Sherman (1995). Manguel (1996) has some useful information about readers' notes, and Kevin Jackson's charming 1992 article in the *Independent* (expanded as a chapter in *Invisible Forms*) should not be missed.

    As an example of intelligent theorizing, Lipking's pioneering essay "Marginal Gloss" (1977) concentrates on printed glosses but offers food for thought about manuscript notes as well. Derrida, being interested in all kinds of dissonance, often uses margins as a metaphor for challenges to the otherwise closed systems of philosophy and of writing in general, but in "Tympan," the first essay in *Margins of Philosophy,* he prints a second text in his own margins, and in *Glas* he constructs a whole volume in two and sometimes more columns and voices. Most of the studies listed in the preceding paragraph are also reflective.

There is a very long tradition of scholars' notes being published in conjunction with another text as commentary or apparatus. Large-scale editions and studies that take the marginalia as primary are relatively rare, but see Blake, Coleridge, Darwin, Keats, Macaulay, and Melville; also Gribben (Twain), Lau (Keats), and O'Shea (Yeats).

By precept and example, Darnton and Grafton encourage historians to make use of the evidence of readers' notes; Martin, among others, is skeptical about the feasibility of recreating reading environments of the past. The issue is discussed in Chapter Eight.

3. Coleridge, *Marginalia*, 1:372, 1:795–97 (quotations from this edition omit cancellations). Lamb's famous essay, "The Two Races of Men," first appeared in the *London Magazine* in December 1820; the "two races" are borrowers and lenders of books. Coleridge is the example of a good borrower who will return your books "enriched with annotations, tripling their value" (p. 26). De Quincey published notes by Coleridge in the *Westmoreland Gazette* (of which he was the editor) in August 1819, and in *Blackwood's Magazine* in 1830—both in Coleridge's lifetime, and the earlier one the first known publication of any of his notes, as Daniel Roberts points out in "Three Uncollected Coleridgean Marginalia," p. 331.

4. Hartley Coleridge, *Essays and Marginalia;* and notes by Sara Coleridge on two sets of memoirs, included in Broughton, ed., *Sara Coleridge and Henry Reed.*

5. Grafton, "Is the History of Reading a Marginal Enterprise?" p. 139. For evidence of the heyday of the reader-response movement, see Tompkins, *Reader-Response,* and Suleiman and Crosman, eds., *Reader in the Text.* Piecemeal—volume by volume—publication of the Coleridge marginalia began in 1980.

6. McKitterick, *Cambridge University Library,* p. 215; see also p. 548. There is some disagreement about the etymology of the term *adversaria*. The *OED* says that it originally meant "things written on the side fronting us (i.e. on one side of the paper)" hence "notes, a commonplace book . . . also commentaries or notes on a text or writing." Glaister's *Glossary of the Book,* however, defines "adversaria" more convincingly as "a collection of notes or commentaries; originally referring to Roman works with the text written on one side of the parchment, the notes on the opposite side" (p. 2). He goes on to explain that "The term was extended both by the Romans and later by the Humanists, to include collections of textual criticisms, also rough note books."

7. For the Darwin example see Stephen Gill, *Wordsworth and the Victorians* (Oxford: Oxford University Press, 1998), according to a reviewer, Daniel Karlin, in *TLS,* 18 September 1998, p. 15. For Dickinson see Sewell, *Life,* 2:678n, and West, "Emily Dickinson's Ambrosian Nights."

Chapter One: Physical Features

1. On the introduction of the footnote see Lipking, "Marginal Gloss," pp. 625–27; Grafton, *The Footnote,* especially pp. 190–222.

2. Complaints about this sort of behavior, as acts of vandalism, go back to the days of the manuscript book. Richard De Bury's *Philobiblon*, written in Latin and completed in 1344, has a chapter entitled (in the English translation) "Of Showing Due Propriety in the Custody of Books" in which he particularly condemns "those shameless youths, who as soon as they have learned to form the shapes of letters" decorate the margins of books with alphabets and similar irrelevancies just to try the "fitness" of their pens.

3. Emily Brontë, *Wuthering Heights*, p. 27.

4. Judith St. John, *The Osborne Collection of Early Children's Books*. Not all the books described in the following paragraphs are listed in the catalogue, for of course the Library continues to collect.

5. Occasionally, of course, adult writers are caught short and do the same thing. A copy of May Sarton's novel *The Small Room* (1961) contains only a few notes, in pencil, on the back endpaper, assigning committee responsibilities for "refreshments this year," "money raiser," and "maybe publicity." Edward Lear's nine-volume set of the letters of Horace Walpole is marked only lightly, but it has a drawing and the outline of an idea for new work on the front endpapers of Vol. 9. Jack London's copy of Stewart Edward White's *The Silent Places* contains ideas for Act II of a play.

6. Iona and Peter Opie, *I Saw Esau*, pp. 31–33.

7. Holbrook Jackson, *Anatomy of Bibliomania*, pp. 370–71. In *The End of the Affair* (pp. 172–73, 179), Graham Greene makes a childish anathema the agent of a miraculous cure.

8. Alan Bennett describes an odd experience that reveals our common understanding of such marking, that it expresses heightened attention in the annotating reader and calls for extra attention from subsequent readers. It is part of a diary entry for 20 December 1993: "I am reading a book on Kafka. It is a library book, and someone has marked a passage in the margin with a long, wavering line. I pay the passage special attention without finding it particularly rewarding. As I turn the page the line moves. It is a long, dark hair" (*Writing Home*, p. 131).

9. Coleridge, *Collected Letters*, 4:837.

10. Ibid., 2:743. The full text of the marginalia appears in Coleridge, *Marginalia*, Vol. 6.

11. Coleridge, *Marginalia*, 5:111.

12. Thackeray, *Vanity Fair*, p. 8.

13. Evelyn B. Tribble, *Margins and Marginality*, p. 10.

14. Simon Singh, *Fermat's Enigma*.

15. F. Tennyson Jesse, *Murder and Its Motives*.

16. Montaigne, "Des livres," *Essais*, 2:89. He quotes a few of these notes at length. Florio's English translation appeared in 1603.

17. Robert E. Gemmett, ed., *Sale Catalogues of Eminent Persons*, Vol. 3.

18. S. T. Coleridge, *On the Constitution of the Church and State*, p. 166; Coleridge, *Marginalia*, 2:519–20.

Chapter Two: History

1. For a fine modern edition that explains and reproduces the conventional layout of such works, see Gratian, *The Treatise on Laws*.

2. Bernard M. Rosenthal's splendid catalogue of 242 annotated books, most of them published before 1600 and each of them illustrated by a photograph, refers repeatedly to the press's provision of space for notes (e.g., pp. 7, 246), and to the annotators' compliance with "the usual distinction between interlinear and marginal notes" (p. 168)—interlinear notes supplying synonyms and translations and marginal notes a more extended commentary (e.g., pp. 302, 307). Tribble describes eighteenth-century printers also as regularly providing large margins for owners' annotations "to books of learning" (Greetham, *Margins*, p. 233). For an example, see fig. 3 (p. 47).

3. Saenger and Heinlen, "Incunable Description," pp. 243–44.

4. Rosenthal, *Rosenthal Collection*, pp. 52, 60–61, 188. Manguel (*History of Reading*, p. 60) describes his own similar experience in Buenos Aires in the middle of the twentieth century: pupils were instructed to take down teachers' dictated comments in the margins of their textbooks.

5. Erasmus, "On the Method of Study," pp. 670, 671. This work was published as *De ratione studii ac legendi interpretandique auctores* in 1511. The commonplace book is recommended at pp. 672–73.

6. Stern, writing about Harvey, p. 144. Cf. Grafton and Jardine on Harvey, and Sherman on Dee (especially pp. 79–100). Hunter describes Evelyn's method of annotation, which was tied to his system of commonplace books, in *John Evelyn in the British Library*, pp. 82–85.

   Samuel Johnson rebelliously cast doubt on the value of marking, in *Idler* 74. Readers who habitually mark up their books, he says, "load their minds with superfluous attention, repress the vehemence of curiosity by useless deliberation, and by frequent interruption break the current of narration or the chain of reason, and at last close the volume, and forget the passages and the marks together."

7. Notes thought to be of an inappropriate kind may also have been removed: Andrew Taylor says that in Renaissance books "Marginal annotations in English are rare and on occasion they have been rubbed out" (Raven, Small, and Tadmor, eds., *Practice*, p. 50).

8. Slights, "Edifying Margins," pp. 685–86.

9. In his complementary study of printed biblical glosses ("'Marginall Notes,'" p. 260), Slights likewise discovers an "undercurrent of interpretative anxiety."

10. Grafton, *Footnote*, p. 115.

11. Steven Zwicker, "Contesting Readers," Modern Language Association session, "Reader *vs* Writer: Marginalia of c 1590, 1690, 1790," Toronto, December 1997. On the evolution of the printed commonplace book see Ann Moss, *Printed Commonplace-Books and the Structuring of Renaissance Thought*.

12. George Crabbe, *The Library* (London: Dodsley, 1781), pp. 6–7. The poem was at first published anonymously. The Bibliography of Annotated Books lists the

copy annotated by Horace Walpole, who noted disparagingly on the title page, "By Mr Crab, bred an Apothecary."

13. The usual phrase is "with MS. Notes" or "with MS. additions" (in the case of a Latin book, "cum Notis Manuscriptis"); it seems to have been desirable but not essential to be able to identify the annotator, and to be all to the good if there were "many" or "a great number of" notes. In catalogues that I have examined dating from the 1740s to the 1820s, the presence of notes is recorded *only* as an asset, along with such features as "an elegant copy," "best edit.," "large paper," and—my favorite—"with his head." The apologetic "some notes, but otherwise a fine copy" belongs to a later period.

14. There seems for once to be some foundation for the legend, though it is only the repetition of an anecdote by one witness. See Appendix A, "General Wolfe and the 'Elegy,'" in Gray, *Elegy*, ed. Stokes, pp. 83–88.

15. Raven, Small, and Tadmor, eds., *Practice*, p. 5.

16. For the survival of the printed gloss in one professional context, see fig. 3 (p. 47); of course it has never entirely disappeared, and endnotes are now in favor again.

17. Tribble in Greetham, *Margins*, pp. 231–32.

18. This is the consensus position of Lipking ("Marginal Gloss"), Tribble *(Margins and Marginality)*, and the contributors to Greetham *(Margins)*. Grafton's book on the footnote is not concerned with the origins or history of the footnote per se, but with the evolution of a particular style and standard of documentation.

19. Maynard Mack, *Alexander Pope: A Life*, p. 85.

20. Pope wrote to his friend Jonathan Richardson, father of the annotator, on 17 June 1737: "I have a particular book for your son of all my Works together, with large Margins, knowing how good an use he makes of them in all his books; & remembring how much a worse writer far, than Milton, has been mark'd, collated, & studied by him" (*Correspondence*, 4:78).

21. Oldham, *Compositions*, 1:lxxx.

22. Filling in the blanks is an obviously useful and entertaining occupation for an annotator. For a twentieth-century example see H. Giles's copy of Weale's alleged eyewitness account of the siege of Peking in 1900, *Indiscreet Letters from Peking*, with the names supplied and this note on the half-title: "This copy contains the names in full of all the persons mentioned by initials only. Passages marked ? are of doubtful historical value."

23. Dennis, *Remarks*, p. 51.

24. Mack, *Alexander Pope*, p. 85.

25. Pope, *Dunciad*, pp. 82–83.

26. Shakespeare, *Works* (1725), 1:xxii–xxiii.

27. Greetham, *Margins*, p. 240.

28. Johnson, *Lives*, 3:112, 119, 241.

29. Walter Ralegh, *The History of the World* (1736), British Library copy.

30. Brand, *Observations* (1777), Bodleian Library copy, note on interleaf facing p. iii. This acknowledgement, lightly edited, did find its way into the 1813 edition revised by Henry Ellis.

31. Granger, *Biographical History* (1779), Bodleian Library copy, 1:277.

32. The song is not printed in the collection but pasted onto a flyleaf by Douce (probably) or the previous owner, William Stukely.

33. This book was brought to my attention by Isobel Grundy in "Books and the Woman," p. 7.

34. Eaves and Kimpel, *Samuel Richardson*, p. 234 (where a sample of the exchange is quoted). The books are now in the Princeton University Library. Stoddard describes a similar case from the sixteenth century as a "dialogue in annotation" (*Marks in Books*, item 51).

35. Johnson, *Letters*, 1:120.

36. Chorley, *Memorials*, 2:108n.

37. Engelsing, *Der Bürger als Leser: Lesergeschichte in Deutschland, 1500–1800*. In the context of France, some doubts were expressed by Darnton (e.g., "First Steps," "Readers Respond") and Chartier (e.g., *The Cultural Uses of Print*, pp. 223–25). Prominent in the Anglo-American context are Sherman (who writes engagingly against what he calls the "Montaigne Model" of solitary withdrawal both in *John Dee* and in "The Place of Reading," p. 70), DeMaria, McGann, and several contributors to Raven, Small, and Tadmor, eds., *Practice*. The reading revolution that Cathy Davidson describes in America *(Revolution and the Word)* is of a different kind.

38. Brewer in Raven, Small, and Tadmor, eds., *Practice*, p. 242.

39. Raven's own contribution, "From Promotion to Proscription," is particularly rich in details about the social character of reading in the period. Chartier (*Cultural Uses*, p. 184) describes similar opportunities for "collective use" of books in France in the seventeenth and eighteenth centuries.

40. A particularly touching example of the familiar souvenir inscription is Charlotte Brontë's note in the front of an anthology of French poetry edited by the Abbé Rabion, recording its association with her beloved tutor: "Given to me by Monsieur Heger on the 1st of Jany. 1845 | The morning I left Brussels | C. Brontë." A rather bizarre one is the inscription that Byron wrote in a copy of Madame de Staël's novel *Corinne:* it is addressed to the owner, Byron's mistress, the Countess Guiccioli, deliberately in a language—English—that she did not understand, Byron foreseeing that she would value the inscription simply for the hand. Byron, *Letters and Journals*, 6:215–16.

41. Halsband, *Life*, p. 116; Montagu, *Essays and Poems*, p. 240.

42. Dodsley, *Collection* (1758), 1:330.

43. Wollstonecraft, *Mary, A Fiction, and The Wrongs of Woman*, pp. 85–90.

44. Or an effort to *arouse* affection, like the wiles of Glorvina O'Dowd when she lays siege to Major Dobbin in Thackeray's *Vanity Fair:* "She was constantly writing notes to him at his house, borrowing his books, and scoring with her

great pencil-marks such passages of sentiment or humour as awakened her sympathy" (pp. 417–18).

45. Millgate, *Thomas Hardy*, pp. 356–57. Helen Spencer married Rolfe Humphries in 1925. In 1923 he had given her a copy of *A Few Figs from Thistles*, by Edna St. Vincent Millay, which she annotated and returned to him, her last note saying, "The whole book knocks me completely dead. . . . Write and tell me what you think—" (p. 39). On Clemens, see Gribben, "'Good Books,'" p. 299. The cases of Larkin and Jones and of Orton and Halliwell are described in Bennett, *Writing Home*, pp. 374–75.

46. Edgar Allan Poe, *The Brevities*, p. 107ff.

47. A very early precedent was set by Sir Walter Scott, who published some notes from manuscript in his edition of Swift's *Works* (1814), but as a few pages in an edition of nineteen volumes they do not seem to have made much of an impression.

48. Beckford's habits are described in Chapter One. For an excellent profile of Walpole's annotating activities see Wilmarth Sheldon Lewis, "Horace Walpole's Library." Ferrier's poem and Dibdin's prose "epistle" both analyzed and heightened the current epidemic of book collecting. For the tension between commercial and social pressures that had prompted an "alarmist reaction" earlier, in the circulating libraries, see Raven in Raven, Small, and Tadmor, eds., *Practice*, pp. 178–79, 181, 187.

49. Matthew, *Gladstone, 1809–1874*, p. 236. John Powell, however, gives a more sympathetic account of Gladstone as a reader, and of the value of his marginalia. The final volume of Matthew's edition of *The Gladstone Diaries* contains a catalogue of Gladstone's reading more than three hundred pages long.

50. Piozzi, *Thraliana*, p. 780.

51. C. Brontë, *Shirley*, 2:243–44.

52. Marguerite Gardiner, Countess of Blessington, *Conversations of Lord Byron* (1834), p. 116.

53. Theobald Wolfe Tone, *Life*, 3:24.

54. Titterton, *Shaw*, endpapers.

55. This state of mind is the subject of Nell's fascinating *Lost in a Book*.

56. Boston College now owns the collection of three thousand books associated with Greene's years in Antibes. See the catalogue by Dennys and McNeil, with an introduction by Dennys.

57. He may well have been Henry Bertram Law Webb, who graduated from Cambridge in 1906, married in 1912 (his wife became famous later as the novelist Mary Webb), and published novels under the pseudonym John Clayton in the 1930s, after his wife's death.

Chapter Three: Motives for Marginalia

1. Peter Green, *Kenneth Grahame, 1859–1932*, pp. 233–34; and Grahame, *Pagan Papers*, pp. 75–81.

2. Blake, *Writings*, 2:1386; Coleridge, *Marginalia*, 4:453; Lamb, *Letters*, 1:79. It is not clear whether Lamb was referring to reading pen in hand, or simply to reading per se. His own discreet annotations tend to be confined to the recording of parallel passages and bibliographical information.

3. These remarks are by Robert Scholes (*Protocols*, p. x) and Alan Kennedy (*Psychology*, p. xiii) respectively.

4. Blake, *Writings*, 2:1464, 1467, 1486 (Reynolds); 2:1445 (Bacon). Hollander, "The Widener Burying-Ground." Kevin Jackson also uses the metaphor of sound when he writes of marginalia as the products of "an unresisted urge to make a noise in the white silence of the page's edge."

5. A group of annotated books in the British Library consists of four copies of Sir James Bland Burges's poem *Richard the First*, a book of 660 pages that was printed but not published in 1800. Burges adopted this method of circulating the work for comment prior to publication. Three copies contain the very detailed observations of different readers; in the fourth Burges transcribed (selectively) the notes from seven annotated copies, including the three extant ones. Herbert Spencer similarly called in experts when he prepared revised editions of his *Principles of Biology*, first published in 1864: the British Library contains at least three interleaved sets annotated at his request.

6. Proust, *On Reading Ruskin*, p. 112.

7. François Roustang's stimulating essay "On Reading Again" uses the word "struggle" to characterize the relation between writer and reader (p. 129); both he and Barthes describe the dynamics of reading as alternately submissive and aggressive. The idea, though thus freshly formulated, is not new. For English readers, Samuel Johnson's observation as recorded by Boswell is a classic expression of a piece of common sense: "People in general do not willingly read, if they can have any thing else to amuse them. . . . The progress which the understanding makes through a book, has more pain than pleasure in it" (Boswell, *Life*, ed. G. B. Hill, 4:218).

8. Booth, *The Rhetoric of Fiction*, especially pp. 71–76, 211–21.

9. In 1997 annotated books in a Dublin bookshop helped the international police to track down a murderer—but perhaps the authorities were concerned with "identity" in a narrow sense and were alerted by the signature in the books rather than by the content of the notes; *The Observer* (London), 22 June 1997.

10. Edgeworth, *Belinda*, pp. 278–79. Stevenson, *Jekyll and Hyde*, pp. 91–92. Amis, *Night Train*, p. 133.

11. See Swift, "Marginalia," in *Prose Works;* Montaigne, *Essais*, 2:89. The Hayward Collection at King's College, Cambridge, includes thirty books from Eliot's library, several of them annotated: see the Handlist in the Modern Archive Centre there. The books are his Ollivier and his Spinoza, in the Bibliography of Annotated Books.

12. Barthes, "Sur la lecture," p. 40: "la lecture ne déborde pas la structure; elle lui est soumise: elle en a besoin, elle la respecte; mais elle la pervertit."

13. McFarland, "Synecdochic Structure," p. 78.

14. De Certeau, "Reading as Poaching," p. 154, describes the traditional separation and hierarchization of writing and reading: "To write is to produce the text; to read is to receive it from someone else without putting one's mark on it, without remaking it."

15. For an excellent survey and analysis of Pound's marginalia see King, "An ABC of E. P.'s Library."

16. For an analysis and generous sampling of Clemens marginalia see Alan Gribben, *Mark Twain's Library: A Reconstruction*, and the two articles by the same author.

17. Reynolds, *Works*, 1:[244].

18. As do more flattering comments. Occasionally, friends or friendly strangers send annotated books back to gratify the authors. James Agate's memoir *Ego 5*, pp. 63, 221–22, records two such gifts, one an annotated copy of his novel *Responsibility* that had survived a fire, the other a copy of *Here's Richness!* annotated "for my own satisfaction" by a friend who then decided that Agate should see what he had had to say. The flattery in these cases depends in part on the conventional assumption that the writer of marginalia can afford to be sincere.

19. Bell, "Waugh," p. 31. The article quotes extensively from the marginalia (which, however, are not overall as intemperate as Bell makes them out to be).

20. Hawtree's article "Footnotes from God" provides a good sampling.

21. De Quincey, "The Lake Poets: William Wordsworth and Robert Southey," 2:314.

22. On Walpole, see Lewis, "Horace Walpole's Library," p. lxiii (where Lewis also makes the general observation, "Annotating one's books is akin to keeping an 'intimate' diary that its author suspects may one day be seen by others").

23. Coleridge, *Marginalia*, 4:612.

24. Ibid., 5:547, 531, 595–97, 662.

25. Only the first chapter in Vol. 1, however, is annotated in this way; Gibbon, *History*, British Library C. 60. m. 1. There are a few revisions in Vols. 4 and 6, but no personal comments. Craddock gives a full account and analysis of corrections in this set. The other annotated British Library copy (C. 135. h. 3.) contains only corrections for a future edition, and only in Vol. 1. In fact none of these notes, whether revisions or reflections, appears to have found its way into a later edition.

26. There are large collections of Macaulay's annotated books at Trinity College, Cambridge; of Waugh's at the University of Texas at Austin; and of Edmund White's at Yale. The Berg Collection of the New York Public Library contains many annotated books from Nabokov's library; Northrop Frye's are in the Pratt Library at Victoria College in the University of Toronto.

Chapter Four: Object Lessons

1. The dealers who sold off the Piozzi library made a special point of annotated books; see Broster, *Collectanea Johnsoniana*, and *Brynbella*. James Clifford esti-

mates that there were "hundreds of volumes" containing her notes, and many survive in public collections, notably the Rothschild Collection at the Wren Library, Trinity College, Cambridge; the John Rylands Library, Manchester; and the Beinecke Library, Yale University (Clifford, *Hester Lynch Piozzi*, p. 449 and n. 5). On the history of publication, see Brownell, "Hester Lynch Piozzi's Marginalia," and the *New Cambridge Bibliography of English Literature*. Piozzi's copy of *Rasselas* was described in a short note by Belloc in 1925 but seems afterward to have dropped out of sight.

2. This account of Conway is indebted to John Tearle's sympathetic biography, *Mrs. Piozzi's Tall Young Beau: William Augustus Conway* (1991).

3. Hayward, ed., *Autobiography*, 1:5.

4. Tearle, *Mrs. Piozzi's Tall Young Beau*, pp. 97, 115, 28. Piozzi's remarkable annotated copy of *The Imperial Family Bible*, now in the British Library, does not appear to have been noticed in the scholarly literature. I quote only the inscription as relevant to the current study: "10 April 1820. | This Book | is the Property of Mrs. Susanna Rudd | Lion Row | Clifton | near Bristol. | It was an imperfect Copy bought cheap for Love of the *Prints;* in 1819, intrusted to my Care; who restored the Text: & wrote Notes to it, for Love of the possessor and *her* Heirs: not those of | H: LP.—"

5. One of Piozzi's friends, Edward Mangin, paid tribute to her annotation and to her handwriting when he made up a special copy of Pettit's *Anecdotes* (1789). He had lent her the book; she returned it with notes written on loose sheets of paper, which he cut into strips so that he could paste the notes in where they belonged, as he explains on a flyleaf: "Mrs. Piozzi borrowed this vol: from me in Jany., 1817, & returned it with the MS. notes which I have pasted in their places, as curious specimens of ye spirited observations & beautiful hand-writing of the ingenious & accomplished annotator—now seventy six."

6. Points of ellipsis in this and subsequent notes are Piozzi's own.

7. Hassall, *Rupert Brooke*, p. 266.

8. See the University of Texas copy in the Bibliography of Annotated Books. Cummings's pencil notes are mostly markings, but he shows considerable interest in certain technical points.

9. Brooke, *Letters*, pp. 11, 156. As for examples of metrical analysis in his college papers, King's keeps a typescript catalogue of the Brooke holdings, and the notebooks M/8, M/12, and M/21 all contain schemes of meter or versification.

10. The line in question, however, is from Coleridge's "Christabel," and Alden could (just) be defended: "The gate that was ironed within and without, / Where an army in battle array had marched out."

11. Hassall, *Rupert Brooke*, pp. 157, 204, 115–16, 177. Brooke's politics come irresistibly even into the Alden marginalia, when he questions one of Alden's general definitions of poetry: "Is it philosophical to judge what <u>poetry is</u> by what the <u>poet feels</u> when he writes it? I suppose it's natural to attach over much importance to the producer, in a Tariff Reform Country" (p. 10).

12. Brooke, *Prose*, p. 111. The review appeared in the *Cambridge Review* of 2 December 1909.
13. *Cambridge Review*, 19 January 1911, p. 209.
14. Brooke, *Letters*, p. 163.
15. Recollecting Brooke about this time, Virginia Woolf treats his poses understandingly in her anonymous review of his posthumously published collected poems, with a memoir: "Like most sensitive people, he had his methods of self-protection; his pretence now to be this and now to be that. But, however sunburnt and slap-dash he might choose to appear at any particular moment, no one could know him even slightly without seeing that he was not only very sincere, but passionately in earnest about the things he cared for" (*TLS*, 8 August 1918; reprinted in Woolf, *Books and Portraits*, p. 87).
16. T. S. Omond, *English Metrists*, p. 148. Brooke recommends Omond (misprinted "Oman") in the Saintsbury review; but he must have meant his basic *Study of Metre* (1903), not *Metrists*.
17. Brooke, *Prose*, p. 112.
18. Hassall, *Rupert Brooke*, pp. 177, 245–46.
19. Rogers, *Rupert Brooke*, p. 11.
20. Omond, *A Study of Metre*, p. 158.
21. Brooke, *Letters*, p. 266, from *Cambridge Review*, 8 December 1910, p. 188.
22. "Some Aspects of English Poetry," a talk written for the classical society, Eranos, at Rugby in July 1906, and repeated in Cambridge in 1908: Modern Archive Centre, King's College, Cambridge, Brooke P / 3, ff 74v–106r. Even as he depended on it, Brooke said Archer's book was "ridiculously incomplete."
23. Rogers, *Rupert Brooke*, p. 13.
24. Saintsbury, *Historical Manual*, p. 337.
25. Omond, *English Metrists of the Eighteenth and Nineteenth Centuries*, pp. 240, 242.
26. Information from M. J. Crump, Head of the Early Collection Series in the British Library.
27. *Catalogue of Books, Manuscripts, and Autograph Letters, Recently Added to the Stock of Thomas Rodd* (London, 1839), p. 10.
28. The name "Scriblerus" appears for example on a flyleaf at the end of Vol. 1, and on 2:499; "Scribbler" on 1:117; "Scribble" on 2:262, "scribbles" on 2:529.
29. For 1791, see 1:516; for 1792, 2:116, 301, 443, 492, 506, 510; for 1797, 2:438.
30. Scriblerus's objections to Johnson's harping occur, for example, at 2:2, 7, 10, 12, 94, 98 (this occasion prompting the protest about Boswell's being an "Idiot," quoted above), 100.
31. His idea about the identity of the orator is confirmed by the editors of the standard edition (ed. Hill, rev. Powell, 1934–50, commonly referred to as "Hill-Powell"), and indeed is fairly obvious; but his annotations contain other identifications not included in Hill-Powell's Table of Anonymous Persons.
32. His own seat was in Wiltshire: he refers to James Harris of Salisbury as "my little Countryman" (2:208).

33. Scriblerus expresses opinions about all sorts of contemporary issues, political, social, and literary, and inadvertently reveals common attitudes and behavior. For example, he takes up the contemporary argument about whether Gay's *Beggar's Opera* had a direct effect on the incidence of crime. Johnson denied it, but Scriblerus cites among other evidence the testimony of a highwayman he met in France: "at Boulogne many years ago I got acquainted with the highwayman (the Milk-boy) who told me his history and how his first idea of being a Highwayman was taken at the beggars opera" (1:488).

34. The Advertisement is quoted in Hill-Powell, 1:13. The corrections introduced in the second edition are conveniently collected in James Boswell, *The Principal Corrections and Additions to the First Edition of Mr. Boswell's Life of Johnson* (London, 1793), where the anonymous annotator (definitely not Scriblerus) is mentioned on page 31.

35. Notably, Add MS 38203, folios 51, 53, 56, 172.

36. Samuel Johnson, *Letters*, 1:129–30; cf. Hill-Powell, 1:60–61.

37. See for example Frances Burney, *Early Journals and Letters*, 1:116 and n. 31.

38. The summary that follows is based on the *Memoirs*, with the addition of information from Frances Burney, *Early Journals and Letters;* Dr. Charles Burney, *Memoirs* and *Letters;* and Roger Lonsdale, *Dr. Charles Burney.*

39. Johnson describes him coming in after dinner, in 1780, as though his presence were to be expected; *Letters*, 3:244–45. Virginia Woolf replays the party scene in "Dr. Burney's Evening Party," *The Common Reader: Second Series*, pp. 108–25.

40. Roger Lonsdale, ed., *Eighteenth-Century Women Poets*, nos. 127–28. Charles Burney, *Letters*, 1:161.

41. The reviews are in *Monthly Review* 68 (1787), 528 and n.s. 3 (1790), 342–43. The latter comes close to revealing Greville's secret and may indeed have made it necessary for Greville to do so himself: "As this gentleman deals much in egotism, some may think it would not have been amiss had he affixed his name: but he has done what amounts to the same thing: he has sufficiently given us to understand, that he is the ingenious author of MAXIMS, &c. a work of considerable reputation."

42. Croft's letter appeared in *Gentleman's Magazine* 57 (1787), 651–52, and the letter from "A.B.C." in 58 (1788), 948, 1152–54.

43. The pamphlet is reviewed in *Monthly Review* n.s. 8 (1792), 570–71; the office copy is at the Bodleian Library, shelf-mark Per 3977. d. 190. This note was drawn to my attention by the entry on Fulke Greville in the old *Cambridge Bibliography of English Literature* (Cambridge, 1940), 2:654.

44. Alan Macdonald's useful article "A Lost Story of Perversion" includes a survey of the White collection at Austin.

45. John Verney, in Warner, *T. H. White*, p. 17.

46. Warner, *T. H. White*, pp. 31, 42, 310, 28, 41–43, 52. In spite of his remark about not being able to love women, White was attracted—and attractive—to them.

In his Chronology, Gallix records several serious relationships between 1935 and 1953, including an engagement in 1946.

47. Warner, *T. H. White,* p. 26. The source is an unpublished autobiographical statement by White's mother, Constance Aston White.

48. Gallix, *T. H. White,* p. 79.

49. White, *Letters to a Friend,* pp. 46, 49, 57–58. In April 1932, White reported to Potts that the book had been rejected by Chatto, and asked him to read it over; in August he promised to send it from Reigate; in January 1933 he thanked him for extensive criticism and said he had made all the changes Potts proposed. He was afraid it might be considered obscene but thought highly of it himself. It went subsequently to I. A. Richards (who did not like it) and was then put aside for thirty years. White revised it again in 1961 but accepted his publisher's advice against publication. The 1961 version is in the White collection at Austin.

50. The "deep well" theory in *The Road to Xanadu* (1927), John Livingston Lowes's study of the genesis of Coleridge's "Rime of the Ancient Mariner," is a celebrated example of the same period.

Chapter Five: Two Profiles

1. Coffman's bibliography of books alleged to have been "owned or read" by Cole-ridge contains more than two thousand titles, and still seems suspiciously narrow.

2. Coleridge, *Letters,* 6:998–1002.

3. Coleridge, *Marginalia,* 1:41.

4. Ibid., 3:805–9. Another noteworthy example of the same kind is James Sedgwick's *Hints to the Public and the Legislature, on the Nature and Effect of Evangelical Preaching* (1810), in which Coleridge wrote an extraordinary set of notes also designed to help Southey with a review; *Marginalia,* 4:619–73.

5. Ibid., 1:741–99; the *Blackwood's* version is at 1:795–99. In annotating Browne's *Religio Medici,* Coleridge had before him the printed precedent of a seventeenth-century commentator, Thomas Keck (1:742). In Part 1 of the *Religio* (i:30), Browne confesses himself a writer of marginalia, quoting a passage of Paracelsus that he declares "I never could pass . . . without an asterisk or annotation."

6. Coleridge, *Marginalia,* 1:lxxxiv–lxxxv; and *Letters,* 3:32.

7. Coleridge, *Marginalia,* 2:118. In Lamb's copy of Donne's *Poems,* annotated in 1811, Coleridge cockily wrote, "N.B. Spite of Appearances, this Copy is the better for the Mss. Notes. The Annotator himself says so" (1:221).

8. Lamb, *Letters,* ed. Lucas, 2:75.

9. Green and Coleridge, living some miles apart from each other, met regularly but also exchanged annotated books to keep in touch. A casual remark in one of Coleridge's letters of 1818 shows that it was not a one-way relationship; having mentioned Novalis's *Heinrich von Ofterdingen,* he says, "(Your short critique on which pencilled at the end of the IInd Vol. contains my full judgement &

convictions thereon)"; Coleridge, *Letters*, 4:870. See also Jackson, "Coleridge's Collaborator."

10. Quoted in Coleridge, *Marginalia*, 1:lxix.

11. Coleridge, *Marginalia*, 4:684–868.

12. Ibid., 3:507–626; the quotation is at 3:512.

13. Ibid., 3:508.

14. Ibid., 4:619, 2:650, 4:161, 5:853–54. Coleridge did not characteristically write in pencil as he did in the book Southey overtraced (by James Sedgwick) and the Malthus—both of which were Southey's books—and he was probably being particularly careful.

    Coleridge did not actually surrender the Richard Field book at the time he inscribed it but kept it by him and continued to make notes in it, as he did with the books annotated for Sara Hutchinson and Charles Lamb mentioned earlier. The inscriptions may have been meant only to ensure that the books would go sooner or later to the right person.

15. Coleridge, *Marginalia*, 5:484.

16. Coleridge, *On the Constitution of the Church and State*, p. 166.

17. The second paragraph of *Biographia Literaria*, for example, begins with the assertion, "In 1794, when I had barely passed the verge of manhood, I published a small volume of juvenile poems" (1:5); the actual date was 1796.

18. Lamb, "Christ's Hospital," p. 21.

19. Quoted from a notebook in Coleridge, *Marginalia*, 1:lxxiii.

20. Coleridge, *Marginalia*, 5:644.

21. Ibid., 5:561–62.

22. In one of his books, Coleridge remarks that when he is reading the words of "a powerful and perspicuous Author (as in the next to inspired Comment[ar]y of Archb. Leighton—for whom God be praised!) I identify myself with the excellent Writer and his thoughts become my thoughts"; *Marginalia*, 6:305.

23. The Bollingen Edition of the *Table Talk* edited by Carl Woodring describes and scrupulously documents these incorporations; for an anthology of reports of Coleridge's conversation see Armour and Howes, *Coleridge the Talker*.

24. Boswell, *Life of Johnson*, ed. G. Birkbeck Hill, rev. L. F. Powell, 1:30. The "loved, or loved to hate" phrase is Steven Lynn's, in reference to Johnson's *Prefaces* (i.e., *Lives of the English Poets*); "Johnson's Critical Reception," p. 242. Like others attempting to summarize trends in the response to Johnson, such as Boulton in his introduction to *Johnson: The Critical Heritage* and Clifford and Greene in *Samuel Johnson: A Survey and Bibliography*, Lynn registers in all periods (a) extremes of adulation and disparagement and (b) stubborn refusal on the part of readers to separate their assessment of the works from their opinion of the man.

25. See Pottle's 1929 survey of major editions in *The Literary Career of James Boswell, Esq.*, reprinted in 1965.

26. Reynolds's copy, signed also by his niece Theophila Gwatkin, is in the Harry E. Widener Collection at Harvard; Hastings's, in the Rare Books Room of the

New York Public Library; the copy inscribed by Elizabeth Boswell, in the Beinecke Library at Yale. The others are as follows (and will not be found in the Bibliography of Annotated Books unless given special mention later): Malone's two revised copies of 1807, in the Beinecke and the British Library; Piozzi's 1807 in the Beinecke, and her 1816 in the Houghton Library at Harvard; Hunt's 1839 in the Huntington; Carlyle's 1874 (Fitzgerald's edition, dedicated to Carlyle) in the Beinecke; Lewes's 1848 in the Yale undergraduate library; Hardy's 1925 in the Humanities Research Center at the University of Texas at Austin; J. P. Morgan's extra-illustrated 1791 in the Morgan Library in New York; C. S. Peirce's 1851 in the Houghton; Willa Cather's 1900 at Austin; Wallace Stevens's 1906 in the Huntington; T. H. White's battered 1867 at Austin; and Elizabeth Bishop's 1931 in Houghton.

27. In the Bibliography of Secondary Works Cited, see Boswell's *Life,* ed. Fletcher.

28. The dog-fighting story is supported by evidence from later in Johnson's life, for example Boswell's report in the *Journal of a Tour to the Hebrides* (*Life,* ed. Hill-Powell, 5:329) that he had heard Johnson say he was "afraid of no dog," and that Beauclerk once saw him deal with a pair of fighting dogs: "Dr. Johnson looked steadily at them for a little while; and then, as one would separate two little boys, who were foolishly hurting each other, he ran up to them, and cuffed their heads, till he drove them asunder."

29. Johnson, "Gray," *Lives,* 3:441.

Chapter Six: Books for Fanatics

1. Ondaatje, *English Patient,* p. 16.

2. The "notebook" of p. 16 becomes "his commonplace book" on p. 96 and p. 231; "the Herodotus journal," p. 156; and "his holy book," p. 294. Since "commonplace" has come to connote dull and hackneyed, sticklers insist on the hyphen that recalls the origins of the "common-place book" in the *topoi* or "common places" of Aristotelian rhetoric.

3. Ondaatje, *English Patient,* pp. 16–17, 58.

4. Ibid., pp. 231–34, 248–49.

5. Ibid., pp. 68, 118, 209.

6. Tribble, *Margins and Marginality,* pp. 51–55.

7. *Catalogue of the Unique Library Formed by Irving Browne, Esq., of Troy, N. Y., Containing the Most Extensive Collection of Extra Illustrated Works Ever Offered by Auction in this Country* (New York, 1878).

8. Holbrook Jackson, *Anatomy of Bibliomania,* gives an entertaining account of grangerizing, with plentiful examples, pp. 576–82, 591–92.

9. The phrase is from the title page of the first edition of his *Biographical History* in two volumes, 1769.

10. Ferriar's *Bibliomania* of 1809, lines 113 and following, describes the "letter'd fop . . . now warm'd by Orford [Walpole], and by Granger school'd" who cuts portraits out of old books to stick in "Paper-books, superbly gilt and tool'd"—

but these sound like albums rather than printed books, and Ferriar does not indicate how long this hobby had existed. The publisher's Advertisement to the fifth edition of Granger (1824) maintains that whereas collectors had earlier expected to have to pay no more than five shillings for a print representing a British figure, "on the appearance of Mr. Granger's work, the rage to illustrate it with portraits was so prevalent, that scarcely a copy of a book ornamented with portraits could be found in an unmutilated state: and books of this description rose in price to five times their original value" (1:iii); but then the publisher has an interest in large claims for the importance of the book he is publishing.

11. Sir William Musgrave's copy, listed in the Bibliography of Annotated Books, was one of them. In the publishers' "Advertisement" to the expanded edition of 1824 they explain that in 1790 a few interleaved copies of the editions of 1775 and 1779 had been especially prepared for eminent print-collectors so that they could enter "information of such Portraits as had escaped the Author's notice, which might happen to be in their own possession, or have come within their knowledge" (1:i). The intent was certainly annotation, not extra-illustration.

12. Daniel Tredwell, who refers to the practice as "private illustration," gives a wry and charming account of the whole process, including rising costs (*Monograph*, pp. 17–25). He recommends maintaining a uniform style—for instance, not mixing prints and photographs—but I find the more unpredictable and less tasteful examples of this art actually more appealing.

13. Dibdin, *Bibliomania*, pp. 61, 62; Tredwell, *Monograph*, p. 11. Dibdin's examples, pp. 62–63, are the Granger in "37 atlas folio volumes" prepared by Richard Bull of Ongar and at that time in the collection of the Marquis of Bute (now at the Huntington, which maintains an index file of extra-illustrated books in its collection); a Clarendon "recently in the metropolis . . . valued at 5000 guineas" (very likely the Sutherland Collection now at the Ashmolean in Oxford); two Shakespeares; Scott's edition of Dryden; and a copy of "the Historical Work of Mr. Fox" enriched not only with the usual engraved portraits but also with an original drawing and "many original notes and letters" by Fox.

14. Granger, *Biographical History* (1824), 1:i; Byron, *English Bards* (1865), p. 17. The pre-printed title page for Granger's *History* appears in the Huntington copy of the fourth edition (1804), included in the Bibliography of Annotated Books.

The advertisement for the Byron assumes that most sizes of print would be accommodated by the large quarto size: quartos could stay as they were, octavos be inlaid, and folios be folded in half and open out to full size.

The Prints and Photographs Collection in the New York Public Library has two extra-illustrated Boswells based on editions by Croker, one published in 1860 and the other in 1866, with specially printed title pages (dated 1868 and 1850 respectively) declaring them to be "Illustrated with Portraits and Views elucidatory of the text." If not identical sets, the illustrations at least exhibit a high degree of overlap, and my working hypothesis is that they were assembled by a bookseller who also dealt in prints. Shelf-marks *KZ 6811–6924 and *KZ 7012–7016. Parkin, *Grangerizing*, points out (p. 2) that the *TLS* of 19 September 1918 describes the small booksellers around Holborn, in London, twenty-five or thirty years earlier as having devoted most of their time to gutting newspapers and illustrated books—"grangerizing for the more well-to-do booksellers."

15. Granger, *Biographical History* (1824), 1:ii.
16. See *Brontëana* in the Bibliography of Annotated Books. There is some uncertainty about the provenance of this volume and some doubt about the connection with Nussey, since the printed title page and "Introduction" are dated 1898 though Nussey died in 1897. The body of the text, however, had been in print since 1889. It is possible that Nussey supplied the illustrative materials and an heir added the printed title page after her death, but more likely that this copy belonged to the original editor (Turner) and found its way into the hands of the collector Michael Sadleir, who was the one to have it extra-illustrated and bound. Sadleir certainly did *some* of the extra-illustrating, for several items in the volume date from the 1930s.
17. Stoddard, *Marks in Books*, item 27.
18. Thomas Gray, *Poems* (1775).
19. See Tennyson, *In Memoriam*, in the Bibliography of Annotated Books.
20. Horseman gave his copy of Maria Edgeworth's *Letters for Literary Ladies* (1799), now at Trinity College Dublin, treatment similar in kind but not in degree.

Chapter Seven: Poetics

1. *A Short Description of . . . the Cathedral Church of Salisbury,* (16 pp.), p. 6.
   Sarah Sophia Banks (called Sophia, and listed as Sophia Sarah in the British Library Catalogue), sister to Sir Joseph Banks, who was President of the Royal Society, was a collector on her own account. On her death in 1818, her brother donated to the British Museum books and objects from her collections that did not duplicate existing holdings *(Dictionary of National Biography)*. The British Library now contains several books with notes in her hand, among which works on archery stand out; see Ascham, *Toxophilus,* Barrington, *Observations on the Practice of Archery in England,* Hargrove, *Anecdotes of Archery,* and Oldfield, *Anecdotes of Archery, Ancient and Modern.*
2. See Clare, *Letters,* pp. 34n, 48n, and Lucas, *John Clare.* It is possible that this copy was only a draft version of the fair copy sent to Radstock.
3. This is a recurrent theme in Coleridge's work, but especially in the "Essays on Genial Criticism."
4. I have not been able to discover Mrs. Trübner's first name. She must have been the wife of the publisher Nikolaus Trübner, whom Lewes wrote for occasionally. *The George Eliot Letters* (including letters by Lewes) records her calling at the house with her husband in 1869 (5:37n).
5. *A Catalogue of the Valuable Library . . . of John Horne Tooke, Esq.* (1813).

6. Coke, *The First Part of the Institutes,* "Editor's Address" (not paginated or foliated). A page from this copy is illustrated in fig. 3 (p. 47).

7. Cecil, *Max,* pp. 371–75; Behrman, *Portrait of Max,* pp. 26–30, 89–97. The quotations are from Cecil, *Max,* p. 374.

    Some of Thackeray's sketches are reproduced in Grego, *Thackerayana* (1875), though in crude copies that hardly do Thackeray justice. The Berg Collection of the New York Public Library has several of the originals.

8. Pickering, *Poems,* pt., 2 p. 53. The volume is separately paginated for each of the three poets; future references give page numbers along with the name of the relevant author.

9. I quote directly from the original at Keats House, citing page references for Keats's notes and book-and-line references for the poem (abbreviated as *PL*).

10. Kafka, *Metamorphosis,* p. 11.

11. Burke, *Observations on a late State of the Nation,* p. 44.

12. *The Rothschild Library,* 1:240–41, describes the volume and prints transcriptions of several notes, as well as a photograph of one annotated page. In *The Library of Edward Gibbon,* Keynes says that he was astonished by the Herodotus, knowing Gibbon's habits (*Library,* p. 33). References to the text of Herodotus in the following pages are to the standard modern divisions of the text, not to those of the edition Gibbon was using.

13. Even disappointment may have a positive side. The imagination makes do with very little. Knowing that there are such actual combinations as Nabokov on Kafka, Bentham on Burke, Wallace Stevens on Wordsworth, E. E. Cummings on Simone de Beauvoir, Gertrude Stein on Harriet Beecher Stowe, and Marie Stopes on the Marquess of Queensberry (on Oscar Wilde) kindles speculation when the reality lets you down. (These are all in the Bibliography of Annotated Books; for Queensberry, see Douglas, *Oscar Wilde and the Black Douglas.*) What *might* those readers have made of those writers? What *should* they have said? Pursue it, and the notion expands to become a thought-experiment something like the "dialogues of the dead" that were popular for many centuries. What *might* X (any reader, say Lewis Carroll) have made of Y (any book, say Newton's *Principia*)?

14. "Bibliomane" in *The Times* (London), 13 May 1999.

15. Sharp published a short addition to this work early in 1772, the title of the sequel incorporating a blunter version of the original title: *An Appendix to the Representation of the Injustice and Dangerous Tendency of Tolerating Slavery, etc.* Francis Hargrave was one of the counsel for Sommersett. He published his views in *An Argument in the Case of James Sommersett a Negro, Lately Determined by the Court of King's Bench: Wherein it is Attempted to Demonstrate the Present Unlawfulness of Domestic Slavery in England* (1772). His own copy of that work is bound together with his copy of Sharp's *Representation*—neither of them, unfortunately, annotated by Hargrave—in British Library 884. k. 26.

16. Collins, *Historical Collections,* p. 212.

Chapter Eight: Book Use or Book Abuse

1. Sendak told this story himself; report by David Allen Brewer, email to SHARP list-serv, 14 February 1996.
2. See Piozzi, Astell, and Coleridge quoted earlier, pp. 74, 64–65, and 155.
3. Coleridge, *Marginalia*, 2:698.
4. Fadiman, *Ex Libris*, pp. 34, 32.
5. Hermione Lee, *Virginia Woolf*, p. 412. The essay remains unpublished; the phrases in quotation marks are quoted by Lee from the manuscript.

   Woolf's system of reading-notebooks has frequently been described: for example, briefly in Lee, *Virginia Woolf*, p. 412; and in detail by Brenda R. Silver, *Virginia Woolf's Reading Notebooks*. For a few exceptions to the general rule of her not annotating books, and for the counterexamples of her husband and her father, see the pamphlet by Laila Miletic-Vejzovic, *A Library of One's Own*. Woolf's father Leslie Stephen often drew animal pictures in his books by way of commentary.
6. Above, p. 73 and n. 48.
7. Lee, *Virginia Woolf*, p. 412.
8. Virginia Woolf, "Writing in the Margin"; the manuscript is untitled and the title supplied by the cataloguer.
9. Lee's term "addiction" must have been based on the idea of habit, but whereas a habit isn't necessarily a bad habit, once you call it an addiction it is. Fadiman, quoted earlier, raises the apprehension of sacrilege against "holy" objects. For the noise metaphor, see p. 83 and n. 4 above. McFarland's assertion that "marginalia always invade the host text" (p. 78) seems to me to invoke both invasion and parasitism (the marginal note cannot stand alone but must feed off a text that can), but it is possible that he was using "host" in the sense of one who offers hospitality and in that case the underlying metaphor is treacherous usurpation.
10. Tribble, *Margins and Marginality*, p. 28; Raven, Small, and Tadmor, eds., *Practice*, pp. 178–81, 187–88, 201.
11. Slights in Greetham, *Margins*, p. 201.
12. Woolf, *The Common Reader: Second Series*, p. 268.
13. Jackson, *The Anatomy of Bibliomania*, p. 503.
14. P. J. O. Taylor, "In the Margin," *Bodleian Library Record* 16 (1998): 365–6.
15. For Gibbon on Herodotus see pp. 227–29 above; for Waugh on Connolly, pp. 93. Stevens comments on the Harvard system of his day in his copy of Samuel Johnson's *Select Essays*, and Hardy on billiards in Captain Crawley's book: for both of these see the Bibliography of Annotated Books.
16. The collection, at the British Library, is Cup. 362. a. 2. (1–76); the book in question is Francis A. K. Douglas's *Oscar Wilde and the Black Douglas*.
17. The leprechaun appears in a copy of Piozzi's own *Retrospection* (1:344), in the Wren Library; the remarks about Bolingbroke, in her *Anecdotes of the late Samuel Johnson* (p. 111), at the Beinecke; the comments about Handel (1:232–

33), about lifting (1:286), and about the Prince Regent (2:130) in John Brady's *Clavis Calendaria,* in the Wren.

18. Davidson, *Revolution,* p. 79.
19. Kintgen, *Reading,* p. 214.
20. Rose, "How Historians Study Reader Response," pp. 195, 209.
21. Kintgen, *Reading,* p. 215; Martin, *History and Power,* p. 346; Machor, *Readers,* pp. x, xxi–xxii.
22. Darnton, *Forbidden Best-Sellers,* p. 85.
23. Darnton, *Kiss of Lamourette,* p. 177.
24. Radway, *Reading the Romance,* p. 11.

Afterword

1. O'Brien, *The Best of Myles,* pp. 17–24. As an example of the highest level of handling, he proposes "suitable passages in not less than fifty per cent of the books to be underlined in good-quality red ink and an appropriate phrase from the following list inserted in the margin, viz: Rubbish! Yes, indeed! How true, how true! I don't agree at all. Why? Yes, but cf. Homer, Od., iii, 151. . . ." (p. 20).

2. In the *New York Times* of 24 October 1999, I was pleased to see creative use of such a find: Vincent Canby's review of Barry Humphries' current one-man show, "Dame Edna: The Royal Tour," spends four paragraphs quoting marginalia from a New York Public Library copy of *My Gorgeous Life*—supposedly the autobiography of Dame Edna Everage—that prove that the annotator believed Dame Edna to be real.

3. Peterson and Standley, "J. S. Mill," uses *three* columns for two sets of marginalia (Mill's and Browning's) to Browning's *Pauline.* I quite like the double-column solution but find three columns taxing.

Bibliography of Annotated Books Cited

Aberdeen School of Domestic Science. *The Aberdeen Cookery Book*. 2nd ed. Aberdeen: Aberdeen Press and Journal Office, 1931. National Library of Scotland. Shelf-mark NG. 837. e. 1.

Adams, Henry. *The Education of Henry Adams*. Boston: Houghton Mifflin, 1918. Humanities Research Center, University of Texas at Austin. Shelf-mark E 175.5 A172 1918. Annotated by O. K. Bouwsma.

Aiken, John, and Anna Laetitia Barbauld. *Evenings at Home; or, The Juvenile Budget Opened*. 2nd ed. London: Johnson, 1794. Osborne Collection, Toronto Public Library.

Alden, Raymond Macdonald. *An Introduction to Poetry for Students of English Literature*. London: George Bell; New York: Henry Holt, 1909. Modern Archive Centre, King's College, Cambridge. Annotated by Rupert Brooke.

———. *An Introduction to Poetry for Students of English Literature*. New York: Henry Holt, 1909. Humanities Research Center, University of Texas at Austin. Shelf-mark PR 1042 A5 HRC CUM. Annotated by E. E. Cummings.

Andrew, Christopher. *Secret Service: The Making of the British Intelligence Community*. London: Heinemann, 1985. Boston College. Annotated by Graham Greene.

The Anti-Jacobin. 20 November 1797–9 July 1798. British Library. Shelf-mark C. 40. l. 2. Annotated by George Canning.

Antoninus, Marcus Aurelius. *Meditations*. Glasgow: Foulis, 1749. Berg Collection, New York Public Library. Annotated by Leigh Hunt.

Ascham, Roger. *Toxophilus*. London, 1545. British Library. Shelf-mark C. 31. e. 29. Annotated by Sarah Sophia Banks.

Austen, Jane. *Emma*. Standard Novels Series. London: Bentley, 1833. Wren Library, Trinity College, Cambridge. Annotated by G. O. Trevelyan.

————. *Mansfield Park*. Standard Novels Series. London: Bentley, 1833. Wren Library, Trinity College, Cambridge. Annotated by T. B. Macaulay and G. O. Trevelyan.

————. *Northanger Abbey; Persuasion*. Standard Novels Series. London: Bentley, 1833. Wren Library, Trinity College, Cambridge. Annotated by T. B. Macaulay and G. O. Trevelyan.

————. *Pride and Prejudice*. Standard Novels Series. London: Bentley, 1833. Wren Library, Trinity College, Cambridge. Annotated by T. B. Macaulay, G. O. Trevelyan, and G. M. Trevelyan.

————. *Sense and Sensibility*. Standard Novels Series. London: Bentley, 1833. Wren Library, Trinity College, Cambridge. Annotated by T. B. Macaulay and G. O. Trevelyan.

The Babes in the Basket. Edinburgh, n.d. Osborne Collection, Toronto Public Library.

Barrington, Daines. *Observations on the Practice of Archery in England*. [N.p., n.d.] British Library. Shelf-mark 797. dd. 13. Annotated by Sarah Sophia Banks.

Bayle, Pierre. *Pensées diverses*. 4th ed. 2 vols. Rotterdam: Leers, 1704. Collection of the Earl of Harrowby. Annotated by Mary Astell.

Bazett, L. M. *After-Death Communications*. London: Kegan Paul, Trench, Trubner, & Co., [1918]. Humanities Research Center, University of Texas at Austin. Shelf-mark BF 1301 B43 1918. Annotated by Arthur Conan Doyle.

Beauvoir, Simone de. *The Second Sex*. Trans. and ed. H. M. Pashley. New York: Knopf, 1953. Humanities Research Center, University of Texas at Austin. Shelf-mark HQ 1208 B352. Annotated by E. E. Cummings.

The Bible: That is, the Holy Scriptures Conteined in the Old and New Testament. London, 1606. British Library. Shelf-mark C. 45. g. 13. Annotated by Edmund Law and others.

Boileau-Despréaux, Nicolas. *The Art of Poetry*. Translated by Sir William Solmes. London: Bentley & Magnes, 1683. Huntington Library. Accession number 49070. Annotated by Alexander Pope.

Book of Common Prayer. London, 1702. British Library. Shelf-mark C. 36. g. 3. Annotated by White Kennett and others.

Boswell, James. *Boswell's Life of Johnson*. Ed. George Birkbeck Hill. 6 vols. Oxford: Clarendon Press, 1887. Harvard University Library. Shelf-mark 16474.11.

————. *Boswell's Life of Johnson*. Ed. George Birkbeck Hill. 6 vols. Oxford: Clarendon Press, 1887. Huntington Library. Accession number 140177.

————. *Boswell's Life of Johnson*. 2 vols. London: Oxford University Press, 1927. English Faculty Library, Cambridge University.

————. *Life of Johnson*. Ed. John Wilson Croker. 10 vols. London: Murray, 1839. Huntington Library. Accession number 471960. Annotated by Leigh Hunt.

————. *The Life of Samuel Johnson, LL.D.* 2 vols. London: Dilly, 1791. Cambridge University Library. Shelf-mark Syn. 4. 79. 15.

———. *The Life of Samuel Johnson, LL.D.* 2 vols. London: Dilly, 1791. British Library. Shelf-mark 633. l. 3,4. Annotated by Fulke Greville.

———. *The Life of Samuel Johnson, LL.D.* 2 vols. London: Dilly, 1791. Rare Books Room, New York Public Library. Shelf-mark *KF 1791 Copy 2. Annotated by Charlotte Beauclerk?

———. *The Life of Samuel Johnson, LL.D.* 2 vols. London: Dilly, 1791. National Library of Scotland. Shelf-mark H. S. 233, 234.

———. *The Life of Samuel Johnson, LL.D.* 3 vols. Dublin: R. Cross et al., 1792. Cambridge University Library. Shelf-mark Hib. 5. 792. 39.

———. *The Life of Samuel Johnson, LL.D.* 3 vols. London: Dilly, 1793. Humanities Research Center, University of Texas at Austin. Shelf-mark PR 3533 B6 1793 Copy 2.

———. *The Life of Samuel Johnson, LL.D.* 2nd ed. 3 vols. London: Dilly, 1793. National Library of Scotland. Shelf-mark F. 7. b. 4. Annotated by "Mr. L."

———. *The Life of Samuel Johnson, LL.D.* 3 vols. Boston: W. Andrews & L. Blake, 1807. National Library of Scotland. Shelf-mark RB. s. 1081. Annotated by Russell, Sarah, and John Bradford.

———. *The Life of Samuel Johnson, LL.D.* 8th ed. 4 vols. London: Cadell & Davies, 1816. Victoria College, University of Toronto. Shelf-mark PR 3533 B6 1816.

———. *The Life of Samuel Johnson, LL.D.* Ed. E. Malone. 5 vols. London: Tegg, 1824. Humanities Research Center, University of Texas at Austin. Shelf-mark Am B657l 1824.

———. *The Life of Samuel Johnson, LL.D.* Ed. E. Malone. London: Jones, 1829. British Library. Shelf-mark 10859. s. 3.

———. *The Life of Samuel Johnson, LL.D.* Ed. J. W. Croker. 5 vols. London: Murray, 1831. Beinecke Library, Yale University. Shelf-mark 1987 150. Annotated by John Gibson Lockhart.

———. *The Life of Samuel Johnson, LL.D.* Ed. J. W. Croker. 10 vols. London: Murray, 1835. British Library. Shelf-mark 1477. a. 7.

———. *The Life of Samuel Johnson, LL.D.* Ed. E. Malone. London: Washbourne, 1848. New York Public Library. Shelf-mark AN.

———. *The Life of Samuel Johnson, LL.D.* 4 vols. London: Office of the National Illustrated Library, n.d. [1851]. Houghton Library, Harvard University. Shelf-mark *AC85.P3533.Zz851b. Annotated by Charles Sanders Peirce.

———. *The Life of Samuel Johnson, LL.D.* Illustrations by Julian Portch. London: Routledge, 1867. Harvard University Library. Shelf-mark 16474. 5. 8.

———. *The Life of Samuel Johnson, LL.D.* Illustrations by Julian Portch. London: Routledge, 1867. Humanities Research Center, University of Texas at Austin. Shelf-mark PR 3533 B6 1867. Annotated by T. H. White.

———. *The Life of Samuel Johnson.* Ed. Roger Ingpen. 2 vols. London: Pitman, 1907. Huntington Library. Accession number 527245. Extra-illustrated.

———. *The Life of Samuel Johnson, LL.D.* New York: Modern Library, 1931. Houghton Library, Harvard University. Shelf-mark *87EB-83. Annotated by Elizabeth Bishop.

Brady, John. *Clavis Calendaria; or, A Compendious Analysis of the Calendar.* 2nd ed. 2 vols. London: Printed for the Author, 1812. Wren Library, Trinity College, Cambridge. Shelf-mark RW. 1. 10–11. Annotated by Hester Piozzi.

Brand, John. *Observations on Popular Antiquities.* Newcastle, 1777. Bodleian Library. Shelf-mark MS. Eng. misc. e. 242. Annotated by John Brand.

Brontëana: Charlotte Brontë's Letters. Ed. J. Horsfall Turner. Bingley, 1898. Houghton Library, Harvard University. Shelf-mark *EC8.B7896.898b. Extra-illustrated, apparently by Michael Sadleir.

Bunyan, John. *Grace Abounding to the Chief of Sinners and The Death of Mr. Badman.* Everyman Library. London & Toronto: Dent, [n.d.] Victoria College Library, University of Toronto. Frye Collection #368. Annotated by Northrop Frye.

Burges, Sir James Bland. *Richard the First: A Poem.* Printed but not published. London, 1800. British Library. Shelf-marks C. 128. h. 9–12. Annotated by William Boscawen, Richard Cumberland, and Christopher Anstey; the last copy (12) contains Burges's transcriptions of notes from their copies and four others.

Burke, Edmund. *Observations on a late State of the Nation.* London: Dodsley, 1769. British Library. Shelf-mark 08138. dd. 50. (1.) Annotated by Jeremy Bentham.

Burke, Kenneth. *A Grammar of Motives.* New York: Prentice-Hall, 1945. Beinecke Library, Yale University. Shelf-mark Za B919 945G copy 2. Annotated by Kenneth Burke and nine others.

Butler, Samuel. *Hudibras . . . to which is added Annotation, with an Exact Index to the Whole.* London, 1726. British Library. Shelf-mark 11626. aaa. 3. Annotated by William Oldys.

The Cathedral Psalter. London, n.d. Beinecke Library, Yale University. Shelf-mark Purdy 132. Annotated by Thomas Hardy.

Cato. *Catonis Disticha de Moribus.* Ed. Charles Hoole. London: Harbin, 1727. Osborne Collection, Toronto Public Library. Annotated by William Curzon.

Chandler, Richard. *Travels in Asia Minor.* Oxford: Clarendon Press, 1775. British Library. Shelf-mark 1782. b. 17. Annotated by Nicholas Revett.

———. *Travels in Greece.* Oxford: Clarendon Press, 1776. British Library. Shelf-mark 1783. a. 23. Annotated by Nicholas Revett.

Cibber, Colley. *An Apology for the Life of Colley Cibber, Comedian . . . with an Historical View of the Stage during his Own Time.* 3rd ed. London: Dodsley, 1750. Fisher Rare Book Library, University of Toronto. Shelf-mark F-10 895. Extra-illustrated by Queen Charlotte.

Clark, Richard. *Reminiscences of Handel, His Grace the Duke of Chandos, Powells the Harpers, The Harmonious Blacksmith, and Others.* London, 1836. British Library. Shelf-mark C. 45. i. 5. (1–3). Extra-illustrated and annotated by Richard Clark.

Coke, Edward. *The First Part of the Institutes of the Laws of England; or, A Commentary upon Littleton.* Ed. Francis Hargrave. London: Kearsley, 1775. British Library. Shelf-mark 508. k. 3. Annotated by Francis Hargrave.

[*Collection of English Poems.*] (Possibly E. Tompkins, ed. *Poems on Various Subjects.* c. 1820.) Humanities Research Center, University of Texas at Austin. Shelf-mark PR 1171 C645 1820z. Annotated by W. M. Thackeray.

Collins, Arthur. *Historical Collections of the Noble Families of Cavendishe, Holles, Vere, Harley, and Ogle.* London: Withers, 1752. British Library. Shelf-mark 1322. ff. 8. Annotated by Horace Walpole.

Cooke, Samuel. *The Complete English Gardener.* London, n.d. British Library. Shelf-mark 7054. b. 25. Annotated by Robert Edmund Sadler Baley.

Cowley, Abraham. *Works.* 12th ed. 2 vols. London, 1721. Berg Collection, New York Public Library. Annotated by Leigh Hunt.

Cowper, William. *The Task.* London: Johnson, 1785. British Library. Shelf-mark C. 71. c. 22. Annotated by Anna Seward.

Crabbe, George. *The Library. A Poem.* London: Dodsley, 1781. Houghton Library, Harvard University. Shelf-mark *EC75 W1654 Zz797p17. Annotated by Horace Walpole.

Crawley, Captain. *Billiards. Its Theory and Practice.* Beinecke Library, Yale University. Shelf-mark Purdy 62. Annotated by Thomas Hardy.

Dante Alighieri. *The New Life.* Translated by Dante Gabriel Rossetti. New York: Crowell, [c. 1904]. Huntington Library. Accession number 331503. Annotated by Witter Bynner.

Dodgson, C. L. *Notes by an Oxford Chiel.* Oxford: Parker, 1874. British Library. Shelf-mark 1855. c. 4. (37.)

Dodsley, R., ed. *A Collection of Poems in Six Volumes by Several Hands.* 5th ed. 6 vols. London: Dodsley, 1758. Bodleian Library. Shelf-mark Percy 93. Annotated by Thomas Percy.

Douglas, Francis A. K., Marquess of Queensberry, with Percy Colson. *Oscar Wilde and the Black Douglas.* London: Hutchinson, 1949. British Library. Shelf-mark Cup. 362. a. 2. (2.) Annotated by Marie Stopes.

Eddington, A. S. *The Nature of the Physical World.* Cambridge: Cambridge University Press, 1928. Trinity College Library, Dublin. Shelf-mark OLS JOH 39. Annotated by Denis Johnston.

Edgeworth, Maria. *Letters for Literary Ladies.* 2nd ed. rev. London: Johnson, 1799. Trinity College Dublin. Shelf-mark OLS B-1-784. Annotated by John Horseman.

Edwards, Jonathan. *A Dissertation Concerning Liberty and Necessity.* Worcester, Mass., 1797. Beinecke Library, Yale University. Shelf-mark K8 Ed9 C797 Copy 2. Annotated perhaps by Samuel Dexter.

Eliot, George. *Middlemarch.* 4 vols. Edinburgh & London: Blackwood, 1873. Beinecke Library, Yale University. Shelf-mark Ip El44 871c. Annotator not identified: probably Mrs. Nikolaus Trübner.

Emerson, Ralph Waldo. *Prose Works*. Vol. 1. Boston: Fields, Osgood, 1870. Beinecke Library, Yale University. Shelf-mark Za Em 34 C869 Copy 3. Annotated by John Muir.

Estwick, Samuel. *Considerations on the Negroe Cause, Commonly So Called*. London: Dodsley, 1772. Beinecke Library, Yale University. Shelf-mark Ntg 45 G5 772E. Annotated by Granville Sharp.

Five Longer Poems. Ed. O. J. Stevenson. Toronto: Copp Clark, 1927. Osborne Collection, Toronto Public Library. Annotated by Carrie Rae.

Fletcher, Joseph. *Situation Ethics: The New Morality*. Philadelphia: Westminster Press, 1966. Author's collection.

Frazer, Sir James George. *The Golden Bough: A Study in Magic and Religion*. 3rd ed. London: Macmillan, 1922–25. Wren Library, Trinity College, Cambridge. Shelf-mark Adv. c. 1–12. 12 vols, interleaved, with notes copied from Frazer's holograph notes in earlier editions, and a few additional notes by Frazer himself.

Gamba, Count. *The Amours, Intrigues, and Adventures of Lord Byron*. Translated by Robert Benson. London, n.d. (1826?). Houghton Library, Harvard University. Shelf-mark *EC8.B9968.Z826b. Extra-illustrated.

Gardiner, Marguerite, Countess of Blessington. *Conversations of Lord Byron with the Countess of Blessington*. London: Colburn, 1834. British Library. Shelf-mark C. 134. e. 3. Annotated by Walter Savage Landor.

Gaskell, Elizabeth. *Life of Charlotte Brontë*. 2 vols. London: Smith, Elder, 1857. Houghton Library, Harvard University. Shelf-mark *EC8.B7896.W857gb. Annotated by Harriet Martineau.

Gemmell, William. *The Diamond Sutra*. London: Kegan Paul, Trench, Trübner & Co., 1912. Trinity College Dublin. Shelf-mark G 12515187 Copy B. Annotated by James Stephens.

Gibbon, Edward. *The History of the Decline and Fall of the Roman Empire*. 6 vols. London: Strahan & Cadell, 1781–88. British Library. Shelf-mark C. 60. m. 1. Annotated by Edward Gibbon. The second BL copy with Gibbon's notes is also a mixed set (volumes from different editions), 1781–88, shelf-mark C. 135. h. 3.

Godwin, William. *Memoirs of the Author of A Vindication of the Rights of Woman*. London: Johnson, 1798. Pforzheimer Collection, New York Public Library. Annotated by John Horseman.

———. *Memoirs of the Author of A Vindication of the Rights of Woman*. 2nd ed. rev. London: Johnson, 1798. British Library. Shelf-mark 1568/4991. Annotated by Benjamin Dockray.

Gosse, Edmund. *The Life of Philip Henry Gosse F.R.S.* London: Kegan Paul, Trench, Trübner & Co., 1890. Cambridge University Library. Shelf-mark Adv. c. 82.5. Extra-illustrated by Philip Gosse.

Granger, James. *A Biographical History of England*. 3 vols. in 5. London: Davies, 1769–74. British Library. Shelf-mark 614. k. 21–5. Annotated and extra-illustrated by Sir William Musgrave.

————. *A Biographical History of England.* 3 vols. in 36. London: Davies, 1769–74. Huntington Library. Accession number 238000. Extra-illustrated by Richard Bull of Ongar.

————. *A Biographical History of England.* 3rd ed. rev. 4 vols. London: Rivington et al., 1779. Bodleian Library. Shelf-mark Douce G 506–509. Annotated by Francis Douce.

————. *A Biographical History of England.* 4th ed. 4 vols. in 8. London: Baynes et al., 1804. With an additional title page "Printed by G. Smeeton," 1812. Huntington Library. Accession number 284147. Extra-illustrated, probably by William George Prescott.

Gray, Thomas. *Elegy, Written in a Country Churchyard.* 9th ed. London: 1754. Thomas Fisher Rare Book Library, University of Toronto. Shelf-mark Wolfe. Annotated by James Wolfe.

————. *Poems. To which are Prefixed Memoirs of his Life and Writings by W. Mason, M.A.* York: J. Todd; London: Dodsley, 1775. Beinecke Library, Yale University. Shelf-mark Im G794 C775 copy 2. Annotated by Isaac Reed and others; extra-illustrated by George Daniel.

Hargrove, E. *Anecdotes of Archery; from the Earliest Ages to the Year 1791.* York, 1792. British Library. Shelf-mark 1040. b. 19. Annotated by Sarah Sophia Banks.

Hawthorne, Nathaniel. *Transformation: or, The Romance of Mount Beni.* Copyright Edition. 2 vols. Leipzig: Tauchnitz, 1860. Berg Collection, New York Public Library. Extra-illustrated.

Heriot, John. *An Historical Sketch of Gibraltar, with an Account of the Siege which that Fortress Stood against the Combined Forces of France and Spain.* London, 1792. British Library. Shelf-mark 10161. e. 20. Annotated by W. Booth.

Herodotus. *Herodoti Halicarnassei Historiarum Libri IX.* Amsterdam: Schouten, 1763. Wren Library, Trinity College, Cambridge. Annotated by Edward Gibbon.

Housman, A. E. *A Shropshire Lad.* London: Grant Richards, 1920. Merton College, Oxford. Beerbohm Collection #3.57. Annotated by Max Beerbohm.

Ide, Simeon. *A Biographical Sketch of the Life of William B. Ide.* Claremont, N.H.: Privately printed, 1880. Huntington Library. Accession number 496937. Annotated by W. M. Boggs.

The Imperial Family Bible. Stourbridge: Heming, 1811. British Library. Shelf-mark C. 61. f. 3. Annotated by Hester Thrale Piozzi.

Jesse, F. Tennyson. *Murder and Its Motives.* London: Pan, 1958. Humanities Research Center, University of Texas at Austin. Shelf-mark HV 6515 J4 1958. Annotated by Miriam Shipley or Ford Shipley.

Johnson, Samuel. *The Diary of a Journey into North Wales, in the Year 1774.* Ed. R. Duppa. London: Jennings, 1816. Bodleian Library. Shelf-mark Arch. H e. 19. Annotated by William Beckford.

————. *The Plan of a Dictionary of the English Language.* London: Knapton et al., 1747. Fisher Rare Book Library, University of Toronto. Shelf-mark E-10 1333. Annotated by Samuel Maude.

————. *The Rambler.* 4th ed. 4 vols. London: Millar, 1756. Bodleian Library. Shelf-mark Percy 77. Annotated by Thomas Percy.

————. *Rasselas.* London: Sharpe, 1818. Houghton Library, Harvard University. Shelf-mark *78–1550. Annotated by Hester Piozzi.

————. *Select Essays.* Ed. George Birkbeck Hill. 2 vols. London: Dent, 1889. Huntington Library. Accession number 440361. Annotated by Wallace Stevens.

Joyce, James. *Ulysses.* New York: Random House, [n.d.]. Trinity College Dublin. Shelf-mark OLS JOH 43. Annotated by Denis Johnston.

Jung, C. G. *Two Essays on Analytical Psychology.* Trans. H. G. and C. F. Baynes. London: Baillière, Tindall & Cox, 1928. Humanities Research Center, University of Texas at Austin. Shelf-mark BF 315 J8 1928b. Annotated by T. H. White.

Justinian. *The Institutes of Justinian; with English Introduction, Translation, and Notes, by Thomas Collett Sandars.* 2nd ed. London: Parker, 1859. British Library. Shelf-mark B.P. 18. Annotated by Charles Wentworth Dilke?

Kafka, Franz. *Metamorphosis.* Trans. A. L. Lloyd. New York: Vanguard, 1946. Berg Collection, New York Public Library. Annotated by Vladimir Nabokov.

Keats, John. *Endymion.* London: Taylor & Hessey, 1818. Berg Collection, New York Public Library. Annotated by Richard Woodhouse.

————. *Poems.* London: Ollier, 1817. Huntington Library. Accession number RB 151852. Annotated by Richard Woodhouse.

Lambert, M. *Little Henry.* London: Harris, 1823. Osborne Collection, Toronto Public Library. Annotated by Ann Owen Hay.

Langbaine, Gerard. *An Account of the English Dramatic Poets.* Oxford, 1691. British Library. C. 45. d. 14. Annotated by Richard Wright and John Haslemere, with copies of notes by William Oldys, Thomas Percy, and George Steevens.

Levesque, René. *An Option for Quebec.* Toronto: McClelland & Stewart, 1968. Victoria College Library, University of Toronto. Shelf-mark JL 27 L482.

Li, Yu Chiao. *In-Kiao-Li: or, the Two Fair Cousins. A Chinese Novel.* 2 vols. London: Hunt & Clarke, 1827. British Library. Shelf-mark C. 60. k. 5. Annotated by Leigh Hunt and Thomas Carlyle.

Macaulay, T. B. *Lays of Ancient Rome: with "Ivry" and "The Armada".* New ed. London: Longman, 1848. Wren Library, Trinity College, Cambridge. Annotated by John James Raven and others. Shelf-mark Macaulay Collection #41.

Marty, A. E., ed. *Ontario High School Reader.* Rev. ed. Toronto: Canada Publishing, 1919. Osborne Collection, Toronto Public Library.

Mathias, T. J. *The Pursuits of Literature.* 13th ed. London: Becket, 1805. Wren Library, Trinity College, Cambridge. Annotated by T. B. Macaulay.

Mauger, Claude. *French Grammar.* 15th ed. London: Bentley, 1693. Huntington Library. Accession number 323251. Annotated by Grizel Baillie.

Millay, Edna St. Vincent. *A Few Figs From Thistles.* New York: Frank Shay, 1922. Beinecke Library. Shelf-mark Za M611 920ff copy 2. Annotated by Rolfe Humphries and Helen Ward Spencer.

Milner, Joseph. *The History of the Church of Christ.* Rev. Isaac Milner. 5 vols. London: Cadell & Davies, 1810. Wren Library, Trinity College, Cambridge. Annotated by T. B. Macaulay.

Milton, John. *Paradise Lost.* 2 vols. Edinburgh: Deas, 1807. Keats House, Hampstead. Shelf-mark KH 24. Annotated by John Keats.

———. *Paradise Lost.* London, 1751. As a second volume, a copy of *Paradise Regained* together with Milton's minor poems, lacking a title page. British Library. Shelf-marks C. 61. a. 5. and C. 61. a. 5*. Annotated by John Lamb, Charles Lamb, and Mary Lamb.

Montaigne, Michel de. *Essais.* Ed. Pierre Coste. 5 vols. Geneva, 1727. Collection of the Earl of Harrowby. Annotated by Lady Mary Wortley Montagu.

Moore, Marianne. *Selected Poems.* New York: Macmillan, 1935. Berg Collection, New York Public Library. Annotated by John St. Edmunds.

———. *Selected Poems.* New York: Macmillan, 1935. Berg Collection, New York Public Library. Annotated by May Lewis (Aline Goldstone).

Mudford, William. *Nubilia in Search of a Husband; Including Sketches of Modern Society, and Interspersed with Moral and Literary Disquisitions.* 4th ed. London: Ridgway et al., 1809. British Library. Shelf-mark 12614. g. 26. Annotated by A. Urquhart?

Muggeridge, Malcolm. *Chronicles of Wasted Time.* 2 vols. London: Collins, 1972–73. Boston College. Annotated by Graham Greene.

Nichol, John. *Byron.* English Men of Letters Series. London: Macmillan, 1883. Berg Collection, New York Public Library. Extra-illustrated by H. Buxton Forman.

Nichols, Philip. *Sir Francis Drake Revived.* London, 1626. British Library. Shelf-mark C. 28. b. 16. Annotated by John Ruskin.

Oldfield, H. G. *Anecdotes of Archery, Ancient and Modern.* London: For the Author, 1791. British Library. Shelf-mark 1040. b. 18. Annotated by Sarah Sophia Banks.

Oldham, John. *Satyrs upon the Jesuits.* 3rd ed. London: Hindmarsh, 1685. British Library. Shelf-mark C. 45. a. 1. Annotated by Alexander Pope and Edward Thompson.

Ollivier, Gabriel. *Une Dynastie millénaire: S.A.S. Rainier III, Prince Souverain de Monaco.* Monaco: Imprimerie nationale, 1949. Modern Archive Centre, King's College, Cambridge. Annotated by T. S. Eliot.

Patmore, Coventry. *The Rod, the Root, and the Flower.* 2nd ed. rev. London: Bell, 1911. Berg Collection, New York Public Library. Annotated by Tennyson Patmore and Derek Patmore.

Pettit, James Andrew. *Anecdotes, &c Ancient and Modern.* Dublin, 1789. British Library. Shelf-mark C. 60. e. 11. Notes by Hester Piozzi pasted in.

Pickering, Priscilla, and John Morfitt. *Poems.* Ed. Joseph Weston. Birmingham, 1794. British Library. Shelf-mark 11633. bb. 33. Annotated by Samuel Parr.

Piozzi, Hester Lynch. *Anecdotes of the late Samuel Johnson, LL.D.* 4th ed. London: Cadell, 1786. Beinecke Library, Yale University. Shelf-mark Im J637 W786d Copy 1. Annotated by Hester Piozzi.

———. *Retrospection: or A Review of the Most Striking and Important Events, Char-*

acters, Situations, and their Consequences, which the Last Eighteen Hundred Years have Presented to the View of Mankind. 2 vols. London: Stockdale, 1801. Wren Library, Trinity College, Cambridge. Shelf-mark RW. 41. 43–4. Annotated by Hester Piozzi.

Pope, Alexander. *Works.* London: Lintot, 1717–35. Berg Collection, New York Public Library. Annotated by Jonathan Richardson, Edmond Malone, and possibly also Pope himself.

Priestley, Joseph. *Disquisitions Relating to Matter and Spirit.* London: Johnson, 1777. British Library. Shelf-mark C. 28. h. 14. Annotated by John Horne.

Pryde, David. *The Highways of Literature; or, What to Read and How to Read.* Edinburgh: Nimmo, 1882. British Library. Shelf-mark 11862. aa. 50. Annotated by Ellen Terry.

Rabelais, Francis. *Works.* Translated by Urquhart. Notes by Motteux. Ed. Ozell. 5 vols. London: Brindley, 1750. British Library. Shelf-mark 12518. b. 1. Annotated by John Mitford.

Rabion, Abbé, ed. *Les Fleurs de la poésie française.* Tours, 1841. Berg Collection, New York Public Library. Annotated by Charlotte Brontë.

Ralegh, Walter. *The History of the World, in Five Books . . . . to which is prefix'd, The Life of the Author, Newly Compil'd, from Materials More Ample and Authentick than have yet been Publish'd; by Mr. Oldys . . . .* 2 vols. London: Conyers et al., 1736. British Library. Shelf-mark 214. e. 13. Additional MS material by William Oldys.

Ratton, Surgeon-Major James J. L. *Syllabus of Lectures on Surgery, Madras Medical College.* Madras, 1885. British Library. Shelf-mark 07482. ee. 46.

Reynolds, Sir Joshua. *Works.* 3 vols. London: Cadell & Davies, 1798. British Library. Shelf-mark C. 45. e. 18–20. Vol. 1 only annotated by William Blake.

Robin Hood's Garland. [N.p., n.d.; c. 1740.] Bodleian Library. Shelf-mark Douce HH 88 (7). Annotated by William Stukely and Francis Douce.

Rochester, John, Earl of. *Poems . . . on Several Occasions: with Valentinian, A Tragedy.* London: Tonson, 1696. Annotated by Alexander Pope.

Rousseau, J. J. *A Treatise on the Social Compact; or The Principles of Politic Law.* New ed. London: Murray, 1791. British Library. Shelf-mark 1608 / 4490. Annotated by H. B. L. Webb and one other.

Sandford, Mrs. Henry (Margaret E.) *Thomas Poole and His Friends.* 2 vols. London & New York: Macmillan, 1888. Huntington Library. Accession number 152302. Extra-illustrated.

Sarton, May. *The Small Room.* New York: Norton, 1961. Beinecke Library, Yale University. Shelf-mark Zab Sa77 961S.

Saunders, Samuel. *A Short and Easy Introduction to Scientific and Philosophic Botany.* London: White, 1792. British Library. Shelf-mark 1507 / 817.

Schreiner, Olive. *Woman and Labour.* London: T. Fisher Unwin, 1911. National Library of Scotland. Shelf-mark JRM 115. Annotated by Ramsay Macdonald.

Selden, John. *Titles of Honour.* London, 1614. British Library. Shelf-mark 884. k. 2. Annotated by Francis Hargrave.

A Short Description of that Admirable Structure, the Cathedral Church of Salisbury, with the Chapels, Monuments, Grave Stones, and other Particulars. Salisbury: Wilks, n.d. British Library. Shelf-mark C. 28. b. 8.

Smiles, Samuel. *Lives of the Engineers, with an Account of their Principal Works.* 3 vols. in 6. London: Murray, 1861–68. Thomas Fisher Rare Book Library, University of Toronto. Shelf-mark sci. Extra-illustrated.

Southcott, Joanna. *The Strange Effects of Faith.* 3rd ed. Exeter, 1801. British Library. Shelf-mark 699. h. 24. (1). Annotated by William George Thompson.

Southey, Robert. *All for Love; and The Pilgrim to Compostella.* London: Murray, 1829. Huntington Library. Accession number 130628. Annotated by William Beckford.

———. *A Vision of Judgment.* London: Longman, 1821. Pierpont Morgan Library. Ray Collection 516. Contains copies of notes by William Beckford.

Spencer, Herbert. *The Principles of Biology.* 2 vols. London: Williams & Norgate, 1884. British Library. Shelf-mark 1650/126 annotated by Sir William Bate Hardy; 1650/124 annotated by Sir William Henry Perkin. The Library also holds a copy of the 1894 edition, shelf-mark 1650/125, annotated by Joseph Thomas Cunningham.

Spinoza, B. *Opera quotquot reperta sunt.* Ed. J. Van Vloten and J. P. N. Land. Vol. 1 (of 3). Hague: Nijhoff, 1895. Modern Archive Centre, King's College, Cambridge. Annotated by T. S. Eliot.

Stein, Gertrude. *The Autobiography of Alice B. Toklas.* London: Bodley Head, 1935. Beinecke Library, Yale University. Shelf-mark Za St34 933Cb (Copy 1). Annotated by Gertrude Stein.

Sterne, Laurence. *A Sentimental Journey through France and Italy. By Mr. Yorick.* 2 vols. in one. London: Becket & De Hondt, 1770. British Library. Shelf-mark G. 13446. Annotated by Edmund Ferrars.

Stewarton, M. *The Revolutionary Plutarch: Exhibiting the Most Distinguished Characters, Literary, Military, and Political, in the Recent Annals of the French Republic.* 5th ed. London: Murray, 1806. Bodleian Library. Shelf-mark Arch. H e. 78. Annotated by William Beckford.

Stock, Joseph. *A Narrative of what passed at Killalla, in the County of Mayo, and the Parts Adjacent, during the French Invasion in the Summer of 1798.* Dublin, 1800. British Library. Shelf-mark 601. h. 22.

Stowe, Harriet Beecher. *Dred; A Tale of the Great Dismal Swamp.* London: S. Low, Marston, & Co., 1907. Beinecke Library, Yale University. Shelf-mark Za St 78 856n. Annotated by Gertrude Stein.

Swinburne, A. *Laus Veneris.* New York: Carleton, 1866. Humanities Research Center, University of Texas at Austin. Shelf-mark PR 5506 L3 PND. Annotated by Ezra Pound.

Tacitus, Cornelius. *Works.* 2 vols. New York: American Book Co., n.d. Huntington Library. Accession number 337538. Annotated by Samuel Clemens.

Tennyson, Alfred, Lord. *In Memoriam.* 17th ed. London: Moxon, 1865. Bound together with Frederick W. Robertson, *Analysis of Mr. Tennyson's "In Memoriam"*

(London: Smith, Elder, 1862) and *An Index to "In Memoriam"* (London: Moxon, 1862). British Library. Shelf-mark 11661. ee. 11. Annotated by James Dykes Campbell and one other.

Third Reader. The Ontario Readers. Toronto: Copp, Clark, 1885. Osborne Collection, Toronto Public Library. Annotated by Robert Odell.

Titterton, W. R. *So This Is Shaw.* London: Douglas Organ, 1945. British Library. Shelf-mark 10862. a. 21. Annotated by John Kirkby.

Tommy Trip's Valentine Gift: A Plan to Enable Children of Sizes and Denominations to Behave with Honour, Integrity, and Humanity. . . . Adorned with Cuts. London: Osborne & Griffin, 1785. Osborne Collection, Toronto Public Library. Annotated by Edwin Griffith.

Tone, Theobald Wolfe. *The Life of Theobald Wolfe Tone, the Founder of the "United Irishmen." Written by Himself and Extracted from his Journals.* Dublin: McCormick, 1845. British Library. Shelf-mark 10817. a. 6. Annotated by Philip MacDermott.

Townsend, Joseph. *The Physician's Vade Mecum.* London: Cox, 1794. British Library. Shelf-mark 1578 / 2973. Annotated by Joshua Earnshaw.

Trimmer, Sarah Kirby. *New and Comprehensive Lessons, Containing a General Outline of the Roman History.* London: Harris, 1818. Osborne Collection, Toronto Public Library. Annotated by Florence Nightingale.

Verral, William. *A Complete System of Cookery.* London: Printed for the Author, 1759. British Library. Shelf-mark C. 28. f. 13. Annotated by Thomas Gray.

Voss, Gerhard. *Poeticarum institutionum, libri tres.* Amsterdam, 1647. Dyce Collection, Victoria and Albert Museum. Annotated by S. T. Coleridge.

Wallace, Alfred Russel. *Contributions to the Theory of Natural Selection.* London: Macmillan, 1870. British Library. Shelf-mark C. 112. b. 6. Annotated by F. T. Palgrave.

Walpole, Horace. *Letters.* Ed. Peter Cunningham. 9 vols. London: Bohn, 1866. Beinecke Library, Yale University. Shelf-mark Ip L477 Zz861w. Annotated by Edward Lear.

Watson, Richard. *A Letter to His Grace the Archbishop of Canterbury.* London: Evans, 1783. Humanities Research Center, University of Texas at Austin. Shelf-mark BX 5165 W3. The Library speculates that the annotator might have been a nineteenth-century owner, Sir Thomas Phillipps (1792–1872), but both content and handwriting suggest a reader closer to the date of publication.

Weale, B. L. Putnam. *Indiscreet Letters from Peking.* 6th ed. London: Hurst & Blackett, [1907?]. Cambridge University Library. Shelf-mark Adv. e. 107.6. Annotated by H. Giles.

Wesley, John. *A Sermon on Mark i.15.* Bristol: Pine, 1767. In a volume of sermons by several authors. Huntington Library. Accession number 80617–28.

Wharton, Grace and Philip. *The Wits and Beaux of Society.* 2 vols. London: Hogg, 1860. Humanities Research Center, University of Texas at Austin. Shelf-mark DA 485 T48. Annotated by T. H. White.

Whitaker, John. *The Ancient Cathedral of Cornwall Historically Surveyed.* 2 vols in 1.

London: Stockdale, 1804. British Library. Shelf-mark C. 28. l. 8. Annotated by Francis Douce.

————. *The History of Manchester*. 2 vols. London: Dodsley, 1771, 1775. British Library. Shelf-mark C. 28. l. 6, 7. Annotated by Francis Douce.

White, Stewart Edward. *The Silent Places*. New York: McClure, Phillips, 1904. Huntington Library. Accession number 323251. Annotated by Jack London.

Williams, Helen Maria. *Sketches of the State of Manners and Opinions in the French Republic towards the Close of the Eighteenth Century*. 2 vols. London: Robinson, 1801. British Library. Shelf-mark Add MS 34991. Annotated by Horatio Nelson.

Wollaston, Francis John Hyde. *A Plan of a Course of Chemical Lectures*. Cambridge: Archdeacon & Burges, 1794. Huntington Library. Accession number 484639.

Wordsworth, William. *Lyric Poems*. Ed. Ernest Rhys. London: Dent, 1897. Huntington Library. Accession number 440408. Annotated by Wallace Stevens.

Wycherley, William. *Plays*. London, 1735. Berg Collection, New York Public Library. Annotated by Charles Lamb, Leigh Hunt, Charles Smith Cheltnam, and one other.

Bibliography of Secondary Works

Cited Including published marginalia

Adler, Mortimer J. "How to Mark a Book." *Saturday Review of Literature* 22 (1940): 80–85.

Agate, James. *Ego 5*. London: Harrap, 1942.

Alston, R. C. *Books with Manuscript: A Short Title Catalogue of Books with Manuscript Notes in the British Library*. London: British Library, 1994.

Altick, Richard D. *The English Common Reader: A Social History of the Mass Reading Public, 1800–1900*. Chicago: University of Chicago Press, 1957.

Amis, Martin. *Night Train*. New York: Vintage, 1997.

Archer, William. *Poets of the Younger Generation*. London: John Lane, The Bodley Head, 1902.

Armour, Richard W., and Raymond F. Howes, eds. *Coleridge the Talker*. Ithaca: Cornell University Press, 1940.

Barney, Stephen A., ed. *Annotation and Its Texts*. New York: Oxford University Press, 1991.

Barthes, Roland. "Sur la lecture." In *Le bruissement de la langue*. Paris: Seuil, 1984. Pp. 37–47.

Behrman, S. N. *Portrait of Max: An Intimate Memoir of Sir Max Beerbohm*. New York: Random House, 1960.

Bell, Alan. "Waugh Drops the Pilot." *Spectator*, 7 March 1987. Pp. 27–31.

Belloc, Hilaire. "Mrs. Piozzi's *Rasselas*." *Saturday Review of Literature* 2 (1925): 38.

Bennett, Alan. *Writing Home*. London: Faber, 1994.

Bennett, Andrew, ed. *Readers and Reading*. London: Longman, 1995.

Blake, William. "Marginalia." In *Writings*. Ed. G. E. Bentley, Jr. 2 vols. Oxford: Clarendon Press, 1978. 2:1349–1518.

Bloomfield, B. C., ed. *A Directory of Rare Books and Special Collections in the United Kingdom and the Republic of Ireland.* 2nd ed. London: Library Association, 1997.

Booth, Wayne C. *The Rhetoric of Fiction.* 2nd ed. Chicago: University of Chicago Press, 1983.

Boswell, James. *Life of Johnson.* Ed. G. Birkbeck Hill. Rev. L. F. Powell. 6 vols. Oxford: Clarendon Press, 1934–50.

―――. *The Life of Samuel Johnson, LL.D. With Marginal Comments and Markings from Two Copies Annotated by Hester Lynch Thrale Piozzi.* Ed. Edward G. Fletcher. 3 vols. London: Limited Editions Club, 1938.

―――. *The Principal Corrections and Additions to the First Edition of Mr. Boswell's Life of Johnson.* London: Dilly, 1793.

Boulton, James T., ed. *Johnson: The Critical Heritage.* London: Routledge & Kegan Paul, 1971.

Brand, John. *Observations on Popular Antiquities.* Rev. Henry Ellis. 2 vols. London: Rivington et al., 1813.

Brewer, John. "Reconstructing the Reader: Prescriptions, Texts, and Strategies in Anna Larpent's Reading." In *Practice and Representation of Reading in England.* Ed. Raven, Small, and Tadmor. Pp. 226–45.

Brontë, Charlotte. *Shirley.* Ed. Temple Scott. 2 vols. Edinburgh: John Grant, 1924.

Brontë, Emily. *Wuthering Heights.* Ed. Temple Scott. Edinburgh: John Grant, 1911.

Brooke, Rupert. *Letters.* Ed. Geoffrey Keynes. London: Faber & Faber, 1968.

―――. *Prose.* Ed. Christopher Hassall. London: Sidgwick & Jackson, 1956.

Broster, John. *Collectanea Johnsoniana: Catalogue of the Library, Pictures, Prints . . . of Mrs. Hester Lynch Piozzi, Deceased.* Chester, 1823.

Broughton, L. N., ed. *Sara Coleridge and Henry Reed.* Ithaca: Cornell University Press, 1937.

Browne, Sir Thomas. *Religio Medici and Other Works.* Ed. L. C. Martin. Oxford: Clarendon Press, 1964.

Brownell, Morris R. "Hester Lynch Piozzi's Marginalia." *Eighteenth-Century Life* 3 (1977): 97–100.

Brynbella. A Catalogue of the Valuable Paintings, Prints, Books . . . the Property of Sir John Salusbury. [n.p.] 1836.

Burney, Charles. *Letters.* Vol. 1. Ed. Alvero Ribiero. Oxford: Clarendon Press, 1991.

―――. *Memoirs.* Ed. Slava Klima et al. Lincoln: University of Nebraska Press, 1988.

Burney, Frances. *Early Journals and Letters.* Ed. Lars E. Troide. Vol. 1. Oxford: Clarendon Press, 1988.

―――. *Memoirs of Dr. Burney.* 3 vols. London: Moxon, 1832.

Byron, George Gordon, Lord. *Byron's Letters and Journals.* Ed. Leslie A. Marchand. Vol. 6: 1818–1819. Cambridge: The Belknap Press of Harvard University Press, 1976.

―――. *English Bards and Scotch Reviewers.* New York: Richardson, 1865.

Catalogue of the Unique Library Formed by Irving Browne, Esq., of Troy, N.Y., Con-

taining the Most Extensive Collection of Extra Illustrated Works Ever Offered by Auction in this Country (New York: Leavitt, 1878).

A Catalogue of the Valuable Library . . . of John Horne Tooke, Esq. London: King & Lochée, 1813.

Cecil, David. *Max: A Biography*. London: Constable, 1964.

Chartier, Roger. *The Cultural Uses of Print in Early Modern France*. Trans. Lydia G. Cochrane. Princeton: Princeton University Press, 1987.

Chorley, Henry. *Memorials of Mrs. Hemans*. London: Saunders & Otley, 1836.

Clare, John. *Letters*. Ed. Mark Storey. Oxford: Clarendon Press, 1985.

Clifford, James L. *Hester Lynch Piozzi (Mrs. Thrale)*. 2nd ed. Oxford: Clarendon Press, 1952.

Clifford, James L., and Donald J. Greene. *Samuel Johnson: A Survey and Bibliography of Critical Studies*. Minneapolis: University of Minnesota Press, 1970.

Coffman, Ralph J. *Coleridge's Library: A Bibliography of Books Owned or Read by Samuel Taylor Coleridge*. Boston: G. K. Hall, 1987.

Coleridge, Hartley. *Essays and Marginalia*. Ed. Derwent Coleridge. 2 vols. London: Moxon, 1851.

Coleridge, Samuel Taylor. *Biographia Literaria*. Ed. James Engell and W. Jackson Bate. 2 vols. Princeton: Princeton University Press, 1983.

———. *Collected Letters*. Ed. Earl Leslie Griggs. 6 vols. Oxford: Clarendon Press, 1956–71.

———. "Essays on the Principles of Genial Criticism." In *Shorter Works and Fragments*. Ed. H. J. Jackson and J. R. de J. Jackson. *Collected Works* Vol. 11. 2 vols. Princeton: Princeton University Press, 1995. 1:353–86.

———. *Literary Remains*. Ed. H. N. Coleridge. 4 vols. London: Pickering, 1836–39.

———. *Marginalia*. Ed. George Whalley and H. J. Jackson. The Collected Works of Samuel Taylor Coleridge 12. Bollingen Series 75. 5 vols. to date, of the projected 6. Princeton: Princeton University Press, 1980– .

———. *On the Constitution of the Church and State*. Ed. John Colmer. Princeton and London: Princeton University Press and Routledge & Kegan Paul, 1976.

———. *Table Talk*. Ed. Carl Woodring. 2 vols. Princeton: Princeton University Press, 1990.

Craddock, Patricia B. "Gibbon's Revision of the *Decline and Fall*." *Studies in Bibliography* 21 (1968): 191–204.

Cunningham, Valentine. "Glossing and Glozing: Bunyan and Allegory." In *John Bunyan: Conventicle and Parnassus*. Ed. N. H. Keeble. Oxford: Clarendon Press, 1988.

Darnton, Robert. "First Steps Toward a History of Reading." In *The Kiss of Lamourette*. Pp. 154–87.

———. *The Forbidden Best-Sellers of Pre-Revolutionary France*. New York: Norton, 1995.

———. *The Kiss of Lamourette: Reflections in Cultural History*. New York: Norton, 1990.

———. "Readers Respond to Rousseau: The Fabrication of Romantic Sensitivity." In *The Great Cat Massacre and Other Episodes in French Cultural History*. New York: Penguin, 1984. Pp. 209–49.

Darwin, Charles. *Marginalia*. Ed. Mario A. Di Grigorio et al. Vol. 1. New York: Garland, 1990.

Davidson, Cathy N. *Revolution and the Word: The Rise of the Novel in America*. New York: Oxford University Press, 1986.

De Bury, Richard. *Philobiblon*. Trans. E. C. Thomas. Ed. Michael MacLagan. Oxford: Shakespeare Head Press, 1960, repr. 1970.

De Certeau, Michel. "Reading as Poaching." Trans. Steven Rendall. Reprinted from *The Practice of Everyday Life*. In *Readers and Reading*. Ed. Bennett. Pp. 150–63.

DeMaria, Robert, Jr. *Samuel Johnson and the Life of Reading*. Baltimore: Johns Hopkins University Press, 1997.

———. "Samuel Johnson and the Reading Revolution." *Eighteenth-Century Life* 16 (1992): 86–102.

Dennys, Nicholas, and Jean McNeil. *The Annotated Library of Graham Greene: A Catalogue*. London: Gloucester Road Bookshop, 1993.

De Quincey, Thomas. "The Lake Poets: William Wordsworth and Robert Southey." In *Collected Writings*. Ed. David Masson. 14 vols. London: Black, 1896. 2:303–32.

Derrida, Jacques. *Glas*. Paris: Editions Galilée, 1974.

———. *Margins of Philosophy*. Trans. Alan Bass. Brighton: Harvester Press, 1982.

Dibdin, Thomas Frognall. *The Bibliomania; or, Book-Madness; Containing Some Account of the History, Symptoms, and Cure of this Fatal Disease. In an Epistle Addressed to Richard Heber, Esq.* London: Longman, 1809.

Eaves, T. C. Duncan, and Ben D. Kimpel. *Samuel Richardson: A Biography*. Oxford: Clarendon Press, 1971.

Edgeworth, Maria. *Belinda*. Introduction by Anne Thackeray Ritchie. London: Macmillan, 1896.

Engelsing, Rolf. *Der Bürger als Leser: Lesergeschichte in Deutschland, 1500–1800*. Stuttgart: J. B. Metzlersche Verlagsbuchhandlung, 1974.

English Poetry: The English Poetry Full-Text Database. CD-ROM. Chadwyck-Healey, 1995.

Erasmus, Desiderius. "On the Method of Study." Trans. Brian McGregor. Ed. Craig R. Thompson. *Collected Works*. Vol. 24. Toronto: University of Toronto Press, 1978. Pp. 661–91.

Fadiman, Anne. *Ex Libris: Confessions of a Common Reader*. London: Allen Lane, The Penguin Press, 1999.

Ferriar, John. *The Bibliomania, an Epistle, to Richard Heber Esq*. London: Cadell & Davies, 1809.

———. *Illustrations of Sterne*. London: Cadell & Davies, 1798.

Gallix, François. *T. H. White: An Annotated Bibliography*. New York: Garland, 1986.

Gemmett, Robert J., ed. *Sale Catalogues of Eminent Persons*. Vol. 3. London: Mansell, 1972.

The George Eliot Letters. Ed. Gordon S. Haight. 8 vols. London: Oxford University Press, 1954–56.

Gladstone, W. E. *The Gladstone Diaries*. Vol. 14. Oxford: Clarendon Press, 1994.

Glaister, Geoffrey Ashall. *Glossary of the Book*. London: George Allen & Unwin, 1960.

Grafton, Anthony. "Discitur ut agatur: How Gabriel Harvey Read His Livy." In *Annotation and Its Texts*. Ed. Barney. Pp. 108–29.

———. *The Footnote*. Cambridge: Harvard University Press, 1997.

———. "Is the History of Reading a Marginal Enterprise? Guillaume Budé and His Books." *Papers of the Bibliographical Society of America* 91:2 (1997): 139–57.

———. *Joseph Scaliger: A Study in the History of Classical Scholarship*. Vol. 1: *Textual Criticism and Exegesis*. Oxford: Clarendon Press, 1983.

Grafton, Anthony, and Lisa Jardine. "'Studied for Action': How Gabriel Harvey Read His Livy." *Past and Present* 129 (1990): 30–78.

Grahame, Kenneth. *Pagan Papers*. 5th ed. London: John Lane, The Bodley Head, 1898.

Granger, James. *A Biographical History of England, from Egbert the Great to the Revolution*. 2 vols. London: Davies, 1769.

———. *A Biographical History of England, from Egbert the Great to the Revolution*. 5th ed. 6 vols. London: Baynes, 1824.

Gratian. *The Treatise on Laws with the Ordinary Gloss*. Translated by Augustine Thompson, O.P., and James Gorley. Washington D.C.: Catholic University Press, 1993.

Gray, Thomas. *An Elegy Written in a Country Church Yard*. Ed. Francis Griffin Stokes. Oxford: Clarendon Press, 1929.

Green, Peter. *Kenneth Grahame, 1859–1932*. London: Murray, 1959.

Greene, Graham. *The End of the Affair*. London: Penguin, 1975.

Greetham, D. C., ed. *The Margins of the Text*. Ann Arbor: University of Michigan Press, 1997.

Grego, Joseph. *Thackerayana: Notes and Anecdotes Illustrated by Nearly Six Hundred Sketches by William Makepeace Thackeray. Depicting Humorous Incidents in His School Life, and Favourite Scenes and Characters in the Books of His Every-day Reading*. London: Chatto & Windus, 1875.

Gribben, Alan. "'Good Books & a Sleepy Conscience': Mark Twain's Reading Habits." *American Literary Realism* 9 (1976): 295–306.

———. "'I kind of love small game': Mark Twain's Library of Literary Hogwash." *American Literary Realism* 9 (1976): 65–76.

———. *Mark Twain's Library: A Reconstruction*. 2 vols. Boston: G. K. Hall, 1980.

Grundy, Isobel. "Books and the Woman: An Eighteenth-Century Owner and Her Libraries." *English Studies in Canada* 20 (1994): 1–22.

A Guide to the Preservation of Archival Materials. [Ottawa]: Public Archives of Canada, 1981.

Halsband, Robert. *The Life of Lady Mary Wortley Montagu.* Oxford: Clarendon Press, 1956.

Hargrave, Francis. *An Argument in the Case of James Sommersett a Negro, Lately Determined by the Court of King's Bench: Wherein it is Attempted to Demonstrate the Present Unlawfulness of Domestic Slavery in England.* London: Printed for the Author, 1772.

Harvey, Gabriel. *Marginalia.* Ed. G. C. Moore Smith. Stratford-upon-Avon: Shakespeare Head Press, 1913.

Hassall, Christopher. *Rupert Brooke: A Biography.* London: Faber & Faber, 1964.

Hawtree, Christopher. "Footnotes from God." *The Times Magazine* (London). 1 January 1994. Pp. 20–23.

Hayward, Abraham, ed. *Autobiography, Letters, and Literary Remains of Mrs. Piozzi (Thrale).* London: Longmans, 1861.

Hazen, Allen T. *A Catalogue of Horace Walpole's Library.* New Haven: Yale University Press, 1969.

Hill, Aaron. *Works.* 4 vols. London: Printed for the Benefit of the Family, 1753.

Hindman, Sandra, ed. *Printing the Written Word: The Social History of Books, circa 1450–1520.* Ithaca: Cornell University Press, 1991.

Hollander, John. "The Widener Burying-Ground." *University of Toronto Quarterly* 61 (1992): 391.

Hunter, Martin. "The British Library and the Library of John Evelyn: With a Checklist of Evelyn Books in the British Library's Holdings." In *John Evelyn in the British Library.* Pp. 82–102.

Index of English Literary Manuscripts. 4 vols. in 11. London: Mansell, 1980–97.

Jackson, H. J. "Coleridge's Collaborator, Joseph Henry Green." *Studies in Romanticism* 21 (1982): 160–79.

———. "Writing in Books and Other Marginal Activities." *University of Toronto Quarterly* 62 (1992): 218–31.

Jackson, Holbrook. *The Anatomy of Bibliomania.* New edition. London: Faber & Faber, 1950.

Jackson, Kevin. "Driven to the Edge of the Page." *The Independent* (London), 8 August 1992.

———. *Invisible Forms.* London: Macmillan, 1999.

John Evelyn in The British Library. London: The British Library, 1995.

Johnson, Samuel. *The Idler and The Adventurer.* Ed. W. J. Bate, John M. Bullitt, and L. F. Powell. New Haven: Yale University Press, 1963.

———. *Letters.* Ed. Bruce Redford. 5 vols. Princeton: Princeton University Press, 1992–94.

———. *Lives of the English Poets.* Ed. George Birkbeck Hill. 3 vols. Oxford: Clarendon Press, 1905.

Keats, John. *Poetical Works and Other Writings.* Ed. H. Buxton Forman. 8 vols. New
York: Scribner's, 1939. Marginalia are at 5:268–320.

Kennedy, Alan. *The Psychology of Reading.* London: Methuen, 1984.

Keynes, Geoffrey. *The Library of Edward Gibbon.* 2nd ed. Godalming: St. Paul's
Bibliographies, 1980.

King, Michael J. "An ABC of E. P.'s Library." *Library Chronicle of the University of
Texas at Austin* n.s. 17 (1981): 31–45.

Kintgen, Eugene R. *Reading in Tudor England.* Pittsburgh: University of Pittsburgh
Press, 1996.

Lamb, Charles. "Christ's Hospital Five and Thirty Years Ago." In *Works.* Ed. E. V.
Lucas. 2:12–22.

———. *The Letters of Charles Lamb, to Which are Added Those of His Sister Mary
Lamb.* Ed. E. V. Lucas. 2 vols. London: Dent, and Methuen, 1935.

———. "Recollections of Christ's Hospital." In *Works.* Ed. E. V. Lucas. 1:139–49.

———. "The Two Races of Men." In *Works.* Ed. E. V. Lucas. 2:22–27.

Lamb, Charles, and Mary Lamb. *Works.* Ed. E. V. Lucas. London: Methuen, 1903–
5.

Lamb, Charles and Mary Anne. *Letters.* Ed. Edwin W. Marrs, Jr. Vol. 1. Ithaca: Cornell University Press, 1975.

Lau, Beth, ed. *Keats's "Paradise Lost."* Gainesville: University Press of Florida,
1998.

Leavis, F. R. *Nor Shall My Sword: Discourses on Pluralism, Compassion, and Social
Hope.* London: Chatto & Windus, 1972.

Lee, Hermione. *Virginia Woolf.* London: Vintage, 1997.

Lewis, May. "Marianne Moore: An Appreciation." *The Forum and Century* 96 (July
1936): 48–49.

Lewis, Wilmarth Sheldon. "Horace Walpole's Library." In Hazen, *Catalogue of
Horace Walpole's Library.* 1:xlvii-xci.

Lipking, Lawrence. "The Marginal Gloss." *Critical Inquiry* 3 (1977): 609–55.

Lonsdale, Roger. *Dr. Charles Burney: A Literary Biography.* Oxford: Clarendon
Press, 1986.

———, ed. *Eighteenth-Century Women Poets.* Oxford: Oxford University Press,
1989.

Lowes, John Livingston. *The Road to Xanadu: A Study in the Ways of the Imagination.* Boston: Houghton Mifflin, 1927.

Luard, Henry Richards. *A Catalogue of Adversaria and Printed Books Containing
MS. Notes, Preserved in the Library of the University of Cambridge.* Cambridge:
Cambridge University Press, 1864.

Lucas, John. *John Clare.* Plymouth: Northcote House, 1994.

Lynn, Steven. "Johnson's Critical Reception." In *The Cambridge Companion to
Samuel Johnson.* Ed. Greg Clingham. Cambridge: Cambridge University Press,
1997. 240–53.

Macaulay, T. B. *The Marginal Notes of Lord Macaulay*. Ed. G. O. Trevelyan. London: Longmans, 1907.

Macdonald, Alan. "A Lost History of Perversion: T. H. White's 'The Witch in the Wood.'" *Library Chronicle of the University of Texas at Austin* 23 (1993): 107–29.

Machor, James L., ed. *Readers in History: Nineteenth-Century American Literature and the Contexts of Response*. Baltimore: Johns Hopkins University Press, 1993.

Mack, Maynard. *Alexander Pope: A Life*. New Haven: Yale University Press, 1985.

Manguel, Alberto. *A History of Reading*. Toronto: Knopf, 1996.

Martin, Henri-Jean. *The History and Power of Writing*. Trans. Lydia G. Cochrane. Chicago: University of Chicago Press, 1994.

Matthew, H. C. G. *Gladstone, 1809–1874*. Oxford: Clarendon Press, 1986.

McFarland, Thomas. "Synecdochic Structure in Blake's Marginalia." *European Romantic Review* 1 (1990): 75–90.

McGann, Jerome J. "How to Read a Book." In *The Textual Condition*. Princeton: Princeton University Press, 1991. Pp. 101–28.

McKitterick, David. *Cambridge University Library: A History*. Cambridge: Cambridge University Press, 1986.

Melville, Herman. *Marginalia*. Ed. Walker Cowen. 2 vols. New York & London: Garland, 1978.

Miletic-Vejzovic, Laila. *A Library of One's Own: The Library of Leonard and Virginia Woolf*. London: Cecil Woolf, 1997.

Millgate, Michael. *Thomas Hardy: A Biography*. New York: Random House, 1982.

Montagu, Lady Mary Wortley. *Essays and Poems and "Simplicity, A Comedy."* Ed. Robert Halsband and Isobel Grundy. Oxford: Clarendon Press, 1993.

Montaigne, Michel de. "Des livres." In *Essais*. 3 vols. Paris: Garnier-Flammarion, 1979. 2:78–90.

Moss, Ann. *Printed Commonplace-Books and the Structuring of Renaissance Thought*. Oxford: Oxford University Press, 1996.

Nell, Victor. *Lost in a Book: The Psychology of Reading for Pleasure*. New Haven: Yale University Press, 1988.

O'Brien, Flann. *The Best of Myles: A Selection from "Cruiskeen Lawn."* Ed. Kevin O' Nolan. London and Sydney: Pan Books, 1977.

Oldham, John. *The Compositions in Prose and Verse of Mr. John Oldham. To which are added Memoirs of his Life, and Explanatory Notes upon some Obscure Passages of his Writings*. Ed. Edward Thompson. 3 vols. London: Flexney, 1770.

Omond, T. S. *English Metrists in the Eighteenth and Nineteenth Centuries*. London: Oxford University Press, 1907.

———. *A Study of Metre*. London: Grant Richards, 1903.

Ondaatje, Michael. *The English Patient*. London: Pan Books, 1992.

Opie, Iona and Peter. *I Saw Esau: Traditional Rhymes of Youth*. London: Williams and Norgate, 1947.

O'Shea, Edward. *A Descriptive Catalog of W. B. Yeats's Library*. New York & London: Garland, 1985.

Parkin, Thomas. *On the Grangerizing and Bowdlerizing of Books.* Hastings: East Sussex Arts Club, 1918.

Peterson, William S., and Fred L. Standley. "The J. S. Mill Marginalia in Robert Browning's *Pauline:* A History and Transcription." *Papers of the Bibliographical Society of America* 66 (1972): 135–70.

Piozzi, Hester L. *Thraliana: The Diary of Mrs. Hester Lynch Thrale (Later Mrs. Piozzi).* Ed. Katharine C. Balderston. 2 vols. Oxford: Clarendon Press, 1942.

Pinker, Stephen. *The Language Instinct.* London: Penguin, 1994.

Plarr, Victor. *Ernest Dowson, 1888–1897: Reminiscences, Unpublished Letters, and Marginalia.* London: Elkin Mathews, 1914.

Poe, Edgar Allan. *The Brevities.* Ed. Burton R. Pollin. *Collected Writings of Edgar Allan Poe.* Vol. 2. New York: Gordian Press, 1985.

Pope, Alexander. *Correspondence.* Ed. George Sherburn. 5 vols. Oxford: Clarendon Press, 1956.

———. *The Dunciad.* Ed. James Sutherland. New Haven and London: Yale University Press and Methuen, 1953.

Pottle, Frederick Albert. *The Literary Career of James Boswell, Esq.* Oxford: Clarendon Press, 1929; reprinted 1965.

Powell, John. "Small Marks and Instinctual Responses: A Study in the Uses of Gladstone's Marginalia." *Nineteenth-Century Prose* 19 (1992): 1–17.

Proust, Marcel. *On Reading Ruskin.* Trans. and ed. Jean Autret, William Burford, and Phillip J. Wolfe. New Haven: Yale University Press, 1987.

Radway, Janice. *Reading the Romance: Women, Patriarchy, and Popular Literature.* Chapel Hill: University of North Carolina Press, 1984.

Raven, James, Helen Small, and Naomi Tadmor, eds. *The Practice and Representation of Reading in England.* Cambridge: Cambridge University Press, 1996.

Roberts, Daniel. "Three Uncollected Coleridgean Marginalia from De Quincey." *Notes and Queries* n.s. 41 (1994): 329–35.

Rogers, Timothy. *Rupert Brooke.* London: Routledge & Kegan Paul, 1971.

Rose, Jonathan. "How Historians Study Reader Response: or, What Did Jo Think of *Bleak House?*" In *Literature in the Marketplace.* Ed. John O. Jordan and Robert L. Patten. Cambridge: Cambridge University Press, 1995. Pp. 195–212.

Rosenthal, Bernard M. *The Rosenthal Collection of Printed Books with Manuscript Annotations.* New Haven: Yale University Press, 1997.

The Rothschild Library: A Catalogue of the Collection of Eighteenth-Century Printed Books and Manuscripts Formed by Lord Rothschild. 2 vols. Cambridge: Privately printed, 1954.

Roustang, François. "On Reading Again." In *The Limits of Theory.* Ed. Thomas M. Kavanagh. Stanford: Stanford University Press, 1989. Pp. 121–38.

The Sacred Books of the New Testament, Recited at Large: and Illustrated with Critical and Explanatory Annotations, Carefully Compiled from the Commentaries and Other Writings of Grotius, Lightfoot, Pool, Calmet, Le Clerc, Lock, Burkit, Sir Isaac Newton, and a Variety of Other Eminent Authors, Ancient and Modern. Embellished with *Ornamental and Useful Representations, Curiously Design'd, and Engraven on Copper.* Vol 1. London: Humphreys, 1739.

Saenger, Paul, and Michael Heinlen. "Incunable Description and Its Implication for the Analysis of Fifteenth-Century Reading Habits." In *Printing the Written Word.* Ed. Hindman. Pp. 225–58.

St. John, Judith. *The Osborne Collection of Early Children's Books.* 2 vols. Toronto: Toronto Public Library, 1958, 1975.

Saintsbury, George. *Historical Manual of English Prosody.* London: Macmillan, 1910.

Sampson, Anthony. *Mandela: The Authorized Biography.* London: HarperCollins, 1999.

Scholes, Robert. *Protocols of Reading.* New Haven: Yale University Press, 1989.

Sewell, Richard B. *The Life of Emily Dickinson.* 2 vols. New York: Farrar, Straus and Giroux, 1974.

Shakespeare, W. *The Works of Shakespear.* Ed. Alexander Pope. 6 vols. London: Tonson, 1725.

Sharp, Granville. *A Representation of the Injustice and Dangerous Tendency of Admitting the Least Claim of Private Property in the Persons of Men, in England.* London, 1769.

Sherman, William H. *John Dee: The Politics of Reading and Writing in the Renaissance.* Amherst: University of Massachussets Press, 1995.

———. "The Place of Reading in the English Renaissance: John Dee Revisited." In *Practice and Representation of Reading in England.* Ed. Raven, Small, and Tadmor. Pp. 62–76.

Silver, Brenda R. *Virginia Woolf's Reading Notebooks.* Princeton: Princeton University Press, 1983.

Singh, Simon. *Fermat's Enigma.* Toronto: Viking, 1998.

Slights, William W. E. "The Cosmopolitics of Reading: Navigating the Margins of John Dee's *General and Rare Memorials.*" In *The Margins of the Text.* Ed. Greetham. Pp. 199–228.

———. "The Edifying Margins of Renaissance English Books." *Renaissance Quarterly* 42 (1989): 682–716.

———. "'Marginall Notes that spoile the Text': Scriptural Annotation in the English Renaissance." *Huntington Library Quarterly* 55 (1992): 255–78.

Stern, Virginia F. *Gabriel Harvey: His Life, Marginalia, and Library.* Oxford: Clarendon Press, 1979.

Stevenson, Robert Louis. *The Strange Case of Dr. Jekyll and Mr. Hyde. With Other Fables.* London: Longmans, 1896.

Stoddard, Roger. *Marks in Books.* Cambridge, Mass.: Houghton Library, 1985.

Suleiman, Susan R., and Inge Crosman, eds. *The Reader in the Text: Essays on Audience and Interpretation.* Princeton: Princeton University Press, 1980.

A Supplement to the Tour through Great-Britain. London: Kearsley, 1787.

Sutherland, Charlotte Hussey. *Catalogue of the Sutherland Collection.* 2 vols. London: Payne & Foss et al., 1837.

Swift, Jonathan. "Marginalia." In *Prose Works*. Ed. Herbert Davis. Vol. 5. Oxford: Blackwell, 1962. Pp. 239–320.

———. *Works*. Ed. Sir Walter Scott. 2nd ed. 19 vols. Edinburgh: Constable, 1824.

Taylor, Andrew. "Into His Secret Chamber: Reading and Privacy in Late Medieval England." In *Practice and Representation of Reading in England*. Ed. Raven, Small, and Tadmor. Pp. 41–61.

Taylor, P. J. O. "In the Margin." *Bodleian Library Record* 16 (1998): 365–66.

Tearle, John. *Mrs. Piozzi's Tall Young Beau: William Augustus Conway*. Rutherford, N.J.: Fairleigh Dickinson University Press, 1991.

Thackeray, William Makepeace. *Vanity Fair*. Ed. John Sutherland. Oxford: Oxford University Press, 1983.

Tompkins, Jane P., ed. *Reader-Response Criticism: From Formalism to Post-Structuralism*. Baltimore: Johns Hopkins University Press, 1980.

Tredwell, Daniel M. *A Monograph on Privately-Illustrated Books. A Plea for Bibliomania*. Brooklyn: Fred. Tredwell, 1881.

Tribble, Evelyn E. "'Like a Looking-Glas in the Frame': From the Marginal Note to the Footnote." In *The Margins of the Text*. Ed. Greetham. Pp. 229–44.

———. *Margins and Marginality: The Printed Page in Early Modern Europe*. Charlottesville: University Press of Virginia, 1993.

Vidal, Gore. "Dinner with the Princess." *The New Yorker*. Joint issue: 24 June and 1 July, 1996. P. 121.

Warner, Sylvia Townsend. *T. H. White: A Biography*. London: Cape, 1967.

West, Michael. "Emily Dickinson's Ambrosian Nights with Christopher North." *Harvard Library Bulletin* n.s. 5 (1994): 67–71.

White, T. H. *Letters to a Friend: The Correspondence Between T. H. White and L. J. Potts*. Ed. François Gallix. New York: Putnam's, 1982.

Wollstonecraft, Mary. *Mary, a Fiction, and The Wrongs of Woman*. Ed. Gary Kelly. London: Oxford University Press, 1976.

Woolf, Virginia. *Books and Portraits*. Ed. Mary Lyon. London: Hogarth Press, 1977.

———. *The Common Reader: Second Series*. London: Hogarth Press, 1932.

———. "Writing in the Margin." In *The Virginia Woolf Manuscripts from the Monks House Papers at the University of Sussex*. Microform Edition. Brighton: Harvester Press, 1985. Reel 2.

ACKNOWLEDGMENTS

The illustrations—in both senses of the word, figures and examples—carry this book, and for them I am indebted to all the libraries cited, specifically to those that gave permission for the reproduction of images: the British Library, the Thomas Fisher Rare Book Library at the University of Toronto, the Harry Ransom Humanities Research Center at the University of Texas in Austin, the Houghton Library at Harvard University, the Osborne Collection of Early Children's Books in the Toronto Public Library, and the Warden and Fellows of Merton College in Oxford. For permission to publish a substantial amount of manuscript material by Hester Piozzi I thank the Houghton Library, Harvard University; for material by Rupert Brooke, the Trustees of the Rupert Brooke Estate; and for material by T. H. White, David Higham Associates. A version of part of Chapter Four appeared originally as an article entitled "An Important Annotated Boswell" in *Review of English Studies*, n.s. 49 (1998), published by Oxford University Press, which holds copyright in that journal.

The human face of library systems can make the difference between an efficient visit and a profitable one and again between a profitable and an agreeable one. Though I have been treated with courtesy everywhere, I am especially grateful to Stephen Crook of the Berg Collection in the New York Public Library, Elisabeth Leedham-Green and David McKitterick at Cambridge, Robert Brandeis and Leslie McGrath in Toronto, and Michael Crump at the British Library, all of whom went out of their way to help me with their own collections and gave me tips that I could apply to other collections as well. It is also a pleasure to recall the generosity of a private owner, the Earl of Harrowby, whose hospitality at Sandon extended well beyond access to books once owned by Lady Mary Wortley Montagu.

Ever since I began to be recognized locally—I fear internationally—as "the marginalia lady," colleagues and friends have not only put up with this obsession but have kindly collected examples on my behalf. Though I know where every one of their contributions lies, there are too many to acknowledge individually and I can only list the names of these indulgent benefactors: John Baker, John Beattie, Susan Beattie, G. E. Bentley, Alan Bewell, Eleanor Cook, Brian Corman, Patricia Fleming, Warwick Gould, Andrew Gray, Isobel Grundy, Heidi Brayman Hackel, Nick Halmi, Jocelyn Harris, Sharon Howe, John Hunter, Marie Korey, Richard Landon, Jill Matus, Jane Millgate, Michael Millgate, Philip Oldfield, Pat Rosenbaum, Bill Sherman, Carmen Socknat, Deirdre Toomey, Stephen Waddams, Steve Zwicker.

For institutional support that made this book possible I am indebted to the Social Sciences and Humanities Research Council of Canada, the Connaught Fund of the University of Toronto, and the School of Advanced Study in the University of London. Finally, my warmest thanks go to those who cast a critical eye over the manuscript as it developed—to John Baird, particularly, and to members of WIPE, the work-in-progress group of the English Department at the University of Toronto, who commented on the first few chapters; to Donna Andrew, Judith Skelton Grant, Robin Jackson, and Bill Slights, who gamely read the whole thing in draft; and to Lara Heimert and Phillip King of Yale University Press, who painstakingly saw it through to its finished state.

Index of Personal Names and Topics

Works may be found through their authors' entries; titles are given only when the author is not known. An asterisk before a page number means that in this case the person is referred to as an annotator.